Windows Phone Recipes

A Problem-Solution Approach

Fabio Claudio Ferracchiati
Emanuele Garofalo

Windows Phone Recipes, Second Edition

ISBN-13 (pbk): 978-1-4302-3371-8

ISBN-13 (electronic): 978-1-4302-3372-5

President and Publisher: Paul Manning
Lead Editor: Ewan Buckingham
Technical Reviewer: Simona Nasetti
Editorial Board: Steve Anglin, Mark Beckner, Ewan Buckingham, Gary Cornell, Morgan Ertel, Jonathan Gennick, Jonathan Hassell, Robert Hutchinson, Michelle Lowman, James Markham, Matthew Moodie, Jeff Olson, Jeffrey Pepper, Douglas Pundick, Ben Renow-Clarke, Dominic Shakeshaft, Gwenan Spearing, Matt Wade, Tom Welsh
Coordinating Editor: Jessica Belanger
Copy Editor: Kimberly Burton
Compositor: Bytheway Publishing Services
Indexer: SPI Global
Artist: SPI Global
Cover Designer: Anna Ishchenko

Distributed to the book trade worldwide by Springer Science+Business Media, LLC., 233 Spring Street, 6th Floor, New York, NY 10013. Phone 1-800-SPRINGER, fax (201) 348-4505, e-mail orders-ny@springer-sbm.com, or visit www.springeronline.com.

For information on translations, please e-mail rights@apress.com or visit www.apress.com.

Apress and friends of ED books may be purchased in bulk for academic, corporate, or promotional use. eBook versions and licenses are also available for most titles. For more information, reference our Special Bulk Sales—eBook Licensing web page at www.apress.com/bulk-sales.

The source code for this book is available to readers at www.apress.com. You will need to answer questions pertaining to this book in order to successfully download the code.

To Simona and Claudia, women of mine —Fabio

To my mommy and daddy, my lighthouse in the fog —Emanuele

Contents at a Glance

Contents

About the Authors

▨ **Fabio Claudio Ferracchiati** is a prolific writer and technical reviewer on cutting-edge technologies. He has contributed to many books on .NET, C#, Visual Basic, SQL Server, Silverlight, and ASP.NET. He is a .NET Microsoft Certified Solution Developer (MCSD) and lives in Rome, Italy. He is employed by Brain Force.

▨ **Emanuele Garofalo** was born at Torre del Greco (Naples), Italy, and now lives in Rome. He is an active member of the DotNetCampania community, and works with Windows Presentation Foundation (WPF), Silverlight, Windows Communication Foundation (WCF), Asp.Net, and Language Integrated Query (LINQ) as principal technologies. He is employed by BCSoft.

About the Technical Reviewer

Simona Nasetti is an expert Microsoft Dynamics CRM and Microsoft SQL Server Business Intelligence consultant. She graduated with a mathematics degree and works at Agic Technology (`www.agic.it`) in Rome, Italy, where she creates vertical solutions and reports for the company's clients.

Acknowledgments

First of all, I'd like to thank Ewan Buckingham. During these years we had working experiences together and he has been always patient, kind, and helpful. I'd also like to thank Emanuele for the great job he did working with me to complete this book. Moreover, the Apress guys, each of you have been great. So, thanks to Jessica Belanger, Dominic Shakeshaft, Christine Ricketts, and Sharon Wilkey. Finally, my wife Simona for her efforts especially trying to quiet my daughter's screams while I was writing the book.

—Fabio Claudio Ferracchiati

Thanks to Alessandra for her patience during the writing of this book, to Fabio for the opportunity to write with him, to Ewan, Jessica, Sharon, and all the staff of Apress for their support, and to Michele Aponte and all the DotNetCampania community for the motivation to study new technologies with the spirit of knowledge-sharing.

—Emanuele Garofalo

About This Book

Are you interested in Windows Phone configuration and development? Learn to build, configure, and distribute your applications through a wide variety of step-by-step recipes. This book contains extensive code samples and detailed walk-throughs. Moreover, the book has been updated for the Windows Phone 7.1 SDK version and the Windows Phone 7.5 operating system.

This second edition covers all the new features—multitasking, networking, creating animated Live Tiles, and much more. Also, the recipes have been updated to show what you have to do to update your applications so that they work on this latest operating system.

CHAPTER 1

Introduction to Windows Phone Application Development

This chapter introduces Windows Phone, including its device hardware characteristics and software development tools. After this introduction, you will learn how to create simple applications and how to deploy them. Finally, you are going to look at the application's distribution via Windows Phone Marketplace. The recipes in this chapter describe how to do the following:

- 1-1: Examine Windows Phone hardware

- 1-2: Examine Windows Phone development tools

- 1-3 and 1-4: Create a simple Windows Phone Silverlight and XNA application

- 1-5: Create a simple Silverlight and XNA mixed application

- 1-6 and 1-7: Deploy a Windows Phone application on both the emulator and device

- 1-8: Put a Windows Phone application into Windows Phone Marketplace

- 1-9: Create a Windows Phone trial application

1-1. Examining Windows Phone

Problem

You have just bought your new Windows Phone 7 device and would like to start developing applications. You need to know the device's hardware characteristics, such as screen resolution and memory capability, but also which sensors and services it provides. Finally, you need to understand what the Windows Phone operating system provides in order to integrate your application in the best way.

Solution

If you have Windows Mobile development experience, please erase it! Joking aside, Microsoft has provided a brand new operating system for its new smartphone: Windows Phone. This operating system has been written from scratch in order to reach—and sometime go beyond—other operating systems' functionalities.

To make an operating system that is reliable and fast and has high performance, Microsoft has dictated hardware requirements. So, every Windows Phone–compatible phone on the market right now and in the future has (or will have) at least minimum common hardware characteristics. For us as developers, this is great news, because we can write code having some certainty of what the smartphone provides.

The Windows Phone device provides a screen resolution of 480×800 pixels in portrait orientation. In the future, mobile vendors plan to release smartphones with smaller screens having a resolution of 320×480 pixels. Having this in mind, you can create a game and draw your sprites knowing that your game will be played on a screen with that resolution—so no scale operations, screen text adaptation, and so forth will be necessary. But even for classic applications showing, for example, text boxes and buttons, this resolution is useful for drawing rich user interfaces.

Every phone provides three hardware buttons, usually at the bottom of the screen, as shown in Figure 1-1. They are the Back button, the Start button, and the Search button. The leftmost button is used to go back to the previous application (just like the Back button on an Internet browser). Moreover, holding the Back button for one second, Windows Phone shows the applications that can be resumed (more on this in Chapter 2). The middle button is used to close the current application and to show the Start menu so that the user can open another application. Holding the Start button you can use the Windows Phone voice recognition to retrieve and call a contact, start an application or dictate an SMS message. The rightmost button is used to access the start screen and start a search. You can do simple text searching using Bing site or search song's information letting Windows Phone hearing the song. Moreover, you can use the Windows Phone camera to retrieve information on items either reading their barcode or letting Windows Phone read text and use Microsoft Tag service.

Figure 1-1. *A generic Windows Phone 7 device*

From a developer's point of view, it is important to understand the impact that these buttons have on an application. When each button is pressed, the running application is either deactivated or killed. A developer has to provide code that responds to those events, perhaps saving data in isolated storage (an application's disk-dedicated storage). To redisplay the application, perhaps after the user pushes the Back button, code has to have been written in order to re-create the same situation present before the deactivation. You can see more on this in Chapter 2.

Windows Phone devices have a Soft Input Panel (SIP) that enables users to write text into text boxes. A hardware keyboard is optional. In both cases, the application will receive text input in the same manner. The same is true for key pressure events. The SIP is shown automatically by Windows Phone when text input is required by the user.

In Figure 1-1, you can see the Windows Phone starting page and its *Metro* user interface. Microsoft designers, with users' feedback, have preferred to put the accent on content and information instead of eye-catching graphics. So the screen is populated with something similar to either metro or airport banners. Every square and rectangle is called a *live tile* and gives access to the *hub*. Each live tile is updated in real time with information taken from the hub. The hub is a sort of aggregator to group similar information such as group photos taken from the web, from the phone itself, and from social networks. For example, the Office tile will show counter indicating the number of incoming e-mail when a new e-mail arrives. So the hub contains an aggregation of information that is both local (on the phone) and remote (on the cloud and from the Internet). For example, the *Pictures hub* contains photos taken from the internal camera and from social networks such as Facebook. There are six hubs provided with Windows Phone 7:

- People
- Office
- Pictures
- Music and Videos
- Marketplace
- Games

By the way, the phone is completely customizable, so you can remove live tiles, add your preferred ones, move tiles, and so on. Users can choose between two graphics themes: dark or light. Each presents a different background color (black and white, respectively), which is important to be aware of as you draw your icons, buttons, and images for an application.

The user can interact with Windows Phone by using its multi-touch screen. Using your fingers to perform various gestures such as taps, you can move the tiles, zoom in and zoom out on text and pictures, and so on. Every vendor that produces Windows Phone devices must provide at least a four-point multi-touch capacitive screen so that you can use at least four fingers on the touch screen.

The Windows Phone device ships with 256 MB or more of RAM and with 8 GB or more of flash storage. The CPU depends on vendors but it must provide at least 1 GHz of frequency.

Finally, the Windows Phone device provides sensors and services to bring the user experience to the next level. Here is a list of the most important ones:

A-GPS: This sensor is the Assisted Global Positioning System. It enables users to retrieve their position in the world in terms of longitude and latitude coordinates taken from both satellite services and cell-site triangulation. The latter is less accurate because it represents the nearest radio network from the phone position but it is useful when satellite signals are low or absent.

Accelerometer: This sensor enables programs to understand when the phone has been moved—for example, either because the user has taken it from the desk to respond to a call, or worse, the phone is falling from the user's hands!

Wi-Fi: This sensor enables the phone to connect to a Wi-Fi spot for an Internet connection.

Camera: This sensor enables users to take photos and videos through a 5-megapixel (or more) camera with flash. New Windows Phone models provide a front-camera (usually less powerful) useful to have video calls and video chat.

Office: This service is not so advertised, but every phone has a very usable and powerful version of Microsoft Office with its common applications such as Word, Excel, Outlook, and PowerPoint. The Office Hub is fully integrated with Office 365, and you can also store your documents directly on your SkyDrive cloud hard drive.

Location: Thanks to this service, a user can be located, and that user's position can be represented via Bing Maps.

Push Notifications: This is a great service that prevents phone to polling information from the Internet. The phone waits to receive notifications from programs that live outside the phone avoiding to continually going to search for new information.

Multitasking: Windows Phone implements multitasking allowing developers to create background agents and task scheduling, background file downloading, and background music playing.

Developers can use all these sensors and services together to create innovative applications and sell them on Windows Phone Marketplace. They do not have to worry about hardware differences (for example, whether a certain cell model has the accelerometer) because every Windows Phone has the same minimum features.

1-2. Understanding the Development Tools

Problem

You want to start developing for Windows Phone. You want to know which tools and which languages you have to use to make an application.

Solution

You have to download the Microsoft Windows Phone Developer Tools.

How It Works

We started Recipe 1-1 saying that if you have Windows Mobile development experience, it is better to erase it! This is a joke, of course, but it is not completely false. In Windows Phone development, you don't have the freedom to create low-level applications with C or C++ languages. Using .NET is the only way allowed by Microsoft to develop your applications for Windows Phone. Even if you find a way to go around this limitation—let's say by injecting some Intermediate Language (IL) code at runtime—you still have to remember that every application will be distributed by Windows Phone Marketplace. And, of course, before users can find your application on Marketplace, that application has to go through different approval steps, and you can be sure that any non-.NET application would not pass the certification process.

You can create three kinds of applications: Silverlight for Windows Phone, XNA for Windows Phone, and combining both technologies together. The first uses a custom Silverlight 4 version in which Microsoft has added some specific features. The second uses XNA libraries and is targeted at creating videogames. The third uses a Silverlight and XNA combination. Usually this is great solution for games where the menu and Internet access for scores sharing is accomplished by Silverlight controls and the game engine with animations, music, etc. is done by XNA.

■ **Note** If you plan to release an application for the old Windows Phone 7 operating system you have to know that you can combine Silverlight and XNA technologies in your application, with the only limitation being the user interface; you can't draw controls by using Silverlight and use XNA to draw sprites at the same time. On the other hand, you can use Silverlight for the user interface and XNA libraries to provide full access to media storage on the phone, to capture audio, and more.

You can use either C# or Visual Basic to write your Windows Phone application.

To start developing, you first have to download the Windows Phone Developer Tools from http://create.msdn.com/en-us/home/getting_started. This setup includes Visual Studio 2010 Express for Windows Phone, Windows Phone Emulator, Silverlight Tools, XNA 4, WCF Data Services Client for Window Phone, Microsoft Advertising SDK for Windows Phone, and Microsoft Expression Blend for Windows Phone. If you already have Visual Studio 2010 installed on your machine, the setup will install only the necessary files and you will see new project templates the next time you start the development tool.

Let's see the necessary steps to install the Microsoft Windows Phone Developer Tools:

1. Launch the installer (vm_web.exe) after having downloaded it.

2. Accept the license agreement.

3. Optionally, choose the Customized installation so you can select a folder in which to install the tools.

4. Wait for the installer to download all the necessary files from the Internet. The number of files downloaded depends on what the installer finds already in your operating system.

5. If you have to install the developer tools on machines not connected to the Internet, you can use the ISO version from http://go.microsoft.com/fwlink/?LinkID=223971.

1-3. Creating a Simple Silverlight Windows Phone Application

Problem

You have to create a Windows Phone application by using Silverlight.

Solution

Use Visual Studio 2010 (either the Express, Professional, or superior edition). Use the Windows Phone Application project template.

How It Works

After opening Visual Studio 2010, you have to create a new project. From the File menu, choose New Item. Project item (or press Ctrl+Shift+N). Figure 1-2 shows the dialog box that appears after launching the New Project command.

Figure 1-2. Visual Studio 2010 New Project dialog box

From the Installed Templates on the left, select Silverlight for Windows Phone. There are five project templates provided by Visual Studio 2010:

- *Windows Phone Application* creates a skeleton code for a generic phone application; no controls or other stuff are added.

- *Windows Phone Databound Application* creates a Windows Phone application, adding List and Navigation controls.

- *Windows Phone Class Library* creates a skeleton code for an external assembly specific to Windows Phone.

- *Windows Phone Panorama Application* creates an application including the Panorama control (see more on that in Chapter 3, Recipe 3-7).

- *Windows Phone Pivot Application* creates an application including the Pivot control (see more on that in Chapter 3, Recipe 3-7).

- *Windows Phone Silverlight and XNA Application* creates an application that uses both Silverlight and XNA technologies (see more on that in Recipe 1-5).

- *Windows Phone Audio Playback Agent* creates a class library with a background agent to play music in background (see more on that in Chapter 8, Recipe 8-6).*Windows Phone Audio Streaming Agent* creates a class library with a background agent to stream audio (see more on that in Chapter 8, Recipe 8-6).

- *Windows Phone Scheduled Task Agent* creates a class library with a background agent to perform scheduled tasks (see more on that in Chapter 2, Recipes 2-8, 2-9, 2-10).

Select the Windows Phone Application project template and type `SimpleSilverlightApplication` in the project's Name text box. Choose a Location where you want to save the project and then click the OK button.

Visual Studio 2010 will ask you to select the target platform for your new Windows Phone application. Select the Windows Phone OS 7.1 item from the dialog box and click the OK button (see Figure 1-3).

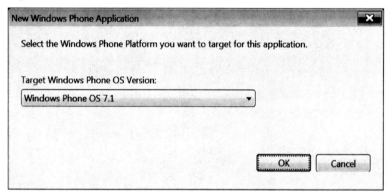

Figure 1-3: Visual Studio 2010 asks to select the target Windows Phone OS version.

■ **Note** Visual Studio 2010 offers the multi-targeting functionality that allows developer to create either old Windows Phone 7 application or the new Windows Phone 7.1 application. If you plan to develop an application that doesn't use new features such as networking, live tiles, etc., you can select the older Windows Phone OS 7.0 version in order to have assurance that your application will run on every phone mounting both the older and newer operating system.

Wait while Visual Studio 2010 writes every file and folder, and after a few seconds you should have `MainPage.xaml` opened in the integrated development environment (IDE) of Visual Studio 2010 (see Figure 1-4).

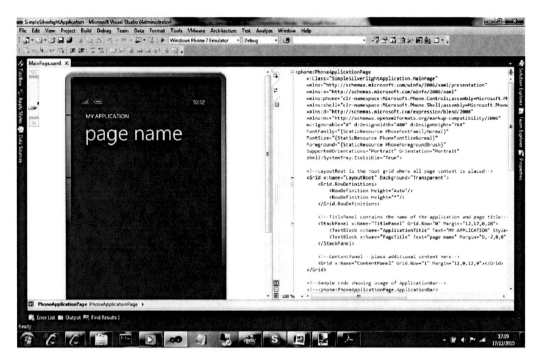

Figure 1-4. `MainPage.xaml` *ready to be edited*

The Code

The project contains two main files: `App.xaml` and `MainPage.xaml`. Two classes are created: the App class and the MainPage class (see class diagram in Figure 1-5). The other files are resources such as a splash screen image, background image, and the application icon. Finally, there is an application manifest file called `WMAppManifest` that contains application data such as the application's title, the resource names, and so forth. It also includes a list of capabilities that you have to specify when you want to use a particular phone feature. For example, if you want to use the phone microphone in your application, you have to add the `ID_CAP_MICROPHONE` capability. The file comes with more than ten capabilities already defined in it; you should remove the ones you don't use.

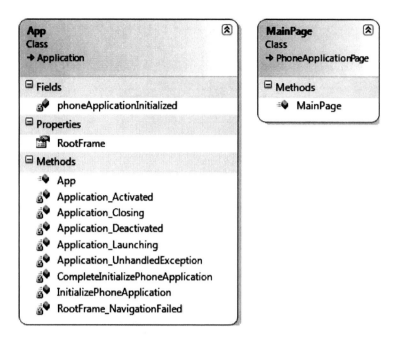

Figure 1-5. The class diagram for the App and MainPage classes

Let's focus our attention on the main two files. The `MainPage.xaml` file contains the Extensible Application Markup Language (XAML) markups that define the main page. At the beginning of the code, all the namespaces used by the application are declared.

```
<phone:PhoneApplicationPage
    x:Class="SimpleSilverlightApplication.MainPage"
    xmlns="http://schemas.microsoft.com/winfx/2006/xaml/presentation"
    xmlns:x="http://schemas.microsoft.com/winfx/2006/xaml"
    xmlns:phone="clr-namespace:Microsoft.Phone.Controls;assembly=Microsoft.Phone"
    xmlns:shell="clr-namespace:Microsoft.Phone.Shell;assembly=Microsoft.Phone"
    xmlns:d="http://schemas.microsoft.com/expression/blend/2008"
    xmlns:mc="http://schemas.openxmlformats.org/markup-compatibility/2006"
```

....

The root tag is `PhoneApplicationPage`, which is the class from which our application derives. The prefix `phone:` is necessary because the `PhoneApplicationPage` name is defined in the namespace `clr-namespace:Microsoft.Phone.Controls;assembly=Microsoft.Phone`. The `x:Class` attribute states that the `MainPage` class is defined in the code-behind and is included in the `SimpleSilverlightApplication` namespace. The first namespace in the XAML code is the main Silverlight namespace; the `x` namespace contains definitions of all extra XAML elements not defined in the previous namespace. The `shell`, `d`, and `mc` namespaces are specific to the Windows Phone application and contain markups for shell instructions, Microsoft Expression Blend, and the Visual Studio designer.

The other attributes of the `<phone:PhoneApplicationPage>` markup are used to define the application's orientation, font, and colors. It is worth noting the use of static resources provided by the

Windows Phone resource dictionary (see `http://msdn.microsoft.com/en-us/library/ff769552(v=vs.92).aspx` for the full list of available resources).

```
....
    mc:Ignorable="d" d:DesignWidth="480" d:DesignHeight="768"
    FontFamily="{StaticResource PhoneFontFamilyNormal}"
    FontSize="{StaticResource PhoneFontSizeNormal}"
    Foreground="{StaticResource PhoneForegroundBrush}"
    SupportedOrientations="Portrait" Orientation="Portrait"
    shell:SystemTray.IsVisible="True">
```

Then the code includes a grid with two rows. In the first row is a stack panel with two text blocks, and in the second row is a content panel where you can add your controls.

```
<!--LayoutRoot is the root grid where all page content is placed-->
<Grid x:Name="LayoutRoot" Background="Transparent">
    <Grid.RowDefinitions>
        <RowDefinition Height="Auto"/>
        <RowDefinition Height="*"/>
    </Grid.RowDefinitions>

    <!--TitlePanel contains the name of the application and page title-->
    <StackPanel x:Name="TitlePanel" Grid.Row="0" Margin="12,17,0,28">
        <TextBlock x:Name="ApplicationTitle" Text="MY APPLICATION"
                   Style="{StaticResource PhoneTextNormalStyle}"/>
        <TextBlock x:Name="PageTitle" Text="page name" Margin="9,-7,0,0"
                   Style="{StaticResource PhoneTextTitle1Style}"/>
    </StackPanel>
    <!--ContentPanel - place additional content here-->
    <Grid x:Name="ContentPanel" Grid.Row="1" Margin="12,0,12,0"></Grid>
</Grid>
```

The other important file is `App.xaml` and its related code-behind `App.xaml.cs` file. The `Application` root tag represents the class from which our App class derives. Again, the `x:Class` attribute contains the name of our class and the namespace in which it is contained. The namespaces are the same as those you have seen before. The `<Application.Resources>` markup is used to add custom resources to the application. But the most important code section is the one included in `<Application.ApplicationLifetimeObjects>`, which defines four event handlers in response to four important events in the application's lifetime. The `Launching` event occurs when the application is started, the `Closing` event occurs before the application is closed, the `Activated` event occurs when the user comes back to the application after having browsed to other phone applications, and the `Deactivated` event occurs when the user leaves the application (for example, by pressing the Back button or answering an incoming call).

```
<Application
    x:Class="SimpleSilverlightApplication.App"
    xmlns="http://schemas.microsoft.com/winfx/2006/xaml/presentation"
    xmlns:x="http://schemas.microsoft.com/winfx/2006/xaml"
```

```
    xmlns:phone="clr-namespace:Microsoft.Phone.Controls;assembly=Microsoft.Phone"
    xmlns:shell="clr-namespace:Microsoft.Phone.Shell;assembly=Microsoft.Phone">

    <!--Application Resources-->
    <Application.Resources>
    </Application.Resources>

    <Application.ApplicationLifetimeObjects>
        <!--Required object that handles lifetime events for the application-->
        <shell:PhoneApplicationService
            Launching="Application_Launching" Closing="Application_Closing"
            Activated="Application_Activated" Deactivated="Application_Deactivated"/>
    </Application.ApplicationLifetimeObjects>
</Application>
```

In the App.xaml.cs code-behind, there is a lot of interesting auto-generated code. First, there are the event handlers, where you have to insert your code to respond to application tombstoning (see more on tombstoning in Chapter 2).

```
    // Code to execute when the application is launching (e.g., from Start)
    // This code will not execute when the application is reactivated
    private void Application_Launching(object sender, LaunchingEventArgs e)
    {
    }

    // Code to execute when the application is activated (brought to foreground)
    // This code will not execute when the application is first launched
    private void Application_Activated(object sender, ActivatedEventArgs e)
    {
    }

    // Code to execute when the application is deactivated (sent to background)
    // This code will not execute when the application is closing
    private void Application_Deactivated(object sender, DeactivatedEventArgs e)
    {
    }

    // Code to execute when the application is closing (e.g., user hit Back)
    // This code will not execute when the application is deactivated
    private void Application_Closing(object sender, ClosingEventArgs e)
    {
    }
```

In the App class's constructor, there are application initialization steps.

```
    public App()
    {
    ...
```

```
        // Standard Silverlight initialization
        InitializeComponent();

        // Phone-specific initialization
        InitializePhoneApplication();
    }
```

In the InitializePhoneApplication method, RootFrame is created. Frame is the topmost control that contains phone pages. It allows page navigation, manages orientation, and reserves space for the system bar and application bar. The Navigated event is used to understand when the application has completed the initialization. Until then, a splash screen is shown. The SplashScreenImage.jpg image will be used as a splash screen, but you can customize it or replace it with another one you prefer.

```
    private void InitializePhoneApplication()
    {
        if (phoneApplicationInitialized)
            return;

        // Create the frame but don't set it as RootVisual yet;
        // this allows the splash
        // screen to remain active until the application is ready to render.
        RootFrame = new PhoneApplicationFrame();
        RootFrame.Navigated += CompleteInitializePhoneApplication;

        // Handle navigation failures
        RootFrame.NavigationFailed += RootFrame_NavigationFailed;

        // Ensure we don't initialize again
        phoneApplicationInitialized = true;
    }
```

Finally, in the CompleteInitializePhoneApplication event handler, the RootVisual property is set to RootFrame. RootVisual is the main application user interface.

```
    private void CompleteInitializePhoneApplication(object sender,
                                            NavigationEventArgs e)
    {
        // Set the root visual to allow the application to render
        if (RootVisual != RootFrame)
            RootVisual = RootFrame;

        // Remove this handler since it is no longer needed
        RootFrame.Navigated -= CompleteInitializePhoneApplication;
    }
```

Usage

Press Ctrl+F5 (or choose Debug Start Without Debugging from the menu).After Visual Studio 2010 compiles the code, the application will start. Visual Studio 2010 will launch the Windows Phone

Emulator application (unless you changed the target from the related combo box that is Windows Phone Emulator by default), and you will be able to see your application running in the emulator, as shown in Figure 1-6.

Figure 1-6. Simple Silverlight for Windows Phone application running in the emulator

1-4. Creating a Simple XNA Windows Phone Application

Problem

You have to create a Windows Phone application by using XNA.

Solution

Use Visual Studio 2010 (either Express, Professional, or superior edition). Use the Windows Phone Game (4.0) project template.

How It Works

Press Ctrl+Shift+N after opening Visual Studio 2010. This brings up the New Project dialog box. Select the XNA Game Studio 4.0 template from the Installed Templates on the left and select the Windows Phone Game (4.0) project template (see Figure 1-7). Type **SimpleXNAApplication** in the project Name text box and then click the OK button.

Figure 1-7. Create a new XNA Windows Phone application by using the Windows Phone Game (4.0) project template.

Click the OK button to select the Windows Phone OS 7.1 platform and after few moments, you will have two projects in the solution. One contains the files to create the game, and the other is specifically for game resources such as sprites, images, and sounds.

The Code

The main file in the project is Game1.cs; it contains the code to create a game in Windows Phone using the Game1 class derived from the Game class (Figure 1-8 shows its own class diagram). The project template does nothing relevant other than creating the code to paint the screen with the CornflowerBlue color. But it is worth noting the class structure and its methods to understand how the XNA game works.

Figure 1-8. The Game1 and Game classes diagram

In the class's constructor, a GraphicsDeviceManager object is created. This object represents the graphic device manager of the Windows Phone and contains properties used to change resolution, toggle full-screen mode, and more. It sets the refreshing frame rate to 30 frames per second (fps), which means that in 1 second, the Update method is called 30 times. Finally, when the phone screen is locked the code saves battery consuming setting the InactiveSleepTime property to one second.

```
public Game1()
{
    graphics = new GraphicsDeviceManager(this);
    Content.RootDirectory = "Content";

    // Frame rate is 30 fps by default for Windows Phone.
```

```
        TargetElapsedTime = TimeSpan.FromTicks(333333);

        // Extend battery life under lock.
        InactiveSleepTime = TimeSpan.FromSeconds(1);
    }
```

The Initialize method is where you have to put the code to initialize your objects.

```
    protected override void Initialize()
    {
        // TODO: Add your initialization logic here

        base.Initialize();
    }
```

The next method that is called by the XNA framework is LoadContent. In this method, you have to load the content previously added to the Content project in the solution. You can add images, sounds, sprites, 3D models, and all your game resources.

```
    protected override void LoadContent()
    {
        // Create a new SpriteBatch, which can be used to draw textures.
        spriteBatch = new SpriteBatch(GraphicsDevice);

        // TODO: use this.Content to load your game content here
    }
```

Finally, the XNA game framework enters into a loop in which two methods are automatically called one by one—first the Update method and then the Draw method. In the Update method, you have to add the code that manages the game's logic, the sprites' movement, a collision algorithm, and so on. The Draw method is where you draw the game objects and you have to be faster to do it. Your game code shouldn't update and check objects in the Draw method.

```
    protected override void Update(GameTime gameTime)
    {
        // Allows the game to exit
        if (GamePad.GetState(PlayerIndex.One).Buttons.Back == ButtonState.Pressed)
            this.Exit();

        // TODO: Add your update logic here

        base.Update(gameTime);
    }

    protected override void Draw(GameTime gameTime)
    {
        GraphicsDevice.Clear(Color.CornflowerBlue);
```

```
        // TODO: Add your drawing code here

        base.Draw(gameTime);
    }
```

There is another method defined in the code that is used to unload the content when the game is closed.

```
    protected override void UnloadContent()
    {
        // TODO: Unload any non ContentManager content here
    }
```

■ **Note** In this book, you will find XNA code used to provide access to Windows Phone features such as the media library and audio files. If you are interested in Windows Phone game development, take a look at *Windows Phone 7 Game Development* by Adam Dawes (Apress, 2010).

Usage

Press Ctrl+F5 to see the game running in the emulator (see Figure 1-9).

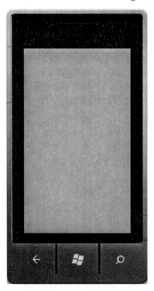

Figure 1-9. SimpleXNAApplication running on the Windows Phone Emulator

1-5. Creating a Simple XNA and Silverlight Mixed Application

Problem

You need to create an application that uses both XNA and Silverlight technologies to manage visuals. For example, you could create a game where menus and the scoreboard are done with Silverlight controls and the game engine and sprites' rendering are accomplished by XNA.

Solution

You can use the Visual Studio 2010's Windows Phone Silverlight and XNA Application template that creates a code skeleton where is implemented the SharedGraphicsDeviceManager class. This class provides static methods useful to retrieve a reference to the graphic device and so to access to its methods and properties.

How It Works

After opening Visual Studio 2010, you have to create a new project. From the File menu, choose New Item Project item (or press Ctrl+Shift+N). As illustrated in Figure 1-10, select the Windows Phone Silverlight and XNA Application template from the New Project dialog box. Specify the SimpleMixedXNASIApplication name in the Name textbox and click on the OK button.

Figure 1-10. Create a mixed XNA and Silverlight Windows Phone application.

The project content is similar to a Windows Phone with Silverlight project but with some additions. First of all, the project contains other two projects. One project is the XNA Content project useful to store images, music, sprites, etc. The other one is a Windows Phone Library that references the XNA Content library.

The main project contains the App.xaml and MainPage.xaml pages as usual but it contains even the GamePage.xaml page. The GamePage.xaml page is where you have to insert the game code using the XNA library. Finally, the main project contains the AppServiceProvider.cs file where the AppServiceProvider class is defined. This class implements the IServiceProvider interface and is useful to add the IGraphicsDeviceService interface to the application.

The Code

To let a Windows Phone with Silverlight application to access to the XNA graphic device and the Content library, where graphic and music are stored, the App class has to implement the IServiceProvider interface. An object that implements this interface is required by the ContentManager class constructor. The App class provides the Content property that has to be set with an object created from the ContentManager class.

The AppServiceProvider class contained in the AppServiceProvider.cs file is the class that implements the IServiceProvider interface:

```
public class AppServiceProvider : IServiceProvider
{
    // A map of service type to the services themselves
    private readonly Dictionary<Type, object> services = new
                                    Dictionary<Type, object>();

    public void AddService(Type serviceType, object service)
    {
        // Validate the input
        if (serviceType == null)
            throw new ArgumentNullException("serviceType");
        if (service == null)
            throw new ArgumentNullException("service");
        if (!serviceType.IsAssignableFrom(service.GetType()))
            throw new ArgumentException("service does not match the
                                    specified serviceType");

        // Add the service to the dictionary
        services.Add(serviceType, service);
    }

    public object GetService(Type serviceType)
    {
        // Validate the input
        if (serviceType == null)
            throw new ArgumentNullException("serviceType");

        // Retrieve the service from the dictionary
        return services[serviceType];
    }
```

```
    public void RemoveService(Type serviceType)
    {
        // Validate the input
        if (serviceType == null)
            throw new ArgumentNullException("serviceType");

        // Remove the service from the dictionary
        services.Remove(serviceType);
    }
}
```

The GetService method is the only method you have to implement in your code to respect the IServiceProvider interface contract. By the way, in the code added to the Visual Studio 2010 project there are other two methods to add and remove services from a class Dictionary variable called services.

The App class code is pretty much the same as you saw in Recipe 1-3 with the addition of an XNA initialization section. In the App class constructor the InitializeXnaApplication method is called. In this method the ApplicationLifetimeObjects collection is used to search for the IGraphicsDeviceService interface. The ApplicationLifetimeObjects returns the application extension services that have been specified in the App XAML code. As you can see from the code below the SharedGraphicsDeviceManager service has been added to the ApplicationLifetimeObjects section. In that way the service will be added to the App class so that the SharedGraphicsDeviceManager class can be used.

```
<Application
    . . .
    xmlns:xna="clr-namespace:Microsoft.Xna.Framework;
            assembly=Microsoft.Xna.Framework.Interop">


    . . .

    <Application.ApplicationLifetimeObjects>
        <!--Required object that handles lifetime events for the
        application-->
        <shell:PhoneApplicationService
            Launching="Application_Launching"
            Closing="Application_Closing"
            Activated="Application_Activated"
            Deactivated="Application_Deactivated"/>

        <!--The SharedGraphicsDeviceManager is used to render with the XNA
            Graphics APIs-->

        <xna:SharedGraphicsDeviceManager />

    </Application.ApplicationLifetimeObjects>
</Application>
```

Once the IGraphicsDeviceService interface is found it is stored into an AppServiceProvider object called Services that is successively used during the ContentManager object's creation.

Finally, a GameTimer object is created and started. The FrameAction event is used to periodically call the Update method. As the code comments say this is necessary to manage XNA events and functionalities.

```
    // Performs initialization of the XNA types required for the
    // application.
```

21

```
private void InitializeXnaApplication()
{
    // Create the service provider
    Services = new AppServiceProvider();

    // Add the SharedGraphicsDeviceManager to the Services as the
    // IGraphicsDeviceService for the app
    foreach (object obj in ApplicationLifetimeObjects)
    {
        if (obj is IGraphicsDeviceService)
            Services.AddService(typeof(IGraphicsDeviceService), obj);
    }

    // Create the ContentManager so the application can load
    // precompiled assets
    Content = new ContentManager(Services, "Content");

    // Create a GameTimer to pump the XNA FrameworkDispatcher
    FrameworkDispatcherTimer = new GameTimer();
    FrameworkDispatcherTimer.FrameAction +=
                            FrameworkDispatcherFrameAction;
    FrameworkDispatcherTimer.Start();
}

// An event handler that pumps the FrameworkDispatcher each frame.
// FrameworkDispatcher is required for a lot of the XNA events and
// for certain functionality such as SoundEffect playback.
private void FrameworkDispatcherFrameAction(object sender,
                                        EventArgs e)
{
    FrameworkDispatcher.Update();
}
```

So now you have access to the XNA graphic device; let's see the GamePage.xaml code to understand how to use the graphic device to render graphics in the application.

In the GamePage class constructor a GameTimer object is created and the Update and Draw events are used to update the game logic and draw the graphics, respectively. The UpdateInterval property is set to manage 30 frames per second. Finally, the Content property provided by the App class is used to retrieve a reference to the ContentManager object that is useful to manage graphic and music game content.

```
public partial class GamePage : PhoneApplicationPage
{
    ContentManager contentManager;
    GameTimer timer;
    SpriteBatch spriteBatch;

    public GamePage()
    {
        InitializeComponent();

        // Get the content manager from the application
```

```
        contentManager = (Application.Current as App).Content;

        // Create a timer for this page
        timer = new GameTimer();
        timer.UpdateInterval = TimeSpan.FromTicks(333333);
        timer.Update += OnUpdate;
        timer.Draw += OnDraw;
    }
```

Next the OnNavigatedTo method is used to initialize some stuff. The OnNavigatedTo method is automatically invoked by the operating system when the page is loaded in the page's frame. Because the page is active, the SetSharingMode is set to true so that in the OnDraw method the XNA graphic device can be used to draw the graphics. Finally, some other initialization code is defined in the OnNavigatedTo method to create a SpriteBatch object and to start the game timer.

```
    protected override void OnNavigatedTo(NavigationEventArgs e)
    {
        // Set the sharing mode of the graphics device to turn on XNA
        // rendering
        SharedGraphicsDeviceManager.Current.GraphicsDevice.
                                        SetSharingMode(true);

        // Create a new SpriteBatch, which can be used to draw textures.
        spriteBatch = new
        SpriteBatch(SharedGraphicsDeviceManager.Current.GraphicsDevice);

        // TODO: use this.content to load your game content here

        // Start the timer
        timer.Start();

        base.OnNavigatedTo(e);
    }

    private void OnDraw(object sender, GameTimerEventArgs e)
    {
        SharedGraphicsDeviceManager.Current.GraphicsDevice.Clear(
            Color.CornflowerBlue);

        // TODO: Add your drawing code here
    }
```

Finally, the OnNavigatedFrom method is added to the code in order to stop the timer and set the SetSharingMode of the SharedGraphicsDeviceManager to false. The OnNavigatedFrom method is the ideal place to specify this kind of code because this method is called just before the page is becoming inactive. Indeed, there is no need to have access to the XNA graphic device when there is nothing to draw!

```
    protected override void OnNavigatedFrom(NavigationEventArgs e)
    {
        // Stop the timer
        timer.Stop();
```

```
                // Set the sharing mode of the graphics device to turn off XNA
                // rendering
                SharedGraphicsDeviceManager.Current.GraphicsDevice.
                                              SetSharingMode(false);

                base.OnNavigatedFrom(e);
        }
```

■ **Note** The Visual Studio 2010 project doesn't contain the code that covers an important aspect of XNA and Silverlight integration. You can add Silverlight controls to the XAML page that uses the XNA library to render graphic objects. In order to render even Silverlight controls you need to add a couple of instructions: a method that is called when the page layout has completed useful to create a UIElementRenderer object. Then in the OnDraw method, where the application graphics is rendered, you can use the UIElementRenderer object and its own Render method that displays Silverlight controls on the page. You can find a couple of good examples in the Code Samples web page at http://msdn.microsoft.com/en-us/library/ff431744(v=VS.92).aspx.

Usage

Press Ctrl+F5 or choose Debug Start Without Debugging. If your code builds correctly, you will see your application running in the Windows Phone Emulator (see Figure 1-11).

Figure 1-11. The SimpleMixedXNASIApplication Main Page

Pressing the Change to game page button the application will show the page that uses the XNA graphic device (see Figure 1-12). In this page the XNA library is used to simply fill the screen with the CornFlowerBlue color.

Figure 1-12. The GamePage.xaml page that uses XNA to render its own graphics

1-6. Deploying the Application to the Windows Phone Emulator

Problem

You have developed your application and want to run it, but you don't have the physical device.

Solution

From Visual Studio 2010—with your phone project loaded—select Windows Phone Emulator from the target combo box (see Figure 1-13).

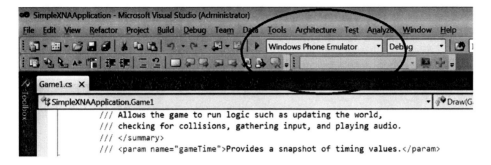

Figure 1-13. The target combo box set to Windows Phone 7 Emulator

Usage

Press Ctrl+F5 or choose Debug   Start Without Debugging. If your code builds correctly, you will see your application running in the Windows Phone Emulator (see Figure 1-14).

Figure 1-14. Windows Phone Emulator

This emulator is very powerful. It supports multi-touch capabilities if your PC monitor supports touching. It supports graphics acceleration if your graphical device supports DirectX 9 or higher. It emulates sensors such as the accelerator, and the A-GPS for the phone location and position. Clicking on the chevron button from the floating menu next to the emulator (see Figure 1-14) the Additional Tools window is shown (see Figure 1-15).

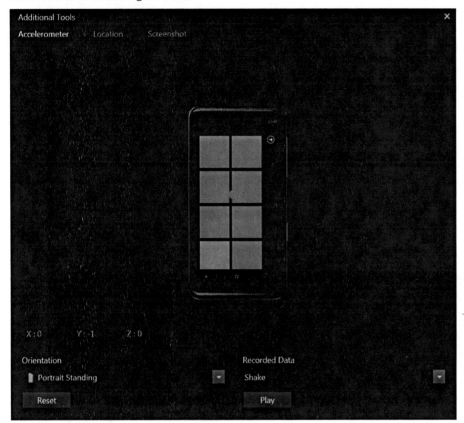

Figure 1-15. The Additional Tools window

The Additional Tools window provides three tabs: Accelerometer, Location, and Screenshot. The accelerometer tool allows developers to simulate the accelerometer sensor. With the Recorded Data functionality you can simulate phone movements such as the phone's shake. The Orientation combo box allows developers to choose the initial phone's orientation. By moving the pink dot in the middle of the 3D phone model you can rotate the phone in the 3D space.

The Location tab provides a map indicating the phone location (see Figure 1-16).

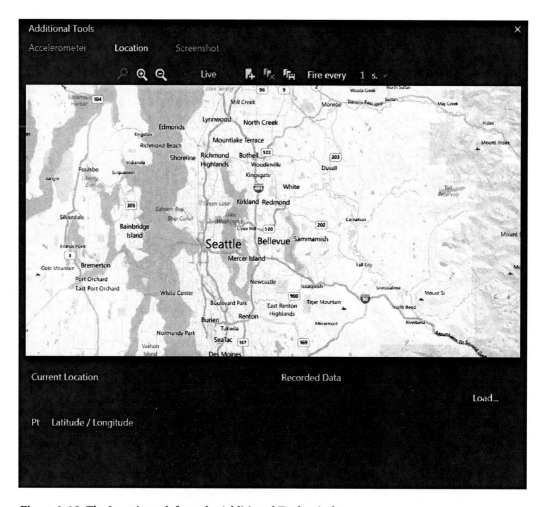

Figure 1-16. The Location tab from the Additional Tools window

You can search for a location by using the Search textbox and then zooming in and out by using lens icons to refine the research. Clicking in the map you set the current location and the related window's area Current Location and Pt Latitude/Longitude will be updated accordingly. You can continue to click on the map to add points creating a sort of path that can be saved on a file and used in a second moment by loading it with the Load… button in the Recorded Data window's area.

The Screenshot tool simply takes screenshots from the emulator and saves them in files. In that way, providing screenshots for your application during Marketplace acceptance phase will be easier.

Note The Multi-Touch Vista library from CodePlex enables users to use multiple mice to simulate fingers. After installing this multi-touch driver, you can test your multi-touch Windows Phone application in the emulator. Download the driver from http://multitouchvista.codeplex.com.

After launching the emulator for the first time, it is convenient to not close it. Every change you make to your code and deploy to the opened emulator will then be visible and testable. With no need to rerun the emulator, the deployment is much faster.

The emulator contains the working version of Internet Explorer 9 plus the Settings application used to change the phone background and styles.

In Figure 1-14, you can see next to the emulator a little floating rectangle with some icons. These buttons are used to close the emulator, minimize it, rotate it, zoom it, and run additional tools. If you choose a 100% zoom level, you will see a large Windows Phone emulator on your monitor. That's because the Windows operating system assumes that your monitor is 96 dpi, while the Windows Phone display has 262 DPI. To enable you to see all the pixels in your monitor, the emulator shows a very large screen.

1-7. Deploying the Windows Phone Application on the Device

Problem

You want to deploy your application to the Windows Phone device because you have to test the sensors' functionalities.

Solution

You have two ways to deploy your application to the phone: using either Visual Studio 2010 or the Application Deployment tool.

How It Works

In both cases, you have to download and install the latest version of Zune software from www.zune.net/en-US/. Zune is an entertainment device—initially available only in the United States—and it is Microsoft's response to Apple's iPod family of devices. You can transfer your music and videos by using the Zune software, but you can use it to deploy your software, too.

Moreover, in both cases, you have to unlock your Windows Phone device with a developer license. You can obtain a license from Microsoft's App Hub site at http://create.msdn.com/en-us/home/membership by paying an annual $99 fee. In the registration, you will associate your Windows Live ID account with an App Hub identifier. This coupling of data is necessary to unlock your Windows Phone device with the help of the Windows Phone Developer Registration tool, which you find within the tools installed with the Windows Phone Developer Tools (see Figure 1-17).

Figure 1-17. The Windows Phone Developer Registration tool used to unlock your phone and deploy applications

---

■ **Note** As you can see in Figure 1-17, Zune software is required to unlock the Windows Phone 7 device.

Okay, after completing these mandatory steps, your device is ready to receive your application. From Visual Studio 2010, you simply have to change the target combo box from Windows Phone Emulator to Windows Phone Device.

Usage

Now, as usual, you can press F5 to start a debug session or press Ctrl+F5 to start the application without the debug. Visual Studio 2010 will compile your application, start Zune software to connect to the Windows Phone device, copy the XAP file to the device, and finally run the application. In your device, you will see your application running.

■ **Note** The Windows Phone Developer Tools includes the WPConnect.exe program. When your application uses the Windows Phone media library or plays a song, it will find those resources locked by Zune software. You have to close Zune software after having connected the phone and then run WPConnect.exe. The device will remain connected, but now you have full access to the phone device.

The second method to deploy your application on the Windows Phone device is to run the Application Deployment tool (see Figure 1-18).

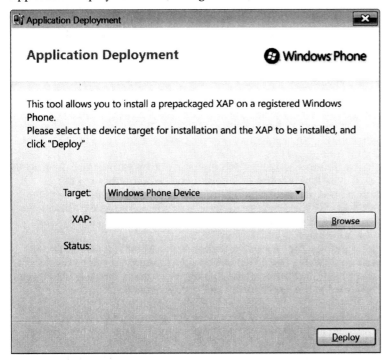

Figure 1-18. The Application Deployment tool used to deploy your application without Visual Studio 2010

The target combo box contains both device and emulator targets. The XAP text box contains the path of your application's XAP file. When you compile your application, Visual Studio 2010 creates the XAP file, which is a compressed file containing everything Windows Phone needs to run the application (EXE, DLLl, images, and so on). After you click the Deploy button, the Application Deployment tool connects to the phone and deploys the application.

1-8. Sending a Windows Phone Application to the Marketplace

Problem

You want to distribute your application by using Windows Phone Marketplace.

Solution

You have to go to the App Hub site and follow the application submission walk-through.

How It Works

Windows Phone Marketplace is the place where you can find applications, music, videos, and more for your device. If you know the Apple Store or Android Market, well, this is the same type of site. The marketplace categorizes applications and lets you download free, trial, and paid applications. When you are satisfied with one application, you can buy it either with electronic payment such as a credit card or by adding the cost to your billing, if your mobile operator lets you do that.

Actually, there is no other way to distribute your application than the marketplace. If you develop an enterprise application and need to distribute it to employees' phones, you have to submit to the marketplace as well. You will probably register the application as private so that it will not be visible to public searching. Informing the employee with the Marketplace link he or she will be able to download the application and install on the phone. The Marketplace application on the phone will inform the employee when an application update is available, automatically.

Every application running on the Windows Phone must be signed with a Microsoft Authenticode certificate. You don't have to sign your application, because it will be signed after Microsoft's review of your application submission. If your application satisfies all the Marketplace conditions, the XAP file will be signed, and the application will be added to the application's category provided during the submission walk-through.

This is not true for application registered as beta; the Marketplace acceptance phase doesn't sign them because they are not completed. A beta application can be downloaded by up to 100 beta testers and the testing period is limited to 90 days.

There is an official document at http://go.microsoft.com/fwlink/?LinkID=183220 called Windows Phone Certification Requirements. It is 27 pages long and contains everything you have to do and avoid doing so that your application satisfies Marketplace conditions. Let's see the most important rules for a developer:

- The maximum XAP size is 225 MB. This file must contain both WMAppManifest.xml and AppManifest.xml files, assemblies, and two icons. By the way, Visual Studio 2010 provides everything you need to create a valid XAP automatically.

- Your application must be developed by using the .NET Framework and cannot use native code. Before submitting the XAP package, you have to build the retail version of your application.

- The application must be reliable. The certification process will check whether the application manages errors, hangs unexpectedly, or has long periods of inactivity caused, for example, by data downloading. In the latter case, you have to provide users a way to cancel the operation and display a progress bar indicating the status of the operation.

- The application must show the first screen within 5 seconds. As you have seen in Recipe 1-3, the Silverlight Windows Phone application provides a splash screen, so you might think that this rule is always satisfied. Sadly, it is not, because the splash screen must disappear within 5 seconds, and the main page has to be rendered. If your application takes longer, you can implement a splash screen with a progress bar, as shown in Chapter 3, Recipe 3-1. The user must use your application within 20 seconds.

- The application must respond correctly to execution model events. When the user presses the Start button, the Windows Phone application should be deactivated; when the user presses the Back button and comes back to your application, it should be activated and should show the same screen information that it was running in the background. Chapter 2 is completely dedicated to the execution model and application tombstoning.

- The application must be usable with the phone's templates, dark and light. So if you have images or other graphics effects working well in one template, you have to implement an algorithm to replace them if the user changes the phone's template.

■ **Note** There is an interesting article at `http://blogs.msdn.com/b/devfish/archive/2010/10/06/ben-s-big-ten-for-wp7-marketplace-acceptance.aspx` that highlights the ten most important rules that you have to satisfy so that your application passes the acceptance process.

Visual Studio 2010 provides the Marketplace Test kit that allows developer to test the application in the same way the Marketplace acceptance phase analyzes the application after the application submitting. See more on this in Chapter 11, Recipe 11-5.

1-9. Creating a Trial Windows Phone Application

Problem

You want to distribute an application that provides a trial version. Also, you want your application to remind users to buy the full version.

Solution

You have to use the Guide class from the GamerServices namespace, which provides properties and methods enabling you to check whether your application is running in trial version mode. Moreover, the Guide class provides methods to simulate both trial mode and buy request when your application is running in either debug mode or in the emulator.

How It Works

Microsoft again helps developers: Marketplace implements a feature enabling users to choose between a trial version and a full version of your application. As a developer, you don't have to provide two versions of your software, but simply check your code to see whether the application is running in trial mode. In fact, when the user chooses to install the trial version of your application, Marketplace adds a trial license file to the directory where the application is installed. If the user decides to buy the application after having tried it, Marketplace replaces the trial license with a full license.

Depending on the framework chosen to write your application, either XNA or Silverlight, there are different ways to check whether the application is running in trial mode. The XNA framework provides the Guide class contained in the GamerServices namespace (see Figure 1-19 for the Guide class diagram). The Silverlight framework provides the LicenseInformation sealed class with the IsTrial method.

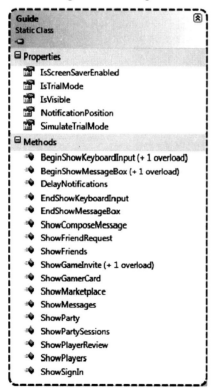

Figure 1-19. *The Guide class diagram*

Your job as a developer in implementing trial mode in the application is to add test conditions in your code, excluding extra application functionalities available only after the user buys the full version of the application. For example, you can show extra menus during the load of the form when the IsTrial method returns false, or you can show an image in your game indicating that the next level is locked if the IsTrialMode property of the Guide class returns true.

As stated before, Marketplace informs the application if it has been bought or if it is in trial mode. So when you test your application in the emulator or from your device, and the application is not being installed by Marketplace, both the IsTrial method and the IsTrialMode property return false. Therefore, it is not so easy to test the application functionalities in trial mode. By the way, there are a lot of solutions that you can implement to resolve this behavior and decide when to run the application in trial mode or full mode. It has been suggested that you could create your own version of the LicenseInformation class, use the var keyword to define the object instanciated from it, and specify via an internal member field whether the application is a trial or not. After testing the code, you could simply remove the class from the project and change a few other code rows. But we don't like this solution, because the XNA framework provides the SimulateTrialMode property from the Guide class, which enables you to specify when the application is in trial mode (by setting the property to true) or not (by setting the property to false).

The Guide class can be used with Silverlight applications too. This is an example of using mixed code between the XNA and Silverlight frameworks. We prefer to use the Guide class in Silverlight because it is already provided by the XNA framework, and even if you have to reference the XNA assembly in your project, using Guide doesn't add any extra space in the XAP application's distribution file.

Finally, it is a good practice to ask users whether they want to buy the full application before exiting from it. If they agree to buy the full application, you have to show the related Marketplace page. This can be accomplished by using either the Marketplace APIs such as the MarketplaceDetailTask and MarketplaceReviewTask classes or the ShowMarketplace method from the Guide class.

We have created two examples to show different trial approaches in Silverlight and XNA Windows Phone applications. Both examples use the Guide class from the Microsoft.Xna.Framework.GamerServices namespace, but they differ in their event handlers. These two applications print a message on the screen telling users that the application is running in trial mode.

In the XNA world, everything is a sprite, so the same is true for text. To print text on the screen, you have to use a sprite font. You can add a font in the Content project (in the example, this is called XNATrialApplicationContent) from Visual Studio 2010 by selecting Project Add New Item. From the dialog box that appears, you then have to select the Sprite Font item and give it a name (see Figure 1-20).

Figure 1-20. *Add a sprite font to the XNA game.*

The .spritefont file added to the project is an XML file containing the font's characteristics such as font family, dimension, and style. You can edit this file to change the font's characteristics. Moreover, the Asset Name property is important because it represents the name of the font that you have to refer to in your code (press F4 to see the font's properties).

SilverlightTrialApplication uses a new text block added to the main content panel, and its text is used to show the message. To add a new text block, you can either drag it from the toolbox or type the XAML code in the editor (see Figure 1-21).

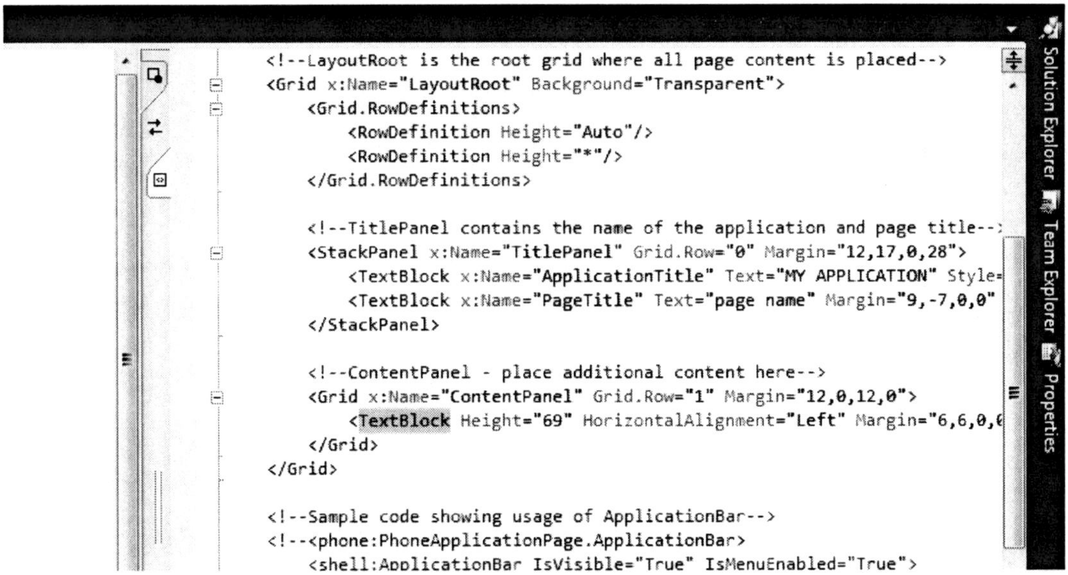

```
<!--LayoutRoot is the root grid where all page content is placed-->
<Grid x:Name="LayoutRoot" Background="Transparent">
    <Grid.RowDefinitions>
        <RowDefinition Height="Auto"/>
        <RowDefinition Height="*"/>
    </Grid.RowDefinitions>

    <!--TitlePanel contains the name of the application and page title-->
    <StackPanel x:Name="TitlePanel" Grid.Row="0" Margin="12,17,0,28">
        <TextBlock x:Name="ApplicationTitle" Text="MY APPLICATION" Style=
        <TextBlock x:Name="PageTitle" Text="page name" Margin="9,-7,0,0"
    </StackPanel>

    <!--ContentPanel - place additional content here-->
    <Grid x:Name="ContentPanel" Grid.Row="1" Margin="12,0,12,0">
        <TextBlock Height="69" HorizontalAlignment="Left" Margin="6,6,0,0
    </Grid>
</Grid>

<!--Sample code showing usage of ApplicationBar-->
<!--<phone:PhoneApplicationPage.ApplicationBar>
    <shell:ApplicationBar IsVisible="True" IsMenuEnabled="True">
```

Figure 1-21. Adding a TextBlock control to the main content panel

The Code

In the XNA game application, we use the Draw event handler to show a message indicating that the application is in trial mode. We add a class Boolean field to store the value from the IsTrialMode property of the Guide class. This is suggested by Microsoft because reading the IsTrialMode property for each instance consumes more time, and in a game, saving time is very important! This operation is accomplished in the Initialize method, where another interesting feature is present. The #DEBUG compiler directive is used to set the SimulateTrialMode property. In that way, when the application is compiled with debug settings, you can simulate the trial mode and test your code.

The Draw method uses the IsTrial property to check that the application is in trial mode and uses the DrawString method in the affirmative case. The DrawString method is necessary for printing information on the screen. This method accepts the sprite font object, the message to show, the X,Y position indicating where to print the message, and the font color to use. The sprite font object is loaded in the LoadContent method.

Finally, in the OnExiting event handler, we add the code to ask users to buy the application. The Guide class provides the ShowMarketplace method to accomplish that. Internally, the method already checks for the IsTrialMode property, so it is not necessary to add this check, too.

```
namespace XNATrialApplication
{
    /// <summary>
    /// This is the main type for your game
    /// </summary>
    public class Game1 : Microsoft.Xna.Framework.Game
    {
```

```
        GraphicsDeviceManager graphics;
        SpriteBatch spriteBatch;
        SpriteFont font;
        bool isTrial = false;

. . .

        /// <summary>
        /// Allows the game to perform any initialization it needs to
        /// before starting to run.
        /// This is where it can query for any required services and load any non-graphic-
        /// related content.  Calling base.Initialize will enumerate through any components
        /// and initialize them as well.
        /// </summary>
        protected override void Initialize()
        {
#if DEBUG
            Guide.SimulateTrialMode = true;
#endif

            isTrial = Guide.IsTrialMode;

            base.Initialize();
        }

        /// <summary>
        /// LoadContent will be called once per game and is the place to load
        /// all of your content.
        /// </summary>
        protected override void LoadContent()
        {
            // Create a new SpriteBatch, which can be used to draw textures.
            spriteBatch = new SpriteBatch(GraphicsDevice);

            // TODO: use this.Content to load your game content here
            font = this.Content.Load<SpriteFont>("Font");
        }

. . .

        /// <summary>
        /// This is called when the game should draw itself.
        /// </summary>
        /// <param name="gameTime">Provides a snapshot of timing values.</param>
        protected override void Draw(GameTime gameTime)
        {
            GraphicsDevice.Clear(Color.CornflowerBlue);

            if (isTrial)
            {
                spriteBatch.Begin();
                spriteBatch.DrawString(font, "The Application is in Trial Mode",
```

```
                                        new Vector2(10, 10), Color.Black);
            spriteBatch.End();
        }

        base.Draw(gameTime);
    }

    protected override void OnExiting(object sender, EventArgs args)
    {
        Guide.ShowMarketplace(PlayerIndex.One);

        base.OnExiting(sender, args);
    }
}
}
```

Writing text in the SilverlightTrialApplication application is easier than XNA application. The lbMessage TextBlock control provides the Text property, where you can specify the string message to print. In the MainPage.xaml code, you can specify the Loaded event, and in the related code-behind method, you can check whether the application is in trial mode. You can add a Buy Me button to the main page in order to call the ShowMarketplace method and let users to buy your application.

```xml
<phone:PhoneApplicationPage
    x:Class="SilverlightTrialApplication.MainPage"
    xmlns="http://schemas.microsoft.com/winfx/2006/xaml/presentation"
    xmlns:x="http://schemas.microsoft.com/winfx/2006/xaml"
    xmlns:phone="clr-namespace:Microsoft.Phone.Controls;assembly=Microsoft.Phone"
    xmlns:shell="clr-namespace:Microsoft.Phone.Shell;assembly=Microsoft.Phone"
    xmlns:d="http://schemas.microsoft.com/expression/blend/2008"
    xmlns:mc="http://schemas.openxmlformats.org/markup-compatibility/2006"
    mc:Ignorable="d" d:DesignWidth="480" d:DesignHeight="768"
    FontFamily="{StaticResource PhoneFontFamilyNormal}"
    FontSize="{StaticResource PhoneFontSizeNormal}"
    Foreground="{StaticResource PhoneForegroundBrush}"
    SupportedOrientations="Portrait" Orientation="Portrait"
    shell:SystemTray.IsVisible="True" Loaded="PhoneApplicationPage_Loaded">

    <!--LayoutRoot is the root grid where all page content is placed-->
    <Grid x:Name="LayoutRoot" Background="Transparent">
        <Grid.RowDefinitions>
            <RowDefinition Height="Auto"/>
            <RowDefinition Height="*"/>
        </Grid.RowDefinitions>

        <!--TitlePanel contains the name of the application and page title-->
        <StackPanel x:Name="TitlePanel" Grid.Row="0" Margin="12,17,0,28">
            <TextBlock x:Name="ApplicationTitle" Text="MY APPLICATION" Style="{StaticResource
PhoneTextNormalStyle}"/>
            <TextBlock x:Name="PageTitle" Text="page name" Margin="9,-7,0,0"
Style="{StaticResource PhoneTextTitle1Style}"/>
```

```xml
        </StackPanel>

        <!--ContentPanel - place additional content here-->
        <Grid x:Name="ContentPanel" Grid.Row="1" Margin="12,0,12,0">
            <TextBlock Height="69" HorizontalAlignment="Left" Margin="6,6,0,0"
Name="lbMessage" Text="" VerticalAlignment="Top" Width="450" />
        <Button Content="Buy Me" Height="72" HorizontalAlignment="Left"
Margin="9,509,0,0" Name="btnBuy" VerticalAlignment="Top" Width="441"
Click="btnBuy_Click" />
        </Grid>
    </Grid>
</phone:PhoneApplicationPage>
```

```csharp
namespace SilverlightTrialApplication
{
    public partial class MainPage : PhoneApplicationPage
    {
        // Constructor
        public MainPage()
        {
            InitializeComponent();

#if DEBUG
            Guide.SimulateTrialMode = true;
#endif
        }

        private void PhoneApplicationPage_Loaded(object sender, RoutedEventArgs e)
        {
            if (Guide.IsTrialMode)
            {
                lbMessage.Text = "The Application is in Trial Mode!";
            }
            else
                btnBuy.Visibility = System.Windows.Visibility.Collapsed;
        }
    }
}
```

When the application is not in Trial Mode the Buy Me button is hidden using the Visibility property set to Collapsed.

Usage

When both applications run, they check for trial mode and then print the appropriate message on the screen. When the XNA application closes, it show a message asking users to buy the application. In the Silverlight application the same behavior is obtained clicking the Buy Me button. In Figure 1-22, you can see both examples' output. On the left is the XNA application, in the middle the Marketplace application page common to both examples, and finally on the right is the Silverlight application. In this case the Marketplace application page displays an error because the application is not been deployed to the Marketplace and doesn't have a valid application ID.

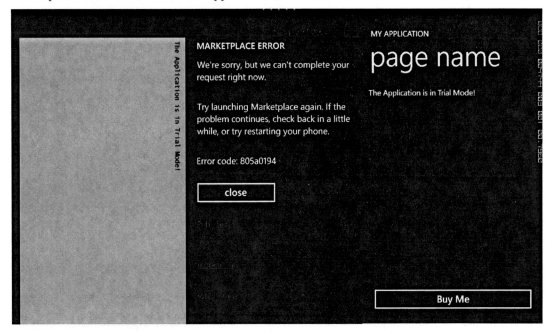

Figure 1-22. XNATrialApplication and SilverlightTrialApplication outputs

CHAPTER 2

Windows Phone Execution Model And Multitasking

In this chapter, you are going to examine the Windows Phone execution model. First, you will examine the navigation of pages in a Windows Phone application. Then you will focus your attention on how the Windows Phone operating system manages running applications.

The recipes in this chapter describe the following:

- 2-1. Navigating the Windows Phone application's pages

- 2-2. Passing parameters through pages

- 2-3. Using global defined variables

- 2-4. Using the State dictionary to store the application's global variables

- 2-5. Managing tombstoning

- 2-6. Managing tombstoning in XNA

- 2-7. Implementing multitasking

- 2-8. Scheduling alarms and reminders

- 2-9. Managing Obscured and Unobscured events

2-1. Navigating Between Pages

Problem

You have a Windows Phone Silverlight application with more than one page and you need to navigate through the pages.

Solution

You have to use the NavigationService class (see Figure 2-1 to see its class diagram) and, optionally, the OnNavigatedTo and OnNavigatedFrom event handlers (see Recipe 2-4 for more on this).

How It Works

The Windows Phone Silverlight application is based on pages and a frame. The latter is the top-level container that provides features such as page orientation and reserves space for the pages' rendering and status bar. The Frame contains one or more pages and provides the navigation service to go through the pages.

A page is a container for Silverlight controls that is rendered in a space reserved by the frame. The page optionally provides the application bar (see Chapter 3), which is used to provide a page menu and a toolbar.

The PhoneApplicationPage class provides developers everything needed to manage a page. On the other hand, the PhoneApplicationFrame class represents the frame.

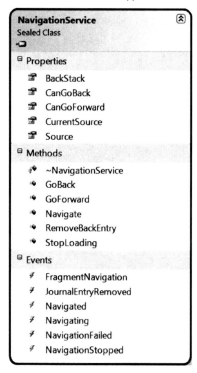

Figure 2-1. The NavigationService class diagram

The NavigationServices property of the PhoneApplicationClass class enables developers to access the frame's navigation service and use the Navigate method. This method has one parameter, which is the Uri object containing the URL of the target page. This Uri constructor has two parameters: the former is the string containing the URL of the page, and the latter is the UriKind enumeration, where you can set whether the URL is relative or absolute.

```
public bool Navigate(
        Uri source
)
```

Another useful method provided by the NavigationServices class is GoBack. This method simulates the hardware Back button press in going one page back. You can use the CanGoBack property to retrieve a Boolean value indicating whether you can go back to the previous page (true) or not (false).

```
public void GoBack()
public bool CanGoBack { get; }
```

▪ **Note** The NavigationServices class provides the GoForward method, too, but because there is no forward navigation in a Windows Phone application, this method always returns an exception.

The Code

To demonstrate simple navigation between two pages, we have created the NavigatingApp Silverlight application.

Start Visual Studio 2010 and choose New Project from the Start page and then select the Windows Phone Application template. In the Name text box of the New Project dialog box, type **NavigatingApp** (see Figure 2-2).

Figure 2-2. Creating the NavigatingApp application

From the Solution Explorer window, right-click the NavigatingApp project name and choose Add New Item.

From the Add New Item dialog box, select the Silverlight for Windows Phone template from the Installed Templates list. Then select Windows Phone Portrait Page. Name the page **Page2.xaml** and then click OK (see Figure 2-3).

Figure 2-3. *Adding a new page to the project*

On both pages, you have to add a hyperlink button. In the MainPage.xaml page, add the following code between the ContentPanel grid tags:

```
. . .
    <!--ContentPanel - place additional content here-->
    <Grid x:Name="ContentPanel" Grid.Row="1" Margin="12,0,12,0">
        <HyperlinkButton x:Name="hbButton1" Content="Navigate to Page 2"
                         Click="hbButton1_Click"/></Grid>
. . .
```

In the Page2.xaml page, insert the following code:

```
. . .
    <!--ContentPanel - place additional content here-->
```

```
<Grid x:Name="ContentPanel" Grid.Row="1" Margin="12,0,12,0">
    <HyperlinkButton x:Name="hbButton2" Content="Go back" Click="hbButton2_Click"/>
```
. . .

Both codes specify the Content attribute, used to define the text that will be shown in the page, and the Click event handler. In the event handler code, we find the navigation logic between the two pages.

In the MainPage.xaml.cs file, we find the Click event handler:

```
private void hbButton1_Click(object sender, RoutedEventArgs e)
{
    this.NavigationService.Navigate(new Uri("/Page2.xaml", UriKind.Relative));
}
```

Because the event handler is defined in the MainPage class that derives from the PhoneApplicationPage class, you can have direct access to the NavigationService property. By using the Navigate method, you can go to Page2.xaml. Note the relative URL attribute specified by the UriKind enumeration. This indicates that the URL is relative to the root application path. Because Page2.xaml is stored at the same level as MainPage.xaml—that is, the root—we can use that simple form.

In the Page2.xaml.cs file, we find the other Click event handler:

```
private void hbButton2_Click(object sender, RoutedEventArgs e)
{
    if (this.NavigationService.CanGoBack)
        this.NavigationService.GoBack();
}
```

First, you check whether you can go back to the previous page; if you can, you call the GoBack method.

▓ **Note** You could use the Navigate method in the Page2 event handler to pointing to MainPage. There is a side effect, however. As with browser navigation, pressing the Back button results in the application showing the previous page in the same state you left it. If you write the URL of the page and navigate to it, the browser shows a brand new page. The same occurs here: by using the Navigate method and specifying the URL of the MainPage.xaml page, you will obtain a fresh, new copy of the MainPage class.

Usage

In Visual Studio 2010, make sure your target is Windows Phone Emulator and then press Ctrl+F5. The emulator will start, briefly showing the splash screen and then the main page. Click the hyperlink button to access the second page. Now click either the hyperlink button or the hardware Back button, and you will return to the main page.

■ **Note** If you use `Navigate` instead of `GoBack` to return to the main page and then press the hardware Back button, the application will not exit as you may expect but will show `Page2` again. That's because each time you call the `Navigate` method, a brand new page is created and loaded, and the replaced page is put on the page stack. Pressing the hardware Back button of the Windows Phone device goes away from the current page and pops the old page off the stack. This stack is managed by the PhoneApplicationFrame class by its BackStack read-only property that contains a list of JournalEntry items representing entries in back or forward page navigation. You can use the BackStack property to retrieve the list of navigated pages and remove pages from the stack calling the RemoveBackEntry method. There is a good example from the Code Samples page at `http://msdn.microsoft.com/en-us/library/hh394012(v=VS.92).aspx`.

2-2. Passing Data Through Pages

Problem

You need to pass data from one page to another.

Solution

You can use the `QueryString` collection provided by the `NavigationContext` property from the `PhoneApplicationPage` class.

How It Works

The source page that has to pass parameters to the destination page can use the URL parameters' syntax:

```
/Page.xaml?param1=value&param2=value&...
```

■ **Note** According to the official documentation at `http://msdn.microsoft.com/en-us/library/z6c2z492(v=VS.95).aspx`, you will receive an exception when the length of the `QueryString` parameter exceeds 65,519 characters.

After the page name, the parameters' definition starts with a question mark and includes a series of key/value pairs separated by the ampersand character.

To retrieve the parameters' values in the destination page, you have to use the QueryString collection provided by the NavigationContext property of the PhoneApplicationPage class.

The Code

To demonstrate navigation between pages with the exchange of parameters, you have to create a new Windows Phone Silverlight application and call it **NavigatingWitParamsApp**. As you did in Recipe 2-1, add a new page and call it **Page2.xaml**.

In MainPage.xaml, you have to add three hyperlink buttons. You then define for each of them a Click event handler. You can take advantage of the TabIndex property to set the value you want to pass to Page2. Let's see the XAML code of the MainPage page:

```
<!--ContentPanel - place additional content here-->
<Grid x:Name="ContentPanel" Grid.Row="1" Margin="12,0,12,0">
    <StackPanel Orientation="Vertical" >
        <HyperlinkButton Content="Option 1" Click="HyperlinkButton_Click"
                         TabIndex="1" />
        <HyperlinkButton Content="Option 2" Click="HyperlinkButton_Click"
                         TabIndex="2" />
        <HyperlinkButton Content="Option 3" Click="HyperlinkButton_Click"
                         TabIndex="3" />
    </StackPanel>
</Grid>
```

In the code of the Click event handler, you can call the Navigate method, passing the parameter that represents the index of the pressed hyperlink button:

```
private void HyperlinkButton_Click(object sender, RoutedEventArgs e)
{
    HyperlinkButton hb = sender as HyperlinkButton;
    string url = string.Format("/Page2.xaml?ID={0}", hb.TabIndex);
    this.NavigationService.Navigate(new Uri(url, UriKind.Relative));
}
```

The sender object passed to the Click event handler represents the hyperlink button that raised the event. You can cast it to a HyperlinkButton object so you can use its TabIndex property and pass it to the Page2 page.

In the Page2.xaml file, you add a TextBlock control that will show a message indicating which button has been pressed in the MainPage page. As you can see in the following code, it is worth noting the PhoneTextTitle3Style static resource that is part of the theme resources for Windows Phone (see Recipe 3-5).

```
<!--ContentPanel - place additional content here-->
<Grid x:Name="ContentPanel" Grid.Row="1" Margin="12,0,12,0">
    <TextBlock x:Name="lbText" Style="{StaticResource PhoneTextTitle3Style}" />
</Grid>
```

In the Page2.xaml.cs file, you have to add the Page_Loaded event handler, where you will retrieve the parameter value passed by the source page.

```
private void PhoneApplicationPage_Loaded(object sender, RoutedEventArgs e)
{
    lbText.Text = string.Format("You clicked the option number {0}",
                                this.NavigationContext.QueryString["ID"]);
}
```

The Loaded event is raised when the page is fully created and every control is loaded. So you are sure here that the TextBlock is ready to show the Text property you set to the message. The event handler name must be specified in the XAML code of Page2.xaml as well:

```
<phone:PhoneApplicationPage
    x:Class="NavigatingWithParamsApp.Page2"
    xmlns="http://schemas.microsoft.com/winfx/2006/xaml/presentation"
    xmlns:x="http://schemas.microsoft.com/winfx/2006/xaml"
    xmlns:phone="clr-namespace:Microsoft.Phone.Controls;assembly=Microsoft.Phone"
    xmlns:shell="clr-namespace:Microsoft.Phone.Shell;assembly=Microsoft.Phone"
    xmlns:d="http://schemas.microsoft.com/expression/blend/2008"
    xmlns:mc="http://schemas.openxmlformats.org/markup-compatibility/2006"
    FontFamily="{StaticResource PhoneFontFamilyNormal}"
    FontSize="{StaticResource PhoneFontSizeNormal}"
    Foreground="{StaticResource PhoneForegroundBrush}"
    SupportedOrientations="Portrait" Orientation="Portrait"
    mc:Ignorable="d" d:DesignHeight="768" d:DesignWidth="480"
    shell:SystemTray.IsVisible="True" Loaded="PhoneApplicationPage_Loaded">

    . . .
```

Usage

From Visual Studio 2010, make sure your target is Windows Phone Emulator and press Ctrl+F5. The emulator will start, briefly showing the splash screen and then the main page (see Figure 2-4).

Figure 2-4. *The source page of the* NavigatingWithParamsApp *application*

Select one option of your choice, and the application will show the Page2 page with a message telling which option you selected. For example, in our case we clicked Option 2; Figure 2-5 shows the related message.

Figure 2-5. *The index of the clicked hyperlink button*

2-3. Navigating Between Pages Using Global Application Variables

Problem

You have to navigate between pages sharing data across them. You want to avoid using a query string because your application has a lot of pages, and you need a smart way to share data between pages.

Solution

You can add a public property to the App class and retrieve its value by using the Current static property provided by the Application class.

How It Works

The Windows Phone Silverlight application always provides a class deriving from the Application class: the App class. This class represents the running application itself with a reference to the root frame and pages. See Recipe 1-3 for more details.

Defining a property in the App class ensures that the property is visible to all pages. At any time and from any page, you can use the Current static property from the Application class to retrieve a reference to the current App object. By using the instance of this object, you can easily either retrieve the property value or set it.

The Code

Create a new Windows Phone Silverlight application called NavigatingWithGlobalVariableApp from Visual Studio 2010. Add two new pages called Page2.xaml and Page3.xaml by choosing Project   Add New Item.

In the App.xaml.cs file, we added a Boolean property that represents the user's choice to have all red pages in the application.

```
public partial class App : Application
{
    /// <summary>
    /// Provides easy access to the root frame of the Phone Application.
    /// </summary>
    /// <returns>The root frame of the Phone Application.</returns>
    public PhoneApplicationFrame RootFrame { get; private set; }

    public bool RedPages { get; set; }

    /// <summary>
    /// Constructor for the Application object.
    /// </summary>
    public App()
    {
. . .
```

In the MainPage.xaml file, we added a check box and two hyperlink buttons. The check box has two event handlers to manage selected and deselected states. When the check box is selected, the background of every page will be red; otherwise, it will be black.

```
. . .
        <!--ContentPanel - place additional content here-->
        <Grid x:Name="ContentPanel" Grid.Row="1" Margin="12,0,12,0">
```

```
        <StackPanel>
            <CheckBox x:Name="chkRedColor" Content="I want all red pages"
                        Checked="chkRedColor_Checked" Unchecked="chkRedColor_Unchecked" />
            <HyperlinkButton Content="Navigate to page2" x:Name="hbToPage2"
                        Click="hbToPage2_Click" />
            <HyperlinkButton Content="Navigate to page3" x:Name="hbToPage3"
                        Click="hbToPage3_Click" />
        </StackPanel>
    </Grid>
. . .
```

In the Checked and Unchecked event handlers' code, we set the RedPages Boolean to true and false, respectively. Moreover, we change the background color properly.

```
private void chkRedColor_Checked(object sender, RoutedEventArgs e)
{
    App a = Application.Current as App;
    a.RedPages = true;
    ContentPanel.Background = new SolidColorBrush(Colors.Red);
}

private void chkRedColor_Unchecked(object sender, RoutedEventArgs e)
{
    App a = Application.Current as App;
    a.RedPages = false;
    ContentPanel.Background = new SolidColorBrush(Colors.Black);
}
```

As usual, both hyperlink buttons' event handlers contain the code to navigate to the other pages.

```
private void hbToPage2_Click(object sender, RoutedEventArgs e)
{
    this.NavigationService.Navigate(new Uri("/Page2.xaml", UriKind.Relative));
}

private void hbToPage3_Click(object sender, RoutedEventArgs e)
{
    this.NavigationService.Navigate(new Uri("/Page3.xaml", UriKind.Relative));
}
```

In Page2.xaml and Page3.xaml, we added the Loaded event handler. In the related code, we retrieved the RedPages Boolean property, setting the page's background color accordingly.

```
private void PhoneApplicationPage_Loaded(object sender, RoutedEventArgs e)
{
    App a = Application.Current as App;
    if (a.RedPages == true)
        ContentPanel.Background = new SolidColorBrush(Colors.Red);
```

```
        }
```

Usage

Run the application from Visual Studio 2010, selecting Windows Phone Emulator as the output target. From the main page, select the I Want All Pages Red check box. The background color turns red (see Figure 2-6).

Figure 2-6. *NavigatingWithGlobalVariableApp in action*

Click the check box again to deselect it, and the main page's background color turns black. Select the check box once more and then press the Navigate to page2 hyperlink button. The Page2 background color is red (see Figure 2-7).

Figure 2-7. Even page 2 has the background color set to red.

2-4. Navigating Between Pages with State

Problem

You have to navigate between pages, and you want to store a complex object that is not suitably stored via the query string method. You need to store the object to prevent tombstoning.

Solution

You should use the State dictionary provided by the PhoneApplicationService class.

How It Works

Sometimes you have to share data between pages that is not suitable for the QueryString property—for instance, when you have to provide a complex object such as an array or list to another page. Moreover, the QueryString property can accept up to 65,519 characters from the Uri object.

Windows Phone helps developers via the State dictionary, which is provided by the PhoneApplicationService class included in the Microsoft.Mobile.Shell namespace.

The PhoneApplicationService class includes the Current static property that retrieves the PhoneApplicationService object related to the current application. By using this object, you can use the State property to store data across pages. Moreover, the PhoneApplicationService automatically manages the application's idle behavior and the application's state when it becomes either active or inactive.

Indeed, managing active and inactive states is an important aspect of Windows Phone life cycle application management that a developer has to consider. During the application usage, a lot of external events may occur, and the developer has to provide the right solutions to avoid a bad user experience. For example, imagine that a user is filling in a form on the page you provided when that user remembers an important e-mail that needs to be sent immediately. The user presses the hardware Start button, and your application becomes inactive. After the e-mail is sent, the user presses the hardware Back button until the application becomes active again. How would the user react if all data in the form were lost?

To provide a complex object to another page, you could use the global application variable technique too (see Recipe 2-3). But what is provided here for free is tombstoning management. When the application is deactivated because of an external event such as the hardware Start button being pressed, the application is put in a dormant state and variables' content are stored in memory. This is true only when the Windows Phone memory is sufficient to run other applications with good user experience. On the other hand, when the Windows Phone memory is not sufficient the last opened application is tombstoned (see more on Recipe 2-5). When an application is tombstoned, the State dictionary is serialized and stored automatically by the Windows Phone operating system. If the application is activated again—not by launching the application from the Start menu, but by going back via the hardware Back button—the State dictionary is deserialized and provided to the application. That's why the State dictionary has to contain only serializable objects.

As already stated in Recipe 2-1, when the Navigate method is called, a brand-new page is created and shown. So if your text boxes are blank by default, when the application is activated from the Windows Phone operating system, the page will show empty text boxes.

To manage this aspect and avoid this application behavior, you can implement the code in the OnNavigatedFrom and the OnNavigatedTo event handlers provided by the PhoneApplicationPage class. The OnNavigatedFrom event is raised just before the user is going to navigate off the page. This event handler is the right place to insert the code that saves your data. The OnNavigatedTo event is raised just after the page is shown because of navigation either from another page or from the Windows Phone operating system.

Both event handlers provide a NavigationEventArgs object that provides some interesting properties such as the Uri of the target page or the target application, and the target Content object. For example, in the OnNavigatedFrom event handler, the Content property contains the MainPage object when you come back to the starting page from page 2. On the other hand, when the application is deactivated, the Content property is null and the Uri is set to the app://external/ value.

Another useful property provided by the PhoneApplicationPage class is State. Do not confuse this with the one provided by the PhoneApplicationService class. The one provided by the page is not shared through the application but is for the page only. This is great for storing page data such as text-box values, check-box selections, and so on. Remember that the Navigate method creates a brand new page so the State property is always empty. The State property of the PhoneApplicationPage class is useful when you come back to a page perhaps using the GoBack method. The main page is the ideal place to use the State property because usually other pages come back to the main page using the GoBack method.

The Code

To demonstrate navigation between pages with a complex data object exchanged, we will create a new Windows Phone Silverlight application called `NavigatingWithStateApp`. In this application, `MainPage` will show a message taking the first name, last name, and city strings provided by the `Page2` page after the user presses the Save button. Those strings are defined in a new class called `Person`.

```
using System;

namespace NavigatingWithStateApp
{
    public class Person
    {
        public string FirstName { get; set; }
        public string LastName { get; set; }
        public string City { get; set; }

        public Person() { }
    }
}
```

The class must be serializable and must provide a public parameterless constructor (if you don't specify it, the compiler will create it for you).

In `MainPage.xaml`, we added a `TextBlock` control to show the message, and a hyperlink button to navigate to the second page.

```
. . .
<!--ContentPanel - place additional content here-->
        <Grid x:Name="ContentPanel" Grid.Row="1" Margin="12,0,12,0">
            <TextBlock x:Name="tbMsg" />
            <HyperlinkButton x:Name="hlNavigate" Content="Navigate to Page 2"
                         Click="hlNavigate_Click"/>
        </Grid>
. . .
```

In the `MainPage.xaml.cs` source code, we added the `Loaded` event handler, which builds the string to be shown only when the `State` dictionary returned by the `PhoneApplicationService`'s `Context` property contains the `Person` object saved in the `Page2`.

```
        private void PhoneApplicationPage_Loaded(object sender, RoutedEventArgs e)
        {
            if (PhoneApplicationService.Current.State.ContainsKey("Person"))
            {
                Person p = (Person)PhoneApplicationService.Current.State["Person"];

                tbMsg.Text = string.Format("Welcome {0} {1} from {2}", p.FirstName,
                                                            p.LastName, p.City);
            }
```

```
    }
```

As already done in previous recipes, we add another page called Page2.xaml. In the Page2.xaml page, we add three TextBox controls and one Button control:

```
. . .
<!--ContentPanel - place additional content here-->
        <Grid x:Name="ContentPanel" Grid.Row="1" Margin="12,0,12,0">
            <StackPanel>
                <TextBox x:Name="txtName" Text="FirstName" GotFocus="txt_GotFocus" />
                <TextBox x:Name="txtLast" Text="LastName" GotFocus="txt_GotFocus" />
                <TextBox x:Name="txtCity" Text="City" GotFocus="txt_GotFocus" />
                <Button x:Name="btnSave" Content="Save" Click="btnSave_Click" />
            </StackPanel>
        </Grid>
. . .
```

Every TextBox control implements GotFocus, so when the TextBox receives the focus, it will select its own text:

```
    private void txt_GotFocus(object sender, RoutedEventArgs e)
    {
        TextBox txt = sender as TextBox;
        txt.SelectAll();
    }
```

■ **Tip** This technique is done to avoid using labels; by showing the string, the text box indicates what its content should be.

The Save button calls the SaveOrUpdate method, which stores the text boxes' text into a Person object. First, the method checks whether the State dictionary of PhoneApplicationService's Current object already contains a Person object. If it does, the method retrieves the object and changes its value. Otherwise, the method creates a brand new object, filling it with the text boxes' values. In both cases, the last instruction is used to store the Person object in the State dictionary of Page2.

Only when the SaveOrUpdate method is called via the Save button is the State dictionary (provided by the Context property of the PhoneApplicationService) populated with the Person object. In this way, the main page will show the message only when the user saves data.

```
    private void SaveOrUpdate()
    {
        Person p = null;

        if (PhoneApplicationService.Current.State.ContainsKey("Person"))
        {
```

```
        p = (Person)PhoneApplicationService.Current.State["Person"];
        p.FirstName = txtName.Text;
        p.LastName = txtLast.Text;
        p.City = txtCity.Text;
    }
    else
    {
        p = new Person();
        p.FirstName = txtName.Text;
        p.LastName = txtLast.Text;
        p.City = txtCity.Text;
    }

    PhoneApplicationService.Current.State["Person"] = p;
}
```

The core of this example is the code in the OnNavigatedFrom and OnNavigatedTo event handlers. In the former, the SavePageLevelData method is called so that when the application is deactivated, the user doesn't lose data. The method will not be called when the user presses the hardware Back button, because in this case its behavior is similar to the Cancel button in a dialog box. Retrieving when the hardware Back button is pressed is accomplished by checking the NavigationMode property of the NavigationEventArgs object passed to the event handler.

You don't have to save data in the State dictionary retrieved by the PhoneApplicationService class when the application is deactivated. You need to store the textboxes values in another dictionary so whether the application is reactivated, you can prompt the values that the user was going to insert into the textboxes. This dictionary can be the State dictionary provided by the PhoneApplicationPage class that is stored locally to the page and is serialized in the same way as the State dictionary provided by the PhoneApplicationService class when the application is tombstoned.

```
protected override void
OnNavigatedFrom(System.Windows.Navigation.NavigationEventArgs e)
{
    if (e.NavigationMode !=
        System.Windows.Navigation.NavigationMode.Back)
    {
        SavePageLevelData();
    }
    else
        this.State["Person"] = null;

    base.OnNavigatedFrom(e);
}

private void SavePageLevelData()
{
    Person p = new Person();
    p.FirstName = txtName.Text;
    p.LastName = txtLast.Text;
    p.City = txtCity.Text;
    this.State["Person"] = p;
}
```

In the `OnNavigatedTo` event handler, we simply check whether the `State` dictionary from the `Page2` class contains the `Person` object and then we eventually fill the text boxes' text with its values. In this case it means the user was inserting some text and the application had been deactivated. On the other hand. the State dictionary is empty and the code checks if the State dictionary from the PhoneApplicationService contains the Person object. This is the case the user had saved the data and the application has to fill the textboxes with saved data.

```
protected override void
OnNavigatedTo(System.Windows.Navigation.NavigationEventArgs e)
{
    if (this.State.ContainsKey("Person"))
    {
        Person p = (Person)this.State["Person"];
        txtName.Text = p.FirstName;
        txtLast.Text = p.LastName;
        txtCity.Text = p.City;
    }
    else if
    (PhoneApplicationService.Current.State.ContainsKey("Person"))
    {
        Person p =
        (Person)PhoneApplicationService.Current.State["Person"];
        txtName.Text = p.FirstName;
        txtLast.Text = p.LastName;
        txtCity.Text = p.City;
    }

    base.OnNavigatedTo(e);
}
```

Finally, the Save button code calls the `SaveOrUpdate` method to save the `Person` object into the PhoneApplicationService's State dictionary.

```
private void btnSave_Click(object sender, RoutedEventArgs e)
{
    SaveOrUpdate();
    this.NavigationService.GoBack();
}
```

Usage

From Visual Studio 2010, run the application after checking that the target is set to Windows Phone Emulator. The main page will be shown briefly with just the link to navigate to the second page (see Figure 2-8).

Figure 2-8. The NavigatingWithStateApp application's first page

By pressing the hyperlink button, you go to the second page, shown in Figure 2-9.

Figure 2-9. The second page contains three text boxes and a button.

Now you can insert your credentials and press the Save button so the application returns to the start page and shows the message (see Figure 2-10).

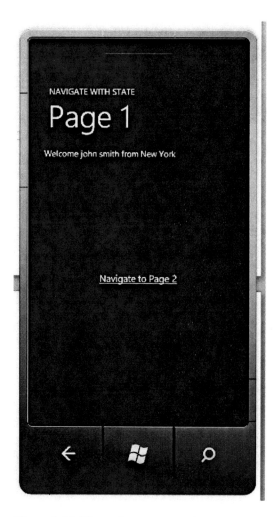

Figure 2-10. The main page greets the person you added from the page 2 form.

Now let's play a bit with the application and explore unexpected situations. Comment the code of the OnNavigatedFrom event handler from Page2.xaml.cs and restart the application. Go to page 2 and add some text to the text boxes. Press the hardware Start button, leaving the application, and then the hardware Back button. The application is resumed and every change is still there. This is because the application has been put in the dormant state and everything has been stored in memory. This could be tricky for you because you think the application works correctly but you have to recall that when memory in not sufficient for the user best experience, the application is tombstoned and if you don't serialize and save your data, you will lose them. So the code in the OnNavigatedFrom event handler is necessary just to save data in the case the tombstone occurs. In order to try the tombstone case, you have to right-click the mouse on the NavigatingWithStateApp project name in the Solution Explorer of Visual Studio 2010 and select the Properties menu item. From the Properties page, select the Debug tab and check the Tombstone upon deactivation while debugging check box. Now each time you launch the Windows Phone application in debug mode you can test the application simulating the tombstoning.

2-5. Managing Tombstoning in Windows Phone Silverlight Applications

Problem

You have to manage tombstoning and store application data permanently so that when the application is either activated or executed, the application can reload data.

Solution

You have to use IsolatedStorage classes (see Chapter 9 for a full coverage on them) together with Application class event handlers: Application_Launching, Application_Activated, Application_Deactivated, and Application_Closing.

How It Works

The Windows Phone operating system doesn't provide support for executing concurrent applications concurrently in the foreground. The application that you run on your phone is the only one executed in foreground. When you press the hardware Start button and run another application, the previous application is put in a dormant state. If there are not sufficient memory resources to run other applications, the Windows Phone operating system terminates runned application, starting from the less recent. This behavior is called *tombstoning*. A tombstoned application is actually terminated but the Windows Phone operating system saves application's states and navigation stack so if the application is reactivated from a tombstone, the application can "cheat" showing the content just as it was left from the user, even if the application actually is a brand new copy.

Let's take a look at an example. Say you press the hardware Start button and launch the Calendar application. You start to note an appointment with Company X, but you don't remember the name of the street where Company X is located. So you press the hardware Search button (in the Calendar application, the Deactivated event is raised), type the name of the company, and press the Enter key. The company site appears, and you click on it so Internet Explorer runs, and the site is shown. You click the Contact Us link and read or copy the company's address. Now you have two options:

- Press the hardware Start button and select the Calendar application again.

- Press the hardware Back button until you reach the Calendar application.

In the former case, you run a fresh new copy of the Calendar application, and everything you wrote before searching for the company's address is gone. In this case, the Launching event is raised.

In the latter case, you should resume the Calendar application from a dormant state. Everything is there just as you left the application pressing the Start button. But, let's say you have already opened some documents on your phone, playing music in background, and the phone's memory is not sufficient, the Windows Phone operating system starts to tombstone less recent application. So there could be the case your application is tombstoned.

For example, you could run a fresh new copy of the Calendar application, but the Windows Phone operating system provides a collection of serializable objects in the State dictionary (as you saw in Recipe 2-4). So you will see your data again in the text boxes because Calendar developers have managed the tombstoning. In this case, the Activated event is raised.

▓ **Note** There is a limit of up to five tombstoned applications. After you have reached that limit, the application is really terminated and every data is lost for good.

There is another way to manage your application. You could store your data permanently. Indeed, the State dictionary is provided only when you activate the application with the hardware Back button and not when you launch it from the Start menu. You can use the four Application event handlers together with isolated storage in order to save data in the memory space reserved for the application.

▓ **Note** There is no limited quota size for the storage of a Windows Phone application. The application itself has to take care of the disk space avoiding useless information. When the application is removed from the phone, the isolated storage is removed as well.

The Code

To demonstrate how to manage the four Application event handlers in conjunction with the isolated storage, we will start to create an application that we will use throughout the book. The 7Drum application provides useful tools to drummers who, for instance, want to plan their practices, record a groove they have in mind, or use a metronome during their drumming.

▓ **Note** You can download this application code and all the source code shown in this book from the Source Code/Download area of the Apress website at www.apress.com.

In this particular case, we will focus our attention on the Training menu of the 7Drum application, where the user can create a training plan specifying an exercise name, a description, and a duration. The application will provide three TextBox controls to contain that information. The code is contained in the Exercise.xaml page. It defines a new Grid with two columns and three rows within the ContentPanel grid. Finally, it adds three TextBox controls and three TextBlock controls as labels. It is worth noting the Description text box, which accepts more than one line of text thanks to the AcceptReturns property being set to true:

. . .

```xml
<!--ContentPanel - place additional content here-->
<Grid x:Name="ContentPanel" Grid.Row="1" Margin="12,0,12,0">
    <StackPanel>
        <Grid>
            <Grid.RowDefinitions>
                <RowDefinition Height="Auto"/>
                <RowDefinition Height="Auto"/>
                <RowDefinition Height="*"/>
            </Grid.RowDefinitions>
            <Grid.ColumnDefinitions>
                <ColumnDefinition Width="Auto" />
                <ColumnDefinition Width="*" />
            </Grid.ColumnDefinitions>

            <TextBlock Grid.Row="0" Grid.Column="0" Text="Name:"
                    Style="{StaticResource PhoneTextNormalStyle}"
                    VerticalAlignment="Center" />
            <TextBox Grid.Row="0" Grid.Column="1" x:Name="txtName" />
            <TextBlock Grid.Row="1" Grid.Column="0" Text="Description:"
                    Style="{StaticResource PhoneTextNormalStyle}"
                    VerticalAlignment="Center" />
            <TextBox Grid.Row="1" Grid.Column="1" x:Name="txtDescription"
                    AcceptsReturn="True" Height="300"/>
            <TextBlock Grid.Row="2" Grid.Column="0" Text="Duration:"
                    Style="{StaticResource PhoneTextNormalStyle}"
                    VerticalAlignment="Center" />
            <TextBox Grid.Row="2" Grid.Column="1" x:Name="txtDuration"
                    InputScope="TelephoneNumber" KeyDown="txtDuration_KeyDown"/>
        </Grid>
    </StackPanel>
</Grid>
```
. . .

In the Exercise.xaml.cs page, we have defined the code to save exercise planning. The Exercise page uses the ApplicationIconBar button (see more on this in Recipe 3-2), which calls the ApplicationBarIconSaveButton_Click event handler when clicked. The code first checks whether the page has to be shown in edit mode or whether the user is going to create a new exercise. This is accomplished by the QueryString property check. If the QueryString property contains an exercise identifier selected in the previous page—the Training page where all exercises are listed—then the user is going to modify the exercise. After that, if the Name and Duration text boxes contain values, a new ExerciseSettings object is created. It will contain values from the related page text boxes. The exercise identifier will be either created by calling the NewGuid static method from the Guid class or set equal to the one that has to be modified. As you will see shortly, the ExerciseSettings class contains everything necessary to store the exercise's information.

Finally, when the Save button is in modify mode, it retrieves the old exercise from the Exercises list, which is stored as a global variable in the Application class by using a LINQ query. This Exercise object is a reference to the stored exercise, so we can change its properties without changing the Guid identifier to modify the exercise.

```csharp
private void ApplicationBarIconSaveButton_Click(object sender, EventArgs e)
```

```
{
    bool bNew = true;

    if (this.NavigationContext.QueryString.ContainsKey("Id"))
        bNew = false;
    else
        bNew = true;

    if (txtName.Text != string.Empty && txtDuration.Text != string.Empty)
    {
        ExerciseSettings exercise = null;

        if (!bNew)
        {
            exercise = (from ex in (Application.Current as App).Exercises
                        where ex.id == new
                        Guid(this.NavigationContext.QueryString["Id"])
                        select ex).SingleOrDefault<ExerciseSettings>();
        }
        else
        {
            exercise = new ExerciseSettings();
            exercise.id = Guid.NewGuid();
        }

        exercise.Description = txtDescription.Text;
        exercise.Name = txtName.Text;
        exercise.Duration = int.Parse(txtDuration.Text);

        if (bNew)
            (Application.Current as App).Exercises.Add(exercise);

        Clean();
    }
    else
        MessageBox.Show("Name and duration fields are mandatory.", "7Drum",
                        MessageBoxButton.OK);
}
```

The ExerciseSettings class is used to store exercise data, and a collection of these objects is stored in the Application page.

```
public class ExerciseSettings
{
    public Guid id { get; set; }
    public string Name { get; set; }
    public string Description { get; set; }
    public int Duration { get; set; }
}
```

```
public partial class App : Application
{
    /// <summary>
    /// Provides easy access to the root frame of the Phone Application.
    /// </summary>
    /// <returns>The root frame of the Phone Application.</returns>
```

. . .

```
    public List<ExerciseSettings> Exercises { get; private set; }

    /// <summary>
```

. . .

Let's discuss of the main part of the code, which handles tombstoning management. We created the ExerciseManager class, which contains the Load and Save methods. These methods, as their names indicate, are used to load exercises stored in isolated storage and to save them, respectively.

The Load static method returns a List<> collection of ExerciseSettings objects when exercises.xml is present in the application isoloated storage. Otherwise, the method returns an empty list.

▪ **Note** This chapter does not cover isolated storage concepts in depth because Chapter 9 is dedicated to that topic.

```
public static List<ExerciseSettings> Load()
{
    List<ExerciseSettings> exercises = new List<ExerciseSettings>();

    IsolatedStorageFile storage = IsolatedStorageFile.GetUserStoreForApplication();

    if (storage.FileExists("exercises.xml"))
    {
        IsolatedStorageFileStream stream = storage.OpenFile("exercises.xml",
                                                            FileMode.Open);
        XmlSerializer xml = new XmlSerializer(typeof(List<ExerciseSettings>));
        exercises = xml.Deserialize(stream) as List<ExerciseSettings>;
        stream.Close();
        stream.Dispose();
    }

    return exercises;
}
```

The Save static method accepts a List<ExerciseSettings> objects collection that is stored in the exercises.xml file.

```
public static void Save(List<ExerciseSettings> exercises)
```

```
    {
        IsolatedStorageFile iso = IsolatedStorageFile.GetUserStoreForApplication();
        IsolatedStorageFileStream stream = iso.CreateFile("exercises.xml");
        StreamWriter writer = new StreamWriter(stream);

        XmlSerializer ser = new XmlSerializer(typeof(List<ExerciseSettings>));

        ser.Serialize(writer, exercises);

        writer.Close();
        writer.Dispose();
    }
```

The final step in managing tombstoning in our application is to call those two methods in the four Application event handlers. When the application is launched from the Start menu, the application calls the Load method from the ExerciseManager class in order to load stored exercises. The same occurs when the application is reactivated from tombstoning. By the way, in this case you have to check the IsApplicationInstancePreserved property in order to know when the application has been reactivated from the dormant state (its value is true) and when the application has been reactivated from a tombstone (its value is false). Only when the application is reactivated from a tombstone you call the Load method. In fact, in the dormant case every variable of the application has been preserved by the operating system, automatically.

On the other hand, when the application is closed by pressing the hardware Back button from the application's main page, the application calls the Save static method from the ExerciseManager class. The same occurs when the application is deactivated that is, the hardware Start button is pressed, or a phone call arrived, or a Chooser is launched (see more on Launchers and Choosers in Chapter 3), or the lock screen is engaged.

```
    public partial class App : Application
    {
        /// <summary>
        /// Provides easy access to the root frame of the Phone Application.
        /// </summary>
        /// <returns>The root frame of the Phone Application.</returns>
. . .

        // Code to execute when the application is launching (e.g., from Start)
        // This code will not execute when the application is reactivated
        private void Application_Launching(object sender, LaunchingEventArgs e)
        {
            Exercises = ExerciseManager.Load();
        }

        // Code to execute when the application is activated (brought to foreground)
        // This code will not execute when the application is first launched
        private void Application_Activated(object sender,
                                            ActivatedEventArgs e)
        {
            if (!e.IsApplicationInstancePreserved)
                Exercises = ExerciseManager.Load();
        }
```

```
    // Code to execute when the application is deactivated (sent to
    // background)
    // This code will not execute when the application is closing
    private void Application_Deactivated(object sender,
                                          DeactivatedEventArgs e)
    {
        ExerciseManager.Save(Exercises);
    }

    // Code to execute when the application is closing (e.g., user hit
    // Back)
    // This code will not execute when the application is deactivated
    private void Application_Closing(object sender, ClosingEventArgs e)
    {
        ExerciseManager.Save(Exercises);
    }

    // Code to execute if a navigation fails
```

. . .

Usage

From Visual Studio 2010, right-click the mouse on the 7Drum project and select the Properties menu item. In the Properties page select the Debug tab on the left of the screen and check the Tombstone upon deactivation while debugging check box. In this way you can simulate the application tombstoning when your application is running in debug mode. Press F5so the application starts and briefly presents the main page and the menu shown in Figure 2-11.

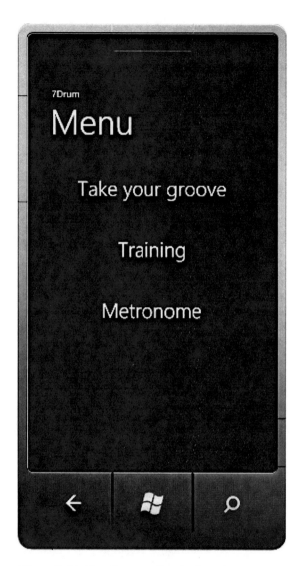

Figure 2-11. The 7Drum application's main page menu

Select the Training menu and then tap the Plus button on the application bar, as shown in Figure 2-12.

Figure 2-12. Add a new exercise by pressing the Plus button.

The Exercise page is shown with the three empty text boxes. Write something, as shown in Figure 2-13, and then click the Save button. The text boxes will be cleaned in order to let the user add another exercise. Press the hardware Back button to come back to the Training page.

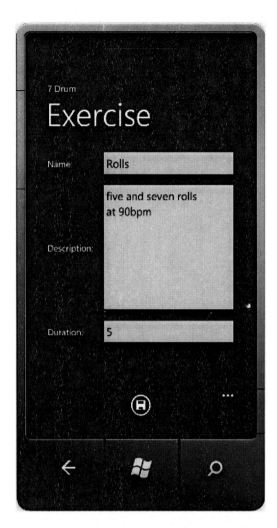

Figure 2-13. Adding a new exercise to the training plan

The Training page will show a list of exercises you added in the previous step. Now let's produce the tombstoning. Press the hardware Start button and again the hardware Back button. The 7Drum application is shown again and you will hopefully see the list of exercises, as you never closed the application (see Figure 2-14).

■ **Note** When you close the Windows Phone Emulator, the isolated storage is deleted along with your application.

Figure 2-14. The Training page contains the list of exercises.

2-6. Managing Tombstoning in Windows Phone XNA Applications

Problem

You need to stop your XNA game when tombstoning occurs on your phone, by showing the game in pause mode.

Solution

You can use both the OnActivated and OnDeactivated event handlers provided by the Game class.

How It Works

Everything you studied in the previous recipes on tombstoning, including State collection, is valid for XNA games too. The big difference is the events raised when the application is tombstoned.

An XNA game responds to the OnActivated event when the application is either run or resumed from dormant or tombstoning. The game responds to the OnDeactivated event when the application is either put in dormant state or closed.

■ **Note** The Game class provides the OnExiting event handler, which is used to know when the application is going to be closed. The OnDeactivated event will be called after OnExiting as well. So in the OnDeactivated event handler, there is no immediate way to know whether the application is going to be closed or it has been put in dormant state.

When the game is tombstoned, the application stores game settings in the State dictionary. When the application is resumed, it loads the game settings and shows a bitmap representing the game in pause mode. Now if the user taps the screen, the game restarts.

The Code

To demonstrate tombstoning management in an XNA application, we have created a bouncing ball game that is paused if the application deactivation occurs. The game provides a pause mode screenshot that is shown after the game is resumed.

The GameSettings class contains three properties to store the ball location, the ball velocity, and a Boolean indicating whether the game is in pause mode (its value is true) or not (its value is false).

```
public class GameSettings
{
    public bool Paused { get; set; }
    public Vector2 Location { get; set; }
    public Vector2 Velocity { get; set; }

    public GameSettings()
    {
        Paused = false;
        Location = Vector2.Zero;
        Velocity = new Vector2(1f, 1f);
    }
}
```

The GameSettingsManager class contains the Load and Save methods, which are used to load game settings from the State dictionary and to save them, respectively. With the Save method, the GameSettings object is stored in the GameSettings key of the State dictionary. With the Load method, we check whether the State dictionary contains the GameSettings key. If it does, the GameSettings object is loaded with the one provided by the State dictionary; otherwise, a brand new object is returned.

■ **Note** The Visual Studio 2010 XNA game project doesn't contain the assemblies needed to use the State dictionary, so you have to add a reference to Microsoft.Phone and System.Windows DLLs.

```
public class GameSettingsManager
{
    public static void Save(GameSettings settings)
    {
        PhoneApplicationService.Current.State["GameSettings"] = settings;
    }

    public static GameSettings Load()
    {
        GameSettings settings = new GameSettings();

        if (PhoneApplicationService.Current.State.ContainsKey("GameSettings"))
            settings = PhoneApplicationService.Current.State["GameSettings"] as
                    GameSettings;

        return settings;
    }

}
```

The Game1.cs file contains the OnActivated and OnDeactivated event handlers. In the former event handler, the Load static method from the GameSettingsManager class is called, and local variables' values are replaced with the stored ones. In the latter event handler, the Save static method is called, providing local variables' values and setting the Paused property to true.

```
protected override void OnActivated(object sender, EventArgs args)
{
    settings = GameSettingsManager.Load();
    spriteLocation = settings.Location;
    spriteVelocity = settings.Velocity;

    base.OnActivated(sender, args);
}

protected override void OnDeactivated(object sender, EventArgs args)
{
    settings.Paused = true;
    settings.Location = spriteLocation;
    settings.Velocity = spriteVelocity;

    GameSettingsManager.Save(settings);

    base.OnDeactivated(sender, args);
}
```

The Update method is the core of the game, where all the logic is calculated, sprite positions are updated and, in this case, the pause mode is checked. When the game is in pause mode, the ball position is not changed and the ball texture is replaced with the Game Paused bitmap. Then the code waits for gesture events—specifically, for a tap on the screen—and when it occurs, the Paused property is set to false and the game restarts (see more on gestures in Chapter 5).

```
protected override void Update(GameTime gameTime)
{
    // Allows the game to exit
    if (GamePad.GetState(PlayerIndex.One).Buttons.Back == ButtonState.Pressed)
        this.Exit();

    // TODO: Add your update logic here
    if (settings.Paused == false)
    {
        spriteLocation = spriteLocation + spriteVelocity;
        spriteTexture = ballTexture;
    }
    else
    {
        spriteLocation = Vector2.Zero;
        spriteTexture = pauseScreen;

        while (TouchPanel.IsGestureAvailable)
        {
            GestureSample gs = TouchPanel.ReadGesture();
            switch (gs.GestureType)
            {
                case GestureType.Tap:
                    settings.Paused = false;
                    spriteLocation = settings.Location;
                    spriteVelocity = settings.Velocity;
                    spriteTexture = ballTexture;
                    break;
            }
        }
    }
. . .
```

Usage

From Visual Studio 2010, select Windows Phone Emulator as the output target and run the application. After few seconds, the emulator will show a bouncing ball moving on the screen (see Figure 2-15).

Figure 2-15. The `XNATombstoning` *application runs, showing a bouncing ball.*

Press the hardware Start button, causing application deactivation. Now press the hardware Back button so that the game is resumed. The application shows the Game Paused bitmap and waits for a tap on the screen (see Figure 2-16).

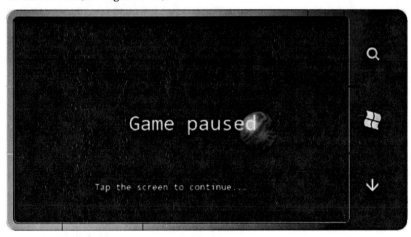

Figure 2-16. The game is in pause mode.

2-7. Implementing Multitasking

Problem

You need to create an application that continues to run tasks either when the user closes or deactivates the application.

Solution

You can use background agents implemented by `PeriodicTask` and `ResourceIntensiveTask` classes.

How It Works

Windows Phone operating system allows just one application running in foreground at a time. When the application is either closed or deactivated the application is put in a dormant state waiting to be resumed.

Windows Phone operating system provides the Fast Switching Application mechanism that allows user to quickly resume an application that has been deactivated. Simply pressing and holding the Back hardware button, the operating system shows a screenshot of every dormant application that can be resumed. Tapping on the application screenshot the selected application is resumed and the user can continue to use the application from the state he or she had left. From a developer point of view there is no need to create code managing the resuming from the dormant state; everything is managed by Windows Phone operating system, automatically.

Often there are situations where the application is closed or deactivated but it needs to continue processing data, check application state's changing, download a file, play music, and so on. In such situations, you can use the background agents. When the process runs for a short amount of time you can use the `PeriodicTask` class. For example, you can use the PeriodicTask agent when you need to update the GPS phone position, or check for new files in the isolated storage.

When the process is long and resource consuming you can use the `ResourceIntensiveTask` class. A classic example of `ResourceIntensiveTask` class usage is when you need to synchronize data from an external source and your application.

There are constraints for both background agents type. The PeriodicTask agent is executed by Windows Phone operating system every 30 minutes, the PeriodicTask agent runs for 25 seconds, but the agent can be terminated early as well. The ResourceIntensiveTask agent runs for 10 minutes but the phone has to be connected to the power source and to either the WiFi or PC. Moreover, the ResourceIntensiveTask agent runs only when the phone's screen is locked.

A rule common to both agents' type regards the phone's battery state. Usually, to save battery life when its state is low the Windows Phone operating system avoids running background agents.

The Windows Phone operating system accepts only one agent per application. This agent can be registered as PeriodicTask, ResourceIntensiveTask, or both. When you register the application to use both types, you have to recall that just one agent's instance will be executed at a time.

There are common constraints to the API that can be called from an agent. For example, an agent cannot call Camera APIs, use the WebBrowser control, use the MessageBox class, implement XNA libraries, and so on.

■ **Note** See the official documentation at `http://msdn.microsoft.com/en-us/library/hh202962(v=VS.92).aspx` for the complete list of unsupported API.

Finally, there are memory usage limitations for the agents. Both periodic and resource intensive tasks can use no more than 6 Mb of memory and tasks are terminated when they don't respect this constraint.

The Code

To demonstrate background agents in action we have created a Windows Phone Silverlight application called MultitaskingApplication.

From Visual Studio 2010, create a new Windows Phone Silverlight application, name it MultitaskingApplication, and press the OK button. Choose the Windows Phone OS 7.1 project template and press the OK button. Now you have to add a second project to the Visual Studio solution so select the File menu and then choose Add aNew Project. This project is called MyAgent and contains the code to implement the background agents. From the New Project dialog box select the Windows Phone Scheduled Task Agent template, name it MyAgent and press the OK button (see Figure 2-17).

Figure 2-17. The Windows Phone Scheduled Task Agent Visual Studio template

Now from the MultitaskingApplication project add a reference to the MyAgent project. Right-click from the MultitaskingApplication project name in the Solution Explorer windows and select the Add

Reference menu item. From the Add Reference dialog box select the Projects tab and then the MyAgent project (see Figure 2-18).

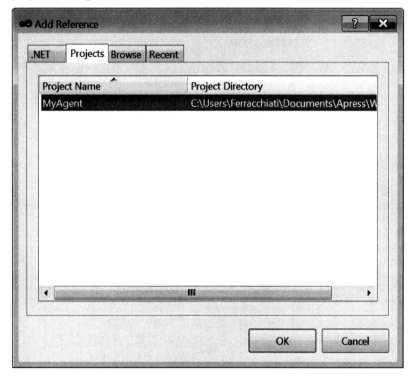

Figure 2-18. *Add a Reference To The MyAgent Project*

The MyAgent project contains the code implementing the background agents and Visual Studio helps you adding a code skeleton to manage background agents in your application. The MyAgent project contains only the ScheduledAgent.cs code file where the ScheduledAgent class is defined. The ScheduledAgent class is derived from the ScheduledTaskAgent class that implements the OnInvoke method called by the Windows Phone operating system when it's time to execute either a PeriodicTask or a ResourceIntensiveTask. The OnInvoke method has a ScheduledTask parameter that you can use to understand whether the invoked task is a PeriodicTask or a ResourceIntensiveTask. Obviously, this check is needed only when your application register both periodic and resource intensive tasks.

In our code, we registered both background agents just to show you how to do it, but only for the PeriodicTask agent is implemented the code. The periodic agent checks a directory in the application-isolated storage for the presence of new files. When the agent finds new files it moves them in a new directory and informs the user that new files are arrived using a toast notification. The resource intensive task could open these files and perhaps add their content to a local database.

Let's see the code within the ScheduledAgent.cs file. As said the ScheduledAgent class inherits from the ScheduledTaskAgent class that is implemented in the Microsoft.Phone.Scheduler namespace. The #define instruction will be useful next when we will force Windows Phone to execute our agents within one minute. So we haven't to wait a lot of minutes for periodic and resource intensive agents execution.

```
#define DEBUG_AGENT

using System.Windows;
using Microsoft.Phone.Scheduler;
using System.IO.IsolatedStorage;
using System;
using Microsoft.Phone.Shell;
using System.IO;

namespace MyAgent
{
    public class ScheduledAgent : ScheduledTaskAgent
    {
```

The OnInvoke method contains the core code of the background agents. The code checks the task type and calls the CheckFile method when the task is a periodic task or the LoadFile method when the task is a resource intensive task. Let's focus on the periodic task code. If the CheckFile method founds new files it moves these files into another folder and returns true. In this case the OnInvoke method code informs the user about new files incoming creating and showing a toast. The toast notification is the unique way to communicate something from the background agent to the user. You can create a toast notification creating an object from the ShellToast class, setting its Title and Content properties with the toast's title and description, respectively. Finally, the Show method of the ShellToast class shows the toast notification.

The ScheduledAgent class has to notify to the Windows Phone operating system the result of its operations calling either NotifyComplete or Abort methods. The former informs that every operation done by the agent was good so the operating system can continue to execute the agent. On the other hand, the latter informs the operating system to stop agent execution because an error is occurred. Stopped agents will not be executed again until the user executes the application again so that the application registers agents again.

Finally, the DEBUG_AGENT constant is checked so to speed up agents' execution from the operating system.

```
        protected override void OnInvoke(ScheduledTask task)
        {
            bool bRes = false;

            if (task is PeriodicTask)
            {
                bRes = CheckFile();
                if (bRes)
                {
                    ShellToast toast = new ShellToast();
                    toast.Title = "New files arrived";
                    toast.Content = "Processing...";
                    toast.Show();
                }
            }
            else
            {
                bRes = LoadFile();
            }
```

```
                    // If debugging is enabled, launch the agent again in one minute.
#if DEBUG_AGENT
              ScheduledActionService.LaunchForTest(task.Name,
                                              TimeSpan.FromSeconds(60));
#endif
              NotifyComplete();
          }
```

The code that informs the Windows Phone operating system where you have implemented the scheduled task agent code is contained in the Tasks section of the WMAppManifest.xml file.

```
. . .
    <Tasks>
      <DefaultTask Name="_default" NavigationPage="MainPage.xaml" />
      <ExtendedTask Name="BackgroundTask">
        <BackgroundServiceAgent Specifier="ScheduledTaskAgent"
                          Name="MyAgent" Source="MyAgent"
                          Type="MyAgent.ScheduledAgent" />
      </ExtendedTask>
    </Tasks>
. . .
```

Finally, the last thing you need to do is use the Add and Remove methods provided by the ScheduledActionService to register background agents in your application. When the application is active and running in the foreground, and your agents have been already executed, you have to register a brand new version of your agents so that they are rescheduled. So you have to choose a method in the application code that allows you to register agents when the application is active. We have chosen the Application class's Launching and Activated event handlers so that the background agents are registered each time the application is launched for the first time and reactivated, respectively.

In both event handlers' code there is the ManageTasks private method call. The code is very similar for registering both background agents. Let's focus on how to register the PeriodicTask agent. First of all, you need to check if the agent has been already executed by the operating system. In the affirmative case, you have to remove the agent and register a brand new one for rescheduling. You can use the Find method provided by ScheduledActionService class to retrieve the PeriodicTask object used by the operating system and pass the object to the Remove method to remove from memory.

Next, you create a brand new PeriodicTask object, set its description so that Windows Phone can show to the user what your agent does, and pass the object to the Add method provided by the ScheduledActionService class.

The Windows Phone operating system gives users the possibility to disable background agents for a specific application. In this case you will receive an InvalidOperationException exception that you have to catch and manage in your application.

```
          private void ManageTasks()
          {
              periodicTask = ScheduledActionService.Find(periodicTaskName) as
                          PeriodicTask;

              if (periodicTask != null)
              {
                  ScheduledActionService.Remove(periodicTaskName);
              }

              periodicTask = new PeriodicTask(periodicTaskName);
```

```
            periodicTask.Description = "MultitaskingApplication periodic
                                        task.";

            try
            {
                ScheduledActionService.Add(periodicTask);

                // If debugging is enabled, use LaunchForTest to launch the
                // agent in one minute.
#if(DEBUG_AGENT)
                ScheduledActionService.LaunchForTest(periodicTaskName,
                                            TimeSpan.FromSeconds(60));
#endif
            }
            catch (InvalidOperationException exception)
            {
                if (exception.Message.Contains("BNS Error: The action is
                                        disabled"))
                {
                    MessageBox.Show("User has disabled background agents for
                                    this application.");
                    return;
                }
            }

            resourceIntensiveTask =
                ScheduledActionService.Find(resourceIntensiveTaskName) as
                ResourceIntensiveTask;

            if (resourceIntensiveTask != null)
            {
                ScheduledActionService.Remove(resourceIntensiveTaskName);
            }

            resourceIntensiveTask = new
                ResourceIntensiveTask(resourceIntensiveTaskName);

            resourceIntensiveTask.Description = "MultitaskingApplication
                                        resource intensive task.";

            try
            {
                ScheduledActionService.Add(resourceIntensiveTask);

                // If debugging is enabled, use LaunchForTest to launch the
                // agent in one minute.
#if(DEBUG_AGENT)
                ScheduledActionService.LaunchForTest(resourceIntensiveTaskName,
                                    TimeSpan.FromSeconds(60));
#endif
```

```
        }
        catch (InvalidOperationException exception)
        {
            if (exception.Message.Contains("BNS Error: The action is
                                        disabled"))
            {
                MessageBox.Show("User has disabled background agents for
                                this application.");
            }
        }
    }
}
```

Usage

From Visual Studio 2010, select Windows Phone Emulator as the output target and press F5 key. The application is started in debug mode showing the main page. The main page indicates that no files are arrived.

Press the Back hardware button so to exit from the application. Now the application is put in dormant state but its own background process are executed. So let's use the Isolated Storage Explorer tool (ISETool.exe) to copy a new file in the application isolated storage (see more on ISETool.exe in Chapter 9, Recipe 9-6).

Launch the command to store locally to your PC the files within the application isolated storage. The ts parameter is to take a snapshot of the application's isolated storage and save to the temp directory. The guid parameter is the application identifier specified in the WMAppManifest.xml file. Finally, the xd parameter indicates that the application has been deployed to the emulator (use sd value if you have deployed to the physical device).

```
ISETool.exe ts xd 49f06382-a11c-4579-b38b-259eb1b33a58 c:\temp
```

Now add an xml file into the IsolatedStore folder and upload the content back to the Windows Phone emulator using the following command. This is pretty similar to the previous command, but here we use the rs parameter to restore the snapshot to the isolated storage.

```
ISETool.exe rs xd 49f06382-a11c-4579-b38b-259eb1b33a58 c:\temp\IsolatedStore
```

When the Windows Phone operating system launches the periodic task (we are in debug mode, so this happens each minute), the agent code finds a new file and informs the user that a new file is arrived (see Figure 2-19).

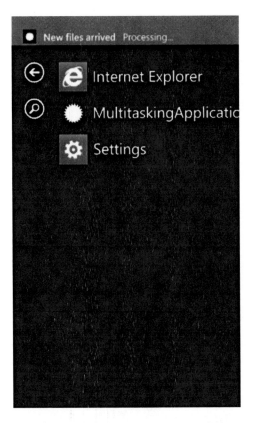

Figure 2-19. A Toast notification indicates new files incoming

You can either tap the toast notification or launch the application manually. In every case the application will show the content of the uploaded xml file (see Figure 2-20).

Figure 2-20: The Main page shows the content of the uploaded XML file

---

■ **Note** To debug resource-intensive tasks, you have to use a physical device, because you have to lock the phone screen and there is no way to simulate lock screen using the emulator.

2-8. Scheduling Alarms and Reminders

Problem

You want to create an application that reminds you about your friends' birthday. Even when the user is not using your application you need to alert the user when a friend has the birthday.

Solution

You can use scheduling notification implementing the Alarm and the Reminder classes.

How It Works

The scheduling notification is a dialog box that appears to remind users about an event to be notified. The scheduling notification is implemented by both the Alarm and Reminder classes. Both classes display a dialog box with a custom message and two buttons to dismiss the notification or postpone it for another reminder. When the user taps on the notification dialog box the application that created it is launched.

The biggest difference between Alarm and Reminder scheduled notifications is that only the Reminder class allows developers to specify an URI pointing to a page of the application and eventually passing parameters using the query string.

On the other hand, the Alarm class doesn't have that feature but it allows developer to customize the ringtone that is played during notification dialog box visualization.

Common classes' characteristics are the possibility to specify some custom text to be shown, the notification can be executed once or multiple times depending on how you have defined in your code the BeginTime, EndTime, and RecurrenceType properties.

After having created either a Reminder or an Alarm object you have to provide it to the Add method of the ScheduledActionService class.

The Code

To demonstrate scheduled notifications, we have created a Windows Phone Silverlight application that reminds to phone user about friends' birthday. The application is focusing on notification reminders management and in particular to the Reminder class.

Open Visual Studio 2010 and create a new Windows Phone Silverlight application called BirthdayApp.

The App class contains the core code for this example. In both the Deactivated and Closing event handlers is called the ManageReminder method.

In the ManageReminder method, first the code checks if the reminder has been already added. In the affirmative case the reminder is first removed and then created again with fresh new information.

We want that the application notifies the birthday from the moment the application is either closed or deactivated to the end of the day. So we used the BeginTime property one minute later to the current time and the EndTime to the 00:00:00 AM of the next day. Finally, the RecurrenceType is set to Daily so that the notification can be prompted for the entire day.

Finally, the Clear.xaml page is indicated in the NavigationUri property as target page when the user taps on the reminder dialog box.

```
private void ManageReminder()
{
    Reminder reminder = ScheduledActionService.Find(reminderName) as
                        Reminder;
    if (reminder != null)
        ScheduledActionService.Remove(reminderName);

    DateTime now = DateTime.Now;
    DateTime tomorrow = now.AddDays(1);
```

```
            reminder = new Reminder(reminderName);
            reminder.BeginTime = now.AddMinutes(1);
            reminder.ExpirationTime = new DateTime(tomorrow.Year,
                                                   tomorrow.Month,
                                                   tomorrow.Day,
                                                   0, 0, 0);

            reminder.Content = "Today is John Smith birthday!";
            reminder.Title = "Birthday App";
            reminder.RecurrenceType = RecurrenceInterval.Daily;
            reminder.NavigationUri = new Uri("/Clear.xaml",
                                             UriKind.Relative);

            ScheduledActionService.Add(reminder);
        }
```

Now, you need to add the Clear.xaml page to the solution. In the Clear page code you need to add the code to clear the reminder. The OnNavigatedTo event handler is the ideal place to specify the code.

```
protected override void
        OnNavigatedTo(System.Windows.Navigation.NavigationEventArgs e)
{
    App a = Application.Current as App;
    a.IsReminderEnabled = false;
}
```

Usage

From Visual Studio 2010, select Windows Phone Emulator as the output target and press CTRL+F5 key. The application is launched showing the main page in Figure 2-21.

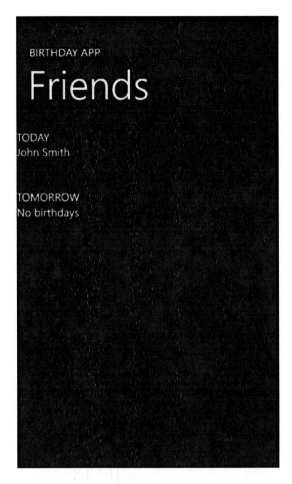

Figure 2-21: *The BirthdayApp application in action*

Now, you can press either the Back or Start hardware buttons to close or to deactivate the application. The application creates the reminder and after one minute you should see the Windows Phone Emulator showing the notification as shown in Figure 2-22.

Figure 2-22: *The scheduled notification*

Now, you can snooze the alarm for 5 minutes or more (you can choose another value from the combo box). Also, you can press the Dismiss button to remove the notification that will not be shown anymore.

Finally, you can tap on the notification dialog box to open a brand new copy of your application and navigate to the Clear.xaml page (see Figure 2-23).

Figure 2-23: The Clear page

2-9. Managing Obscured and Unobscured Events

Problem

You need to create an application that continues to run either when the Windows Phone operating system locks the phone screen or you receive a phone call. During those events, you have to power off some battery-consuming resources. Then, when the screen is unlocked or the phone call ends, you have to turn those resources on again.

Solution

You have to use the `ApplicationIdleDetectionMode` property provided by the `PhoneApplicationService` class and register both `Obscured` and `Unobscured` event handlers defined in the `PhoneApplicationFrame` class.

How It Works

`ApplicationIdleDetectionMode` is a property that is defined in the `PhoneApplicationService` class and that has its default value set to `IdleDetectionMode.Enabled`. This means that the application is suspended when the operating system finds it idle. You can set the property to `IdleDetectionMode.Disabled` so that your application will continue to run even when the operating system locks the screen.

■ **Note** The lock screen idle time is defined in the Settings of your physical phone and is not configurable from the emulator.

The `Obscured` event is raised when the phone screen is locked by the Windows Phone operating system or when you receive a phone call. The `Unobscured` event is raised when the phone screen is unlocked or when the phone call is terminated.

When the `IdleDetectionMode` property of `ApplicationIdleDetectionMode` is set to `Disabled`, you can use those two methods to stop power-consuming resources (such as the accelerometer, screen animations, FM radio service, and so on) and then start them again when the lock screen is removed. In the `Obscured` event handler, you should specify the code to stop services that your application is not going to use because the phone screen is locked. So if your application uses the StoryBoard to show an animated progress bar, you will stop the animation but upgrade the progress bar logic. You should stop other services to reduce battery consumption.

When `IdleDetectionMode` is set to `Disabled`, you can use `Obscured` and `Unobscured` event handlers to manage particular events that are not raised with tombstoning. Indeed, the phone lock screen and phone calls don't raise tombstoning events. So, for example, if you have created a game with Silverlight and you want to show a pause screen after a phone call ends, you have to use the `Obscured` and `Unobscured` events.

■ **Note** The `OnDeactivated` event handler from the XNA `Game` class receives the phone screen lock and the phone call events. So it is not necessary to implement the `Obscured` and `Unobscured` event handlers to stop a game. The `OnDeactivated` event handler remains necessary when you disable idle detection mode.

You should set the IdleDetectionMode property to Disabled only for very particular cases, when you are not able to accomplish application functionalities using background agents, scheduled notifications, background audio playback, and background file transfers. Indeed, the Windows Phone operating system resuming functionalities that speed up application restoring, fast application switching, and the like are not working on applications that have disabled the idle detection mode. With the idle detection disabled, the phone locks the screen but the Windows Phone operating system doesn't put the application in a dormant state.

Finally, in your application you have to ask to the user whether he or she wants to disable the idle detection and not assuming the user always accept it.

The Code

Open Visual Studio 2010 and create a new Windows Phone Silverlight application called ObscuredUnobscuredApp. In MainPage.xaml.cs, we added the code to the MainPage constructor in order to register the Obscured and Unobscured event handlers and to set the IdleDetectionMode.Disabled value to ApplicationIdleDetectionMode.

```
public MainPage()
{
    InitializeComponent();

    PhoneApplicationService.Current.ApplicationIdleDetectionMode =
                                        IdleDetectionMode.Disabled;
    PhoneApplicationFrame rootFrame = ((App)Application.Current).RootFrame;
    rootFrame.Obscured += new EventHandler<ObscuredEventArgs>(rootFrame_Obscured);
    rootFrame.Unobscured += new EventHandler(rootFrame_Unobscured);
}
```

▦ **Note** A restart application is required if you change the IdleDetectionMode value twice at runtime. The official documentation indicates that this behavior could change in future operating system releases.

The Obscured event handler provides the ObscuredEventArgs parameter, which defines the IsLocked property used to know if the event is raised either by the phone screen lock (its value is true) or by the phone call (its value is false).

In the Obscured and Unobscured event handlers, we are going to disable and then enable the battery's power-consuming services, respectively.

```
void rootFrame_Unobscured(object sender, EventArgs e)
{
    FMRadio.Instance.PowerMode = RadioPowerMode.On;
    acc.Start();
    geoW.Start();
}

void rootFrame_Obscured(object sender, ObscuredEventArgs e)
{
    FMRadio.Instance.PowerMode = RadioPowerMode.Off;
    acc.Stop();
    geoW.Stop();
```

```
        }
```

Usage

There is no way to test the application by using the Obscured and Unobscured event handlers in the emulator. So press F5 only if you changed the output target to the Windows Phone device. You have to put two breakpoints in the Obscured and Unobscured code so you can see that events are raised.
The application will start, briefly showing the main page. Now you can call your phone with another phone or wait while the Windows Phone operating system locks the screen. Note the application hitting breakpoints.

CHAPTER 3

User Interface

A user's first impression of a computer application's user interface is critical. Users will immediately decide to uninstall an application if it is too complex or if it not do what it promises to do. When comparing two user interfaces, users will often choose the more eye-catching one.

The Windows Phone user interface is not exempt from this type of user behavior. In addition, there are lot of applications on the Marketplace, so the competition is ruthless. The user might try your application, but you will have to convince that user to buy it.

In this chapter and in the next (which is about Expression Blend), you will find a lot of recipes on the user interface. You will see how to use Silverlight common controls and Silverlight features such as bindings, but also how to implement eye-catching effects including an animated splash screen and navigation between pages.

The recipes in this chapter describe how to do the following:

- 3-1. Create an animated splash screen

- 3-2. Use the `ApplicationBar` control

- 3-3. Detect changes in the theme template

- 3-4. Customize the Soft Input Panel keyboard to accept only numbers

- 3-5. Use the Windows Phone predefined styles

- 3-6. Localize your application

- 3-7. Use `Panorama` and `Pivot` controls

- 3-8. Spice up the user interface with the Silverlight for Windows Phone Toolkit

- 3-9. Use launchers and choosers

- 3-10. Access to Contacts library

- 3-11. Add advertising to your application

3-1. Creating an Animated Splash Screen

Problem

Your application starts connecting to a web page, and you need to show a splash screen with an animated progress bar in order to inform users that they need to wait a few seconds before using the application.

Solution

You can create a user control and use it with the `Child` property provided by the `Popup` class. The `ProgressBar` control has the `IsIndeterminate` property set to `true`.

How It Works

The splash screen provided by the Visual Studio 2010 Windows Phone Silverlight Application project template is static, a simple PNG image shown during the application launch. To create an animated splash screen, you need to remove the `SplashScreen.png` file from the project and use a trick: the `Popup` class.

Usually, the `Popup` class is used to show tooltips during mouse activities in desktop applications. However, with a Windows Phone application, you can use it to show a generic `UIElement` object, perhaps either a common control or a user control. User controls are often used when you need to compose more than one common control within a unique control having its own logic. Instead of using dozens of controls to create a complex user interface, you can separate functionality into user controls and thereby achieve code reusability too.

In this case, you are going to create a user control composed of a full-screen image—480×800 pixels—some text, and a progress bar. The `Popup` class provides the `Child` property used to specify the `UIElement` that has to be shown. In this case, the `Child` property will be set to the `MySplashScreen` object defined by the user control.

The `ProgressBar` control within the user control has the `IsIndeterminate` property set to `true` because the loading time of the web page cannot be estimated. Indeed, when your application starts, you make a call to a web page, and because you don't know whether the phone is connected to Wi-Fi or to General Packet Radio Service (GPRS), or whether some network traffic delays might occur, you cannot estimate the loading time.

When the application is launched, the pop-up will fill the entire screen surface, and the progress bar will display across the screen. Behind the scenes, the `WebBrowser` control (see Recipe 3-2) will load the page and then raise the `Navigated` event. Trapping the `Navigated` event will allow you to hide the pop-up and show the user interface that is underneath.

The Code

To demonstrate the animated splash screen example, you are going to create a `FlickrPhotoAlbum` application. This application uses the Flickr.NET library (see `http://flickrnet.codeplex.com`) and the phone camera to take a picture and upload it to a Flickr gallery.

Before uploading Flickr.NET API calls to the destination, users have to be authenticated to Flickr and have to accept that your application will use their resources.

Our application accomplishes these steps by redirecting the WebControl content to an URL page returned by the AuthCalcUrl method call. In this case, the animated splash screen is really useful in enabling you to avoid having the user interface show blank WebControl content until the page is loaded. Indeed, by using the Navigated event handler, you know exactly when the page has finished loading and can hide the splash screen. Let's examine the code from the FlickrPhotoAlbum application.

In the MySplashScreen.xaml file, you defined the user control's user interface. It is composed of a full-screen image, a TextBlock control showing the Loading text, and a ProgressBar:

```
<UserControl x:Class="FlickrPhotoAlbum.MySplashScreen"
    xmlns="http://schemas.microsoft.com/winfx/2006/xaml/presentation"
    xmlns:x="http://schemas.microsoft.com/winfx/2006/xaml"
    xmlns:d="http://schemas.microsoft.com/expression/blend/2008"
    xmlns:mc="http://schemas.openxmlformats.org/markup-compatibility/2006"
    mc:Ignorable="d"
    FontFamily="{StaticResource PhoneFontFamilyNormal}"
    FontSize="{StaticResource PhoneFontSizeNormal}"
    Foreground="{StaticResource PhoneForegroundBrush}"
    d:DesignHeight="800" d:DesignWidth="480">

    <Grid x:Name="LayoutRoot" Background="White" Width="480" Height="800">
        <ProgressBar HorizontalAlignment="Left" Margin="47,692,0,89" Name="pbProgress"
        Width="383"  />
        <Image Height="512" HorizontalAlignment="Left" Margin="114,75,0,0" Name="imgScreen"
        Stretch="Fill" VerticalAlignment="Top" Width="272" Source="images/screen.png" />
        <TextBlock HorizontalAlignment="Left" Margin="185,656,0,114" Text="Loading..."
        Width="111" Foreground="Black" FontSize="22" />
    </Grid>
</UserControl>
```

▨ **Note** The screen.png image is included in the project inside the images folder and has the Build Action property set to Content. In this way, you can use the relative path in the Source attribute of the Image tag.

The IsIndeterminate property value is set to true in the MySplashScreen constructor:

```
namespace FlickrPhotoAlbum
{
    public partial class MySplashScreen : UserControl
    {
        public MySplashScreen()
        {
            InitializeComponent();
            this.pbProgress.IsIndeterminate = true;
        }
    }
}
```

In the `MainPage.xaml.cs` file, you define the `MainPage` class constructor in which the `Popup` object is created, its `Child` property is set to an object of the `MySplashScreen` class, and the `IsOpen` property is set to true, causing the splash screen to be shown:

```
public partial class MainPage : PhoneApplicationPage
{
    Popup popup = null;

    // Constructor
    public MainPage()
    {
        InitializeComponent();

. . .

        popup = new Popup();
        popup.Child = new MySplashScreen();
        popup.IsOpen = true;
    }
```

The `IsOpen` property is set to `false` in the `Navigated` event handler that is raised by the `WebBrowser` control after having completely loaded the web page:

```
private void wbBrowser_Navigated(object sender,
                                 System.Windows.Navigation.NavigationEventArgs e)
{
    this.popup.IsOpen = false;
}
```

The instruction to trap the `Navigated` event is declared in the `phone:WebBrowser` XAML tag by using the `Navigated` attribute:

```
<phone:WebBrowser x:Name="wbBrowser" Grid.Row="0" Navigated="wbBrowser_Navigated"/>
```

Usage

In Visual Studio 2010, select Windows Phone Emulator as the target output and press Ctrl+F5. The emulator displays the animated splash screen, as shown in Figure 3-1.

Figure 3-1. The animated splash screen in action

The splash screen automatically disappears when the web page is loaded, showing the user interface beneath (see Figure 3-2).

Figure 3-2. *The splash screen is automatically hidden, and the application is ready to authenticate the user on Flickr.*

3-2. Using the ApplicationBar Control

Problem

You need to add the application bar to your application.

Solution

You have to add an `ApplicationBar` section to the XAML of your page provided by `PhoneApplicationPage` within the phone namespace. Within this new tag, you can include one or more `ApplicationBar` tags provided—this time—by the shell namespace. The code generated by Visual Studio already contains a commented section in which `ApplicationBar` is defined with some buttons and menu items. You can simply uncomment and customize the code to obtain your goal.

How It Works

`ApplicationBar` is a Windows Phone control created just for Windows Phone devices. It allows you to have a sort of toolbar and menu in the application. The application bar is completely managed by the operating system, so it is placed at the bottom of the page when the application is in Portrait mode, and moved to one side when the phone is put in Landscape mode (which side depends on the direction in which you rotate your phone).

The application bar should contain at least four icons, and you should use the ones provided with the SDK. In the `%Program Files%\Microsoft SDKs\Windows Phone\v7.1\Icons` path, you can find both dark and light versions of application bar icons. You should use different icon colors depending on the selected theme (see Recipe 3-3). In the case user selects the light Windows Phone theme and you used the dark version, the operating system will take care of changing icons to light version for you, automatically. If you don't find the icon you need, you can use Microsoft Expression Blend for Windows Phone to draw your own.

The application bar also can contain menu items that will be shown when the user selects the ellipses at the top-right of the bar. You should not specify too many menu items, however, because the application bar will expand toward the top to show all items and could cover important parts of the user interface control. The official documentation sets this limit to at most five menu items. You have to set the `IsMenuEnabled` property to `true` to enable menu items in the application bar (see Figure 3-3 for the class diagram).

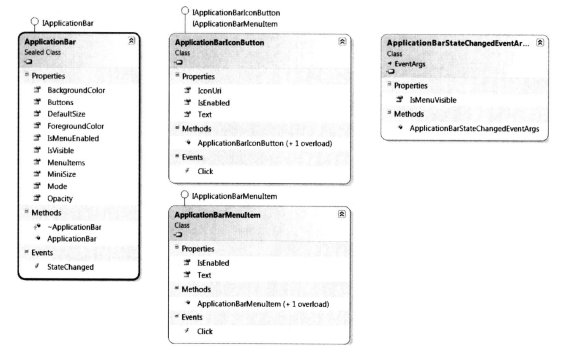

Figure 3-3. The ApplicationBar *class diagram*

The ApplicationBar control has the Opacity property, which affects the rectangle that contains the icons, not the icons themselves. This property accepts a decimal value between 0 and 1. When you set this property to 1, the frame resizes the page's content in order to reserve space for the application bar. On the other hand, when you set this property to a value less than 1, the application bar and its buttons will be drawn over the page content.

The IsVisible property is used to set when the application bar has to be shown (true) and when it does not (false).

The Mode property is used to set the application bar size between the default size and the mini size modes. The last option is particularly adapted to Windows Phone applications that need to save screen space and show mainly their content. For example, Windows Phone pages using Panorama and Pivot controls are indicated to implement mini application bars.

Although you can assign a name to both menu items and application bar buttons, you can't use those names to access related properties. You have to use the Buttons and MenuItems collections provided as properties by the ApplicationBar class to retrieve a reference to those buttons and menu items. Usually, you can use the page class constructor to map application bar items to relative names.

As already said, ApplicationBar can contain both ApplicationBarIconButton and ApplicationBarMenuItem controls. ApplicationBarIconButton has some interesting properties, such as IconUri, which specifies the URI relative to a path where the image is stored.

■ **Note** Remember to change the icon's `Build Actions` property from `Resource` to `Content` so that you can specify a relative URI path to the image.

The Text property is used to specify a very short button's description that will be shown when the user selects the ellipses button. Finally, `IsEnabled` is used to either enable or disable the button. `ApplicationBarMenuItem` uses the `Text` property to specify the menu item text that will be shown when the user displays the application bar by clicking the ellipses button.

Usually in your application, you implement a different application bar for each page you create (or some pages never need an application bar). You might have a case where you need to implement the same application bar in different application pages. This global application bar can be created in the App.xaml file, between the `<Application.Resources>` and `</Application.Resources>` tags. Finally, in each page where you need the application bar, you have to add this instruction

```
ApplicationBar = "{StaticResource AppBarName}"
```

where `AppBarName` is the application bar name you assigned in the XAML code and you have to specify this instruction as an attribute of the `<phone:PhoneApplicationPage>` tag.

The Code

You will find a lot of applications using the `ApplicationBar` control in this book. To demonstrate this recipe, we are implementing the `ApplicationBar` in the 7Drum application, specifically in the Training page. This page allows you to add, edit, and delete an exercise.

In the `Training.xaml` page, you define an `ApplicationBar` control with four buttons and one menu item:

```
. . .
<!--Sample code showing usage of ApplicationBar-->
    <phone:PhoneApplicationPage.ApplicationBar>
        <shell:ApplicationBar IsVisible="True" IsMenuEnabled="True">
            <shell:ApplicationBarIconButton IconUri="/images/dark/appbar.new.rest.png"
            Text="new" Click="ApplicationBarIconNewButton_Click" x:Name="btnNew" />
            <shell:ApplicationBarIconButton
            IconUri="/images/dark/appbar.transport.play.rest.png"
            Text="start" IsEnabled="False" Click="ApplicationBarIconPlayButton_Click"
            x:Name="btnPlay"/>
            <shell:ApplicationBarIconButton IconUri="/images/dark/appbar.edit.rest.png"
            Text="edit" IsEnabled="False" Click="ApplicationBarIconEditButton_Click"
            x:Name="btnEdit"/>
            <shell:ApplicationBarIconButton IconUri="/images/dark/appbar.delete.rest.png"
            Text="delete" IsEnabled="False" Click="ApplicationBarIconDeleteButton_Click"
            x:Name="btnDelete"/>
            <shell:ApplicationBar.MenuItems>
                <shell:ApplicationBarMenuItem Text="Exercise of the day"
                Click="ApplicationBarMenuItem_Click"/>
            </shell:ApplicationBar.MenuItems>
        </shell:ApplicationBar>
```

```
    </phone:PhoneApplicationPage.ApplicationBar>
. . .
```

In the Training.xaml.cs code, you use the constructor to map application bar buttons to related names so you can use variables to manage the buttons' properties throughout the entire code. The Buttons collection indexes correspond to the order you specified the buttons in the XAML code. So, the first New button will have the 0 index, the Play button will have the 1 index, and so on:

```
public partial class Training : PhoneApplicationPage
{
    public Training()
    {
        InitializeComponent();
        btnNew = ApplicationBar.Buttons[0] as ApplicationBarIconButton;
        btnPlay = ApplicationBar.Buttons[1] as ApplicationBarIconButton;
        btnEdit = ApplicationBar.Buttons[2] as ApplicationBarIconButton;
        btnDelete = ApplicationBar.Buttons[3] as ApplicationBarIconButton;
    }
. . .
```

Finally, you can use the buttons' names in other methods such as the lbExercise_SelectionChanged event handler that is raised when the user select an exercise from the list box. This event handler either enables or disables application bar buttons:

```
        private void lbExercise_SelectionChanged(object sender,
                                        SelectionChangedEventArgs e)
    {
        if (lbExercise.SelectedItems.Count > 0)
        {
            btnPlay.IsEnabled = true;
            btnEdit.IsEnabled = true;
            btnDelete.IsEnabled = true;
        }
        else
        {
            btnPlay.IsEnabled = false;
            btnEdit.IsEnabled = false;
            btnDelete.IsEnabled = false;
        }
    }
}
```

Usage

In Visual Studio 2010, load the 7Drum project from the companion code and then press Ctrl+F5. If your target output is the Windows Phone Emulator, you will see it running briefly. Tap the Training menu so that you go to the Training page shown in Figure 3-4. At the bottom of the screen, you can see the application bar with the Add button enabled and the others disabled.

Figure 3-4. *The application bar contains four buttons, but only one is enabled.*

Clicking the ellipses button at the top-right corner of the application bar causes the button descriptions and the menu items to appear (see Figure 3-5).

Figure 3-5. *Clicking the ellipses button the application bar shows the buttons' text and menu items.*

3-3. Detecting Changes in the Theme Template

Problem

You need to detect when the user changes the Windows Phone theme from Dark to Light or vice versa so you can change icons, buttons, and background colors accordingly.

Solution

You can use the `ResourceDictionary` class provided by the `Resources` property from the `Application` class.

How It Works

The `Application` class has a static property called `Resources` that returns a `ResourceDictionary` object filled with Windows Phone resources representing, for example, the chosen fonts, the background color, the foreground color, and so on.

In this recipe, you will use the `PhoneBackgroundBrush` resource to retrieve the chosen background theme color. If the theme is set to *Dark*, this value will be equal to the black color (Red Green Blue values set to 0). Otherwise, it will be set to the white color (Red Green Blue values set to 255) for the *Light* theme.

The Code

To demonstrate this recipe, you will create the `DetectingThemeChanging` Silverlight for Windows Phone application. The application has a main page on which two application bar buttons are set with the dark image version. During the `Loaded` event handler, the application checks what color is stored in the `PhoneBackgroundBrush` key within the `Resources` dictionary. Based on the returned value, the icons are taken from either the dark or the light relative path.

In the `MainPage.xaml` file, the application bar is defined with two buttons:

```
. . .
<phone:PhoneApplicationPage.ApplicationBar>
     <shell:ApplicationBar IsVisible="True" IsMenuEnabled="False" Opacity="0">
          <shell:ApplicationBarIconButton x:Name="btnPlay"
          IconUri="/Images/dark/appbar.transport.play.rest.png" Text="Play"/>
          <shell:ApplicationBarIconButton x:Name="btnStop"
          IconUri="/Images/dark/appbar.stop.rest.png" Text="Stop"/>
     </shell:ApplicationBar>
  </phone:PhoneApplicationPage.ApplicationBar>
. . .
```

In the `MainPage.xaml.cs` code file, the `Loaded` event handler is hooked so you can call the `UpdateUI` method, which is the core method of this recipe. The `IsDarkTheme` static property from the `ThemeDetector` class is checked to retrieve whether the current background theme is the Dark theme. If it is, the icons are picked from the dark directory; otherwise, the icons are picked from the Light directory.

```
        private void UpdateUI()
        {
            if (ThemeDetector.IsDarkTheme)
            {
                btnPlay.IconUri = new Uri("/Images/dark/appbar.transport.play.rest.png",
                                    UriKind.Relative);
                btnStop.IconUri = new Uri("/Images/dark/appbar.stop.rest.png",
                                    UriKind.Relative);
```

```
            PageTitle.Text = "Dark Theme";
        }
        else
        {
            btnPlay.IconUri = new Uri("/Images/light/appbar.transport.play.rest.png",
                                UriKind.Relative);
            btnStop.IconUri = new Uri("/Images/light/appbar.stop.rest.png",
                                UriKind.Relative);
            PageTitle.Text = "Light Theme";
        }
    }
```

The ThemeDetector class has only one property, which returns a Boolean value indicating when the Dark background theme is in use:

```
public class ThemeDetector
{
    public static bool IsDarkTheme
    {
        get
        {
            SolidColorBrush backgroundBrush =
            Application.Current.Resources["PhoneBackgroundBrush"] as SolidColorBrush;
            if (backgroundBrush.Color == Color.FromArgb(255, 0, 0, 0)) // Black color
                return true;
            else
                return false;
        }
    }
}
```

▪ **Tip** You can use the ThemeDetector class in your projects to retrieve the current background theme and to change your buttons' colors, icons, and so forth.

Usage

From Visual Studio 2010, select the Windows Phone Emulator as your target output and then press Ctrl+F5. The emulator starts, briefly displaying the application with the application bar shown in Figure 3-6. As you can see, the application uses the page title to inform the user about the background theme it has found in the operating system.

Figure 3-6. The application has detected the Dark theme.

Press the hardware Start button and then go to the application list by pressing the right arrow at the top-right corner of the screen. Select the Settings tile, tap the Theme list item, and change the Background value from Dark to Light.

Now the emulator has the white background color; go back to the application by running a new application instance. The application retrieves the current background theme as the Light theme and changes the icon accordingly (see Figure 3-7).

Figure 3-7. *The application detects the new background and changes the icons and page title.*

3-4. Customizing the Soft Input Panel Keyboard to Accept Only Numbers

Problem

You need to provide a virtual keyboard (also called a Soft Input Panel, or SIP) that accepts only numbers so users can insert numeric values into a text field.

Solution

You can use the InputScope property provided by the TextBox control and use the KeyDown event to exclude keys that are not needed.

How It Works

When the user has to insert information in your application and taps on a text field, a SIP keyboard appears, allowing the input of text. By using the InputScope attribute in your XAML code, you can customize the SIP in order to help users during text input.

You can use one of the values available from the InputScopeNameValue enumerator, as shown in Table 3-1. For example, if you use the TelephoneNumber value, the tapped text box will show the panel used to compose a telephone number.

■ **Note** There are more than 50 values in the InputScopeNameValue enumerator, and most of them either are useless or cause no changes to the SIP. Table 3-1 lists the most common values that are specific to the Windows Phone.

Table 3-1. *The Most Common InputScope Enumerator Values*

Value	Description
Chat	Used for chat messaging, SIP recognizes pre-stored abbreviations.
Digits	Specifies digits.
EmailNameOrAddress	Specifies e-mail names and addresses, because some shortcut keys such as the *at* character (@) and the *.com* key will be added to the main keyboard.
CurrencyAmount	Specifies currency amount values.
Date	Inserts a calendar date.
Maps	Specifies a map location.
NameOrPhoneNumber	Specifies the destination address of a Short Message Service (SMS) text message.
Number	The SIP shows just number and dot separator to specify numbers.
Password	Specifies password text.
Text	The standard SIP layout for inserting text.

Url	Specifies an Internet address.

You can use a combination of the InputScope attribute and the KeyDown event handler to customize the SIP behavior.

This recipe creates a SIP layout that accepts only numeric digits.

The Code

To demonstrate this recipe, you have to open the 7Drum project from the companion code by using Visual Studio 2010 and then focus on the Exercises page. It contains some data describing the exercise, such as the exercise's name and duration. It is the Duration text box that has to be numeric and accept only numeric digits.

In the Exercise.xaml file, you define the text box fields that compose the input form to specify an exercise. Note that the Duration text box field has the InputScope set to the Number value:

```
. . .
    <!--ContentPanel - place additional content here-->
    <Grid x:Name="ContentPanel" Grid.Row="1" Margin="12,0,12,0">
        <StackPanel>
            <Grid>
                <Grid.RowDefinitions>
                    <RowDefinition Height="Auto"/>
                    <RowDefinition Height="Auto"/>
                    <RowDefinition Height="*"/>
                </Grid.RowDefinitions>
                <Grid.ColumnDefinitions>
                    <ColumnDefinition Width="Auto" />
                    <ColumnDefinition Width="*" />
                </Grid.ColumnDefinitions>
                <TextBlock Grid.Row="0" Grid.Column="0"
                 Text="Name:" Style="{StaticResource PhoneTextNormalStyle}"
                 VerticalAlignment="Center" />
                <TextBox Grid.Row="0" Grid.Column="1" x:Name="txtName" />
                <TextBlock Grid.Row="1" Grid.Column="0" Text="Description:"
                Style="{StaticResource PhoneTextNormalStyle}"
                VerticalAlignment="Center" />
                <TextBox Grid.Row="1" Grid.Column="1" x:Name="txtDescription"
                AcceptsReturn="True" Height="300"/>
                <TextBlock Grid.Row="2" Grid.Column="0" Text="Duration (min):"
                Style="{StaticResource PhoneTextNormalStyle}"
                VerticalAlignment="Center" />
                <TextBox Grid.Row="2" Grid.Column="1" x:Name="txtDuration"
                InputScope="Number" />
            </Grid>
        </StackPanel>
    </Grid>
. . .
```

Usage

Press Ctrl+F5 from Visual Studio 2010 so that the application is deployed to either the Windows Phone Emulator or the Windows Phone device. The application starts. Select the Training menu item from the main page and then select the Add application bar button to add a new exercise.

The Exercise page loads, and you will see the text boxes shown in Figure 3-8.

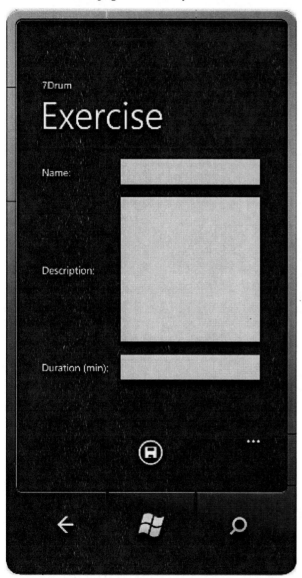

Figure 3-8. The Exercise page with the Duration numeric field

Now tap the Duration text box, and the Number layout of the Soft Input Panel virtual keyboard appears (see Figure 3-9).

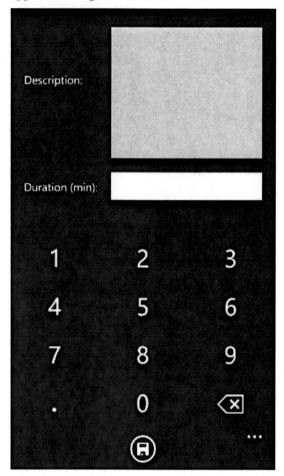

Figure 3-9. The Number virtual keyboard

Try to press numeric and non-numeric keys, and you will see that only the former are allowed.

3-5. Using the Windows Phone Predefined Styles

Problem

You need to develop a Windows Phone application that provides a dynamic user interface that changes based on the user's choices of theme and font.

Solution

You can use the Windows Phone predefined styles so that you are sure your user interface will change fonts and colors according to your user's setting changes.

How It Works

When you define the user interface of your Silverlight for Windows Phone application, it is very common to add text blocks, text boxes, links, and so forth. You can specify their dimensions, colors, and positions, but you need to pay attention to the changes made by the user in the Settings system page (see Figure 3-10).

Figure 3-10. *The emulator's Settings page*

For example, by selecting the Theme menu item, the user can change the Phone Accent color. If your user interface provides links to other pages or external web pages, this color should be used to specify this information. By using those predefined styles, you can be sure that your link's color will change to the new user selection automatically.

■ **Note** The full list of predefined styles is available at the MSDN official page: `http://msdn.microsoft.com/en-us/library/ff769552(v=VS.92).aspx`.

As you saw in Recipe 3-4, the Windows Phone theme is a set of resources such as background colors and phone accent color used to customize the phone's look. By using the predefined resource dictionary provided by the phone, you can be sure to maintain the consistency and compatibility of your application. Moreover, you can be pretty sure that your application will pass Marketplace approval.

When you need to use your own colors, fonts, and so forth, you can override the static resource in your application. Obviously, this change will be applied only to your application and not to the entire phone system.

You can specify the static resource either in an XAML file or in a code file. In the former, you can use the {StaticResource} markup extension together with the static resource name. This static resource will be added to your application when it starts. In the latter case, you can use the Resources property from the Application class, specifying the static resource name (as seen in Recipe 3-4).

The Code

To demonstrate this recipe, you will create the PreDefinedSystemStylesDemo Silverlight for Windows Phone application. It uses the Pivot control (which you can learn more about in Recipe 3-7) to separate application content in different categories such as Brushes, Text Boxes, Fonts, and Text Styles.

The application is simply a visual reference to the static resource styles provided by the phone, so the code is pretty simple, all defined in the MainPage.xaml file.

It starts defining all the Brush styles applicable to a control such as the Rectangle. The Fill property of the Rectangle control contains different static resource styles defined by the Brush style.

```
<Grid x:Name="LayoutRoot" Background="YellowGreen">
    <controls:Pivot Title="Predefined styles">
        <controls:PivotItem Header="Brushes">
            <ListBox Margin="0,0,-12,0">
                <StackPanel Orientation="Vertical" Margin="0,0,0,17">
                    <StackPanel Orientation="Horizontal" Margin="0,0,5,5">
                        <Rectangle Width="100" Height="100"
                        Fill="{StaticResource PhoneAccentBrush}" />
                        <TextBlock Margin="5,0,0,0" Text="PhoneAccentBrush"
                        FontSize="{StaticResource PhoneFontSizeNormal}" />
                    </StackPanel>
                    <StackPanel Orientation="Horizontal" Margin="0,0,5,5">
                        <Rectangle Width="100" Height="100"
                        Fill="{StaticResource PhoneForegroundBrush}" />
                        <TextBlock Margin="5,0,0,0" Text="PhoneForegroundBrush"
                        FontSize="{StaticResource PhoneFontSizeNormal}" />
                    </StackPanel>
```

```
<StackPanel Orientation="Horizontal" Margin="0,0,5,5">
    <Rectangle Width="100" Height="100" Fill="{StaticResource
    PhoneBackgroundBrush}" />
    <TextBlock Margin="5,0,0,0" Text="PhoneBackgroundBrush"
    FontSize="{StaticResource PhoneFontSizeNormal}" />
</StackPanel>
<StackPanel Orientation="Horizontal" Margin="0,0,5,5">
    <Rectangle Width="100" Height="100" Fill="{StaticResource
    PhoneContrastBackgroundBrush}" />
    <TextBlock Margin="5,0,0,0" Text="PhoneContrastBackgroundBrush"
    FontSize="{StaticResource PhoneFontSizeNormal}" />
</StackPanel>
<StackPanel Orientation="Horizontal" Margin="0,0,5,5">
    <Rectangle Width="100" Height="100" Fill="{StaticResource
    PhoneContrastForegroundBrush}" />
    <TextBlock Margin="5,0,0,0" Text="PhoneContrastForegroundBrush"
    FontSize="{StaticResource PhoneFontSizeNormal}" />
</StackPanel>
<StackPanel Orientation="Horizontal" Margin="0,0,5,5">
    <Rectangle Width="100" Height="100"
    Fill="{StaticResource PhoneDisabledBrush}" />
    <TextBlock Margin="5,0,0,0" Text="PhoneDisabledBrush"
    FontSize="{StaticResource PhoneFontSizeNormal}" />
</StackPanel>
<StackPanel Orientation="Horizontal" Margin="0,0,5,5">
    <Rectangle Width="100" Height="100"
    Fill="{StaticResource PhoneSubtleBrush}" />
    <TextBlock Margin="5,0,0,0" Text="PhoneSubtleBrush"
    FontSize="{StaticResource PhoneFontSizeNormal}" />
</StackPanel>
<StackPanel Orientation="Horizontal" Margin="0,0,5,5">
    <Rectangle Width="100" Height="100"
    Fill="{StaticResource PhoneBorderBrush}" />
    <TextBlock Margin="5,0,0,0" Text="PhoneBorderBrush"
    FontSize="{StaticResource PhoneFontSizeNormal}" />
</StackPanel>
<StackPanel Orientation="Horizontal" Margin="0,0,5,5">
    <Rectangle Width="100" Height="100"
    Fill="{StaticResource TransparentBrush}" />
    <TextBlock Margin="5,0,0,0" Text="TransparentBrush"
    FontSize="{StaticResource PhoneFontSizeNormal}" />
</StackPanel>
<StackPanel Orientation="Horizontal" Margin="0,0,5,5">
    <Rectangle Width="100" Height="100"
    Fill="{StaticResource PhoneSemitransparentBrush}" />
    <TextBlock Margin="5,0,0,0" Text="PhoneSemitransparentBrush"
    FontSize="{StaticResource PhoneFontSizeNormal}" />
</StackPanel>


<StackPanel Orientation="Horizontal" Margin="0,0,5,5">
    <Rectangle Width="100" Height="100"
```

```
                    Fill="{StaticResource PhoneChromeBrush}" />
                    <TextBlock Margin="5,0,0,0" Text="PhoneChromeBrush"
                    FontSize="{StaticResource PhoneFontSizeNormal}" />
                </StackPanel>
            </StackPanel>
        </ListBox>
    </controls:PivotItem>
```

The second Pivot control contains the styles applicable to text boxes:

```
<controls:PivotItem Header="TextBoxes">
    <ListBox Margin="0,0,-12,0">
        <StackPanel Orientation="Vertical" Margin="0,0,0,17">
            <TextBox BorderBrush="{StaticResource PhoneTextBoxEditBorderBrush}"
             Background="{StaticResource PhoneTextBoxEditBackgroundBrush}"
             Foreground="{StaticResource PhoneTextBoxForegroundBrush}"
             SelectionForeground="{StaticResource
                                    PhoneTextBoxSelectionForegroundBrush}" />
            <TextBlock TextWrapping="Wrap"
             Text="TextBox with PhoneTextBoxEditBorderBrush,
                    PhoneTextBoxEditBackgroundBrush,
                    PhoneTextCaretBrush, PhoneTextBoxForegroundBrush, and
                    PhoneTextBoxSelectionForegroundBrush styles." />
        </StackPanel>
        <StackPanel Orientation="Vertical" Margin="0,0,0,17">
            <TextBox IsReadOnly="True"
             Background="{StaticResource PhoneTextBoxReadOnlyBrush}"
             Text="I'm a read-only textbox"/>
            <TextBlock TextWrapping="Wrap"
             Text="Read only TextBox with PhoneTextBoxReadOnlyBrush" />
        </StackPanel>
    </ListBox>
</controls:PivotItem>
```

The third Pivot control contains the Fonts static resource styles. The FontFamily and FontSize properties of the TextBlock control are used to show the Font static resource styles:

```
<controls:PivotItem Header="Fonts">
    <ListBox Margin="0,0,-12,0">
        <StackPanel Orientation="Vertical" Margin="0,0,0,17">
            <TextBlock FontFamily="{StaticResource PhoneFontFamilyNormal}"
                        FontSize="{StaticResource PhoneFontSizeSmall}"
                        Text="PhoneFontFamilyNormal with PhoneFontSizeSmall" />
            <TextBlock FontFamily="{StaticResource PhoneFontFamilyNormal}"
                        FontSize="{StaticResource PhoneFontSizeNormal}"
                        Text="PhoneFontFamilyNormal with PhoneFontSizeNormal" />
            <TextBlock FontFamily="{StaticResource PhoneFontFamilyNormal}"
                        FohntSize="{StaticResource PhoneFontSizeMedium}"
                        Text="PhoneFontFamilyNormal with PhoneFontSizeMedium" />
            <TextBlock FontFamily="{StaticResource PhoneFontFamilyNormal}"
```

```
                    FontSize="{StaticResource PhoneFontSizeMediumLarge}"
                    Text="PhoneFontFamilyNormal with
                            PhoneFontSizeMediumLarge" />
<TextBlock FontFamily="{StaticResource PhoneFontFamilyNormal}"
           FontSize="{StaticResource PhoneFontSizeLarge}"
           Text="PhoneFontFamilyNormal with PhoneFontSizeLarge" />
<TextBlock FontFamily="{StaticResource PhoneFontFamilyNormal}"
       FontSize="{StaticResource PhoneFontSizeExtraLarge}"
       Text="PhoneFontFamilyNormal with PhoneFontSizeExtraLarge" />
<TextBlock FontFamily="{StaticResource PhoneFontFamilyNormal}"
     FontSize="{StaticResource PhoneFontSizeExtraExtraLarge}"
     Text="PhoneFontFamilyNormal with PhoneFontSizeExtraExtraLarge" />
<TextBlock FontFamily="{StaticResource PhoneFontFamilyNormal}"
           FontSize="{StaticResource PhoneFontSizeHuge}"
           Text="PhoneFontFamilyNormal with PhoneFontSizeHuge" />

<TextBlock FontFamily="{StaticResource PhoneFontFamilyLight}"
           FontSize="{StaticResource PhoneFontSizeSmall}"
           Text="PhoneFontFamilyLight with PhoneFontSizeSmall" />
<TextBlock FontFamily="{StaticResource PhoneFontFamilyLight}"
           FontSize="{StaticResource PhoneFontSizeNormal}"
           Text="PhoneFontFamilyLight with PhoneFontSizeNormal" />
<TextBlock FontFamily="{StaticResource PhoneFontFamilyLight}"
           FontSize="{StaticResource PhoneFontSizeMedium}"
           Text="PhoneFontFamilyLight with PhoneFontSizeMedium" />
<TextBlock FontFamily="{StaticResource PhoneFontFamilyLight}"
         FontSize="{StaticResource PhoneFontSizeMediumLarge}"
         Text="PhoneFontFamilyLight with PhoneFontSizeMediumLarge" />
<TextBlock FontFamily="{StaticResource PhoneFontFamilyLight}"
           FontSize="{StaticResource PhoneFontSizeLarge}"
           Text="PhoneFontFamilyLight with PhoneFontSizeLarge" />
<TextBlock FontFamily="{StaticResource PhoneFontFamilyLight}"
       FontSize="{StaticResource PhoneFontSizeExtraLarge}"
       Text="PhoneFontFamilyLight with PhoneFontSizeExtraLarge" />
<TextBlock FontFamily="{StaticResource PhoneFontFamilyLight}"
     FontSize="{StaticResource PhoneFontSizeExtraExtraLarge}"
     Text="PhoneFontFamilyLight with PhoneFontSizeExtraExtraLarge" />
<TextBlock FontFamily="{StaticResource PhoneFontFamilyLight}"
           FontSize="{StaticResource PhoneFontSizeHuge}"
           Text="PhoneFontFamilyLight with PhoneFontSizeHuge" />
<TextBlock FontFamily="{StaticResource PhoneFontFamilySemiLight}"
           FontSize="{StaticResource PhoneFontSizeSmall}"
           Text="PhoneFontFamilySemiLight with PhoneFontSizeSmall" />
<TextBlock FontFamily="{StaticResource PhoneFontFamilySemiLight}"
           FontSize="{StaticResource PhoneFontSizeNormal}"
           Text="PhoneFontFamilySemiLight with PhoneFontSizeNormal" />
<TextBlock FontFamily="{StaticResource PhoneFontFamilySemiLight}"
           FontSize="{StaticResource PhoneFontSizeMedium}"
           Text="PhoneFontFamilySemiLight with PhoneFontSizeMedium" />
<TextBlock FontFamily="{StaticResource PhoneFontFamilySemiLight}"
      FontSize="{StaticResource PhoneFontSizeMediumLarge}"
      Text="PhoneFontFamilySemiLight with PhoneFontSizeMediumLarge" />
```

```xml
                    <TextBlock FontFamily="{StaticResource PhoneFontFamilySemiLight}"
                        FontSize="{StaticResource PhoneFontSizeLarge}"
                        Text="PhoneFontFamilySemiLight with PhoneFontSizeLarge" />
                    <TextBlock FontFamily="{StaticResource PhoneFontFamilySemiLight}"
                         FontSize="{StaticResource PhoneFontSizeExtraLarge}"
                         Text="PhoneFontFamilySemiLight with PhoneFontSizeExtraLarge" />
                    <TextBlock FontFamily="{StaticResource PhoneFontFamilySemiLight}"
                    FontSize="{StaticResource PhoneFontSizeExtraExtraLarge}"
                    Text="PhoneFontFamilySemiLight with PhoneFontSizeExtraExtraLarge" />
                    <TextBlock FontFamily="{StaticResource PhoneFontFamilySemiLight}"
                            FontSize="{StaticResource PhoneFontSizeHuge}"
                            Text="PhoneFontFamilySemiLight with PhoneFontSizeHuge" />

                    <TextBlock FontFamily="{StaticResource PhoneFontFamilySemiBold}"
                            FontSize="{StaticResource PhoneFontSizeSmall}"
                            Text="PhoneFontFamilySemiBold with PhoneFontSizeSmall" />
                    <TextBlock FontFamily="{StaticResource PhoneFontFamilySemiBold}"
                            FontSize="{StaticResource PhoneFontSizeNormal}"
                            Text="PhoneFontFamilySemiBold with PhoneFontSizeNormal" />
                    <TextBlock FontFamily="{StaticResource PhoneFontFamilySemiBold}"
                            FontSize="{StaticResource PhoneFontSizeMedium}"
                            Text="PhoneFontFamilySemiBold with PhoneFontSizeMedium" />
                    <TextBlock FontFamily="{StaticResource PhoneFontFamilySemiBold}"
                        FontSize="{StaticResource PhoneFontSizeMediumLarge}"
                        Text="PhoneFontFamilySemiBold with PhoneFontSizeMediumLarge" />
                    <TextBlock FontFamily="{StaticResource PhoneFontFamilySemiBold}"
                            FontSize="{StaticResource PhoneFontSizeLarge}"
                            Text="PhoneFontFamilySemiBold with PhoneFontSizeLarge" />
                    <TextBlock FontFamily="{StaticResource PhoneFontFamilySemiBold}"
                         FontSize="{StaticResource PhoneFontSizeExtraLarge}"
                         Text="PhoneFontFamilySemiBold with PhoneFontSizeExtraLarge" />
                    <TextBlock FontFamily="{StaticResource PhoneFontFamilySemiBold}"
                     FontSize="{StaticResource PhoneFontSizeExtraExtraLarge}"
                     Text="PhoneFontFamilySemiBold with PhoneFontSizeExtraExtraLarge" />
                    <TextBlock FontFamily="{StaticResource PhoneFontFamilySemiBold}"
                            FontSize="{StaticResource PhoneFontSizeHuge}"
                            Text="PhoneFontFamilySemiBold with PhoneFontSizeHuge" />
                </StackPanel>
            </ListBox>
        </controls:PivotItem>
```

The last Pivot control contains the static resource styles that are applicable to the text. In this case, you use the TextBlock control to demonstrate the effect of those resource styles:

```xml
        <controls:PivotItem Header="Text Styles">
            <ListBox Margin="0,0,-12,0">
                <StackPanel Orientation="Vertical" Margin="0,0,0,17">
                    <TextBlock Style="{StaticResource PhoneTextBlockBase}"
                     Text="PhoneTextBlockBase" />
                    <TextBlock Style="{StaticResource PhoneTextNormalStyle}"
                     Text="PhoneTextNormalStyle" />
                    <TextBlock Style="{StaticResource PhoneTextTitle1Style}"
```

```
                            Text="PhoneTextTitle1Style" />
                    <TextBlock Style="{StaticResource PhoneTextTitle2Style}"
                     Text="PhoneTextTitle2Style" />
                    <TextBlock Style="{StaticResource PhoneTextTitle3Style}"
                     Text="PhoneTextTitle3Style" />
                    <TextBlock Style="{StaticResource PhoneTextLargeStyle}"
                     Text="PhoneTextLargeStyle" />
                    <TextBlock Style="{StaticResource PhoneTextExtraLargeStyle}"
                     Text="PhoneTextExtraLargeStyle" />
                    <TextBlock Style="{StaticResource PhoneTextGroupHeaderStyle}"
                                Text="PhoneTextGroupHeaderStyle" />
                    <TextBlock Style="{StaticResource PhoneTextSmallStyle}"
                                Text="PhoneTextSmallStyle" />
                    <TextBlock Style="{StaticResource PhoneTextContrastStyle}"
                                Text="PhoneTextContrastStyle" />
                    <TextBlock Style="{StaticResource PhoneTextAccentStyle}"
                                Text="PhoneTextAccentStyle" />
                </StackPanel>
            </ListBox>
        </controls:PivotItem>
    </controls:Pivot>
</Grid>
```

This changes the application background color to YellowGreen so that system colors can be visible. Finally, all the predefined system resources are specified by using the {StaticResource} markup extension so as to have a visual representation of those resources at runtime.

Usage

From Visual Studio 2010, run the application by pressing Ctrl+F5. Depending on the target output, the application deploys either on the Windows Phone Emulator or the Windows Phone device.

The application starts showing all the available brushes; you have to scroll up and down to see them all. Flicking to the left brings you to the next page, which shows text box styles. Going further to the left shows all the predefined font styles. Finally, the last page shows the predefined text styles (see Figure 3-11).

Figure 3-11. The `PreDefinedSystemStylesDemo` *application shows all the static resources provided by the phone.*

3-6. Localizing Your Application

Problem

You need to create an application that changes the user interface depending on the language and regional settings of the Windows Phone operating system.

Solution

You can use the `CultureInfo` class and its `Name` property to retrieve the current language and regional settings. Moreover, by using the `Resources` files from Visual Studio 2010, you can define constant strings in different languages that can be shown according to the selected Windows Phone operating system language.

How It Works

Localizing your application is an important task because by implementing different languages, you can distribute your application in various markets. Also, you can obtain automatic formatting of information that differs from country to country, such as dates, calendars, and money. Actually, Windows Phone manages 22 different cultures (see the full list at http://msdn.microsoft.com/en-us/library/hh202918(v=VS.92).aspx).

Visual Studio 2010 and Windows Phone SDK give you all the necessary tools to easily implement a localized application. The `CultureInfo` class includes properties and methods to retrieve the current culture set in the user phone (see Figure 3-12 for the class diagram). An instance of the `CultureInfo` class is retrieved by using the `CurrentThread` static property provided by the `Thread` class. This class is defined in the `System.Threading` namespace, while the `CultureInfo` class is defined in the `System.Globalization` namespace.

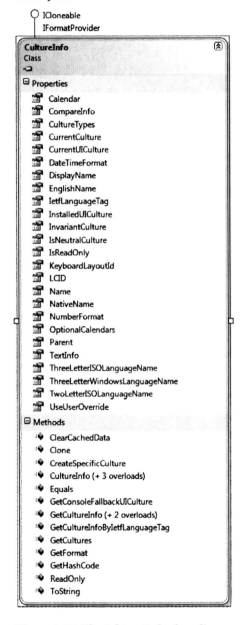

Figure 3-12. The `CultureInfo` class diagram

The `Name` property of the `CultureInfo` class returns the culture name. This value has a standard format such as en-US, it-IT, fr-FR, and so on. The name is divided into a lowercase two-letter part that indicates the language and an uppercase two-letter part that indicates the country or region. So, for example, the en-US name indicates the English language used in the United States, and the en-CA name indicates the English language in Canada.

By using Visual Studio 2010, you can add resource files in which you can put strings and constant values. If you specify the culture name in the resource filename (for example, the `MyResources.fr-FR.resx` filename), you can ensure that those values are automatically used when the user's phone is set to use French culture and language.

So when you build the user interface of your application, you should not use fixed values for text block names, button captions, and so forth, but instead use resource strings. You have to pay attention to text blocks, buttons, and general controls showing text because what will be shown in one language will not be the same in another language. For example, a button showing the text OK when using English should be sized to contain different text when another language is selected.

Using Visual Studio 2010, you have to create an invariant culture resource file that is used by default when no other localized resources are found in the application, and that doesn't have any culture specified in the filename. Finally, you will add a resource file for each culture you want to manage in your application.

The Code

To demonstrate this recipe, you will create the `LocalizationDemo` Silverlight for Windows Phone application. Depending on the selected language and regional settings in the Windows Phone operating system, the application changes its title, button captions, and image.

So, create a new Silverlight for Windows Phone application and call it `LocalizationDemo`. Then select Add New Item from the Project menu and select the Resource File template from the Add New Item dialog box. You can give your own name to the file (we chose `Resource.resx`). Repeat this operation to add another resource file, but this time you have to append the culture name and region. In our case, being Italian, we added the resource file `Resource.it-IT.resx`.

Specify the same keys in the resource file but with different values. Figure 3-13 compares the two resource files.

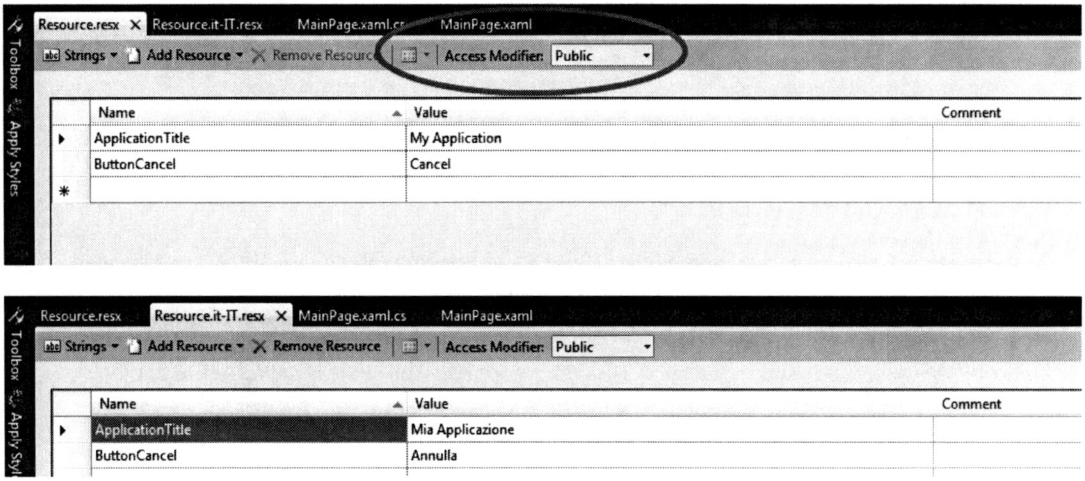

Figure 3-13. The resource files compared

The circled Access Public combo box in Figure 3-13 has to be set to Public so that Visual Studio 2010 generates a class for you. This class—which has the same resource filename without the file extension—can be used directly in your code so that you can specify resources in the XAML file.

The Resource class (generated from the Resource.resx resource file) is instantiated into the custom LocalizedString class. In the class constructor, a new Resource object is created, and by using the LocalizedResource property, is returned to the caller. This class will be used in MainPage.xaml to retrieve keys from the resource file.

```
public class LocalizedString
{
    private Resource m_LocalizedResource;

    public LocalizedString()
    {
        m_LocalizedResource = new Resource();
    }

    public Resource LocalizedResource { get { return m_LocalizedResource; } }
}
```

Before designing the user interface and specifying resources, you have to inform the application that you want to use the resources. This is accomplished by specifying the class name containing the Resource class instance between the Application.Resource tags in the App.xaml file:

```
<Application
    x:Class="LocalizationDemo.App"
    xmlns="http://schemas.microsoft.com/winfx/2006/xaml/presentation"
    xmlns:x="http://schemas.microsoft.com/winfx/2006/xaml"
    xmlns:phone="clr-namespace:Microsoft.Phone.Controls;assembly=Microsoft.Phone"
```

```
xmlns:shell="clr-namespace:Microsoft.Phone.Shell;assembly=Microsoft.Phone"
xmlns:local="clr-namespace:LocalizationDemo">

<!--Application Resources-->
<Application.Resources>
    <local:LocalizedString x:Key="LocalizedString" />
</Application.Resources>
```
. . .

In the `MainPage.xaml` page, you add a button and an image control. The image will be changed depending on the selected language and region in the code, while the button's content string will be changed automatically by reading the strings from the resource. To obtain this behavior, you have to specify to bind the button's content to the `ButtonCancel` key returned by the `LocalizedResource` property that the runtime engine can find in the `LocalizedString` source. The same is valid for the application title that points to the `ApplicationTitle` resource key.

. . .

```
<!--ContentPanel - place additional content here-->
<Grid x:Name="ContentPanel" Grid.Row="1" Margin="12,0,12,0">
    <StackPanel>
        <Image x:Name="imgBanner" />
        <Button Content="{Binding Path=LocalizedResource.ButtonCancel,
                Source={StaticResource LocalizedString}}" />
    </StackPanel>
</Grid>
```

In the `MainPage.xaml.cs` file, you define the `Loaded` event handler, where you use the `CurrentCulture` property to retrieve an instance from the `CultureInfo` class. The `CurrentCulture` property is provided by the `Thread` class with its own static `CurrentThread` property. You use the `Name` property of the `CultureInfo` class to format the string used by the `Uri` class's constructor. This is accomplished in order to retrieve the localized image you have stored in the appropriate folder. For example, if the application retrieves the user using the Italian language and regional settings, the `it-IT` culture name is used to pick the right image from the `it-IT` folder created in the Visual Studio solution.

```
private void PhoneApplicationPage_Loaded(object sender, RoutedEventArgs e)
{
    CultureInfo ci = Thread.CurrentThread.CurrentCulture;
    imgBanner.Source = new BitmapImage(new Uri(string.Format("{0}/amazon.png",
                                       ci.Name), UriKind.Relative));
}
```

Usage

Press Ctrl+F5 to execute the application. The application deploys either on the emulator or the device, depending on the target output chosen.

In our case, the emulator starts with the English language set as the culture, so the application shows the title, the button caption, and the image taken from the English resource file (see the left part of Figure 3-14).

> ▨ **Note** This is the invariant culture resource file, so you will see the English language even if you chose other unsupported languages such as French or Spanish.

Figure 3-14. The LocalizationDemo application showing both supported languages

Now go to the Start menu by pressing the hardware Start button. Tap the top-right circled arrow to access the application list and then tap the Settings app. From the Region & Language menu, select the Italiano language. Finally, tap the Tap Here To Accept Changes And Restart Your Phone link to accept the new language (see Figure 3-15).

Figure 3-15. *The Region & Language settings page*

The phone restarts, and you can go to the application list and again execute the LocalizationDemo application. This time, it will show the Italian language and the localized image (see the right part of Figure 3-14).

3-7. Using Panorama and Pivot Controls

Problem

You need to develop an application that shows a lot of information that is separated into categories or groups. You don't want to put this information on separate pages and provide a navigation system; you would prefer to have them on the same main page of the application.

Solution

You can use either a `Panorama` control or a `Pivot` control provided by the `Microsoft.Phone.Controls` assembly.

How It Works

Both controls are similar in their programming and final output, so you can choose which one to use in your application. Each provides a `Title` property used to specify a title for the application. Each also provides the xxxItem child control (where xxx can be either a `Pivot` or `Panorama` control) used to specify a category or a group of information. You can specify whatever you want within this child control because it derives from `ContentControl`. The common implementation provides a `ListBox` control with its own template providing an image and some related text.

In the Windows Phone operating system, you can see the `Panorama` control in action, executing the Marketplace application. On the other hand, execute the `Settings` application to see the `Pivot` control in action. As you can see, the main difference between these two controls is the background image provided by the `Panorama` control. The `Title` property in the `Panorama` control uses a larger font respect to the one provided by the `Pivot` control. Indeed, with the `Panorama` control, the title gives the panorama effect, because the full title is readable only by scrolling between panorama's items.

The Code

In this recipe, you will create an application that shows today's BBC program schedule by using both a `Panorama` and a `Pivot` control. The TV schedule is provided by a web service from the `www.bleb.org` site (see more on how to use web services in your application in Chapter 10).

The first operation to perform is to add a reference to the `Microsoft.Phone.Controls.dll` assembly, only if you haven't created the application from the Windows Phone Panorama Application or the Windows Phone Pivot Application Visual Studio 2010 template.

In this case, we started the TvSchedule7 application (and the TvSchedulePivot7 application too) from the Visual Studio 2010 template, so we already have all that is needed to use both `Panorama` and `Pivot` controls. This template implements the Model-View-ViewModel (MVVM) architecture, so you will find the `ViewModels` folder in the Visual Studio solution containing two files: `ItemViewModel.cs` and `MainViewModel.cs`. Thanks to this architecture, you can separate data into its visual representation.

In `ItemViewModel.cs`, you have to describe and define the item's characteristics. So you have to define properties representing your data. In this case, a TV program is defined by a title, a description, and the scheduled time. So you add three properties into the `ItemViewModel.cs` file:

```csharp
public class ItemViewModel : INotifyPropertyChanged
{
    private string _title;
    /// <summary>
    /// Programme title
    /// </summary>
    /// <returns></returns>
    public string Title
    {
        get
        {
            return _title;
        }
        set
        {
            if (value != _title)
            {
                _title = value;
                NotifyPropertyChanged("Title");
            }
        }
    }

    private string _startEnd;
    /// <summary>
    /// Programme start end.
    /// </summary>
    /// <returns></returns>
    public string StartEnd
    {
        get
        {
            return _startEnd;
        }
        set
        {
            if (value != _startEnd)
            {
                _startEnd = value;
                NotifyPropertyChanged("StartEnd");
            }
        }
    }


    private string _description;
    /// <summary>
    /// Sample ViewModel property; this property is used in the view to display its
    /// value using a Binding.
    /// </summary>
```

```
        /// <returns></returns>
        public string Description
        {
            get
            {
                return _description;
            }
            set
            {
                if (value != _description)
                {
                    _description = value;
                    NotifyPropertyChanged("Description");
                }
            }
        }

        public event PropertyChangedEventHandler PropertyChanged;
        private void NotifyPropertyChanged(String propertyName)
        {
            PropertyChangedEventHandler handler = PropertyChanged;
            if (null != handler)
            {
                handler(this, new PropertyChangedEventArgs(propertyName));
            }
        }
    }
```

In the MainViewModel.cs code file, you add the logic to gather information from the web service. First of all, you define an ObservableCollection generic collection for each group of items you need to show:

```
    public class MainViewModel : INotifyPropertyChanged
    {
        public MainViewModel()
        {
            this.BBC1Items = new ObservableCollection<ItemViewModel>();
            this.BBC2Items = new ObservableCollection<ItemViewModel>();
            this.ITV1Items = new ObservableCollection<ItemViewModel>();
        }


        /// <summary>
        /// A collection for ItemViewModel objects.
        /// </summary>
        public ObservableCollection<ItemViewModel> BBC1Items { get; private set; }
        public ObservableCollection<ItemViewModel> BBC2Items { get; private set; }
        public ObservableCollection<ItemViewModel> ITV1Items { get; private set; }
```

. . .

Then in the LoadData method, you define the code to load the TV schedule from the web service. So you create a new WebClient object and hook its own DownloadStringCompleted event. This is raised when the call to the DownloadStringAsync method is completed. You call this method to retrieve information from the web service. The last method parameter represents a user token string that is passed as a parameter to the DownloadStringCompleted event handler. You use it to determine which TV channel is required for the web service and which is the next channel to retrieve.

```
public void LoadData()
{
    web = new WebClient();

    web.DownloadStringAsync(new Uri("http://www.bleb.org/tv/data/listings/0/bbc1.xml"),
                            "BBC1");
    web.DownloadStringCompleted +=
                new DownloadStringCompletedEventHandler(web_DownloadStringCompleted);
}
```

The real data loading is in the DownloadStringCompleted event handler. Because the web service returns XML content, you use the LINQ to XML library to load and manage this result. A snippet of the XML content is shown here:

```
<?xml version="1.0" encoding="UTF-8"?>
<!-- produced for the bleb.org TV system at Sun Mar  6 08:39:03 2011 -->
<channel id="bbc1" source="XMLTV" date="06/03/2011">
  <programme>
    <flags>(S)</flags>
    <desc>The latest news, sports, business and weather from the BBC's Breakfast
        team.</desc>
    <title>Breakfast</title>
    <end>0735</end>
    <start>0600</start>
    </programme>
. . .
```

The Parse method from the XElement class loads and parses the XML and then goes through its programme elements filling the MainViewModel collections with related items. Then, checking the user token string, you again call the DownloadStringAsync method to retrieve the next TV channel schedule.

▓ **Note** It is not possible to call the DownloadStringAsync method again, until the DownloadStringCompleted event is raised. Otherwise, the application retrieves an exception.

Finally, you set the IsDataLoaded property to true to indicate that the loading operations are concluded:

```
void web_DownloadStringCompleted(object sender, DownloadStringCompletedEventArgs e)
{
    if (e.Error != null && e.Error.Message != string.Empty)
        return;

    if (e.Cancelled)
        return;

    string result = e.Result;
    XElement xml = XElement.Parse(result);

    if (xml != null)
    {
        foreach (XElement programme in xml.Descendants("programme"))
        {
            ItemViewModel item = new ItemViewModel();
            item.Description = programme.Element("desc").Value;
            item.Title = programme.Element("title").Value;
            item.StartEnd = programme.Element("start").Value + " - " +
                            programme.Element("end").Value;

            switch ((string)e.UserState)
            {
                case "BBC1":
                    this.BBC1Items.Add(item);
                    break;
                case "BBC2":
                    this.BBC2Items.Add(item);
                    break;
                case "ITV1":
                    this.ITV1Items.Add(item);
                    break;
            }
        }
    }

    switch ((string)e.UserState)
    {
        case "BBC1":
            web.DownloadStringAsync(
                new Uri("http://www.bleb.org/tv/data/listings/0/bbc2.xml"), "BBC2");
            break;
        case "BBC2":
            web.DownloadStringAsync(
                new Uri("http://www.bleb.org/tv/data/listings/0/itv1.xml"), "ITV1");
            break;
    }

    this.IsDataLoaded = true;
}
```

The code shown to this point is common to both the `Panorama` and `Pivot` examples because it manages the model and data part of the MVVM architecture. Now you can focus your attention on how to visually represent this data.

Both the `Panorama` and `Pivot` item children controls have defined a `ListBox` with a template including an image control, and two `TextBlocks` within a stack panel. The `ListBox`—as with most of the controls—provides the binding feature used to populate the control reading data from a data source. The `ItemsSource` attribute from the `ListBox` control accepts the binding to the collections defined in the `MainViewModel` properties such as `BBC1Items`, `BBC2Items`, and `ITV1Items`. The binding mechanism is pretty smart to add a `ListBox` item for each related item in the collection. We don't need to write any code lines. By always using the binding feature, you can specify which `ItemViewModel` property to use to print the text blocks' text:

```
. . .
<ListBox Margin="0,0,-12,0" ItemsSource="{Binding BBC1Items}"
    SelectionChanged="lb_SelectionChanged" x:Name="lbBBC1">
    <ListBox.ItemTemplate>
        <DataTemplate>
            <StackPanel Orientation="Horizontal" Margin="0,0,0,17">
                <Image Source="images/bbc1.png" Height="100" Width="100" />
                <StackPanel Width="311">
                    <TextBlock Text="{Binding Title}" TextWrapping="Wrap"
                               Style="{StaticResource PhoneTextExtraLargeStyle}"/>
                    <TextBlock Text="{Binding StartEnd}" TextWrapping="Wrap"
                               Margin="12,-6,12,0"
                               Style="{StaticResource PhoneTextSubtleStyle}"/>
                </StackPanel>
            </StackPanel>
        </DataTemplate>
    </ListBox.ItemTemplate>
</ListBox>
. . .
```

▪ **Note** The `ListBox` control defines the `SelectionChanged` event handler used to retrieve when the user taps on a list item. In this application, this event handler is used to show program details. By the way, this is not the proper implementation if you want to write code using the pure MVVM pattern. Chapter 11 covers the MVVM pattern.

Now let's see the differences in the XAML code in order to define either a `Panorama` or a `Pivot` control. The `Panorama` has a background that is not provided by the `Pivot`, but the rest of code is really similar.

Here is the `Pivot` control definition with one item:

```
. . .
    <!--LayoutRoot is the root grid where all page content is placed-->
    <Grid x:Name="LayoutRoot" Background="Transparent">
        <!--Pivot Control-->
```

```
    <controls:Pivot Title="TvSchedule7">
        <!--Pivot item one-->
        <controls:PivotItem Header="BBC1">
            <!--Double line list with text wrapping-->
```
. . .

And here is the Panorama definition:

. . .
```
    <!--LayoutRoot is the root grid where all page content is placed-->
    <Grid x:Name="LayoutRoot" Background="Transparent">

        <!--Panorama control-->
        <controls:Panorama Title="TvSchedule7">
            <controls:Panorama.Background>
                <ImageBrush ImageSource="PanoramaBackground.png"/>
            </controls:Panorama.Background>

            <!--Panorama item one-->
            <controls:PanoramaItem Header="BBC1">
```
. . .

That's it. The code defines the other two control items with the other two TV channels, but the code is pretty much the same (it differs only in its ID and header text).

Usage

We have two projects: TvSchedule7 that uses the Panorama control, and TvSchedulePivot7 that uses the Pivot control. So open two Visual Studio 2010 program instances and load these two projects. Press Ctrl+F5 from one Visual Studio 2010 instance and wait until the application is deployed and started. For example, starting with the TvSchedule7 example, you will see the Panorama control showing a background with BBC1 TV scheduled programs and part of BBC2 TV scheduled programs (see the left part of Figure 3-16). You can flick to the left so that the Panorama control shows some other part of the title and the BBC2's program schedules. When you reach the last item of the Panorama control and flick again to the left, the control will show you the first page.

Leaving the emulator in execution, launch the other project. The Pivot control will briefly show the same information but with a different user interface (see the right-hand side of Figure 3-16). The title is fully readable, and there are more list box items visible. Even with the Pivot control, you can flick either left or right to navigate through items.

Figure 3-16. Panorama vs Pivot controls

3-8. Spicing Up the User Interface with the Silverlight Toolkit

Problem

You would like to enhance your user interface with some new controls but don't want to spend time making them.

Solution

You can use the Silverlight for Windows Phone Toolkit, which is available from CodePlex at http://silverlight.codeplex.com.

How It Works

The `Microsoft.Phone.Controls.Toolkit.dll` assembly that you download from the CodePlex site has 20 controls. Some are new controls, and others are enhanced versions of existing controls.

At the time of this writing, the Silverlight for Windows Phone Toolkit is the August 2011 version. Among others, it contains the following controls:

- The `AutoCompleteBox` control is an enhanced version of the `TextBox` control that implements the autocomplete feature. While you are writing text, a pop-up appears, suggesting similar words.

- The `ContextMenu` control , as its name indicates, provides a context menu. Tapping and holding a control results in a pop-up being shown with menu items. You can define different event handlers to respond to menu item selection.

- The `DatePicker` and `TimePicker` controls allow users to easily select a date and a time, respectively.

- The `DateTimeConverters` converter classes allow users to easily convert date and time to a variety of strings. For example, using the `RelativeTimeConverter` class, you can retrieve the text indicating the elapsed time relatively to the present.

- The `ExpanderView` control allows users to collapse and expand items in a list. The Windows Phone operating system uses a similar control in the mail client (Outlook, Gmail, and the like).

- The `GestureService/GestureListener` controls help developers to easily manage gestures in a Silverlight application (see Recipe 5-4 in Chapter 5).

- The `HubTile` control allows developer to add animated tiles to the application.

- The `ListPicker` control is a sort of combo box allowing users to pick a value from a list. Depending on its attributes, the list can either be shown as a pop-up or can fill the full screen.

- The `LongListSelector` control, as its name suggests, provides a list that is capable of containing a lot of items and of automatically adding a scrollbar when needed.

- The `Page Transitions` are a set of classes dedicated to adding page transition effects during page navigation.

- The `PerformanceProgressBar` control is an enhanced version of the `ProgressBar` control that uses the compositor thread to paint itself. Differing from the user interface thread, the compositor is a separate thread that manages animation and other dedicated tasks. This thread performs better than the user interface thread, and this control uses it to create the progress bar animation.

- The `TiltEffect` control provides a highly required animation from the Internet community: the tilt effect. The tilt animation is applied to controls that implement the `Click` event adding a shaking effect when the control is clicked. The `TiltEffect` control provides an attached property set to a container control such as the `Page` that adds the tilt effect to its own controls.

- The ToggleSwitch control is used to turn on or off settings or features that you have added to your application. For example, the Windows Phone 7 operating system uses this control on its Settings page to activate or deactivate Airplane mode.

- The WrapPanel control is an enhanced version of the StackPanel that implements a wrap feature for the controls it contains.

The Code

To demonstrate this recipe, we have borrowed the official example that ships with the Silverlight for Windows Phone Toolkit library. To use it in your code, you first need to add a reference to the library that usually is installed in the %Program Files%\Microsoft SDKs\Windows Phone\v7.1\Toolkit path.

The PhoneToolkitSample application has a main page with 17 clickable list items. Each of them points to a control demo.

The AutoCompleteBox control is defined in the AutoCompleteBoxSample.xaml page. First of all, it is worth noting the toolkit namespace added to the Page tag (this is common to all pages using the toolkit controls):

```
<phone:PhoneApplicationPage
    x:Class="PhoneToolkitSample.Samples.AutoCompleteBoxSample"
    xmlns="http://schemas.microsoft.com/winfx/2006/xaml/presentation"
    xmlns:x="http://schemas.microsoft.com/winfx/2006/xaml"
    xmlns:phone="clr-namespace:Microsoft.Phone.Controls;assembly=Microsoft.Phone"
    xmlns:shell="clr-namespace:Microsoft.Phone.Shell;assembly=Microsoft.Phone"
    xmlns:toolkit="clr-
        namespace:Microsoft.Phone.Controls;assembly=Microsoft.Phone.Controls.Toolkit"
. . .
```

The usual ContentPanel grid is replaced by a stack panel containing two TextBlock controls and two AutoCompleteBox controls. The ItemSource property is used to define the source from which suggestions are picked and shown. The second AutoCompleteBox control uses a two-line suggestion, such as the one used by Internet Explorer that shows both page title and its URL.

```
<StackPanel x:Name="ContentPanel" Grid.Row="1" Margin="12,0,12,0">
    <TextBlock Text="AutoCompleteBox, single-line items"
     Style="{StaticResource PhoneTextNormalStyle}"/>
    <toolkit:AutoCompleteBox VerticalAlignment="Top"
     ItemsSource="{StaticResource words}" Margin="0,12"/>
    <TextBlock Text="AutoCompleteBox, double-line items"
     Style="{StaticResource PhoneTextNormalStyle}"/>


    <toolkit:AutoCompleteBox
        InputScope="Url"
        ItemsSource="{StaticResource websites}"
        Margin="0,12"
        ValueMemberPath="Item1">
        <toolkit:AutoCompleteBox.ItemTemplate>
```

```
                    <DataTemplate>
                        <StackPanel Margin="0,7">
                            <TextBlock
                                Margin="8,0"
                                Text="{Binding Item1}"/>
                            <TextBlock
                                FontSize="{StaticResource PhoneFontSizeNormal}"
                                Foreground="#ff666666"
                                Margin="8,-6,8,2"
                                Text="{Binding Item2}"/>
                        </StackPanel>
                    </DataTemplate>
                </toolkit:AutoCompleteBox.ItemTemplate>
            </toolkit:AutoCompleteBox>
        </StackPanel>
```

The ContextMenu control is demonstrated in the ContextMenuSample.xaml page. The menu items composing the context menu have to be defined within the ContextMenu tags. Those tags have to be nested within the ContextMenuService.ContextMenu tags. Each menu item is defined by the MenuItem tag that provides the Header attribute used to specify the menu item text and the Click event handler.

. . .

```
<ScrollViewer x:Name="ContentPanel" Grid.Row="1" Margin="12,0,12,0">
        <StackPanel VerticalAlignment="Top">
            <StackPanel Orientation="Horizontal">
                <TextBlock Text="last selection:"
                            Style="{StaticResource PhoneTextSubtleStyle}"/>
                <TextBlock Text="none"
                            x:Name="lastSelection"
                            Style="{StaticResource PhoneTextNormalStyle}"/>
            </StackPanel>

            <Button Margin="0,0"
                    VerticalAlignment="Center"
                    Padding="12"
                    Content="ContextMenu"
                    FontSize="18">
                <toolkit:ContextMenuService.ContextMenu>
                    <toolkit:ContextMenu>
                        <!-- You can suppress tilt on indivudal menu items with
TiltEffect.SuppressTilt="True" -->
                        <toolkit:MenuItem Header="this is a menu item"
Click="MenuItem_Click"/>
                        <toolkit:MenuItem Header="this is another menu item"
Click="MenuItem_Click"/>
                        <toolkit:MenuItem Header="this is a yet another menu item"
Click="MenuItem_Click"/>
                    </toolkit:ContextMenu>
                </toolkit:ContextMenuService.ContextMenu>
```

```xml
                        </Button>
                        <Button Margin="0,0"
                                VerticalAlignment="Center"
                                Padding="12"
                                Content="ContextMenu with items bound to ICommands"
                                FontSize="18">
                            <toolkit:ContextMenuService.ContextMenu>
                                <toolkit:ContextMenu>
                                    <toolkit:MenuItem Header="Always-on item" Command="{Binding
AlwaysCommand}"/>
                                    <toolkit:MenuItem Header="Intermittent item" Command="{Binding
IntermittentCommand}"/>
                                    <toolkit:MenuItem Header="Always-on item with param"
                                                      Command="{Binding AlwaysCommand}"
                                                      CommandParameter="param1"/>
                                    <toolkit:MenuItem Header="Intermittent item with param"
                                                      Command="{Binding IntermittentCommand}"
                                                      CommandParameter="param2"/>
                                    <toolkit:MenuItem Header="option 3" Click="MenuItem_Click"/>
                                </toolkit:ContextMenu>
                            </toolkit:ContextMenuService.ContextMenu>
                        </Button>
                        <Button Margin="0,0"
                                VerticalAlignment="Center"
                                Padding="12"
                                Content="ContextMenu with IsFadeEnabled=false"
                                FontSize="18">
                            <toolkit:ContextMenuService.ContextMenu>
                                <toolkit:ContextMenu IsFadeEnabled="False">
                                    <toolkit:MenuItem Header="option 1" Click="MenuItem_Click"/>
                                    <toolkit:MenuItem Header="option 2" Click="MenuItem_Click"/>
                                    <toolkit:MenuItem Header="option 3" Click="MenuItem_Click"/>
                                </toolkit:ContextMenu>
                            </toolkit:ContextMenuService.ContextMenu>
                        </Button>
                        <Button Margin="0,0"
                                VerticalAlignment="Center"
                                Padding="12"
                                Content="ContextMenu with IsZoomEnabled=false"
                                FontSize="18">
                            <toolkit:ContextMenuService.ContextMenu>
                                <toolkit:ContextMenu IsZoomEnabled="false">
                                    <toolkit:MenuItem Header="option 1" Click="MenuItem_Click"/>
                                    <toolkit:MenuItem Header="option 2" Click="MenuItem_Click"/>
                                    <toolkit:MenuItem Header="option 3" Click="MenuItem_Click"/>
                                </toolkit:ContextMenu>
                            </toolkit:ContextMenuService.ContextMenu>
                        </Button>
                    </StackPanel>
                </ScrollViewer>
```

The DatePicker control and TimePicker control are shown in the DateTimePickerSample.xaml page. Within the ContentPanel code section, the DatePicker and TimePicker are defined with the ValueChanged event management.

```
. . .
        <StackPanel x:Name="ContentPanel" Grid.Row="1" Margin="12,0,12,0">
            <TextBlock Text="select date" Style="{StaticResource PhoneTextNormalStyle}"/>
            <toolkit:DatePicker ValueChanged="DatePicker_ValueChanged"/>
            <TextBlock Text="select time" Style="{StaticResource PhoneTextNormalStyle}"/>
            <toolkit:TimePicker ValueChanged="TimePicker_ValueChanged"/>
            <TextBlock Text="note" Style="{StaticResource PhoneTextLargeStyle}"/>
            <TextBlock TextWrapping="Wrap" Style="{StaticResource PhoneTextNormalStyle}">
                <TextBlock.Text>
                    To see the correct ApplicationBar icons in the DatePicker and
                    TimePicker, you will need to create a folder in the root of your project
                    called "Toolkit.Content" and put the icons in there. You can copy them
                    from this project. They must be named "ApplicationBar.Cancel.png" and
                    "ApplicationBar.Check.png", and the build action must be "Content".
                </TextBlock.Text>
            </TextBlock>
        </StackPanel>
. . .
```

The ListPickerSample.xaml file contains the demonstration of the ListPicker control. Five list pickers are defined. The first is the simple version providing the Header attribute that is shown as a title and some fixed values defined as system strings. The second list is similar to the first, but adds a FullModeItemTemplate tag that shows list items in full-screen mode. The third list picker control is composed of two item templates: the ItemTemplate tag defines the item when the value has been selected and the list picker is closed, and the FullModeItemTemplate tag defines the list of available items that will be shown in full-screen mode. The fourth list picker control implements the SelectionMode attribute set to Multiple. When the list picker control is tapped, the full-screen list is shown and its items can be selected by checkboxes. The last list picker control is the RecurringDaysPicker control that lets you to select days of the week.

The following is the code for the third list picker control; both item templates define a rectangle and a text block with predefined colors:

```
. . .
        <StackPanel Grid.Row="1" Margin="12,0,12,0">
            <!-- For best performance, set the CacheMode on items below a ListPicker -->
            <!-- that will be dropping down. -->

            <toolkit:ListPicker ItemsSource="{Binding}" Header="accent color"
                FullModeHeader="ACCENTS" CacheMode="BitmapCache">
                <toolkit:ListPicker.ItemTemplate>
                    <DataTemplate>
                        <StackPanel Orientation="Horizontal">
                            <Rectangle Fill="{Binding}" Width="24" Height="24"/>
                            <TextBlock Text="{Binding}" Margin="12 0 0 0"/>
                        </StackPanel>
                    </DataTemplate>
                </toolkit:ListPicker.ItemTemplate>
```

```
                </toolkit:ListPicker.ItemTemplate>
                <toolkit:ListPicker.FullModeItemTemplate>
                    <DataTemplate>
                        <StackPanel Orientation="Horizontal" Margin="16 21 0 20">
                            <Rectangle Fill="{Binding}" Width="43" Height="43"/>
                            <TextBlock Text="{Binding}" Margin="16 0 0 0" FontSize="43"
                                    FontFamily="{StaticResource PhoneFontFamilyLight}"/>
                        </StackPanel>
                    </DataTemplate>
                </toolkit:ListPicker.FullModeItemTemplate>

            </toolkit:ListPicker>
```

The LongListSelector control is shown in the LongListSelectorSample.xaml file. This page implements the Pivot control you saw in the previous recipe. In the first part of the LongListSelectorSample.xaml code, the resources used to populate the LongListSelector control are defined. Data is taken from reading some external source text files and using classes contained in the Data folder of the project. As shown in the following code, the data is movie resources.

```
. . .
    <phone:PhoneApplicationPage.Resources>
        <!-- MOVIE RESOURCES -->

        <!-- The template for the list header. This will scroll as a part of the list. -->
        <DataTemplate x:Key="movieListHeader">
            <TextBlock Text="new releases"
                    Margin="8,-24,0,0"
                    Style="{StaticResource PhoneTextTitle1Style}"/>
        </DataTemplate>

        <!-- The group header template, for groups in the main list -->
        <DataTemplate x:Key="movieGroupHeader">
            <TextBlock Text="{Binding Key}" FontSize="{StaticResource PhoneFontSizeLarge}"
                    Foreground="{StaticResource PhoneAccentBrush}" Margin="12,28,0,24"/>
        </DataTemplate>

        <!-- The template for groups when they are items in the "jump list". Not setting -->
        <!-- the GroupItemTemplate property will disable "jump list" functionality. -->
        <DataTemplate x:Key="groupItemHeader">
            <Border Background="{StaticResource PhoneAccentBrush}"
                    Width="432" Height="62"
                    Margin="6" Padding="12,0,0,6">
                <TextBlock Text="{Binding Key}"
                        Foreground="#FFFFFF" FontSize="26.667"
                        HorizontalAlignment="Left"
                        VerticalAlignment="Bottom"
                        FontFamily="{StaticResource PhoneFontFamilySemiBold}"/>
                <Border.Projection>
                    <PlaneProjection RotationX="-60"/>
                </Border.Projection>
```

```
            </Border>
        </DataTemplate>

        <!-- The template for movie items -->
        <DataTemplate x:Key="movieItemTemplate">
            <Grid Margin="{StaticResource PhoneTouchTargetOverhang}">
                <Grid.ColumnDefinitions>
                    <ColumnDefinition Width="Auto"/>
                    <ColumnDefinition Width="*"/>
                </Grid.ColumnDefinitions>
                <Image Width="110" Height="150" Source="{Binding ImageUrl}"
VerticalAlignment="Top"/>
                <StackPanel Grid.Column="1" VerticalAlignment="Top">
                    <TextBlock Text="{Binding Title}" Style="{StaticResource
PhoneTextLargeStyle}" FontFamily="{StaticResource PhoneFontFamilySemiBold}"
TextWrapping="Wrap" Margin="12,-12,12,6"/>
                    <TextBlock Text="{Binding Stars}" Style="{StaticResource
PhoneTextNormalStyle}" TextWrapping="Wrap" FontFamily="{StaticResource
PhoneFontFamilySemiBold}"/>
                    <TextBlock Text="{Binding Information}" Style="{StaticResource
PhoneTextSmallStyle}" FontFamily="{StaticResource PhoneFontFamilySemiBold}"/>
                    <TextBlock Text="{Binding Description}" Style="{StaticResource
PhoneTextNormalStyle}" TextWrapping="Wrap" FontFamily="{StaticResource
PhoneFontFamilySemiLight}"/>
                </StackPanel>
            </Grid>
        </DataTemplate>

        <data:MoviesByCategory x:Key="movies"/>
        <data:MoreCommand x:Key="moreCommand" />

        <!-- BUDDIES RESOURCES -->
        <data:PeopleByFirstName x:Key="buddies"/>
        <data:GroupToBackgroundBrushValueConverter x:Key="GroupBackground"/>
        <data:GroupToForegroundBrushValueConverter x:Key="GroupForeground"/>
    </phone:PhoneApplicationPage.Resources>
```

In the linq Pivot item, the basic version of the LongListSelector is used to show movies separated by categories. These data are retrieved by using a LINQ query that is assigned to the ItemSource property in the code. Each LongListSelector section is associated to the resources defined in the preceding code. The ListHeaderTemplate is used to add some header text to the list. The GroupHeaderTemplate and GroupItemTemplate are used when a grouping operation is accomplished on the data. The GroupViewOpened and GroupViewClosing event handlers are used to track when the user taps on the category. Finally, ItemTemplate is the template used to show items.

```
    <Grid x:Name="LayoutRoot" Background="Transparent">
        <controls:Pivot Title="LONGLISTSELECTOR SAMPLES">
            <controls:PivotItem Header="linq">
                <toolkit:LongListSelector x:Name="linqMovies"
                    Background="Transparent"
                    ListHeaderTemplate="{StaticResource movieListHeader}"
```

145

```
                    GroupHeaderTemplate="{StaticResource movieGroupHeader}"
                    GroupItemTemplate="{StaticResource groupItemHeader}"
                    ItemTemplate="{StaticResource movieItemTemplate}"
                    GroupViewOpened="LongListSelector_GroupViewOpened"
                    GroupViewClosing="LongListSelector_GroupViewClosing"/>
        </controls:PivotItem>
```

The code `Pivot` item provides a `LongListSelector` that has a `GroupFooterTemplate` defined to add a button that shows other results when pressed.

```
<controls:PivotItem Header="code">
    <toolkit:LongListSelector x:Name="codeMovies"
     Background="Transparent"
     ItemsSource="{StaticResource movies}"
     ListHeaderTemplate="{StaticResource movieListHeader}"
     GroupHeaderTemplate="{StaticResource movieGroupHeader}"
     GroupItemTemplate="{StaticResource groupItemHeader}"
     ItemTemplate="{StaticResource movieItemTemplate}"
     GroupViewOpened="LongListSelector_GroupViewOpened"
     GroupViewClosing="LongListSelector_GroupViewClosing">
    <!-- The group footer template, for groups in the main list -->
        <toolkit:LongListSelector.GroupFooterTemplate>
          <DataTemplate>
            <Button DataContext="{Binding}"
                    Content="{Binding GetMore}"
                    Command="{StaticResource moreCommand}"
                    CommandParameter="{Binding}"/>
          </DataTemplate>
        </toolkit:LongListSelector.GroupFooterTemplate>
    </toolkit:LongListSelector>
</controls:PivotItem>
```

The buddies `Pivot` item contains a `LongListSelector` control in which each section is defined by a `DataTemplate` different from the one defined in the resources. This is because the information to show is different; in this case, a list of people is retrieved by using the `PeopleByFirstName` class. The `LongListSelector` provides the item's selection too. In the code behind the XAML file, in the class's constructor, the `SelectionChanged` event is hooked and the personal details are shown on a different page.

```
<controls:PivotItem Header="buddies">
    <toolkit:LongListSelector x:Name="buddies" Background="Transparent"
                              Margin="0,-8,0,0"
                              GroupViewOpened="LongListSelector_GroupViewOpened"
                              GroupViewClosing="LongListSelector_GroupViewClosing"
                              ItemsSource="{StaticResource buddies}">
        <toolkit:LongListSelector.GroupItemsPanel>
            <ItemsPanelTemplate>
                <toolkit:WrapPanel Orientation="Horizontal"/>
            </ItemsPanelTemplate>
        </toolkit:LongListSelector.GroupItemsPanel>
```

```
                <toolkit:LongListSelector.GroupItemTemplate>
                    <DataTemplate>
                        <Border Background="{Binding Converter={StaticResource
GroupBackground}}"
                                Width="99" Height="99" Margin="6"
IsHitTestVisible="{Binding HasItems}">
                            <TextBlock Text="{Binding Key}"
                                       FontFamily="{StaticResource
PhoneFontFamilySemiBold}"
                                       FontSize="48"
                                       Margin="8,0,0,0"
                                       Foreground="{Binding Converter={StaticResource
GroupForeground}}"
                                       VerticalAlignment="Bottom"/>
                            <Border.Projection>
                                <PlaneProjection RotationX="-60"/>
                            </Border.Projection>
                        </Border>
                    </DataTemplate>
                </toolkit:LongListSelector.GroupItemTemplate>
                <toolkit:LongListSelector.GroupHeaderTemplate>
                    <DataTemplate>
                        <Border Background="Transparent" Margin="12,8,0,8">
                            <Border Background="{StaticResource PhoneAccentBrush}"
                                    Padding="8,0,0,0" Width="62" Height="62"

                                    HorizontalAlignment="Left">
                                <TextBlock Text="{Binding Key}"
                                           Foreground="#FFFFFF"
                                           FontSize="48"
                                           FontFamily="{StaticResource
PhoneFontFamilySemiLight}"
                                           HorizontalAlignment="Left"
                                           VerticalAlignment="Bottom"/>
                            </Border>
                        </Border>
                    </DataTemplate>
                </toolkit:LongListSelector.GroupHeaderTemplate>
                <toolkit:LongListSelector.ItemTemplate>
                    <DataTemplate>
                        <Grid Margin="12,8,0,8">
                            <Grid.ColumnDefinitions>
                                <ColumnDefinition Width="Auto"/>
                                <ColumnDefinition Width="*"/>
                            </Grid.ColumnDefinitions>
                            <Image Width="110" Height="150" Source="{Binding ImageUrl}"
VerticalAlignment="Top"/>
                            <StackPanel Grid.Column="1" VerticalAlignment="Top">
                                <TextBlock Text="{Binding FullName}"
Style="{StaticResource PhoneTextLargeStyle}" FontFamily="{StaticResource
PhoneFontFamilySemiBold}" Margin="12,-12,12,6"/>
```

```
                                        <TextBlock Text="{Binding Email}" Style="{StaticResource
PhoneTextNormalStyle}" TextWrapping="Wrap" FontFamily="{StaticResource
PhoneFontFamilySemiBold}"/>
                                        <StackPanel Orientation="Horizontal">
                                            <TextBlock Text="Mobile:" Style="{StaticResource
PhoneTextSmallStyle}"/>
                                            <TextBlock Text="{Binding Mobile}"
Style="{StaticResource PhoneTextSmallStyle}" FontFamily="{StaticResource
PhoneFontFamilySemiBold}"/>
                                        </StackPanel>
                                        <StackPanel Orientation="Horizontal">
                                            <TextBlock Text="Home:" Style="{StaticResource
PhoneTextSmallStyle}"/>
                                            <TextBlock Text="{Binding Home}"
Style="{StaticResource PhoneTextSmallStyle}" FontFamily="{StaticResource
PhoneFontFamilySemiBold}"/>
                                        </StackPanel>
                                    </StackPanel>
                                </Grid>
                            </DataTemplate>
                        </toolkit:LongListSelector.ItemTemplate>
                    </toolkit:LongListSelector>
                </controls:PivotItem>
            </controls:Pivot>
        </Grid>
. . .
```

The `PerformanceProgressBar` control is defined in the `PerformanceProgressBarSample.xaml` file. This is an enhanced version of the `ProgressBar` control because it uses the compositor thread. Its usage is very simple; you can specify the `PerformanceProgressBar` tag as shown in the following code.

▪ **Note** The `PhoneApplicationPage` provides the `ProgressIndicator` property used to show a progress indicator on the system tray. Even this progress indicator uses the compositor thread so has a better animation (see Recipe 3-10).

```
. . .
    <toolkit:PerformanceProgressBar
        VerticalAlignment="Top"
        x:Name="_performanceProgressBar"/>
. . .
```

This progress bar is activated by setting its `IsIndeterminate` property to `true`, and deactivated by setting it to `false`. In this example, this property is both activated and deactivated by a check box that uses a Silverlight binding feature. It binds its own `IsChecked` Boolean property to the `IsIndeterminate` property so that when the check box is selected, the progress bar appears at the top of the screen.

. . .

```
    <CheckBox Content="Show performance progress bar"
            IsChecked="{Binding IsIndeterminate,
                    ElementName=_performanceProgressBar, Mode=TwoWay}"/>
```

. . .

The ToggleSwitch control is shown in the ToggleSwitchSample.xaml file. This control is a switch that assumes two states: on and off. It provides the Header property used to show text associated with the control. When you need to show more text or other controls near the switch control, you can define how the template should look by using both the HeaderTemplate and the ContentTemplate.

```
<StackPanel x:Name="ContentPanel" Grid.Row="1" Margin="12,0,12,0">
    <toolkit:ToggleSwitch Header="Wi Fi networking"/>
    <toolkit:ToggleSwitch Header="Set automatically"/>
    <toolkit:ToggleSwitch Header="5:45 AM">
        <toolkit:ToggleSwitch.HeaderTemplate>
            <DataTemplate>
                <ContentControl FontSize="{StaticResource PhoneFontSizeLarge}"
                  Foreground="{StaticResource PhoneForegroundBrush}"
                  Content="{Binding}"/>
            </DataTemplate>
        </toolkit:ToggleSwitch.HeaderTemplate>
        <toolkit:ToggleSwitch.ContentTemplate>
            <DataTemplate>
                <StackPanel>
                    <StackPanel Orientation="Horizontal">
                        <TextBlock Text="Alarm: "
                          FontSize="{StaticResource PhoneFontSizeSmall}"/>
                        <ContentControl HorizontalAlignment="Left"
                          FontSize="{StaticResource PhoneFontSizeSmall}"
                          Content="{Binding}"/>
                    </StackPanel>
                    <TextBlock Text="every schoolday"
                     FontSize="{StaticResource PhoneFontSizeSmall}"
                     Foreground="{StaticResource PhoneSubtleBrush}"/>
                </StackPanel>
            </DataTemplate>
        </toolkit:ToggleSwitch.ContentTemplate>
    </toolkit:ToggleSwitch>
</StackPanel>
```

The TiltEffect control is demonstrated in the TiltEffectSample.xaml file. Activating the tilt effect on a page is as easy as adding a PhoneApplicationPage attribute. Every control that responds to a tapping gesture will automatically provide the tilt effect animation.

```
<phone:PhoneApplicationPage
    x:Class="PhoneToolkitSample.Samples.TiltEffectSample"
    xmlns="http://schemas.microsoft.com/winfx/2006/xaml/presentation"
```

```
        xmlns:x="http://schemas.microsoft.com/winfx/2006/xaml"
        xmlns:phone="clr-namespace:Microsoft.Phone.Controls;assembly=Microsoft.Phone"
        xmlns:shell="clr-namespace:Microsoft.Phone.Shell;assembly=Microsoft.Phone"
        xmlns:d="http://schemas.microsoft.com/expression/blend/2008"
        xmlns:mc="http://schemas.openxmlformats.org/markup-compatibility/2006"
        xmlns:toolkit="clr-
namespace:Microsoft.Phone.Controls;assembly=Microsoft.Phone.Controls.Toolkit"
        FontFamily="{StaticResource PhoneFontFamilyNormal}"
        FontSize="{StaticResource PhoneFontSizeNormal}"
        Foreground="{StaticResource PhoneForegroundBrush}"
        SupportedOrientations="PortraitOrLandscape"
        Orientation="Portrait"
        mc:Ignorable="d" d:DesignHeight="768" d:DesignWidth="480"
        shell:SystemTray.IsVisible="True"
        toolkit:TiltEffect.IsTiltEnabled="True">
. . .
```

The Transitions effects are shown in the TransitionsSample.xaml file. The Silverlight for Windows Phone Toolkit library gives you two possibilities: the transition between pages during the navigation and the transition effect on the page itself. In the TransitionsSample.xaml file (and in all the pages seen until now as well), between the PhoneApplicationPage tags, are the NavigationInTransition and NavigationOutTransition tags, which define the transition effects when the page is loaded and before it is unloaded, respectively.

```
. . .
        <toolkit:TransitionService.NavigationInTransition>
            <toolkit:NavigationInTransition>
                <toolkit:NavigationInTransition.Backward>
                    <toolkit:TurnstileTransition Mode="BackwardIn"/>
                </toolkit:NavigationInTransition.Backward>
                <toolkit:NavigationInTransition.Forward>
                    <toolkit:TurnstileTransition Mode="ForwardIn"/>
                </toolkit:NavigationInTransition.Forward>
            </toolkit:NavigationInTransition>
        </toolkit:TransitionService.NavigationInTransition>
        <toolkit:TransitionService.NavigationOutTransition>
            <toolkit:NavigationOutTransition>
                <toolkit:NavigationOutTransition.Backward>
                    <toolkit:TurnstileTransition Mode="BackwardOut"/>
                </toolkit:NavigationOutTransition.Backward>
                <toolkit:NavigationOutTransition.Forward>
                    <toolkit:TurnstileTransition Mode="ForwardOut"/>
                </toolkit:NavigationOutTransition.Forward>
            </toolkit:NavigationOutTransition>
        </toolkit:TransitionService.NavigationOutTransition>
. . .
```

The TransitionsSample.xaml file contains two buttons and two list picker controls. One button starts the transition effect on the page itself, picking the transition type from both the list pickers. The other button shows page navigation transition effects in the same way as described earlier. So let's focus on the first button and the code behind the Click event.

The See method is called when the button is clicked so that the selected transition from the family list picker is started. The code checks whether the selected transition type (or family) is Roll, because that is the only transition type that doesn't have an associated transition mode. The Roll effect simply rolls the page in a unique way; there is no way to choose the way it rolls. On the other hand, the other transition families have different modes. Those families are Rotate, Slide, Swivel, and Turnstile and support different modes. They are returned from the EnumConverter class that, depending on the transition family, returns a List collection filled with all the supported modes.

Depending on the selected transition family, a new transition object is created and associated to the page. The available classes are RollTransition, RotateTransition, SlideTransition, SwivelTransition, and TurnstileTransition. Each class—except the RollTransition class—accepts a transition mode as the class constructor's parameter. Finally, the reference to the PhoneApplicationPage is used to associate the new transition that is started by calling the Begin method. When the transition is completed, the Completed event is raised and the Stop method is called.

```
private void See(object sender, RoutedEventArgs e)
{
    string family = (string)Family.SelectedItem;
    string mode = (string)Mode.SelectedItem;
    TransitionElement transitionElement = null;
    if (family.Equals("Roll"))
    {
        transitionElement = new RollTransition();
    }
    else
    {
        transitionElement = TransitionElement(family, mode);
    }
    PhoneApplicationPage phoneApplicationPage =
(PhoneApplicationPage)(((PhoneApplicationFrame)Application.Current.RootVisual)).Content;
    ITransition transition = transitionElement.GetTransition(phoneApplicationPage);
    transition.Completed += delegate
    {
        transition.Stop();
    };
    transition.Begin();
}


public class EnumConverter : IValueConverter
{
    public object Convert(object value, Type targetType, object parameter,
                        CultureInfo culture)
    {
        string s = value as string;
        if (s == null)
        {
            return null;
        }
        switch (s)
        {
            case "Roll":
```

```
                    return new List<string>();
            case "Rotate":
                return new List<string>
                {
                    "In90Clockwise",
                    "In90Counterclockwise",
                    "In180Clockwise",
                    "In180Counterclockwise",
                    "Out90Clockwise",
                    "Out90Counterclockwise",
                    "Out180Clockwise",
                    "Out180Counterclockwise"
                };
            case "Slide":
                return new List<string>
                {
                    "SlideUpFadeIn",
                    "SlideUpFadeOut",
                    "SlideDownFadeIn",
                    "SlideDownFadeOut",
                    "SlideLeftFadeIn",
                    "SlideLeftFadeOut",
                    "SlideRightFadeIn",
                    "SlideRightFadeOut"
                };
            case "Swivel":
                return new List<string>
                {
                    "FullScreenIn",
                    "FullScreenOut",
                    "ForwardIn",
                    "ForwardOut",
                    "BackwardIn",
                    "BackwardOut"
                };
            case "Turnstile":
                return new List<string>
                {
                    "ForwardIn",
                    "ForwardOut",
                    "BackwardIn",
                    "BackwardOut"
                };
        }
        return null;
    }
}
```

The WrapPanel is shown in the WrapPanelSample.xaml page. Depending on the Orientation property value, the items are aligned from left to right (or from top to bottom), breaking them in a new line when the container edge is reached. Adding to your page is as easy as specifying the WrapPanel tag in the page.

```
<toolkit:WrapPanel x:Name="wrapPanel" Orientation="Vertical"/>
```

Usage

From Visual Studio 2010, press Ctrl+F5 and then check that the target output is set to Windows Phone Emulator. The application deploys to the emulator and starts, briefly showing the main page, as in Figure 3-17.

Figure 3-17. The Silverlight for Windows Phone Toolkit official application

The application is composed of 17 clickable list items that you can see if you drag up and down the page. If you tap one list item, you will navigate to the related page containing that control. For example, to see the AutoCompleteBox in action, tap the AutoCompleteBox button and you will be redirected to the AutoCompleteBoxSample.xaml page (see Figure 3-18).

Figure 3-18. The AutoCompleteBox *control showing both one-line and two-line suggestions*

You can continue by trying every control and seeing it in action on the related page.

3-9. Using Launchers and Choosers

Problem

You have to add interaction between your application and external phone applications such as Phone, Search, and Marketplace.

Solution

You can add interaction between your application and your phone applications by using launchers and choosers classes.

How It Works

Windows Phone applications have their own private storage and cannot interact with other applications installed on the phone. In some cases, you need to perform a particular task in your application that requires use of existing Windows Phone applications. In those cases you can use both launchers and choosers to add interaction with particular Windows Phone applications.

Indeed, there is no way to add interaction between two applications with launchers and choosers. You can only integrate into your application common tasks such as a phone call, an e-mail composer, the Marketplace, the photo camera, the web browser, and the search function.

The main difference between launchers and choosers is that launchers don't return any kind of data to the application caller. The choosers implement an asynchronous event handler that is called after the operation is completed, returning the data to the application caller.

After having used a launcher or a chooser, the application caller is closed, so it's very important to correctly manage tombstoning (see Recipe 2-5 and Recipe 2-6 in Chapter 2). Indeed, when the launcher or chooser has completed its operations, the application caller is launched again with the tombstoning feature.

In Table 3-2 and Table 3-3, you can find the names and descriptions of each launcher and chooser available from the `Microsoft.Phone.Tasks` namespace, respectively.

Table 3-2. *launchers Available from the Windows Phone SDK*

Launcher	Description
BingMapsDirectionsTask	Launches the Bing Maps application displaying driving directions between a start and an end point.
BingMapsTask	Launches the Bing Maps application, showing a location specified as a search string.
ConnectionSettingsTask	Launches the network connection settings panel.
EmailComposeTask	Launches the e-mail application and optionally fills an e-mail field such as Body, To, Cc, and so on.

Launcher	Description
MarketplaceDetailTask	Launches the Marketplace application, showing details either on the current application or the application specified by its identifier.
MarketplaceHubTask	Launches the Marketplace application, showing either the Application section or the Music section.
MarketplaceReviewTask	Launches the Marketplace application, showing the review form to add a comment to your application.
MarketplaceSearchTask	Launches the Marketplace application, showing the search form with results based on the text you provided.
MediaPlayerLauncher	Launches the Media Player application playing the specified media file.
PhoneCallTask	Launches the Phone application, showing the phone number and display name. The phone call is not automatically started.
SearchTask	Launches the Search application, performing the query with the provided text.
ShareLinkTask	Launches the share link panel that allows the user to share a link on a social network.
ShareStatusTask	Launches the share status panel where the user can add text and select social networks where to publish the message.
SmsComposeTask	Launches the Messaging application with a new SMS filled with provided arguments such as the Body and To data.
WebBrowserTask	Launches the Internet Explorer application, displaying the provided URL.

Table 3-3. Choosers Available from the Windows Phone SDK

Chooser	Description
AddressChooserTask	Launches the Contacts application. If the user selects a contact, the contact's address is returned to the application caller.
CameraCaptureTask	Launches the Camera application, and if the user takes the photo, the photo is returned to the application caller.
EmailAddressChooserTask	Launches the Contact application, allowing users to select a contact

	whose e-mail is returned to the application caller.
GameInviteTask	Launches the game invite screen, allowing the user to invite other players to join the game in a multiplayer game session.
PhoneNumberChooserTask	Launches the Contact application, allowing users to select a contact whose phone number is returned to the application caller.
PhotoChooserTask	Launches the Photo Picker application, allowing users to pick a photo from the media library.
SaveContactTask	Launches the Concact application, allowing users to save a contact.
SaveEmailAddressTask	Saves the provided e-mail address into the Contact application.
SavePhoneNumberTask	Saves the phone number into the Contact application.
SaveRingtoneTask	Launches the Ringtones application, allowing the user to save the audio file to the phone ringtones list.

The Code

In this recipe, you will create a Silverlight for Windows Phone application called LaunchersAndChoosersDemo that implements the Pivot control with two items, launchers and choosers. Every pivot item contains a ListBox with an item for each launcher and for each chooser. After the user selects a list box item the application will launch either the related launcher or chooser.

In the MainPage.xaml file, the Pivot control contains two items, both of which fill a ListBox with the complete list of launchers and choosers. The SelectionChanged event from the ListBox is managed to retrieve the selected item and show the related launcher or chooser.

```
. . .
        <controls:Pivot Title="LAUNCHERS AND CHOOSERS">
            <!--Pivot item one-->
            <controls:PivotItem Header="Launchers">
                <!--Double line list with text wrapping-->
                    <ListBoxItem x:Name="iBingMapsDirectionsTask"
                        Content="BingMapsDirectionsTask"
                        HorizontalAlignment="Center" Height="55"/>
                    <ListBoxItem x:Name="iBingMapsTask"
                        Content="BingMapsTask"
                        HorizontalAlignment="Center" Height="55"/>
                    <ListBoxItem x:Name="iConnectionSettingsTask"
                        Content="ConnectionSettingsTask"
                        HorizontalAlignment="Center" Height="55"/>
                    <ListBoxItem x:Name="iEmailComposeTask"
                        Content="EmailComposeTask"
```

```
                              HorizontalAlignment="Center" Height="55"/>
                <ListBoxItem x:Name="iMarketplaceDetailTask"
                    Content="MarketplaceDetailTask"
                    HorizontalAlignment="Center" Height="55" />
                <ListBoxItem x:Name="iMarketplaceHubTask"
                    Content="MarketplaceHubTask"
                    HorizontalAlignment="Center" Height="55"/>
                <ListBoxItem x:Name="iMarketplaceReviewTask"
                    Content="MarketplaceReviewTask"
                    HorizontalAlignment="Center" Height="55"/>
                <ListBoxItem x:Name="iMarketplaceSearchTask"
                    Content="MarketplaceSearchTask"
                    HorizontalAlignment="Center" Height="55"/>
                <ListBoxItem x:Name="iMediaPlayerLauncher"
                    Content="MediaPlayerLauncher"
                    HorizontalAlignment="Center" Height="55"/>
                <ListBoxItem x:Name="iPhoneCallTask"
                    Content="PhoneCallTask"
                    HorizontalAlignment="Center" Height="55"/>
                <ListBoxItem x:Name="iSearchTask"
                    Content="SearchTask"
                    HorizontalAlignment="Center" Height="55"/>
                <ListBoxItem x:Name="iShareLinkTask"
                    Content="ShareLinkTask"
                    HorizontalAlignment="Center" Height="55"/>
                <ListBoxItem x:Name="iShareStatusTask"
                    Content="ShareStatusTask"
                    HorizontalAlignment="Center" Height="55"/>
                <ListBoxItem x:Name="iSmsComposeTask"
                    Content="SmsComposeTask"
                    HorizontalAlignment="Center" Height="55"/>
                <ListBoxItem x:Name="iWebBrowserTask"
                    Content="WebBrowserTask"
                    HorizontalAlignment="Center" Height="55"/>                 </ListBox>
    </controls:PivotItem>

    <!--Pivot item two-->
    <controls:PivotItem Header="Choosers">
        <ListBox x:Name="SecondListBox" Margin="0,0,-12,0"
                SelectionChanged="SecondListBox_SelectionChanged">
            <ListBoxItem x:Name="iAddressChooserTask"
                Content="AddressChooserTask"
                HorizontalAlignment="Center" Height="55"
                VerticalAlignment="Center" />
            <ListBoxItem x:Name="iCameraCaptureTask"
                Content="CameraCaptureTask"
                HorizontalAlignment="Center" Height="55"
                VerticalAlignment="Center" />
            <ListBoxItem x:Name="iEmailAddressChooserTask"
                Content="EmailAddressChooserTask"
                HorizontalAlignment="Center" Height="55"
                VerticalAlignment="Center"  />
```

```
                <ListBoxItem x:Name="iGameInviteTask"
                    Content="GameInviteTask" HorizontalAlignment="Center"
                    Height="55" VerticalAlignment="Center"  />
                <ListBoxItem x:Name="iPhoneNumberChooserTask"
                    Content="PhoneNumberChooserTask"
                    HorizontalAlignment="Center" Height="55"
                    VerticalAlignment="Center" />
                <ListBoxItem x:Name="iPhotoChooserTask"
                    Content="PhotoChooserTask"
                    HorizontalAlignment="Center" Height="55"
                    VerticalAlignment="Center" />
                <ListBoxItem x:Name="iSaveContactTask"
                    Content="SaveContactTask"
                    HorizontalAlignment="Center" Height="55"
                    VerticalAlignment="Center" />
                <ListBoxItem x:Name="iSaveEmailAddressTask"
                    Content="SaveEmailAddressTask"
                    HorizontalAlignment="Center" Height="55"
                    VerticalAlignment="Center" />
                <ListBoxItem x:Name="iSavePhoneNumberTask"
                    Content="SavePhoneNumberTask"
                    HorizontalAlignment="Center" Height="55"
                    VerticalAlignment="Center" />
                <ListBoxItem x:Name="iSaveRingtoneTask"
                    Content="SaveRingtoneTask"
                    HorizontalAlignment="Center" Height="55"
                    VerticalAlignment="Center" />                </ListBox>
        </controls:PivotItem>
    </controls:Pivot>
. . .
```

In the `MainPage.xaml.cs` file, there is the `SelectionChanged` event handler for both list boxes. Within the event handlers, a switch case is used to retrieve the selected item and execute the related launcher or chooser. Let's start analyzing each launcher.

The first case pertains to the `BingMapsDirectionsTask` that launches the Bing Maps application with driving instructions to go from the Start location to the End location. Both the Start and End locations are `LabeledMapLocation` class types. The `LabeledMapLocation` class's constructor accepts two parameters. The former is a string indicating the location name, and the latter is a `GeoCoordinate` object pointing to the location's latitude and longitude. Setting the `GeoCoordinate` parameter to null, the location name is used as searching text in the Bing Maps application. Finally, omitting the Start property, the phone's location retrieve by GPS sensor will be used as Start location.

The `BingMapsTask` case launches the Bing Maps application searching for the location specified in the `SearchTerm` property. The Zoom property indicates the map zoom level.

The `ConnectionSettingsTask` case shows the connection settings of WiFi, Bluetooth, Cellular, and Airplane mode allowing the user to change them.

```
    private void FirstListBox_SelectionChanged(object sender,
                                     SelectionChangedEventArgs e)
    {
        switch ((e.AddedItems[0] as ListBoxItem).Name)
        {
```

```
        case "iBingMapsDirectionsTask":
            BingMapsDirectionsTask bmdt = new
                                     BingMapsDirectionsTask();
            bmdt.Start = new LabeledMapLocation("Rome, Italy", null);
            bmdt.End = new LabeledMapLocation("Milan, Italy", null);
            bmdt.Show();
            break;
        case "iBingMapsTask":
            BingMapsTask bmt = new BingMapsTask();
            bmt.SearchTerm = "Buckingham Palace, London";
            bmt.ZoomLevel = 400;
            bmt.Show();
            break;
        case "iConnectionSettingsTask":
            ConnectionSettingsTask cst = new
                                     ConnectionSettingsTask();
            cst.ConnectionSettingsType = ConnectionSettingsType.WiFi;
            cst.Show();
            break;
```

When the iEmailComposeTask list box item is selected, a new EmailComposeTask object is created and its own properties are filled with values. You can specify the destination address by using the To property, the e-mail subject by using Subject, the e-mail body by using Body, and eventually a carbon copy address by using the Cc property. Finally, by calling the Show method, the launcher is executed and a new e-mail is created.

. . .

```
        case "iEmailComposeTask":
            EmailComposeTask ect = new EmailComposeTask();
            ect.To = "some.email@address.com";
            ect.Subject = "Some subject";
            ect.Body = "email content here";
            ect.Show();
            break;
```

. . .

The next launchers are used to interact with the Marketplace. The MarketplaceDetailTask class provides two properties: the ContentType can be set only to the MarketplaceContentType.Applications value, and the ContentIdentifier can be either omitted to retrieve detail for the current application or set to an application identifier.

The MarketplaceHubTask class provides the ContentType property that can be set to either MarketplaceContentType.Applications or MarketplaceContentType.Music so that the Marketplace application starts by showing either the Applications section or the Music section, respectively.

The MarketplaceReviewTask class provides only the Show method, because it opens the Marketplace, allowing users to review the current application.

The MarketplaceSearchTask class provides the SearchTerms property for specifying the text that has to be searched in the context set by the ContentType property.

. . .

```
            case "iMarketplaceDetailTask":
                MarketplaceDetailTask mdt = new MarketplaceDetailTask();
                mdt.ContentType = MarketplaceContentType.Applications;
                mdt.Show();
                break;
            case "iMarketplaceHubTask":
                MarketplaceHubTask mht = new MarketplaceHubTask();
                mht.ContentType = MarketplaceContentType.Applications;
                mht.Show();
                break;
            case "iMarketplaceReviewTask":
                MarketplaceReviewTask mrt = new MarketplaceReviewTask();
                mrt.Show();
                break;
            case "iMarketplaceSearchTask":
                MarketplaceSearchTask mst = new MarketplaceSearchTask();
                mst.ContentType = MarketplaceContentType.Music;
                mst.SearchTerms = "Radiohead";
                mst.Show();
                break;
...
```

The MediaPlayerLauncher class provides the Media property, which is used to specify the URL of the media file to be played. The file has to be saved in the isolated storage either by the application itself or when the application is deployed on the phone. The Location property defines where the media file is located, either in the installation file (its value is set to Install) or in the isolated storage (its value is set to Data). Finally, the Controls property is used to specify which buttons the media player has to show.

```
...
            case "iMediaPlayerLauncher":
                MediaPlayerLauncher mpl = new MediaPlayerLauncher();
                mpl.Media = new Uri("Notes_INTRO_BG.wmv",
                                    UriKind.Relative);
                mpl.Location = MediaLocationType.Install;
                mpl.Controls = MediaPlaybackControls.Pause |
                               MediaPlaybackControls.Stop |
                               MediaPlaybackControls.Rewind;
                mpl.Show();
                break;
...
```

The PhoneCallTask launcher provides the PhoneNumber property used to specify the phone number to call and the DisplayName property to display the contact name.

```
...
            case "iPhoneCallTask":
                PhoneCallTask pct = new PhoneCallTask();
                pct.DisplayName = "My contact";
                pct.PhoneNumber = "55512345678";
```

```
                    pct.Show();
                    break;
. . .
```

The SearchTask launcher provides the SearchQuery property used to specify the text to search both on the Web and locally.

```
. . .
                case "iSearchTask":
                    SearchTask st = new SearchTask();
                    st.SearchQuery = "Facebook";
                    st.Show();
                    break;
. . .
```

The ShareLinkTask and ShareStatusTask launchers show a panel to share link and status message on the social networks. The link is specified using the LinkUri property. You can set the link's title and a comment setting the Title and Message properties, respectively.

The status message is set using the Status property.

```
. . .
                case "iShareLinkTask":
                    ShareLinkTask slt = new ShareLinkTask();
                    slt.Title = "AS Roma scored";
                    slt.Message = "What a shot!";
                    slt.LinkUri = new Uri("http://www.youtube.com/",
                                        UriKind.Absolute);
                    slt.Show();
                    break;
                case "iShareStatusTask":
                    ShareStatusTask sst = new ShareStatusTask();
                    sst.Status = "I'm writing Windows Phone Recipe book!";
                    sst.Show();
                    break;
. . .
```

The SmsComposeTask launcher provides classic properties such as To and Body to fill the message recipient and message content fields. If you don't specify these properties, an empty message will be created. The message will not be sent until the user sends it.

```
. . .
                case "iSmsComposeTask":
                    SmsComposeTask sct = new SmsComposeTask();
                    sct.To = "My contact";
                    sct.Body = "sms content";
                    sct.Show();
                    break;
. . .
```

The WebBrowserTask class provides the Uri property to specify which Internet address has to be shown in the web browser application.

■ **Note** The URL property provided by the WebBrowserTask is obsolete.

. . .

```
            case "iWebBrowserTask":
                WebBrowserTask wbt = new WebBrowserTask();
                wbt.Uri = new Uri("http://www.apress.com",
                                UriKind.Absolute);                    wbt.Show();
                break;
        }
    }
```

■ **Note** Each launcher class and each chooser class provides the Show method that is responsible for performing the related action, such as showing the web browser, opening the e-mail composer, and so on.

In the other SelectionChanged event handler of the Choosers list box, there is another switch case that is executed by the code related to the user's choice. The first two cases are just an introduction; in Chapter 8, these two choosers are explained more completely.

```
    private void SecondListBox_SelectionChanged(object sender,
                                        SelectionChangedEventArgs e)
    {
        switch ((e.AddedItems[0] as ListBoxItem).Name)
        {
            case "iCameraCaptureTask":
                MessageBox.Show("See recipe 8-1 for
                                CameraCaptureTask chooser explanation.");
                break;
            case "iPhotoChooserTask":
                MessageBox.Show("See recipe 8-3 for
                                PhotoChooserTask chooser explanation.");
                break;
. . .
```

The EmailAddressChooserTask executes the Contact application and raises the Completed event after the user has chosen a contact.

. . .

```
            case "iEmailAddressChooserTask":
                EmailAddressChooserTask eact = new EmailAddressChooserTask();
                eact.Completed +=
                    new EventHandler<EmailResult>(EmailAddressChooserTask_Completed);
                eact.Show();
                break;
    . . .
```

The Completed event handler provides the EmailResult parameter with the Email property containing the e-mail address of the selected contact.

```
        void EmailAddressChooserTask_Completed(object sender, EmailResult e)
        {
            if (e.TaskResult == TaskResult.OK)
                MessageBox.Show(e.Email);
        }
```

Similar to the previous chooser, the PhoneNumberChooserTask class opens the Contact application and raises the Completed event when the user has finished selecting a contact. This time, the returning parameter of the Completed event handler will be the contact's phone number.

```
    . . .
            case "iPhoneNumberChooserTask":
                PhoneNumberChooserTask pnct = new PhoneNumberChooserTask();
                pnct.Completed +=
                  new EventHandler<PhoneNumberResult>(PhoneNumberChooserTask_Completed);
                pnct.Show();
                break;
    . . .

        void PhoneNumberChooserTask_Completed(object sender, PhoneNumberResult e)
        {
            if (e.TaskResult == TaskResult.OK)
                MessageBox.Show(e.PhoneNumber);
        }
```

The SaveEmailAddressTask and SavePhoneNumberTask choosers save a new e-mail address and a new phone number when adding a new contact, respectively. Neither chooser returns a value from the Completed event handler—just the result of whether the operation has been completed successfully or has been aborted by the user.

```
    . . .
            case "iSaveEmailAddressTask":
                SaveEmailAddressTask seat = new SaveEmailAddressTask();
                seat.Completed +=
                    new EventHandler<TaskEventArgs>(SaveEmailAddressTask_Completed);
                seat.Email = "some.email@address.com";
                seat.Show();
```

```
                    break;
            case "iSavePhoneNumberTask":
                SavePhoneNumberTask spnt = new SavePhoneNumberTask();
                spnt.PhoneNumber = "55512345678";
                spnt.Completed +=
                        new EventHandler<TaskEventArgs>(SavePhoneNumberTask_Completed);
                spnt.Show();
                break;
        }
    }

    void SavePhoneNumberTask_Completed(object sender, TaskEventArgs e)
    {
        if (e.TaskResult == TaskResult.OK)
            MessageBox.Show("Phone numeber saved correctly");
        else if (e.TaskResult == TaskResult.Cancel)
            MessageBox.Show("Save operation cancelled");
    }


    void SaveEmailAddressTask_Completed(object sender, TaskEventArgs e)
    {
        if (e.TaskResult == TaskResult.OK)
            MessageBox.Show("Email saved correctly");
        else if (e.TaskResult == TaskResult.Cancel)
            MessageBox.Show("Save operation cancelled");
    }
```

The GameInviteTask chooser sends an invite to join to a game to both contacts and xlive friends. The SessionId property is used to specify the network session identifier. The GameInviteTask_Completed event handler provides the TaskEventArgs parameter with the sending invite result.

```
            case "iGameInviteTask":
                GameInviteTask git = new GameInviteTask();
                git.Completed += new
                    EventHandler<TaskEventArgs>(GameInviteTask_Completed);
                git.SessionId = "Join my game network";
                git.Show();
                break;

    void GameInviteTask_Completed(object sender, TaskEventArgs e)
    {
        if (e.TaskResult == TaskResult.OK)
            MessageBox.Show("Invite sent successfully");
        else
            MessageBox.Show("Invite not sent");
    }
```

The SaveContactTask chooser launches the Contacts application, allowing user to add a contact. Before showing the Contacts application, you can set a lot of contact's information—such as first name, last name, e-mail, phone, and the like. After the Contacts application execution, the user can add contact photo, a ringtone, and more. You know whether the user has added the contact or has cancelled the saving operation checking the SaveContactResult parameter provided by the Completed event.

```
            case "iSaveContactTask":
                SaveContactTask sct = new SaveContactTask();
                sct.Completed += new
                 EventHandler<SaveContactResult>(
                                SaveContactTask_Completed);
                sct.FirstName = "Ewan";
                sct.LastName = "Buckingham";
                sct.Company = "Apress";
                sct.Show();
                break;

    void SaveContactTask_Completed(object sender, SaveContactResult e)
    {
        if (e.TaskResult == TaskResult.OK)
            MessageBox.Show("Contact added successfully");
        else
            MessageBox.Show("Contact not added");
    }
```

Finally, the SaveRingtoneTask chooser displays the save ringtone panel, allowing the user to save the ringtone provided by the application in the phone's ringtone library, and eventually set the ringtone as the default. The Source property is used to point to the ringtone audio file that can be provided with the application XAP file or saved in the isolated storage after a file download. In the former case, you have to set the Uri path with the appdata: prefix; in the latter case, you have to specify the isostore: prefix. We have included the Ringstone 10.wma file in our project, so we used the appdata: prefix to the Uri path. The audio file has to be either MP3 or WMA (Windows Media Audio) file format, and the file audio has to be less than 1 MB in size. Finally, the audio file has to be less than 40 seconds in length and without digital rights management (DRM) protection.

The DisplayName property is useful to provide a name to the ringtone that is shown by the phone's ringtone panel.

You know whether the user has saved the ringtone in the phone ringtone application checking the TaskEventArgs parameter provided by the SaveRingtoneTask_Completed event handler.

```
            case "iSaveRingtoneTask":
                SaveRingtoneTask srt = new SaveRingtoneTask();
                srt.Completed += new
                                EventHandler<TaskEventArgs>(
                                  SaveRingtoneTask_Completed);
                srt.DisplayName = "Ringtone from code";
                srt.Source = new Uri("appdata:/Ringtone 10.wma");
                srt.Show();
                break;

    void SaveRingtoneTask_Completed(object sender, TaskEventArgs e)
    {
        if (e.TaskResult == TaskResult.OK)
            MessageBox.Show("Ringtone added successfully");
        else
            MessageBox.Show("Ringtone not added");
    }
```

Usage

From Visual Studio 2010, press Ctrl+F5. Depending on the target output, the application deploys either on the physical device or the emulator.

The LaunchersAndChoosersDemo application will run, briefly showing the Launchers pivot item with its own list box filled with launchers (see Figure 3-19).

Figure 3-19. The LaunchersAndChoosersDemo application in action

If you flick to the left, the application will show the second pivot item filled with all the available choosers (see Figure 3-20).

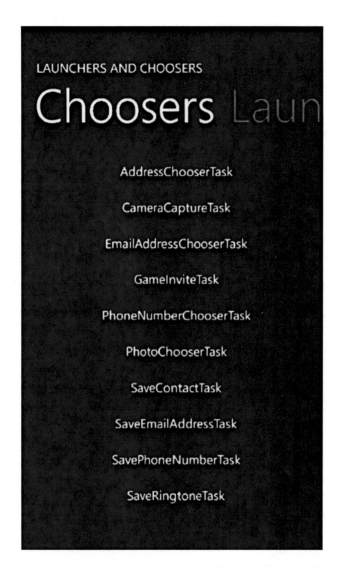

Figure 3-20. The Choosers pivot item showing all available choosers

Now you can tap a list box item and see the related functionality. For example, Figure 3-21 shows the MarketplaceSearchTask launcher.

Figure 3-21. The MarketplaceSearchTask launcher in action

■ **Note** The `EmailComposeTask` launcher cannot be tested on the emulator because it doesn't provide an e-mail composer application. Moreover, the `MarketplaceDetailTask` launcher doesn't work in either target output until the Marketplace accepts your application.

3-10. Accessing to the Contacts Library

Problem

Your application needs to access contacts stored in your phone.

Solution

You can search and retrieve phone contacts using the `Contacts` class.

How It Works

The Windows Phone operating system aggregates contacts data from different sources, including the phone itself, social networks such as Facebook, Windows Live, e-mail accounts, and so on. You can retrieve information on phone contacts using the `Contacts` class, which works on a read-only snapshot data, so you have to use the class again when you need fresh information.

The `Contacts` class contains the `SearchAsync` method and the `SearchCompleted` event. Using the `SearchAsync` method in your code, you can specify the query string that can be used during the search. It's recommended to use the `SearchAsync` method to filter contacts respect to LINQ, because the `SearchAsync` method uses indexed queries, so the query result is more efficient and fast against the LINQ query. By the way, the `SearchAsync` method has indexes filter only on contact's display name, e-mail address, phone number, and on contacts that have been pinned to the phone start screen. When you need different information, such as a contact's birthday, you have to retrieve all contacts and use a LINQ query to filter the results.

You don't know how many contacts are stored on the user's phone, so it's mandatory to inform the user about the searching progress status.

Finally, you need to add the `ID_CAP_CONTACTS` capability to the `WMAppManifest.xml` file when you create an application that searches for contacts.

Note This chapter doesn't cover phone's Calendar searches, because they are pretty similar to Contacts searches. Using the `Appointments` class, you can query the phone Calendar data retrieving appointements for a range of dates specified in the SearchAsync method.

The Code

In this recipe, you will modify the Silverlight for Windows Phone application created in Chapter 2, Receipe 2-8: the BirthdayApp application.

The BirthdayApp application reminds user about friends' birthday. In chapter 2, we focused on how to use the Reminder class so friends and birthdays are fixed in the code and not retrieve from Contacts.

Let's modify this code to retrieve contacts from the phone contacts store. In the `MainPage.xaml` page, we specified two listboxes to contain today and tomorrow birthdays. Listbox items are designed to show the `DisplayName` property provided by the Contact class.

. . .

```xml
<!--ContentPanel - place additional content here-->
<Grid x:Name="ContentPanel" Grid.Row="1" Margin="12,0,12,0">
    <TextBlock Height="30" HorizontalAlignment="Left"
            Margin="12,6,0,0" Name="textBlock1"
            Text="TODAY" VerticalAlignment="Top" />
    <ListBox Height="216" HorizontalAlignment="Left"
            Margin="0,45,0,0" Name="lbToday"
            VerticalAlignment="Top" Width="460">
        <ListBox.ItemTemplate>
            <DataTemplate>
                <StackPanel Orientation="Horizontal">
                    <TextBlock Text="{Binding DisplayName}" />
                </StackPanel>
            </DataTemplate>
        </ListBox.ItemTemplate>
    </ListBox>
    <TextBlock Height="30" HorizontalAlignment="Left"
            Margin="8,267,0,0" Name="textBlock2"
            Text="TOMORROW" VerticalAlignment="Top" />
    <ListBox Height="216" HorizontalAlignment="Left"
            Margin="-4,306,0,0" Name="lbTomorrow"
            VerticalAlignment="Top" Width="460">
        <ListBox.ItemTemplate>
            <DataTemplate>
                <StackPanel Orientation="Horizontal">
                    <TextBlock Text="{Binding DisplayName}" />
                </StackPanel>
            </DataTemplate>
        </ListBox.ItemTemplate>
    </ListBox>
</Grid>
```

. . .

In the `MainPage.xaml.cs` page, we added the code to search for all the contacts stored in the phone. We used the last parameter of the `SearchAsync` method to distinguish between the query for today and tomorrow birthdays. The other two parameters of the `SearchAsync` method are provided to retrieve all the contacts. So the `FilterKind` enumeration is set to None and no search text is provided.

```csharp
protected override void
    OnNavigatedTo(System.Windows.Navigation.NavigationEventArgs e)
{
    piBar.IsVisible = true;

    lbToday.Items.Clear();
    lbTomorrow.Items.Clear();

    Contacts birthdays = new Contacts();
    birthdays.SearchCompleted += new
```

```
                    EventHandler<ContactsSearchEventArgs>(
                    birthdays_SearchCompleted);
        birthdays.SearchAsync(string.Empty, FilterKind.None, "today");
        birthdays.SearchAsync(string.Empty, FilterKind.None, "tomorrow");

        base.OnNavigatedTo(e);
    }
```

When the searching operation is completed, the birthdays_SearchCompleted event handler is called and we can search for the contacts today and tomorrow birthdays. In both cases, a LINQ query is used to filter contacts' birthdays. The Contact class provides the Birthdays collection that can be queried by LINQ to retrieve today and tomorrow birthdays. Finally, the birthdays collection is used as ItemsSource data source for both today and tomorrow listboxes.

```
    void birthdays_SearchCompleted(object sender,
                                   ContactsSearchEventArgs e)
    {
        IEnumerable<Contact> contacts = e.Results;
        IEnumerable<Contact> birthdays = null;
        App app = Application.Current as App;

        if (e.State.ToString() == "today")
        {
            birthdays = from b in contacts
                        where b.Birthdays.FirstOrDefault().Month ==
                            DateTime.Now.Month &&
                            b.Birthdays.FirstOrDefault().Day ==
                            DateTime.Now.Day
                        select b;

            lbToday.ItemsSource = birthdays;

            if (birthdays.Count() > 0)
            {
                app.msgReminder = "Today is ";
                app.msgReminder += birthdays.First().DisplayName;
                app.msgReminder += " birthday!";
            }
        }
        else
        {
            DateTime tomorrow = DateTime.Now.AddDays(1);
            birthdays = from b in contacts
                        where b.Birthdays.FirstOrDefault().Month ==
                            tomorrow.Month &&
                            b.Birthdays.FirstOrDefault().Day ==
                            tomorrow.Day
                        select b;

            lbTomorrow.ItemsSource = birthdays;
```

```
        }

        piBar.IsVisible = false;
    }
```

Usually, the user phone contacts store is huge because the store is an aggregation of many contact's sources. So, the query time is long and it is different from phone to phone. It is mandatory that you inform the user about the query in progress. There are different ways to do this. We used the ProgressIndicator class that implements a progress indicator within the phone system tray. You can also indicate some text that is shown together with the progress indicator.

In the MainPage class constructor we created a ProgressIndicator object. We set its Text property to a message shown with the progress indicator. The IsIndeterminate property is set to true so that the progress indicator animation is looped and not limited for a range of time. The progress indicator is strictly tied to the phone system tray. So you have to use the SystemTray class and its own SetIsVisible and SetProgressIndicator static methods. Finally, you have to use the IsVisible property from the ProgressIndicator class to show and to hide the progress indicator bar.

```
public partial class MainPage : PhoneApplicationPage
{
    ProgressIndicator piBar = null;

    // Constructor
    public MainPage()
    {
        InitializeComponent();

        SystemTray.SetIsVisible(this, true);
        piBar = new ProgressIndicator();
        piBar.Text = "Searching...";
        piBar.IsIndeterminate = true;

        SystemTray.SetProgressIndicator(this, piBar);
    }
```

Usage

From Visual Studio 2010, press Ctrl+F5 after having set the target output to Windows Phone Device option. This is necessary because the eight contacts provided by the Windows Phone emulator doesn't have specified birthdays.

When the application is shown, you can see the contacts birtdays. If you don't see any contact you can lauch the Contacts application, select a contact, tap on the modify application bar button, and add the birthday information. Then you can lauch the BirthdayApp again to see it on the list.

3-11. Adding Advertising to Your Application

Problem

You want to create a free application, but you want to earn money as well.

Solution

You can add the AdControl on the Windows Phone page and use your Microsoft pubCenter account to register your application and start to monetize.

How It Works

The Microsoft Advertising SDK has been included in the Windows Phone 7.1 SDK version allowing an easy integration between your Windows Phone applications and the Microsoft pubCenter site that provides ads service.

Before you start monetizing with your application, you have to register an account to the Microsoft pubCenter site at `http://pubcenter.microsoft.com`. After the account is registered, you can add application registrations to the site. You can have more than one registered application and for each application you can require one or more ad units. An ad unit corresponds to either a banner text or a banner image. Also, you can select one or more ad categories (for example, Sports, Travel, and so on), and a subcategory (for example, Boxing, Soccer, and the like). Once you have saved an ad unit in your registered application you have to use the application identifier and the ad unit identifier in your code so that the application can download the banner once is running in the phone.

The Microsoft Advertising SDK provides the `Microsoft.Advertising.Mobile.dll` and `Microsoft.Advertising.Mobile.UI.dll` assemblies to add ads management in your Windows Phone application. In detail, the `Microsoft.Advertising.Mobile.UI` assembly provides the AdControl control that can be added to the Windows Phone page and accepts the application identifier and ad unit identifier as properties. The AdControl control is responsible to show either the banner image or banner text and the related ads sites opening the Internet Explorer mobile browser.

The AdControl control size has to be equal either to 480x80 or 300x50 pixels accordingly to the ad unit created in the pubCenter site. If you don't use these sizes, the AdControl doesn't show the ad banner.

When you add the AdControl control to the Windows Phone page, you have to follow some simple user interface rules. For example, the default page template created by Visual Studio has a layout grid that has some margins and when you place the AdControl control over the page you automatically cut some pixels. So you can either remove the grid's margins or place the AdControl control outside the grid. It's a best practice putting the ad banner either on top or bottom of the page so the final result is more discrete than having an ad banner in the middle of the page.

During the testing phase of your application you can use application test identifier and ad unit test identifier. This is pretty useful when you need to create the application user interface and you still haven't registered your application in the pubCenter site.

You have to specify the `test_client` string value in the ApplicationId property and you can choose the ad unit from three different types of values: the `TextAd` ad unit identifier diplays a 480x80 pixels text banner, the `Image480_80` ad unit identifier displays an XXL image banner (480x80 pixels), and the `Image300_50` ad unit identifier displays an X-Large image banner (300x50 pixels).

Finally, the AdControl control provides useful events that can be cached by your application. Among the others, the application can register the Tap event in order to know whether users have tapped on the banner, or use the `AdRefreshed` event that is raised when the banner has refreshed its content.

■ **Note** Windows Phone games using XNA Framework cannot use the AdControl control, but they have to implement the AdGameComponent and DrawableAd classes contained in the `Microsoft.Advertising.Mobile.Xna.dll` assembly.

The Code

In this recipe, we will create the Windows Phone main page filled with an advertising banner and we force the user to select the banner before starting to use the application.

In the `MainPage.xaml` page we added the AdControl control after having removed the Grid's margin attribute and added the import of the `Microsoft.Advertising.Mobile.UI` namespace.

```
<phone:PhoneApplicationPage
    x:Class="AdvertisingApp.MainPage"
. . .
xmlns:my="clr-
namespace:Microsoft.Advertising.Mobile.UI;assembly=Microsoft.Advertising.Mobile.UI">

    <!--LayoutRoot is the root grid where all page content is placed-->
    <Grid x:Name="LayoutRoot" Background="Transparent">
        <Grid.RowDefinitions>
            <RowDefinition Height="Auto"/>
            <RowDefinition Height="*"/>
        </Grid.RowDefinitions>

        <!--TitlePanel contains the name of the application and page title-->
        <StackPanel x:Name="TitlePanel" Grid.Row="0" Margin="12,17,0,28">
            <TextBlock x:Name="ApplicationTitle" Text="ADVERTISING APP" Style="{StaticResource
PhoneTextNormalStyle}"/>
            <TextBlock x:Name="PageTitle" Text="Ads page" Margin="9,-7,0,0"
Style="{StaticResource PhoneTextTitle1Style}"/>
        </StackPanel>

        <!--ContentPanel - place additional content here-->
        <Grid x:Name="ContentPanel" Grid.Row="1">
            <my:AdControl AdUnitId=" Image480_80" ApplicationId="test_client" Height="80"
HorizontalAlignment="Left" Margin="0,521,0,0" Name="adControl1" VerticalAlignment="Top"
Width="480" Tap="adControl1_Tap" />
        </Grid>
    </Grid>
```

In the `MainPage.xaml.cs` code, we have overridden the `OnNavigatedTo` method, so we can check whether the user has tapped the banner and in the affirmative case show the Page2 page.

```
protected override void OnNavigatedTo(System.Windows.Navigation.NavigationEventArgs e)
{
    if (PhoneApplicationService.Current.State.ContainsKey("ads"))
    {
        NavigationService.Navigate(new Uri("/Page2.xaml", UriKind.Relative));
    }
```

```
    }
```

We know when the user has tapped the ad banner because we have registered the Tap event handler and we use the event handler code to add the ads key in the State dictionary provided by the PhoneApplicationService class.

```
    private void adControl1_Tap(object sender, GestureEventArgs e)
    {
        if (!PhoneApplicationService.Current.State.ContainsKey("ads"))
            PhoneApplicationService.Current.State.Add("ads", "");
    }
```

Finally, in the `Page2.xaml.cs` code, we have cached the `OnNavigatedTo` event so we can remove the `MainPage` page from the `BackStack` page stack. This is very important because when the user presses the hardware Back button from `Page2` the application must exit and not show again the `MainPage` where the banner has been placed. Moreover, since the `MainPage` has the `OnNavigatedTo` method that navigates to Page2, the application navigation system would enter in a loop and the user would not be able to exit from the application.

```
    protected override void OnNavigatedTo(System.Windows.Navigation.NavigationEventArgs e)
    {
        NavigationService.RemoveBackEntry();
    }
```

Usage

From Visual Studio 2010, select either the Windows Phone Emulator or the Windows Phone Device option as your target output and then press Ctrl+F5. The application starts showing the advertising page as shown in Figure 3-22.

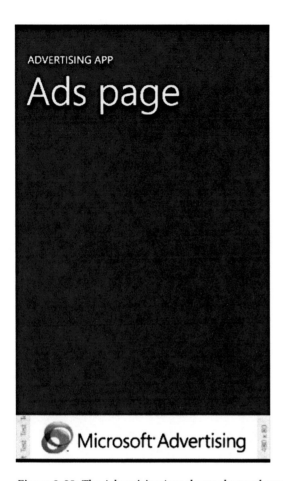

Figure 3-22: The AdvertisingApp shows the test banner

Now you can tap on the ad banner so that the Bing page is opened in the Internet browser. Now click the hardware Back button and you will see that the advertising page is gone and the application shows the real main page. Now, if you click the hardware Back button again, the application exits.

CHAPTER 4

User Interface with Expression Blend

This chapter explains how easy it is to customize controls in Silverlight for Windows Phone. We also wanted to show the use of special effects, but unfortunately, the fact that in the official release haven't been included requires us to not include them in this chapter.

But before starting with the recipes, you need to remember some fundamental concepts, such as the importance of a good user experience. In addition, it is essential for you to follow the user interface guidelines provided by Microsoft to ensure that your application is not rejected from the Marketplace, even if it is extremely functional. Before starting with the customization of controls, read the "UI Design and Interaction Guide for Windows Phone 7" document published by Microsoft and available at `http://msdn.microsoft.com/en-us/library/ff637515(v=vs.92).aspx`. This site also includes a series of templates for Photoshop®.

The recipes in this chapter describe how to do the following:

- 4-1. Create a data template that will enable your application to display well with a light or dark theme

- 4-2. Change the skin of your app

- 4-3. Create some cool animation

- 4-4. Customize a control

4-1. Getting Ready for Light and Dark

Problem

You want your application to display a list of items inside a list box. This list box needs a custom layout that enables you to display a rectangle next to each list item. The rectangle will appear when the item is selected. You also want to test the display of the list box by using various combinations of themes allowed by Windows Phone.

Solution

To create the layout of your list, you must create an `ItemTemplate` template and an `ItemContainerTemplate`. Then you must interact with the Device panel in Expression Blend to change between various combinations of themes.

How It Works

The data template is a powerful tool that provides developers and designers significant control over customizing UI elements (including, for example, a list box). These templates allow you to create a custom organization of UI elements that is based on the way you want users to visualize the information and that allows users to easily find what they need. By combining the power of the data template with the Device panel of Blend at design time, you can try out various combinations of themes and accent colors to determine what the user's feedback will be.

The Code

It is important that your application be able to adapt to the user's visual choices. If you don't use a color scheme suited to the theme chosen by the user, your application could become unused. Of course, some applications can impose a schema of color that differs from the choices of the user, while still providing a great user experience, by adapting the needs of the user to that graphic style (look at Facebook). In other cases, however, you won't be able to boast with such boldness and you'll want your application to be in line with the user's choices.

Suppose your application has a list box on the main page. Without having any customization on brushes, you use system colors. Then, when the user changes the theme, your application is still in line with it.

Problems arise when you decide that you don't want to design an application similar to others. Instead, you want one that reflects, for example, the web version of your application. You want to use your color scheme, and would like it if we use the light or dark theme.

Well, the first thing to know is that you don't need to make ongoing changes to the settings of your device or emulator. Blend already supports (at design time) the change of themes by providing an instant preview. So before we show you how to customize your application, we will show you how to use the Device panel of Microsoft Expression Blend (shown in Figure 4-1)—because it's important to become familiar with the tool that you will be using over the course of this chapter.

Figure 4-1. Device panel inside Blend

By clicking one of the two buttons highlighted in Figure 4-2, you can rotate the preview in landscape or portrait orientation, and then immediately test whether the application is ready for the two display modes. Of course, if your application doesn't need to rotate in the hands of the user, this option is not for you.

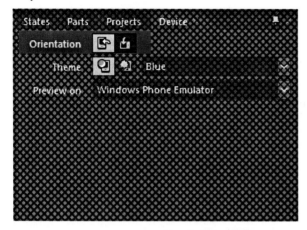

Figure 4-2. Orientation buttons

Similarly, you can change the appearance (dark or light) and the accent color matching PhoneAccentBrush, which will allow you to keep the display in line with the "mood" of the user. The Device panel enables you to try various combinations of themes and accent colors, as you can see highlighted in Figure 4-3. However, in addition to enabling you to see whether your layout works with various accent colors, the Display panel also enables you to monitor how the various brushes that you have defined in your application are compatible with dark and light themes.

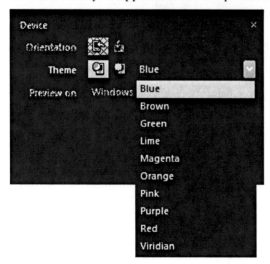

Figure 4-3. Theme selection

■ **Note** Just like the physical device, the emulator selects the dark theme by default.

You have reached nearly the central point of this book, but you will also consider applications from other chapters (also later) for customize it.

For this example, you will use the feed reader from Chapter 9 (Recipe 9-2). At first, it has only a list box. You will edit the item template with Blend: right-click the list box and then choose Edit Additional Templates ↗ Edit Generated Items ↗ Edit A Copy.

A screen similar to Figure 4-4 appears and asks where you want to create the resource. We recommend that you always create a dictionary in which you can enter all the data template and container styles. We make this recommendation for several reasons. First, if you create a template and your application consists of many pages, you will want to reuse the template for data of the same type. It would be equally available in profiles in the app.xaml file, but is our best practice to leave this as clean as possible. By using the Resources panel in Blend, you have available all the resources from various dictionaries merged into a single point. Then, if you're editing the template, you already know where to go to find it. We do not recommend using the template defined inside the control, because it is more difficult to see the template while you are creating the application, without selecting the template again, and because this template will not be easily reusable.

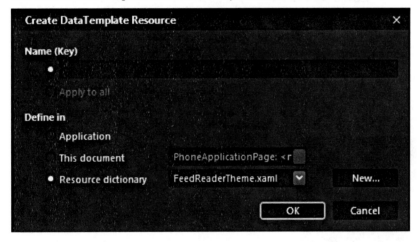

Figure 4-4. Creating a data template

So create a new dictionary named FeedReaderTheme.xaml and create a new template named NewsItemTemplate. In this case, we opted for a simple template that has a stack panel with a text block to show the title of the news, and a hyperlink button to open the link to the news in a browser. The XAML is as follows:

```
...
<DataTemplate x:Key="NewsItemTemplate">
  <StackPanel>
    <TextBlock Text="{Binding Title}" Style="{StaticResourceNewsTitleTextBlockStyle}" />
    <HyperlinkButtonHorizontalAlignment="Left" Content="{Binding Link}"
            Click="HyperlinkButton_Click"/>
  </StackPanel>
</DataTemplate>
...
```

Refer to Chapter 10 to learn more about the concept of binding, which is explained together with preliminary information about implementing the Model-View-ViewModel (MVVM) pattern.

As you can see in the following code, you also retrieve the style of the text block that displays the title, and for this we have chosen a Tahoma (Bold) 12-point font, with a foreground color based on the PhoneAccentBrush color that represents the color chosen by the user for him phone.

```
...
<Style x:Key="NewsTitleTextBlockStyle" TargetType="TextBlock">
  <Setter Property="Foreground" Value="{StaticResource PhoneAccentBrush}" />
  <Setter Property="FontWeight" Value="Bold"/>
  <Setter Property="FontFamily" Value="Tahoma" />
  <Setter Property="FontSize" Value="16"/>
</Style>
...
```

In this way, we have defined the style for the TextBox inside the ItemTemplate, and we have chosen to use the PhoneAccentBrush as the foreground color according to the user mood. You can test the result against all the colors available, simply by switching the accent color from the **Device** panel using the options highlighted in Figure 4-3.

After defining the style of the elements contained in the list, you will customize the itemContainer for the selection of an item that appears as a rectangle outline. Again, right-click the list box and then choose Edit Additional Template ↗ Edit Generated Item Container ↗ Edit A Copy. Call the style NewsListItemContainerStyle.

The template will appear very simple, but complete enough. In Blend's States panel, you can see the states that currently can take this control. What interests us is the Selected status. If you select it, the interface is put in "recording" and the text is displayed with the color that you chose for the accent brush. (Now you get to play with the Device panel in Blend.)

In the States panel, select the element Base, to which you will add a rectangle without fill. Set the outline color to Accent Color, and then set the opacity to 0% so that in all cases the rectangle will be transparent. Then select Selected status, but this time for working more comfortable press F6 to change the layout of panels and enter in Storyboard Creation modality. Select the rectangle, and if you do not see the storyboard, click the Show Timeline button shown in Figure 4-5. Now you want the rectangle to appear with a fading effect with a delay of 5 seconds, so select the rectangle and move the playhead along the timeline up to 500 milliseconds, as shown in Figure 4-6. In the Properties panel, edit the property opacity to 100%.

Figure 4-5. Show Timeline button

Figure 4-6. Timeline

In this way, you just created a storyboard, which will result in the following XAML:

```
...
<VisualState>
  <Storyboard>
    <ObjectAnimationUsingKeyFrames Storyboard.TargetProperty="Foreground"
        Storyboard.TargetName="ContentContainer">
      <DiscreteObjectKeyFrame KeyTime="0" Value="{StaticResource PhoneAccentBrush}"/>
    </ObjectAnimationUsingKeyFrames>
    <ObjectAnimationUsingKeyFrames Storyboard.TargetProperty="(UIElement.Visibility)"
        Storyboard.TargetName="rectangle">
      <DiscreteObjectKeyFrame KeyTime="0">
        <DiscreteObjectKeyFrame.Value>
          <Visibility>Visible</Visibility>
        </DiscreteObjectKeyFrame.Value>
      </DiscreteObjectKeyFrame>
    </ObjectAnimationUsingKeyFrames>
    <DoubleAnimationUsingKeyFrames Storyboard.TargetProperty="(UIElement.Opacity)"
        Storyboard.TargetName="rectangle">
      <EasingDoubleKeyFrame KeyTime="0" Value="0"/>
      <EasingDoubleKeyFrame KeyTime="0:0:0.5" Value="1"/>
    </DoubleAnimationUsingKeyFrames>
  </Storyboard>
</VisualState>
...
```

Obviously, it is much easier for a designer to create an animation with a few simple clicks than to write the XAML. Although it is not difficult, it requires more time (and in the real world, when you work on a project, time is too valuable to waste).

The portion of XAML storyboards that most interests us is included in the item `DoubleAnimationUsingKeyFrames`—which, contrary to what it may seem, is an animation in which you define changes to properties that have values of type `Double`.

Storyboard.TargetProperty indicates to the storyboard what properties of the element specified in Storyboard.TargetName apply the changes keyframe by keyframe. In fact, you specify which are keyframes for us (at time 0 and 0.5), and declare that at time 0, the value of the property is 0, while at time 0.5, the value is 1 (100%). Then you're finished, because an animation declared in this way (with EasingDoubleKeyFrame) will increase with a linear function.

Usage

From Blend, select the target of your test in the Device panel. Press F5 or Ctrl+F5 and wait for the application to take the information from the Web. Select an element and watch the rectangle's opacity increase. Then select another and watch the unfocused element return to normal.

4-2. Changing the Skin of Your App

Problem

You want to customize your application with a different resource dictionary, depending on whether the light or dark theme is selected, and you want to test it with fake data.

Solution

You must create different dictionaries with your brushes. Then you select PhoneLightThemeVisibility and apply the theme that you prefer, using sample data created inside Blend.

How It Works

This recipe is achievable in part only with Blend. In Visual Studio, you can edit only the app.xaml.cs code, and then from one of the two instruments you create a new project for Windows Phone (in Blend, as you can see in Figure 4-7).

Once you have created the project, add a folder named Skins, and add to this folder two dictionaries, DarkTheme.xaml and LightTheme.xaml. Next, edit the app.XAML file, which will be automatically linked to the dictionary taking care to comment the two lines representing the themes to be applied (unfortunately, not at design time, but at runtime). If you also have settings that are shared by both themes, you could add a resource dictionary that contains the shared keys.

```
...
<ResourceDictionary.MergedDictionaries>
<!--<ResourceDictionary Source="Skins/DarkTheme.xaml" />-->
<!--<ResourceDictionary Source="Skins/LightTheme.xaml" />-->
</ResourceDictionary.MergedDictionaries>
...
```

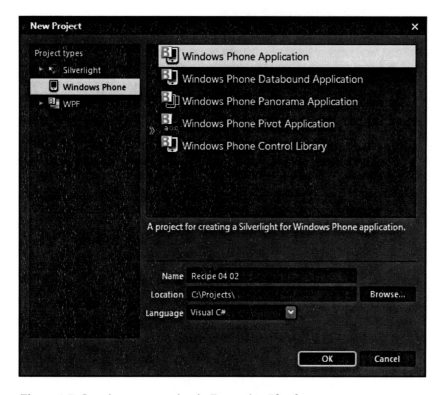

Figure 4-7. Creating a new project in Expression Blend

At this point, you use Blend's Data panel, which enables you to manage your application data sources and to generate sample data to test your pages. Another very nice feature offered by this panel is the creation of data representation from data. Follow along step by step:

Click the ![button] button to displays the menu in Figure 4-8. From this menu, select New Sample Data. A dialog box appears, where you can choose the data source's name, the point at which to define the scope, and the data source's visibility.

Call the data source `SampleDataSource`. If you are using a domain-oriented approach, consider creating the data source at the project level so that you can reuse it in another view. And because this is an application that is simply allowing you to take into consideration these features offered by Blend, enable the sample data at runtime.

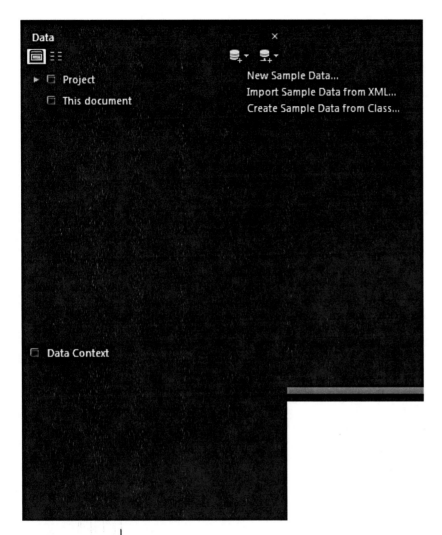

Figure 4-8. Data panel inside Blend

At this point, the base template has generated a data source called `SampleDataSource`, which (through the template hierarchy that you see in Figure 4-8) will have a complex type called `SampleDataSource`. Within the complex type, you can find a collection of objects composed of two properties called `Property1` and `Property2` (which will be the ones that are going to change).

To simulate an application domain, think of your application as an organizer that lets you keep track of your money. Rename the two properties automatically generated by the tool as `Reason` and `Money`, and add another by clicking the plus (+) symbol next to collection and naming it `Date`.

At this point, by clicking the Edit Sample Value button ![button], you can edit the values that the properties must take. For `Date`, you define a type `String ↗ Date` (remember that Windows Phone doesn't have `StringFormat` in binding). For `Money`, you define a type `String ↗ Price`, and for `Reason`, you use

187

String ↗ loremipsum. From this screen, you can specify the number of items that must be contained in your collection. To have a good amount of data, we have chosen 30.

Assuming that it was up to the developer to create the sample data source, it's now up to the designer to create a view template. (It is true that often these two job titles merge into one person, but it's always nice to talk of an ideal world.) And assuming that you are the designer, in this case, we inform that this professional figure needs a lot of inventiveness, and the use of a lot of noncode tool.

In fact, you can just drag the collection contained in the data source on the page where you want it to display the list to create a list box that already has an `ItemTemplate`. Unfortunately, the basic template is not as appealing as a designer might hope, but it still saves a bit of work.

```
...
<DataTemplate x:Key="ItemTemplate">
  <StackPanel>
    <TextBlock Text="{Binding Date}"/>
    <TextBlock Text="{Binding Money}"/>
    <TextBlock Text="{Binding Reason}"/>
</StackPanel>
</DataTemplate>
...
```

Starting from this template, you want to get a table design, and then you will delete the `StackPanel` to get a `Grid` to define columns from 182/76/200 pixels (above the list box, you will create another `Grid` with the same columns to make the header of the grid).

Then the XAML for your template must be similar to this:

```
<DataTemplate x:Key="ItemTemplate">
        <Grid>
  <Grid.ColumnDefinitions>
                <ColumnDefinition Width="182" />
    <ColumnDefinition Width="76" />
    <ColumnDefinition Width="200" />
  </Grid.ColumnDefinitions>
  <TextBlock Text="{Binding Date}" />
  <TextBlock Text="{Binding Money}" Grid.Column="1" />
  <TextBlock Text="{Binding Reason}" Grid.Column="2" />
</Grid>
</DataTemplate>
```

▪ **Note** For more information about data binding, see Chapter 10.

At this point, the information is displayed in white on black, and vice versa, depending on the theme. Create your theme and try it to see if you like the result. The wisest choice is to uncomment the chosen theme and use the Device panel to change the theme of your phone. So, first you define within the dark theme the following brushes:

```
...
<SolidColorBrush x:Key="DateBrush" Color="#FFFFFFFF" />
<SolidColorBrush x:Key="ReasonBrush" Color="#FBBEBE00" />
<SolidColorBrush x:Key="MoneyBrush" Color="#FFFF0000" />
...
```

In the light theme, the brushes are defined the same way, but with different colors:

```
...
<SolidColorBrush x:Key="DateBrush" Color="#FF160FF9" />
<SolidColorBrush x:Key="ReasonBrush" Color="#FBE707AB" />
<SolidColorBrush x:Key="MoneyBrush" Color="#FFA90000" />
...
```

You now have two themes and you have tested them in various combinations for the phone. The last thing to do is apply them at runtime. Unlike everything you've done so far, this task must be done by hand with code at runtime, because only at this time can you know which theme has been chosen by the user.

Within the `App.xaml.cs` file, create a private method that has the scope to apply the theme and call it (with extreme imagination) `ApplyTheme()`. This method should be invoked to raise either of the events `Launching` or `Activated` for the simple reason that, in case your application has been simply reactivated following a tombstoning, you must be ready to acknowledge any change in theme settings made by the user in the meantime.

```
...
private void Application_Launching(object sender, LaunchingEventArgs e)
{
        ApplyTheme();
}

private void Application_Activated(object sender, ActivatedEventArgs e)
{
        ApplyTheme();
}

private void ApplyTheme()
{
  Visibility vis = (Visibility)Application.Current.Resources["PhoneLightThemeVisibility"];
  ResourceDictionary dict = new ResourceDictionary();
  dict.Source = new Uri((vis == System.Windows.Visibility.Visible)
      ? "/Skins/LightTheme.xaml"
      : "/Skins/DarkTheme.xaml", UriKind.Relative);

  Application.Current.Resources.MergedDictionaries.Clear();
  Application.Current.Resources.MergedDictionaries.Add(dict);
}
...
```

The method `ApplyTheme()` checks the value of the system resource `PhoneLightThemeVisibility`. If `Visible` loads the dictionary for the theme, the application uses the light theme; otherwise it uses dark. After this, it cleans the `MergedDictionaries` collection of the application and adds the dictionary you have just loaded. This enables you to have different views, depending on the theme that the user has chosen.

Usage

You can run the project from Blend or Visual Studio by pressing F5. Look for the information displayed according to the color scheme you've chosen with respect to the mood of the user. Now go back to the start page, pressing the windows button. Enter the settings and change the theme to light or dark depending on what you had before. Go back into your application and view it in the theme with the mood chosen, but with the colors changed for better display.

4-3. Creating Some Cool Animation

Problem

You want to add animations to your application, to make the interaction with the user more interesting.

Solution

You will consider the idea of creating storyboard-based animations, and bind them to the various states of your controls.

How It Works

You will modify `7Drum`, our pilot project, and change the three text blocks into three buttons. You will add a different effect to each button by creating a template for each and applying transformations to the elements that make up the template. The interface will then become animated, offering the user a more interactive experience.

The Code

Open the `7Drum` project from Blend and open the main page. Let's start with the comment on the three text blocks:

```
<!--
<TextBlock x:Name="tbRecordGroove" Text="Take your groove" Style="{StaticResource
    PhoneTextExtraLargeStyle}" ManipulationStarted="tbRecordGroove_ManipulationStarted"
    HorizontalAlignment="Center" VerticalAlignment="Center" Padding="0 34" />

<TextBlock x:Name="tbTraining" Text="Training" Style="{StaticResource
    PhoneTextExtraLargeStyle}" ManipulationStarted="tbTraining_ManipulationStarted"
```

```
            HorizontalAlignment="Center" VerticalAlignment="Center" Padding="0 34" />

<TextBlock x:Name="tbMetronome" Text="Metronome" Style="{StaticResource
    PhoneTextExtraLargeStyle}" ManipulationStarted="tbMetronome_ManipulationStarted"
    HorizontalAlignment="Center" VerticalAlignment="Center" Padding="0 34" />
-->
```

Then add the three buttons:

```
<Button x:Name="RecordGrooveButton" Content="Take your groove" />
<Button x:Name="TrainingButton" Content="Training" />
<Button x:Name="MetronomeButton" Content="Metronome" />
```

For the first button, you want its size to decrease and then increase at regular intervals when the button is pressed.

First you have to convert the base template button in a custom template. Right-click RecordGrooveButton and choose Edit Template ↗ Edit A Copy, naming it GrooveButtonTemplate. As always, we prefer the dictionary-based approach to organize our styles. Then, in the screen of creating the dictionary, you create a dictionary called SevenDrumButtonTemplates, because that's where you will put the template to use for the various buttons. You now have a template on which to work.

First you access the animation mode of the Blend interface by pressing F6 on your keyboard. For this first button, you do not need to add elements to the template for this type of animation, but you do have to select the state of all that you want to animate. In the States panel, select the state Pressed and then select the Border element called ButtonBackground, which contains the element ContentControl that acts as a container for the content you choose. Even before you have changed something, you expand the node of the tree view to display the children of ButtonBackground, note that has already set an animation, which develops all in the instant 0 in the timeline, when the button changes its color when touched.

Once you have selected ButtonBackground, move the yellow playhead along the timeline at instant 0.1 (the animation grows in a short time). In the Properties panel, select the Transform section from the list of sections and then tab Scales (as in Figure 4-9), bringing the values of X and Y to about 0.8

In this way, you have created the first part of the animation. Unfortunately, the animation is limited to execute only once, without then increase again the proportions as we have planned before. So select the animation of the RenderTransform property on the value of ScaleX and edit the XAML (this method is faster than having to select the various property and edit values in the Properties panel) to set the AutoReverse property to true, so that the animation will re-create the condition of the button enlargement, and set the RepeatBehavior to Forever so that there is a loop in the animation.

```
...
<DoubleAnimationUsingKeyFrames
Storyboard.TargetProperty="(UIElement.RenderTransform).(CompositeTransform.ScaleX)"
Storyboard.TargetName="ButtonBackground" AutoReverse="True" RepeatBehavior="Forever">
      <EasingDoubleKeyFrame KeyTime="0" Value="1"/>
      <EasingDoubleKeyFrame KeyTime="0:0:0.1" Value="0.8"/>
</DoubleAnimationUsingKeyFrames>

<DoubleAnimationUsingKeyFrames
Storyboard.TargetProperty="(UIElement.RenderTransform).(CompositeTransform.ScaleY)"
Storyboard.TargetName="ButtonBackground"  AutoReverse="True" RepeatBehavior="Forever">
      <EasingDoubleKeyFrame KeyTime="0" Value="1"/>
```

```
    <EasingDoubleKeyFrame KeyTime="0:0:0.1" Value="0.8"/>
</DoubleAnimationUsingKeyFrames>
...
```

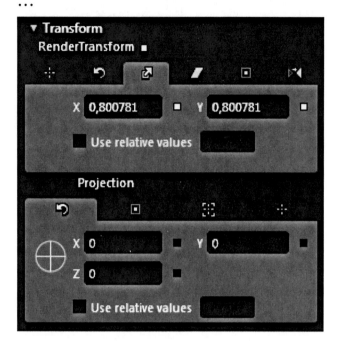

Figure 4-9. Transform section inside the Properties panel

Now your first animation of the button is ready, and you can move on to the next animation. In this case, you want the button area to become smaller and will be only a rectangle that widens and narrows to do animation.

As before, your first task is to edit a copy of the button's current template, placing it in the resource dictionary that you created earlier. Call the template `TrainingButtonTemplate`. Unlike before, this time you will go deeper into the study of why you need to modify the template by adding a `Rectangle` that will create the button animation that you desire. The template consists of a main `Grid` control.

```
...
<ControlTemplateTargetType="Button">
  <Grid Background="Transparent">
...
```

Inside of is set the value of the attached property `VisualStateManager.VisualStateGroups`, which defines the various states that the control can assume. If you read it, you will find that it contains various `Storyboard` that we have defined. Immediately under the definition of this attached property, you will put a rectangle that will have as its margin the system resource `PhoneTouchTargetOverhang` and the `PhoneAccentBrush` as `Stroke` color to fit just the size of the border `ButtonBackground`, like a unique element.

```
...
<Rectangle Margin="{StaticResourcePhoneTouchTargetOverhang}"
Stroke="{StaticResourcePhoneAccentBrush}" />
<Border x:Name="ButtonBackground"
...
```

Now you have the controls that you need and you can proceed with the creation of the storyboard.

Select from the States panel the `Pressed` state and select `ButtonBackground` that you want to remain smaller for all the time of the pressure. Move the playhead along the timeline to 0.04 seconds (if you have difficulty doing so, you need to disable snapping to the timeline), as you did with the previous button size climbing up to 0.8, but in this case, you do not want your storyboard to be performed cyclically, so you will not define `RepeatBehavior`, and you don't want to run back, so you will not define the autoreverse (which by default is set to `false`).

So for this animation, you have this XAML:

```
<DoubleAnimationUsingKeyFrames
    Storyboard.TargetProperty="(UIElement.RenderTransform).(CompositeTransform.ScaleX)"
    Storyboard.TargetName="ButtonBackground">
  <EasingDoubleKeyFrame KeyTime="0" Value="1"/>
  <EasingDoubleKeyFrame KeyTime="0:0:0.04" Value="0.8"/>
</DoubleAnimationUsingKeyFrames>
<DoubleAnimationUsingKeyFrames
    Storyboard.TargetProperty="(UIElement.RenderTransform).(CompositeTransform.ScaleY)"
    Storyboard.TargetName="ButtonBackground">
  <EasingDoubleKeyFrame KeyTime="0" Value="1"/>
  <EasingDoubleKeyFrame KeyTime="0:0:0.04" Value="0.8"/>
</DoubleAnimationUsingKeyFrames>
```

Now you just have to animate the rectangle that you added earlier. Therefore, always remaining within the editing of the `Pressed` state, select the rectangle and move the playhead to the beginning of the timeline if it isn't there already. You create a keyframe and then, moving along the timeline at the level of 0.20 seconds, scale the rectangle to 0.8 for both the x- and y-axis. In this case, however, you define an infinite loop, and set `Autoreverse` to `true` so that the animation will expand and shrink the rectangle continuously, until the finger is on the button. Your XML should look like this:

```
<DoubleAnimationUsingKeyFrames AutoReverse="True" RepeatBehavior="Forever"
    Storyboard.TargetProperty="(UIElement.RenderTransform).(CompositeTransform.ScaleX)"
    Storyboard.TargetName="rectangle">
  <EasingDoubleKeyFrame KeyTime="0" Value="1"/>
  <EasingDoubleKeyFrame KeyTime="0:0:0.2" Value="0.8"/>
</DoubleAnimationUsingKeyFrames>
<DoubleAnimationUsingKeyFrames AutoReverse="True" RepeatBehavior="Forever"
    Storyboard.TargetProperty="(UIElement.RenderTransform).(CompositeTransform.ScaleY)"
    Storyboard.TargetName="rectangle">
  <EasingDoubleKeyFrame KeyTime="0" Value="1"/>
  <EasingDoubleKeyFrame KeyTime="0:0:0.2" Value="0.8"/>
</DoubleAnimationUsingKeyFrames>
```

It's time to animate the last button. This time, the animation will be a bit more 3D. As the user presses the button, it will flip along the y-axis.

As with the other buttons, you have to edit the template in the usual way, so right-click the button and edit the template as `MetronomeButtonTemplate`. You are using this naming convention because you are applying this style exclusively to the button itself. However, from the perspective of reusing these animations, you should indicate the name of the animation so that in your future projects, you can link in `app.xaml` the dictionary with templates and animations so you can use them anywhere.

Because you're editing the Metronome button, you want to give the button an oscillating movement in order to stay in the topic, and then select as usual the `Pressed` status and the `ButtonBackground Border` to edit the properties of the latter in time.

In the Properties panel under the transform section, you have other kinds of transformations to apply to objects, including projection that is the arrangement of control along the x-, y- and z-axis.

At instant 0:00.1, you set the Y value of the `Projection` property to 18. Then in the instant 0: 00.3, you set it to -18. Finally, at instant 0:00.4, you reset it to 0. In this way, there is perpetual movement and adjustments over time. You also have to set `RepeatBehavior` to `Forever` for this animation to be ready.

The XAML resulting from these steps is as follows:

```
<DoubleAnimationUsingKeyFrames RepeatBehavior="Forever"
Storyboard.TargetProperty="(UIElement.Projection).(PlaneProjection.RotationY)"
Storyboard.TargetName="ButtonBackground">
        <EasingDoubleKeyFrame KeyTime="0" Value="0"/>
   <EasingDoubleKeyFrame KeyTime="0:0:0.1" Value="18"/>
   <EasingDoubleKeyFrame KeyTime="0:0:0.3" Value="-18"/>
   <EasingDoubleKeyFrame KeyTime="0:0:0.4" Value="0"/>
</DoubleAnimationUsingKeyFrames>
```

This animation presents a lot to consider, including the fact that it develops with regular intervals, just like a metronome. In this way, the animation draws the user's attention to what awaits when he or she clicks that button. The animation itself completes in a short time, adding a visual benefit to the user. (An animation with too much time on a control that should just manage the TAP does not make sense.)

Now you have to perform the developer's task and create the event handler to manage the `Click` event of all three buttons, so they do what they were doing before the text blocks.

Then the three event handlers will be so:

```
private void RecordGrooveButton_Click(object sender, System.Windows.RoutedEventArgs e)
{
        this.NavigationService.Navigate(new Uri("/VirtualDrum.xaml", UriKind.Relative));
}

private void TrainingButton_Click(object sender, RoutedEventArgs e)
{
        this.NavigationService.Navigate(new Uri("/Training.xaml", UriKind.Relative));
}

private void MetronomeButton_Click(object sender, RoutedEventArgs e)
{
        this.NavigationService.Navigate(new Uri("/Metronome.xaml", UriKind.Relative));
}
```

Usage

From Expression Blend, run the project by pressing F5 or Ctrl+F5. Click all three buttons to test that all the animations work, and relative event handler.

4-4. Customizing a Control

Problem

You would like to have a customized button that shows an image instead of the usual written text.

Solution

You have several solutions to this problem, each with its pros and cons. We will be listing them all, and then providing a definitive template that reflects what we want from this customization.

How It Works

With XAML, you have the ability to create multiple controls together—so, for example, items in a list box can be a series of check boxes. You can also use XAML to set the contents of a button to be an image rather than text. Finally, you can customize the behavior of a check box so that it has a different symbol than the standard by editing the template to modify the path representing the usual check mark.

The Code

From Expression Blend, create a new project for Windows Phone and call it `PlayWithControlTemplate`. Do not create a pilot project for this recipe, because you could use this information in all your applications, and consequently bring your template around your products. (Suppose you have created a suite of products and you want each product within the suite to have a uniform look so your users are automatically comfortable using each one.)

In this project, the first thing you do is add an `Images` folder and add an image named `TestImage.png` (Look at this link if you want some information about this image format: `www.libpng.org/pub/png/pngintro.html`). In this example, the image is the one shown in Figure 4-10, but you are free to choose another.

Figure 4-10. *Our icon*

The first thing you want to get is an image that works just like a button. There are several ways to achieve this goal, but the easiest is to use an image instead of text as the content of the button. Here is an example:

```
<Button x:Name="ImageButton" Height="84" >
  <Image Source="Images/TestImage.png" />
</Button>
```

This code creates a button, shown in Figure 4-11, which is apparently already a button that is acceptable, but lacks some specialties. For example, if it has kept the edge to the content, then we have to edit the template of the button to remove the Board and add to our button some small effect to make it complete. Then, as always, right-click the button and edit the template, calling it `ImageButtonTemplate`.

First, you need to locate `ButtonBackground`, which currently is an element of type `Border`. You want to delete it or replace it with a common `Grid`, whose `Background` remains bound to the template. Then this `Grid` will add a rectangle that you will call `OverlayRectangle` and will fill with black so that its opacity is 100% not visible initially.

Figure 4-11. An image as content

The addition of this rectangle to afford when the button is disabled, showing an overlay on the image (or any other custom content).

Then the XAML that you need to use is similar to the following:

```
<Gridx:Name="ButtonBackground"Background="{TemplateBinding Background}"
    Margin="{StaticResource PhoneTouchTargetOverhang}">
        <ContentControl x:Name="ContentContainer" ContentTemplate="{TemplateBinding
            ContentTemplate}" Content="{TemplateBinding Content}" Foreground="{TemplateBinding
            Foreground}" HorizontalContentAlignment="{TemplateBinding
            HorizontalContentAlignment}" Padding="{TemplateBinding Padding}"
            VerticalContentAlignment="{TemplateBinding VerticalContentAlignment}"/>
        <Rectangle x:Name="OverlayRectangle" Fill="#B0000000" Visibility="Collapsed" />
</Grid>
```

Now you have to edit the statuses disabled and pressed. (This step is avoidable if you don't remove the `Border`, but as you change it with the `Grid`, remember that if you do, it will result in an error in the storyboard, because unlike the `Grid`, it does not have a border attribute as `BorderBrush`.) To complete this custom control, press F6 to toggle to storyboard mode and select the `Pressed` state, and then the grid, changing the background to `{StaticResourcePhoneForegroundBrush}`. Just as before, the button will change color from black to white (and vice versa), depending on the visual theme chosen by the user (which should always be taken into account). The XAML for this effect should be similar to this:

```
<VisualState x:Name="Pressed">
  <Storyboard>
    <ObjectAnimationUsingKeyFrames Storyboard.TargetProperty="Background"
Storyboard.TargetName="ButtonBackground">
```

```
        <DiscreteObjectKeyFrame KeyTime="0" Value="{StaticResource PhoneForegroundBrush}"/>
      </ObjectAnimationUsingKeyFrames>
    </Storyboard>
  </VisualState>
```

You are changing the foreground color because you are thinking of abstracting this template compared to contents (contrary to what is chosen for the naming convention of the templates) so that if you apply this style to a button with text as its content, you would get the same result, a reversal of the background and foreground color. The aim is always the same: to have consistent behavior across the various elements that make up the user interface so that they are part of one big picture.

Well, you just have to manage the `Disabled` state of your templates, so that the rectangle forming the overlay to show "inert" our elements to change their visibility in visible, then once again select the element and change the visibility into property in order to obtain automatically the XAML like this:

```
<VisualState x:Name="Disabled">
  <Storyboard>
    <ObjectAnimationUsingKeyFrames Storyboard.TargetProperty="(UIElement.Visibility)"
Storyboard.TargetName="OverlayRectangle">
      <DiscreteObjectKeyFrame KeyTime="0">
        <DiscreteObjectKeyFrame.Value>
          <Visibility>Visible</Visibility>
        </DiscreteObjectKeyFrame.Value>
      </DiscreteObjectKeyFrame>
    </ObjectAnimationUsingKeyFrames>
  </Storyboard>
</VisualState>
```

Note: If you have previously changed the `Border` control in XAML to a `Grid` control and then haven't deleted the storyboard attached to it, you'll end up with a change of the foreground color in this case. However, it does nothing more than what is already done by the rectangle, except that in this case it also applies to images, and in either case applies only to text.

The template is ready, as you have customized the button template. Earlier, we said that you could create this template in several ways—and there is also a reverse way that could come in handy if you wanted to give a background image to your button while keeping a "normal" behavior compared to textual content.

This template will depart from using an item image for a button control. The process is virtually automatic thanks to Blend, and allows you to achieve satisfactory results with regard to the user experience. Our image for the button, shown in Figure 4-12, represents a prototype idea of a circular button.

Insert it into your own XAML as a normal image:

```
<Image Source="Images/Circle Button Red.png" />
```

So now you just have to right-click and choose the menu item Make Into Control. At this point, you will see a screen for selecting the controls that you can achieve starting from this image. In our case, we chose a button, but if you had a different image that represented, for example, a sheet of notebook paper, you might have considered using a list box.

Figure 4-12. The base image for our button

Name the template CircleButtonTemplate. If you try to, you will realize that the button is inert; it does not react to changes in state, to user pressure, or to being disabled. So you have to define the behavior under these conditions. Although this is unlike the type of template that you created earlier, it's not a big problem. All you have to do to start is add two ellipses to the template that will overlay the button's Pressed and Disabled states. You could also use a rectangle to achieve this goal, but just to let you see that you can achieve the same result in this manner, this example uses an ellipse.

The first ellipse, PressedEllipse, will overlay the image when the button is pressed. The second ellipse, DisabledEllipse, will, as its name suggests, overlay the image when the button is disabled.

Both ellipses must have their visibility set to Collapsed. Their opacity mask must be the image that you used to create the button. The fill color is white for the pressed state and gray for the disabled state. Both are not entirely opaque and have a good level of transparency.

```
<Ellipse x:Name="PressedEllipse" Visibility="Collapsed" Fill="#72DEDADA" >
        <Ellipse.OpacityMask>
    <ImageBrush Stretch="Uniform" ImageSource="Images/Circle Button Red.png"/>
  </Ellipse.OpacityMask>
</Ellipse>
<Ellipse x:Name="DisabledEllipse" Visibility="Collapsed" Fill="#B2787878" >
        <Ellipse.OpacityMask>
    <ImageBrush Stretch="Uniform" ImageSource="Images/Circle Button Red.png"/>
  </Ellipse.OpacityMask>
</Ellipse>
```

At this point, edit the Pressed state storyboard, and set the PressedEllipse visibility to Visible, and do the same for the Disabled state on DisabledEllipse in order to obtain an interactive button.

At the end of this edit, your XAML should be like this:

```
...
<VisualState x:Name="Pressed">
  <Storyboard>
    <ObjectAnimationUsingKeyFrames Storyboard.TargetProperty="(UIElement.Visibility)"
Storyboard.TargetName="PressedEllipse">
      <DiscreteObjectKeyFrame KeyTime="0">
        <DiscreteObjectKeyFrame.Value>
```

```
      <Visibility>Visible</Visibility>
    </DiscreteObjectKeyFrame.Value>
  </DiscreteObjectKeyFrame>
</ObjectAnimationUsingKeyFrames>
</Storyboard>
</VisualState>

<VisualState x:Name="Disabled">
  <Storyboard>
    <ObjectAnimationUsingKeyFrames Storyboard.TargetProperty="(UIElement.Visibility)"
Storyboard.TargetName="DisabledEllipse">
      <DiscreteObjectKeyFrame KeyTime="0">
        <DiscreteObjectKeyFrame.Value>
          <Visibility>Visible</Visibility>
        </DiscreteObjectKeyFrame.Value>
      </DiscreteObjectKeyFrame>
    </ObjectAnimationUsingKeyFrames>
  </Storyboard>
</VisualState>
...
```

Now you have a fully functional button. And now that you've learned how to customize the data template, button, and interaction with these tools, understanding how to change the template of a check box will be much easier.

A check box template is composed of various elements: a content container, which allows you to specify the text to display (as you may have guessed, even in this case you could use an image); a path (a sequence of points connected by lines that make up a figure) that is made visible when the check box is selected; and a rectangle that is made visible in the case of an indeterminate state (as in the case of three state check box).

Suppose that for your application, you want your check box to be marked with an X instead of the usual check mark. You also want to display a question mark instead of a square for the indeterminate state. The first thing to do is get the path that reflects this forms. We recommend using Microsoft Expression Design for this purpose because creating a path by hand can be too difficult. To create an X, the code would be written as follows:

```
<Path x:Name="CheckMark" Fill="{StaticResource PhoneRadioCheckBoxCheckBrush}" Width="25"
Height="25" Canvas.Left="0" Canvas.Top="0" Stretch="Fill" StrokeLineJoin="Round"
Stroke="#FF000000" Data="F1 M 0.5,2.47917L 2.46875,0.5L 12.4687,10.4792L 22.4687,0.500002L
24.5,2.47917L 14.4687,12.4792L 24.5,22.4792L 22.4687,24.5L 12.4687,14.4792L 2.46875,24.5L
0.5,22.4792L 10.4687,12.4792L 0.5,2.47917 Z "/>
```

The path to get the question mark will more or less take this form:

```
<Path x:Name="IndeterminateMark" Fill="{StaticResourcePhoneRadioCheckBoxCheckBrush}"
Width="11.2721" Height="21.6238" Canvas.Left="0" Canvas.Top="0" Stretch="Fill" Data="F1 M
3.33606,15.3168C 3.24626,15.0697 3.16511,14.7475 3.09259,14.3501C 3.02006,13.9528
2.9838,13.5571 2.9838,13.1629C 2.9838,12.5529 3.1228,12.0015 3.40081,11.5087C 3.67881,11.016
4.02589,10.5546 4.44203,10.1244C 4.85817,9.69425 5.31144,9.28051 5.80183,8.8832C
6.29223,8.48589 6.7455,8.08388 7.16164,7.67719C 7.57778,7.27049 7.92486,6.84502
```

```
8.20286,6.40078C 8.48087,5.95655 8.61987,5.46538 8.61987,4.92729C 8.61987,4.47054
8.51885,4.06462 8.31683,3.70955C 8.1148,3.35447 7.83852,3.05726 7.48799,2.81794C
7.13747,2.57861 6.73254,2.39951 6.27323,2.28063C 5.81392,2.16175 5.32698,2.10231
4.81241,2.10231C 2.96135,2.10231 1.35722,2.80308 0,4.20462L 0,1.48288C 1.67493,0.494293
3.41203,0 5.21129,0C …
```

It does not seem necessary to continue with all the points contained in this path. We introduce it only to explain how much important is for a designer who intends to customize his own interface, the use of a tool such as Design to get XAML like this.

Usage

To use this recipe, use an alternative form to create a dictionary in which you insert all the effects, styles, and templates that were shown. Then apply them to 7Drum or some other application. Note how important (and clever) it is as a designer to create your own dictionary of effects (while always trying to improve the graphics rendering) to keep in touch in the creation of an application. And if you're a developer, you can do the same thing, if you want to do without a designer on your next application.

CHAPTER 5

Gestures

With the introduction of the touch screen on phones, the way users interact with these devices has radically changed as compared to traditional mouse usage on personal computers. The same is true for the pen stylus input device, used for example, with BlackBerry phones; however, although the pen stylus emulates the mouse, it doesn't offer any new way to interact with the device.

The input interface revolution was born with the iPhone and iPod Touch devices, on which you can use your fingers to zoom in or zoom out on pictures, scroll text, and much more. Windows Phone inherits iPhone input interface directives, enabling similar gestures to accomplish user interaction with the phone.

In this chapter, you will learn which gestures are provided by Windows Phone and how to use them in your application. The recipes in this chapter describe how to do the following:

- 5-1. Manage gestures in a Silverlight Windows Phone application

- 5-2. Add gestures management to Click-less Silverlight controls

- 5-3. Handle gestures in a graphical context, such as a game menu

- 5-4. Manage gestures from the Silverlight for Windows Phone toolkit

5-1. Managing Gestures in a Silverlight Windows Phone Application

Problem

You need to understand what gestures are and how to use them in your Silverlight Windows Phone application.

Solution

Various techniques are available for enabling you to know where a user touched the screen and how many fingers were used. You can use the Touch static class, which provides the FrameReported event rose when the screen is touched. Along with the Touch static class, you can use the GetTouchPoints method from the TouchFrameEventArgs argument provided by the FrameReported event handler. The

GetTouchPoints method returns a TouchPointCollection collection filled with TouchPoint objects representing touched screen points.

But using the TouchPointCollection to understand gestures is not so easy. You have to study the collection to understand how the user's fingers have moved on the screen and what that user's intentions could be. You should use—along with the Touch.FrameReported event handler—the TouchPanel class included in the XNA framework. The TouchPanel class, along with the GestureSample structure, really simplifies the recognition of gestures by your application (see Figure 5-1 for diagrams of these classes).

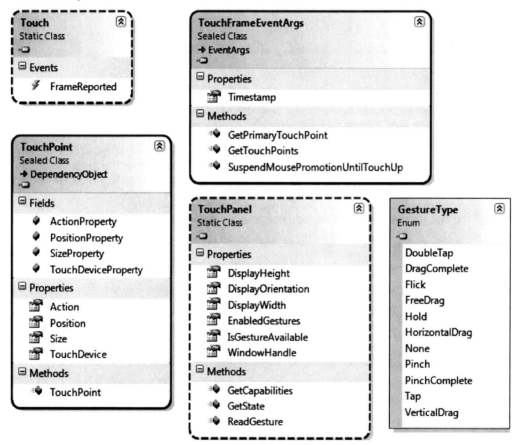

Figure 5-1. *Class diagram for gesture classes*

How It Works

Gestures are operations carried out with one or more fingers on the phone's touch screen. Windows Phone supports having at least four fingers on the screen. A finger can touch the screen and immediately rise up, or it can touch the screen and move in any direction while remaining pressed on the screen.

Each operation that the user's fingers perform on the touch screen represents a gesture. In Table 5-1, you can see the list of supported gestures. The most used are Tap, Double Tap, Pinch and Flick.

Most Silverlight controls provide Click and Double Click event handlers when the user taps and double-taps on the control itself, but you might need other gestures in your application. For example, imagine a book reader application in which the user needs to scroll through pages quickly. Implementing a Tap gesture to scroll page by page would be frustrating for the user. Much better: the Flick gesture, which returns finger-moving speed with the Delta property provided by the GestureSample structure. You could use this Vector2 value returned by the Delta property to enable the user to move faster across the book pages.

Table 5-1. All the Gestures Provided by the GestureType Enumeration

Gesture	Description
Tap	The finger touches and immediately rises up from the touch screen.
Double Tap	The same as the Tap gesture, but touching and rising two times, one right after the other.
Horizontal Drag	The finger touches the screen, continues to press it, and moves horizontally.
Vertical Drag	The same as Horizontal Drag, but the movement is vertical.
Free Drag	The finger touches the screen, continues to press it, and moves freely.
Drag Complete	The finger starts a drag gesture and completes it by raising the finger.
Flick	The finger touches the screen and moves either up or down very fast. This is the gesture used to quickly remove the lock screen.
Pinch	Two fingers touch the screen, moving either apart or together. This is the gesture used to either zoom into or zoom out from an image.
Pinch Complete	Two fingers start the Pinch gesture and complete it by raising both fingers.
Hold	The finger touches the screen and continues to press it without moving.

To use gestures in your application, you first need to complete the following steps:

1. Add a reference to both the `Microsoft.Xna.Framework.dll` and `Microsoft.Xna.Framework.Input.Touch.dll` assemblies.

2. Define a `FrameReported` event handler.

3. Define all the gestures you want to trap in your application by specifying them in the `EnabledGestures` property from the `TouchPanel` class separated by the `OR` logical operator.

4. In the `FrameReported` event handler, check whether a gesture is available by using the `IsGestureAvailable` property from the `TouchPanel` class.

5. Define a `GestureSample` object that receives gestures from the `ReadGesture` method provided by the `TouchPanel` class.

6. Use the gesture accordingly in your application.

The Code

To demonstrate every gesture provided by the phone, we have created a simple application that writes the gesture type on the page title.

Start Visual Studio 2010 and create a new Silverlight Windows Phone application called GesturesDemo. In the `MainPage.xaml` file, add a row definition to the content grid, specifying a new row with the `Height` property equal to `Auto`. Inside the content grid, add an image that fills the entire grid.

```
. . .
<!--ContentPanel - place additional content here-->
       <Grid x:Name="ContentPanel" Grid.Row="1" Margin="12,0,12,0">
           <Grid.RowDefinitions>
               <RowDefinition Height="Auto" />
           </Grid.RowDefinitions>

           <Image x:Name="imgBackground" Grid.Row="0" Stretch="Fill"
               Source="/images/background.png"/>
       </Grid>
. . .
```

░ **Note** We have added an image control just to give to the application a better look, but the image control is not necessary to retrieve gestures. The `Touch.FrameReported` event is the only one that catches gestures because it is implemented into the `PhoneApplicationFrame` class.

The `MainPage.xaml.cs` file—more specifically, in the `MainPage` constructor—contains the necessary instructions for defining the gestures that you need to catch. In our case, we want to catch all the available gestures, so we specify them all, separating them by the `OR` logical operator in the

EnabledGestures property. Moreover, the FrameReported event is defined and managed by the Touch_FrameReported event handler.

```
. . .
// Constructor
      public MainPage()
      {
          InitializeComponent();
          Touch.FrameReported += new TouchFrameEventHandler(Touch_FrameReported);
          TouchPanel.EnabledGestures = GestureType.Tap
                                  | GestureType.DoubleTap
                                  | GestureType.Flick
                                  | GestureType.Pinch
                                  | GestureType.HorizontalDrag
                                  | GestureType.VerticalDrag
                                  | GestureType.PinchComplete
                                  | GestureType.DragComplete
                                  | GestureType.Hold
                                  | GestureType.FreeDrag;
      }
```

In the Touch_FrameReported event handler, the IsGestureAvailable property is checked to determine whether a gesture has been caught by the frame. If it has, the ReadGesture method is used to retrieve a GestureSample object. This object contains useful information (via the GestureType property) indicating which gesture has been performed by the user, and eventually extra information depending on the gesture type. For example, in our code when the Flick gesture occurs, we also print on the screen the Delta property.

The TouchFrameEventArgs parameter provided by the FrameReported event contains some cool information, such as a TimeSpan value set to the time—when the gesture has occurred. This gesture has been used in the 7Drum application to store drum component playing sequences and the times when they occur.

```
      void Touch_FrameReported(object sender, TouchFrameEventArgs e)
      {
          if (TouchPanel.IsGestureAvailable)
          {
              GestureSample gesture = TouchPanel.ReadGesture();

              PageTitle.Text = gesture.GestureType.ToString();

              if (gesture.GestureType == GestureType.Flick)
                  PageTitle.Text += " " + gesture.Delta.ToString();
          }
      }
```

Usage

In this recipe, you need a physical device to test the application. Indeed, the emulator is not able to intercept multi-touch gestures such as the Pinch.

Connect your unlocked device (see Recipe 1-6 for more information on how to unlock devices) and run the application from Visual Studio 2010, ensuring that the output target is set to Windows Phone Device. The application will start, showing the output in Figure 5-2.

Figure 5-2. The GesturesDemo *application in action*

At this point, you can start playing with your phone. In Figure 5-3, we performed a very rapid Flick, as demonstrated by the page title showing the gesture type and the Delta property value.

Figure 5-3. The page title shows that a Flick gesture has occurred.

5-2. Adding Gestures Management to Click-less Silverlight Controls

Problem

You need to add gestures to the controls that don't provide the Click event.

Solution

You need to use the Behavior class defined in the System.Windows.Interactivity.dll assembly.

How It Works

Almost all Silverlight controls in Windows Phone have the Tap and Double Tap gestures associated to the Click and Double Click events. By the way, there are controls such as Grid (which inherits from the Panel control) that provide neither the Click nor Double Click events.

Examining the parent classes from which the Panel class derives, we arrive at the UIElement class that provides mouse events. Obviously, a Windows Phone doesn't have a mouse, but the events are fired the same when a finger touches the screen. You can manage MouseLeftButtonDown and MouseLeftButtonUp events to simulate the Tap or the Double Tap gestures on controls that derive from the UIElement class. In your code, you have to specify the response to mouse events for each control you need to manage. This is not the best approach to have when you need to add gestures to elements that don't provide them. It would be nice to have generic and reusable code that could be applied in XAML code to every control that needs it. This can be created by using the Behavior class.

The Behavior class (see its class diagram in Figure 5-4) provides the methods to create a behavior that is applicable to controls. Each control that derives from the class specified as generic type during the behavior definition will have that behavior. It provides the OnAttached method, where you can specify the event handlers that you want to trap. You can release those event handlers in the OnDetaching method provided by the Behavior class.

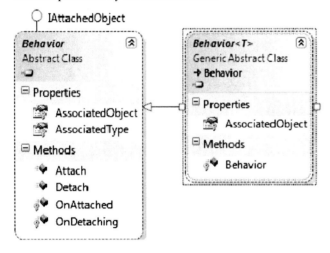

Figure 5-4. The Behavior class diagram

The Code

In the code for this recipe, you are going to add both the Tap and Hold gestures to the Grid control. Let's create a new Silverlight Windows Phone application called AddGestureDemo from Visual Studio 2010.

The first operation you are going to perform is to add a new class to the project called AddTap. You can accomplish this step from Visual Studio 2010 by choosing Project Add Class. The skeleton of AddTap class is generated.

The next thing to do is to add a reference to the System.Windows.Interactivity.dll assembly. From the Solution Explorer, right-click the project name and select Add Reference from the context menu. From the Add Reference dialog box, select the .NET tab and search for System.Windows.Interactivity.

Now you can add the using directive in the AddTap class to point to the
System.Windows.Interactivity namespace. In that way, you can derive the AddTap class from the
Behavior<UIElement> class.

Next you override the OnAttached and OnDetaching methods. For the former, you are going to define
event handlers for the MouseLeftButtonDown and MouseLeftButtonUp events. For the latter, you will detach
them.

You will use the MouseLeftButtonDown event to store the ticks from the DateTime.Now property. Those
ticks will be subtracted from the ticks picked in the MouseLeftButtonUp event and compared to the ticks
equal to 1 second. In this way, you can tell when the user taps the screen (button down and up in less
than 1 second) or when user holds a finger on the screen (button down and up in more than 1 second).
So in the former case, the DoTap event will be raised, and in the latter case, the DoHold event will be fired.

▒ **Note** We chose 1 second as the time limit to distinguish a Tap gesture from a Hold gesture, but you can change
this value simply by changing the TimeSpan.TicksPerSecond value in the if condition within the
AssociatedObject_MouseLeftButtonUp event handler.

```
. . .

using System.Windows.Interactivity;

namespace AddGestureDemo
{
    public class AddTap : Behavior<UIElement>
    {
        public event EventHandler Tap;
        public event EventHandler Hold;
        private bool _IsMousePressed;
        private TimeSpan _mouseLeftButtonDownTime;

        protected override void OnAttached()
        {
            this.AssociatedObject.MouseLeftButtonDown +=
                new MouseButtonEventHandler(AssociatedObject_MouseLeftButtonDown);
            this.AssociatedObject.MouseLeftButtonUp +=
                new MouseButtonEventHandler(AssociatedObject_MouseLeftButtonUp);
            base.OnAttached();
        }

        protected override void OnDetaching()
        {
            this.AssociatedObject.MouseLeftButtonDown -=
                AssociatedObject_MouseLeftButtonDown;
            this.AssociatedObject.MouseLeftButtonUp -= AssociatedObject_MouseLeftButtonUp;
            base.OnDetaching();
        }

        void AssociatedObject_MouseLeftButtonDown(object sender, MouseButtonEventArgs e)
```

```
    {
        _IsMousePressed = true;
        _mouseLeftButtonDownTime = TimeSpan.FromTicks(DateTime.Now.Ticks);
    }

    void AssociatedObject_MouseLeftButtonUp(object sender, MouseButtonEventArgs e)
    {
        TimeSpan _elapsedTime = TimeSpan.FromTicks(DateTime.Now.Ticks) -
                                _mouseLeftButtonDownTime;


        if (_IsMousePressed && _elapsedTime.Ticks < TimeSpan.TicksPerSecond)
            DoTap();
        else
            DoHold();

        _IsMousePressed = false;
    }

    void DoTap()
    {
        if (Tap != null)
            Tap(AssociatedObject, EventArgs.Empty);
    }

    void DoHold()
    {
        if (Hold != null)
            Hold(AssociatedObject, EventArgs.Empty);
    }
    }
}
```

In the MainPage.xaml file, you can add some directives to use the AddTap class with the content grid. First, in the namespaces definition, you have to add two new namespaces: tap and i.

Between the ContentPanel's Grid tags, you can use our new behavior by adding the following instructions:

```
<i:Interaction.Behaviors>
    <tap:AddTap Tap="AddTap_Tap" Hold="AddTap_Hold"/>
</i:Interaction.Behaviors>
```

As you will see in the following code, the i namespace is added to the PhoneApplicationPage to point to the System.Windows.Interactivity assembly.

In that way, you declare that the new behavior is associated to the grid, and it will respond to the public Tap and Hold events defined in the AddTap class.

```
<phone:PhoneApplicationPage
    x:Class="AddGestureDemo.MainPage"
```

```
    xmlns="http://schemas.microsoft.com/winfx/2006/xaml/presentation"
    xmlns:x="http://schemas.microsoft.com/winfx/2006/xaml"
    xmlns:phone="clr-namespace:Microsoft.Phone.Controls;assembly=Microsoft.Phone"
    xmlns:shell="clr-namespace:Microsoft.Phone.Shell;assembly=Microsoft.Phone"
    xmlns:d="http://schemas.microsoft.com/expression/blend/2008"
    xmlns:mc="http://schemas.openxmlformats.org/markup-compatibility/2006"
    xmlns:tap="clr-namespace:AddGestureDemo"
    xmlns:i="clr-namespace:System.Windows.Interactivity;assembly=System.Windows.Interactivity"
. . .



    <!--ContentPanel - place additional content here-->
        <Grid x:Name="ContentPanel" Grid.Row="1" Margin="12,0,12,0" Background="White">
            <i:Interaction.Behaviors>
                <tap:AddTap Tap="AddTap_Tap" Hold="AddTap_Hold"/>
            </i:Interaction.Behaviors>
        </Grid>
</Grid>
```

Finally, when the Tap and Hold events are raised, you simply show a MessageBox message indicating which gesture has been performed.

Usage

Press Ctrl+F5 from Visual Studio 2010, and be sure to select the Windows Phone Emulator as the output target. The emulator will start, briefly showing the application, as you can see in Figure 5-5.

ADD GESTURE

Add Tap

Figure 5-5. The AddGesture *application shows a white background for the content grid.*

Now press and then rapidly release the left mouse button over the white zone. A message box showing *You tapped the grid* is shown.

Now press and hold for more than 1 second the left mouse button over the white zone and then release it. A message box showing *Hold gesture in the grid* appears.

5-3. Handling Gestures in a Graphical Context, Such as a Game Menu

Problem

You have an image with sensible touch zones—for example, a graphical game menu—and you need to manage gestures only when they occur in those zones.

Solution

You can create a mask image and use the `WriteableBitmap` class to retrieve the chosen pixel color. In your code, you associate a color to an operation.

How It Works

In this recipe, we are going further with the 7Drum application developed throughout this book. In this case, you are going to examine the virtual drumming functionality. An image of a drum kit is shown on the screen, and the user can tap the drum components and hear the related sounds.

Because drum components have different sizes and shapes, memorizing their positions on the screen is not really the best thing to do. You can retrieve the position of the tap, but then you have to check which drum component has those coordinates. Because a drum component cannot have a linear shape, this is really a bad approach.

You can use the `WriteableBitmap` class, which provides the `Pixels` array used to retrieve a pixel to a provided x and y coordinate. You can create a mask image from the original image, load it in memory without showing it in your application, and use the `Pixels` array to retrieve the color of the chosen pixel. In your code, you have associated a color to an operation or a menu item, so you know what to do.

In our case, the drum-kit mask image contains different-colored zones related to drum components (see Figure 5-6). The drum-kit image shown to the user is definitely much better (see Figure 5-7).

Figure 5-6. The drum kit mask image

Figure 5-7. *The drum kit shown to the user*

When the user taps the snare, the code retrieves the pixel with blue color and plays the snare sound (see Recipe 7-3 to read more on playing sound).

■ **Note** To produce the mask image, we used the Paint.NET free drawing tool (you can download it from www.getpaint.net). You load the main image in the tool and add a new layer. You start to draw over the sensitive picture zones, giving each a different color. You remove the layer (the background, in this case) where you set the original image, remaining with the mask. Finally, you have to save the mask image in either a 16- or 256-color bitmap format so that pixels use solid colors.

The Code

To demonstrate this technique, we have added the virtual drumming functionality to the 7Drum application. Open the 7Drum project and add a Windows Phone Landscape Page called VirtualDrum.xaml. Create an images folder with the original image and the related mask image. Select the Content value from the Build Action property in the Property window. In this way, images will be added to the final XAP file as distinct files and not inserted as resources. This is done so that in the Image control, you can set the Source attribute to the image's relative path.

```
<phone:PhoneApplicationPage
    x:Class="_7Drum.VirtualDrum"
    xmlns="http://schemas.microsoft.com/winfx/2006/xaml/presentation"
```

```
xmlns:x="http://schemas.microsoft.com/winfx/2006/xaml"
xmlns:phone="clr-namespace:Microsoft.Phone.Controls;assembly=Microsoft.Phone"
xmlns:shell="clr-namespace:Microsoft.Phone.Shell;assembly=Microsoft.Phone"
xmlns:d="http://schemas.microsoft.com/expression/blend/2008"
xmlns:mc="http://schemas.openxmlformats.org/markup-compatibility/2006"
mc:Ignorable="d" d:DesignWidth="800" d:DesignHeight="480"
FontFamily="{StaticResource PhoneFontFamilyNormal}"
FontSize="{StaticResource PhoneFontSizeNormal}"
Foreground="{StaticResource PhoneForegroundBrush}"
SupportedOrientations="Landscape" Orientation="Landscape"
shell:SystemTray.IsVisible="False">

<Image x:Name="imgDrum" Source="images/Drum_Kit_480x800.jpg" Width="800" Height="480" />

</phone:PhoneApplicationPage>
```

In the `VirtualDrum.xaml.cs` file, you use the constructor code to load the mask image and add the
`FrameReported` event handler:

```
// Constructor
public VirtualDrum()
{
    InitializeComponent();

    bmpMask = new BitmapImage(new Uri("images/mask_480x800.png", UriKind.Relative));
    bmpMask.CreateOptions = BitmapCreateOptions.None;

. . .

    Touch.FrameReported += new TouchFrameEventHandler(Touch_FrameReported);
}
```

In the `Touch_FrameReported` event handler, the `GetTouchPoints` method is used to retrieve the
collection of touched points within the `TouchPointCollection` object. Next, a foreach loop goes through
the retrieved collection, checking only those points having `Action` set to the `TouchAction.Down`
enumerable value. This is necessary because the `TouchPointCollection` contains points for every kind of
operation such as drag, pinch, and so on.

The position of the tapped screen is passed to the `PickTappedColor` private method, which returns
the `Color` object of the pixel. A LINQ query is used to retrieve the drum-kit component associated to the
picked color, and the related sound is played.

```
void Touch_FrameReported(object sender, TouchFrameEventArgs e)
{
    TouchPointCollection tpc = e.GetTouchPoints(this);

    foreach (TouchPoint t in tpc)
    {
        if (t.Action == TouchAction.Down)
        {
```

```
                    System.Windows.Media.Color pickedColor = PickTappedColor(t.Position.X,
                                                                              t.Position.Y);

DrumKitComponent component = (from d in drum
                             where d.maskColor == pickedColor
                             select d).SingleOrDefault<DrumKitComponent>();

            if (component != null)
            {
                // Play sound
            }
        }
    }
}
```

Let's take a look at the PickTappedColor method in detail. An object from the WriteableBitmap class is created from the bitmap mask stored in memory. The WriteableBitmap contains the Pixels array but—surprise—it is not a two-dimensional one, so we cannot use x and y as array indexes. We need a simple math formula to transform x and y coordinates into one dimensional index. The formula is the y coordinate by the sum of the x coordinate with the bitmap width dimension.

After having retrieved the pixel, we can return the related Color by using the FromArgb static method provided by the Color class.

```
        private System.Windows.Media.Color PickTappedColor(double X, double Y)
        {
            wbmp = new WriteableBitmap(bmpMask);
            int pixel = (int)Y * (int)wbmp.PixelWidth + (int)X;
            int i = wbmp.Pixels[pixel];
            System.Windows.Media.Color color = System.Windows.Media.Color.FromArgb(255,
                                     (byte)((i >> 16) & 0xFF),
                                     (byte)((i >> 8) & 0xFF),
                                     (byte)(i & 0xFF));

            return color;
        }
```

Usage

This may be one of the most fun "Usage" sections of the entire book. We can make a lot of noise with a virtual drum! From Visual Studio 2010, press Ctrl+F5 and wait a few moments until the emulator starts (check that Windows Phone Emulator is the current output target).

From the main menu, choose Take Your Groove. The drum kit appears, as shown in Figure 5-8.

Figure 5-8. *The virtual drum in action*

Now you can tap on one or more drum components to hear the related sound.

5-4. Managing Gestures from the Silverlight for Windows Phone Toolkit

Problem

You need to implement drag-and-drop in your Silverlight Windows Phone application.

Solution

You have different options here, including using the gestures and techniques explained in the previous recipes. However, this time we suggest another solution to accomplish drag-and-drop or other gestures management: GestureListener, provided by the Silverlight for Windows Phone toolkit.

How It Works

As you saw in Chapter 3, you can download the Silverlight for Windows Phone toolkit from CodePlex at http://silverlight.codeplex.com. This toolkit provides the GestureService class, which exposes the GestureListener property. You can use this property to specify the gesture you want to manage in your application. Indeed, GestureListener provides a public event for each gesture supported by the phone, plus two more events indicating when the gesture begins and when the gesture is completed.

The Code

To demonstrate the drag-and-drop function in a Silverlight Windows Phone application, we have created the GesturesWithToolkit project. You are going to create an application in which a rectangle can be dragged around the screen. When the drag is completed, the code checks whether the rectangle has been dropped over another rectangle.

Create a new Visual Studio 2010 Silverlight Windows Phone application called GesturesWithToolkit. Add a reference to the Microsoft.Phone.Controls.Toolkit assembly. You should find it in the %Program%\ \Microsoft SDKs\Windows Phone\v7.1\Toolkit\Aug11\Bin directory.

In MainPage.xaml, you have to add a new namespace declaration to use the toolkit.

```
<phone:PhoneApplicationPage
    x:Class="GesturesWithToolkit.MainPage"
    xmlns="http://schemas.microsoft.com/winfx/2006/xaml/presentation"
    xmlns:x="http://schemas.microsoft.com/winfx/2006/xaml"
    xmlns:phone="clr-namespace:Microsoft.Phone.Controls;assembly=Microsoft.Phone"
    xmlns:shell="clr-namespace:Microsoft.Phone.Shell;assembly=Microsoft.Phone"
    xmlns:d="http://schemas.microsoft.com/expression/blend/2008"
    xmlns:mc="http://schemas.openxmlformats.org/markup-compatibility/2006"

    xmlns:toolkit="clr-
namespace:Microsoft.Phone.Controls;assembly=Microsoft.Phone.Controls.Toolkit"

. . .
```

Then you have to add the GestureService tag between the tags of the control used to manage the gestures. For example, we added those tags to the Rectangle control defined inside Canvas. The GestureListener tag enables us to define which gestures can be managed by our application specifying the related event handler. We have specified to retrieve DragStarted, DragDelta, and DragComplete events.

The two rectangles are placed into a Canvas control at fixed positions. The dragable rectangle has the ZIndex property greater than the other rectangle, so it will not disappear under the dragged rectangle when they overlap.

```
. . .
<!--ContentPanel - place additional content here-->
        <Canvas x:Name="ContentPanel" Margin="12,0,12,0">
            <Rectangle Fill="Red" x:Name="rSource" Width="100" Height="100" Grid.Row="0"
                    Canvas.Left="0" Canvas.Top="160" Canvas.ZIndex="1">

                <toolkit:GestureService.GestureListener>
                    <toolkit:GestureListener DragStarted="GestureListener_DragStarted"
                            DragDelta="GestureListener_DragDelta"
                            DragCompleted="GestureListener_DragCompleted" />
                </toolkit:GestureService.GestureListener>

            </Rectangle>
            <Rectangle Fill="Yellow" x:Name="rTarget" Height="100" Width="460"
                    Canvas.Left="0" Canvas.Top="660" Canvas.ZIndex="0" />
        </Canvas>
. . .
```

In the MainPage.xaml.cs file, we implemented the code to respond to the gesture events. In the GestureListener_DragStarted event handler, we simply inform the application that a drag operation has started. This is informs the other event handlers to accomplish their operation only when a drag is started. Despite the name, the CaptureMouse method is used to capture the tap on the control that uses it. So, the controls will receive tap and drag information whether or not the user's finger is in control's borders.

The GestureListener_DragDelta event handler is used to paint the rectangle to the newer coordinates. Those are calculated by adding the actual Left and Top rectangle positions in the Canvas to the VerticalChange and HorizontalChange values provided by the DragDeltaGestureEventArgs parameter.

```
private void GestureListener_DragStarted(object sender,
                                    DragStartedGestureEventArgs e)
{
    Rectangle rect = sender as Rectangle;
    _isDrag = true;
    rect.CaptureMouse();
}

private void GestureListener_DragDelta(object sender, DragDeltaGestureEventArgs e)
{
    if (_isDrag)
    {
        Rectangle rect = sender as Rectangle;
        rect.SetValue(Canvas.TopProperty,
                (double)rect.GetValue(Canvas.TopProperty) + e.VerticalChange);
        rect.SetValue(Canvas.LeftProperty,
                (double)rect.GetValue(Canvas.LeftProperty) + e.HorizontalChange);
    }
}
```

Finally, in the GestureListener_DragCompleted event handler, we inform the application that the drag operation has ended. Moreover, we check whether the two rectangles have collided by calling the CollisionDetected method. If the rectangles have collided, we will show a MessageBox message informing the user that a collision between rectangles has been detected.

```
private void GestureListener_DragCompleted(object sender,
                                    DragCompletedGestureEventArgs e)
{
    Rectangle rect = sender as Rectangle;
    _isDrag = false;
    rect.ReleaseMouseCapture();

    if (CollisionDetected())
        MessageBox.Show("Collision detected!");
}
```

The CollisionDetected method simply checks the vertical position of the rectangle adding to the position the rectangle's height. If this value is equal to or greater than the vertical position of the destination rectangle, then a collision is detected and the method returns a Boolean true value.

```
private bool CollisionDetected()
{
    double rSourcePos = rSource.Height +
                        (double)rSource.GetValue(Canvas.TopProperty);
    if (rSourcePos >= 660)
        return true;
    else
        return false;
}
```

Usage

From Visual Studio 2010, press Ctrl+F5 and wait for the emulator to start. The application shown in Figure 5-9 displays.

Figure 5-9. The GestureWithToolkit application shows the red rectangle ready to be dragged over the yellow one.

Now you can press and hold the left mouse button and start to move it around the screen emulator. When you drop the red rectangle over the yellow one, you will see a message appear onscreen, as shown in Figure 5-10.

Figure 5-10. The collision between the red and yellow rectangle has been detected.

CHAPTER 6

Sensors

This chapter covers the use of sensors on Windows Phone. The base requirements for manufacturers are the accelerometer, compass, proximity sensor, light, and A-GPS. In this version of Windows Phone, you have access to Accelerometer, Compass, and Gyroscope.

An accelerometer measures acceleration forces, such as gravity or movement. The accelerometer, like the other sensors, is built extending the class SensorBase<TSensorReading>, where TSensorReading implements the interface ISensorReading. When we have access to the other sensors exposed by the API, we will use them all in the same way. The accelerometer data are exposed by the AccelerometerReadingEventArgs class, which exposes three properties for the x-, y-, and z-axis that assume values between -2 and 2 (the sign is used to interpret the direction of the vector of force).

The A-GPS is part of the Location Service, which enables us to obtain the position of the phone on the planet. To find the position, the device can use GPS, Wi-Fi, and cellular radio, each with a different (decreasing) level of precision, balanced by the phone according to the state of battery and precision required by the application.

The compass sensor measures the position angle of the phone compared to the magnetic north pole, and provides data only relative to one axis. If you want to retrieve information on all axes, you must use the Motion class and its property RotationMatrix.

Gyroscope provides information about the velocity of your device on each axis. Using the gyroscope, you will retrieve information about how quickly the user moves the device.

In the sensors framework, you have access to a new class called Motion that handles the three sensors mentioned previously in one place, giving you information that combines raw data in a matrix of value that helps you to evaluate device's yaw, pitch, and roll.

The recipes in this chapter describe how to do the following:

- 6-1. Resetting a form by shaking the phone

- 6-2. Create a seismograph

- 6-3. Indicating the user's position on a map

- 6-4. Displaying the time of sunrise and sunset

- 6-5. Indicating the user's position with coordinates

- 6-6. Using the radio

- 6-7. Building an augmented reality application

6-1. Resetting a Form by Shaking the Phone

For this first recipe, we chose to create a cool user interaction, in order to provide a better user experience (UX). When the device is shaken, we want all the text in the text boxes to be erased. As you know, people are fascinated by features that make a device's functionality more interesting. In this example, you will use a data form, but you could take this code and put it, for example, in a Sudoku game. In that case, creating a new schema when shaking the phone would be simple, and would require only a change of the algorithm inside the method that resets the text boxes.

Problem

You need to detect the shaking of the device along the x-axis.

Solution

You must use the `Accelerometer` class, subscribe to the event `ReadingChanged`, and manage the phone's movements.

How It Works

An accelerometer is an instrument capable of detecting and/or measuring acceleration. The accelerometer of Windows Phone is accessible thanks to the `Accelerometer` class that extends the base class of all sensors `SensorBase` (shown in Figure 6-1), which simply exposes methods to begin (`Start`) and end (`Stop`) the use of the accelerometer, and the event that will notify you that the values read from the device have changed. A fundamental thing to be taken into consideration is the scale of values that can be reported by the instrument along the x-, y-, and z-axis, which have a lower limit of -2 and an upper limit of 2.

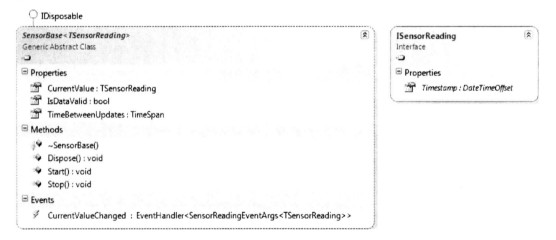

Figure 6-1. SensorBase and ISensorReading class diagram

The Code

There's no need to repeat how to create a new project at this point in the book, and so we'll start directly with the code that interests us, then start creating a new Silverlight application for Windows Phone.

For the user interface (UI), you will have only a set of four text boxes that contain information for Name, Surname, Street, and City:

```
<Grid x:Name="ContentPanel" Grid.Row="1" Margin="12,0" Grid.RowSpan="6">
  <Grid.RowDefinitions>
    <RowDefinition Height="80"/>
    <RowDefinition Height="80" />
    <RowDefinition Height="80" />
    <RowDefinition Height="80" />
    <RowDefinition Height="80" />
    <RowDefinition Height="*" />
  </Grid.RowDefinitions>
  <TextBox Name="NameTextBox" Text="TextBlock" />
  <TextBox Name="SurnameTextBox" Text="TextBlock" Grid.Row="1" />
  <TextBox Name="StreetTextBox" Text="TextBlock" Grid.Row="2" />
  <TextBox Name="CityTextBox" Text="TextBlock" Grid.Row="3" />
  <TextBlock Text="Shake to reset" Grid.Row="4" VerticalAlignment="Center"
                                    HorizontalAlignment="Center"/>
</Grid>
```

The first class that you must know about is `Accelerometer`, which allows you to access the functionality that you need. It's important to say how the movements are interpreted by the device. Assuming that you have your Windows Phone in your hand in portrait position, the movement along the x-axis is considered positive if you move the phone to the right (and negative if you move the phone to the left). Movement along the y-axis is relative to moving the phone up (in a positive direction) and down (in a negative direction). Movement along the z-axis occurs when you move the phone toward you (positive) and away from you (negative).

■ **Note** The `Accelerometer` class (which gives you access to accelerometer functionality) is contained in the namespace `Microsoft.Device.Sensors`. To use it, you must add a reference to the `Microsoft.Device.Sensors` assembly.

As you can see from the class diagram shown in Figure 6-2, there is an event to be subscribed to (`ReadingChanged`). This event is triggered every time the reference values of the accelerometer change (and based on the accelerometer's high degree of accuracy, those values will change often).

At the class level, you need to declare these members:

```
...
Accelerometer accelerometer = null;
```

```
//represents the time of the first significant movement
DateTimeOffset movementMoment = new DateTimeOffset();

double firstShakeStep = 0; //represents the value of the first significant movement
...
```

You will see soon why you need these two members.

Next you will write a private method named initAccelerometer that you will call just after InitializeComponents in the page constructor. This method will be responsible for initializing all you need for the accelerometer, such as the subscription to the ReadingChanged event.

```
...
private void initAccelerometer()
{
        accelerometer = new Accelerometer();
        accelerometer.ReadingChanged += new
EventHandler<AccelerometerReadingEventArgs>(Accelerometer_ReadingChanged);
        accelerometer.Start(); //this can be done in a button_click
}
...
```

The preceding code is self-explanatory, but note that with the last line you actually started the use of the accelerometer. But let's show in detail what you will do with this accelerometer, by using the event handler:

```
void Accelerometer_ReadingChanged(object sender, AccelerometerReadingEventArgs e)
{
        //put here the code to detect a shake
}
```

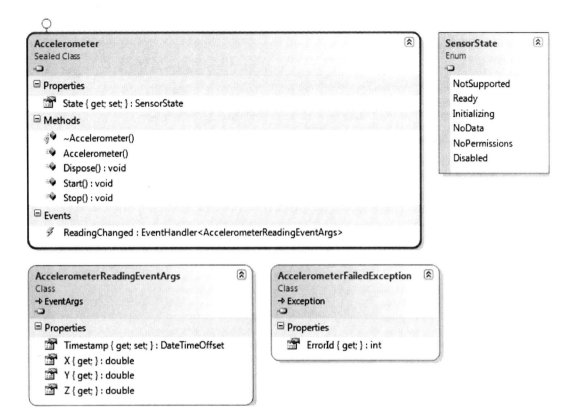

Figure 6-2. *Diagram of classes used by the accelerometer*

Assuming that by *shake* we mean a fast movement, large enough along the x-axis, the code that allows us to identify a movement of this type makes use of a precise timestamp, in order to access the actual position (relative to the starting point) of the phone at all times.

This code is as follows:

```
...
void Accelerometer_ReadingChanged(object sender, AccelerometerReadingEventArgs e)
{
  //if the movement takes less than 500 milliseconds
  if (e.Timestamp.Subtract(movementMoment).Duration().TotalMilliseconds <= 500)
  {
    if ((e.X <= -1 || e.X >= 1) && (firstShakeStep <= Math.Abs(e.X)))
      firstShakeStep = e.X;

    if (firstShakeStep != 0)
    {
      firstShakeStep = 0;
      Deployment.Current.Dispatcher.BeginInvoke(() => ResetTextBox());
    }
  }
}
```

```
    movementMoment = e.Timestamp;
}
...
```

All this code is based on a mathematical calculation to determine the magnitude of movement along the x-axis (you can test it moving the phone along the y- and z-axis). But why do you need to write `Deployment.Current.Dispatcher.BeginInvoke(() => ResetTextBox())`? It's simple:

- `() => ResetTextBox()` represents a delegate to the `ResetTextBox` method.

- `Deployment.Current.Dispatcher.BeginInvoke` is used to execute `Action` on the same thread of the UI. If you try to call a method that works on UI elements without this methodology, you will receive an "Invalid cross-thread access" error.

Finally, you must implement the `ResetTextBox` method:

```
...
private void ResetTextBox()
{
    this.NameTextBox.Text = "";
    this.SurnameTextBox.Text = "";
    this.StreetTextBox.Text = "";
    this.CityTextBox.Text = "";
}
...
```

There is something important to note about this code: with it, you started to use the accelerometer, but you never stopped it. That means you will be using this sensor for the entire time that your application is working. This is a bad practice because the application will consume too much battery power. It is becoming increasingly important to offer the best user experience possible. If the user thinks that the application requires an excessive use of resources, that user might simply delete it.

Usage

In this recipe, you can follow two paths: you can test the application on a physical device and produce the movement or use additional tools of Windows Phone emulator and simulate the shake in one click.

To follow the first way: connect your unlocked device (see Recipe 1-6 for more information on how to unlock devices) and run the application from Visual Studio 2010. Make sure that the target output is set to Windows Phone Device. Write something in the text boxes, shake the phone, and then check that your form has been erased.

If you want to use additional tools run the application on the emulator then when is ready click the last button on the right of the emulator, as shown in Figure 6-3.

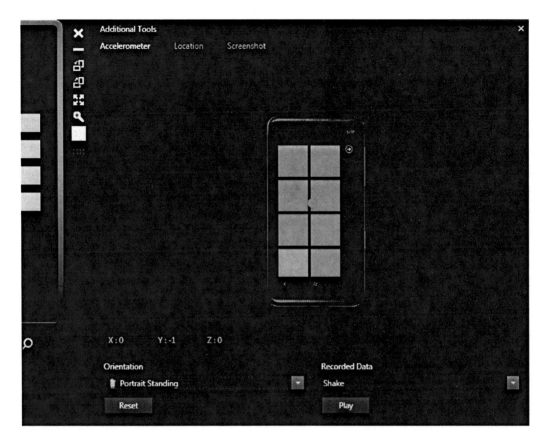

Figure 6-3. *Opening additional tools*

These tools will help you to simulate some behaviors that otherwise require a physical device; for example, you can simulate movements of device, or you can simulate a movement on the planet when you want to test an application that uses A-GPS, and you can take a screenshot of your application.

Now to test your application all you have to do is click on the Play button to reproduce the shaking movement (remember that the emulator will not actually shake).

6-2. Creating a Seismograph

Problem

You want to create a seismograph by merging into a single project the use of Microsoft XNA drawing capabilities with the sensitivity of the accelerometer (the accelerometer has a limited range, from -2 to +2 on the scale of values on the three axes, but has a high precision of floating-point numbers beyond the point).

Solution

You need to use the accelerometer capabilities in association with the XNA framework.

How It Works

The use of the accelerometer in our applications is a standard now. Users require greater interaction with devices. Think of these devices as trendy consoles on which users want more control and participation; they are no longer the old Commodore 64 joysticks. Shakes and finger gestures are just some of the interactions that users want, in order to feel at the heart of what they are doing. It is time to adapt our applications to keep in sync with the times and provide a richer user experience.

Okay, it's time to get serious. In this example, you will learn how to access and use the accelerometer in your games, to provide user interaction. By following the concepts used in these recipes, you can make high-interaction games, for a better experience for your gamers. So that we don't lose too much time in explaining what games you can create and how, you can use your own ideas. So enough with the talk. Let's start to write code.

The Code

This section does not explain the basics for working with XNA, because doing so would require another entire book. Instead, it explains what you need to do in order to read the oscillations of the phone and to turn those oscillations into a line on the screen. Obviously, that read data can be applied to every other aspect of any other application that you want to write.

So let's go! As a first step, add a new SpriteFont in the project of the contents (automatically created by project template), which with his default content must be good enough.

```
<XnaContent xmlns:Graphics="Microsoft.Xna.Framework.Content.Pipeline.Graphics">
  <Asset Type="Graphics:FontDescription">

    <!--
    Modify this string to change the font that will be imported.
    -->
    <FontName>Segoe UI Mono</FontName>

    <!--
    Size is a float value, measured in points. Modify this value to change
    the size of the font.
    -->
    <Size>14</Size>

    <!--
    Spacing is a float value, measured in pixels. Modify this value to change
    the amount of spacing in between characters.
    -->
    <Spacing>0</Spacing>

    <!--
    UseKerning controls the layout of the font. If this value is true, kerning
    Information will be used when placing characters.
```

```
    -->
    <UseKerning>true</UseKerning>

    <!--
    Style controls the style of the font. Valid entries are "Regular", "Bold", "Italic",
    and "Bold, Italic", and are case sensitive.
    -->
    <Style>Regular</Style>

<!--
CharacterRegions control what letters are available in the font. Every character from Start to
End will be built and made available for drawing. The default range is from 32 (ASCII space)
to 126 ('~'), covering the basic Latin character set. The characters are ordered according to
the Unicode standard.
-->
    <CharacterRegions>
      <CharacterRegion>
        <Start>&#32;</Start>
        <End>&#126;</End>
      </CharacterRegion>
    </CharacterRegions>
  </Asset>
</XnaContent>
```

After creating this font, the other content you need is a 1×1 pixel image that will be the texture of your line. At this point, there is nothing in the design of Contents, so go to the heart of the action: to the code in the .cs file of our game.

First of all, remember to resolve `Microsoft.Devices.Sensors`, and then add (always at the class level) a member of type `Accelerometer` that will be the data provider. This time you have an available method that is called `Initialize`, which is the ideal place to do all your initializations:

```
...
accelerometer = new Accelerometer();
accelerometer.ReadingChanged += new
EventHandler<AccelerometerReadingEventArgs>(accelerometer_ReadingChanged);
accelerometer.Start();
...
```

In the event handler, the first thing you do is calculate the magnitude of oscillation, increasing by 100 the scale because, as you recall, the accelerometer is extremely sensitive, but assumes values from -2 to +2 for each axis. Then you need to convert it to an acceptable value if compared to the screen resolution:

```
...
void accelerometer_ReadingChanged(object sender, AccelerometerReadingEventArgs e)
{
   double magnitude = Math.Sqrt(Math.Pow(e.X, 2) + Math.Pow(e.Y, 2) + Math.Pow(e.Z, 2))* 100;
}
...
```

But what do you do with this magnitude after it is calculated? Well, it's clear! It will be the value of reference for your swing. But before using it to draw, you need to take a few preliminary steps. First, at the class level, define some members as follows:

```
...
        VertexBuffer vertexBuffer = null;
        Texture2D pointTexture = null;
        List<VertexPositionColor> vertices = null;
        SpriteFont font = null;

        double actualX;
        double actualY;
        double actualZ;
        float maxMagnitude = 0;
        float yPosition = 240;
...
```

The most important members that we need to talk about are the following:

- yPosition represents the offset relative to the y-axis of the graph. (Otherwise, you would have a chart that stays too high on the screen.)

- vertexBuffer is your "summits" buffer, where you will load the vertices to be drawn.

- vertices is the vertex list that you'll draw. (Keep in mind that you could use an array for greater consistency with the methods used, but we are more comfortable working with a list and then converting the array when necessary.)

- pointTexture and font are part of the topics that are not covered in this chapter in detail. You need to know only that the class will be used to load the texture (created earlier in the Contents project) and to load the preceding fonts.

We would dare call the other fields *diagnostic*, and you need them to see the onscreen information about the status of the accelerometer as you go forward in the execution.

Next, with all these elements set to null, something in the initialization method must be changed, as follows:

```
...
vertexBuffer = new VertexBuffer(graphics.GraphicsDevice,
                                typeof(VertexPositionColor),
                                1000,
                                BufferUsage.None);
vertices = new List<VertexPositionColor>();
...
```

There are still loads of fonts and textures. The best place for them is the LoadContent method:

```
...
pointTexture = this.Content.Load<Texture2D>("point");
```

```
font = this.Content.Load<SpriteFont>("SismoFont");
...
```

And the code of the event handler becomes somewhat more full bodied:

```
...
void accelerometer_ReadingChanged(object sender, AccelerometerReadingEventArgs e)
{
 double magnitude = Math.Sqrt(Math.Pow(e.X, 2) + Math.Pow(e.Y, 2) + Math.Pow(e.Z, 2)) * 100;
 if (magnitude > maxMagnitude)
   maxMagnitude = (float)magnitude;

 VertexPositionColor vertex = new VertexPositionColor(new Vector3(0, yPosition +
                                             (float)magnitude, 1), Color.White);
 vertices.Add(vertex);

 actualX = e.X;
 actualY = e.Y;
 actualZ = e.Z;

 List<VertexPositionColor> newVertices = new List<VertexPositionColor>();
 for (int i = 0; i < vertices.Count; i++)
 {
    VertexPositionColor ver = vertices[i];
    ver.Position.X += 1;
    newVertices.Add(ver);
 }
 vertices = newVertices;

 if (vertices.Count > 799)
    vertices.RemoveAt(0);
}
...
```

Step by step, what you do is as follows:

1. Calculate as before the magnitude of the vibration.

2. Check if it is greater than the event occurred; if yes, you keep it in the variable.

3. Create a new vertex with x = 0, and y = magnitude + (your offset).

4. Set the fields with the values of the disclosures made by the accelerometer.

5. Create a list of the same type of summits, where items are taken from the original list increasing the value on the x-axis by one (that means that you are shifting them) then allocate (and replace) the original list.

6. With the last two line of code you ensure that you will never have more vertices needed to show the information onscreen (in this case, we are not at all interested in having a history of what happened).

So far, you have calculated the position of the various summits, and this means that now the vertices are ready to be drawn. As you know, XNA is based on two methods (Update and Draw) that are invoked cyclically, about 30 times per second. In the Update method, you will prepare the data in the buffer to be drawn, while Draw will actually do the work of showing vertexes on video.

```
protected override void Update(GameTime gameTime)
{
  // Allows the game to exit
  if (GamePad.GetState(PlayerIndex.One).Buttons.Back == ButtonState.Pressed)
    this.Exit();

  //force reading accelerometer data
  //accelerometer_ReadingChanged(null, null);
  if (vertices.Count > 0 && vertices.Count < 800)
    vertexBuffer.SetData<VertexPositionColor>(vertices.ToArray()); ;
  base.Update(gameTime);
}
```

This is not complicated to understand: you are setting data in vertexBuffer and taking them from the vertices collection. Although things do get complicated (but are also short) in the Draw method:

```
protected override void Draw(GameTime gameTime)
{
  GraphicsDevice.Clear(Color.Black);
  spriteBatch.Begin();
  if (vertices.Count > 1)
  {
    for (int i = 0; i < vertices.Count - 1; i++)
    {
      VertexPositionColor v1 = vertices[i];
      VertexPositionColor v2 = vertices[i + 1];
      drawLine(
        new Vector2(v1.Position.X, v2.Position.X),
        new Vector2(v1.Position.Y, v2.Position.Y), v1.Color);

    }
    spriteBatch.DrawString(font, string.Format("Count: {0}",vertices.Count),
                      new Vector2(20, 20), Color.Red);

    spriteBatch.DrawString(font, string.Format("X:{0}", actualX), new Vector2(20, 40),
                      Color.PeachPuff);

    spriteBatch.DrawString(font, string.Format("Y:{0}", actualY), new Vector2(20, 60),
                      Color.PeachPuff);

    spriteBatch.DrawString(font, string.Format("Z:{0}", actualZ), new Vector2(20, 80),
                      Color.PeachPuff);

    spriteBatch.DrawString(font, string.Format("MaxMagnitude:{0}", maxMagnitude),
                      new Vector2(20, 100), Color.PeachPuff);
```

```
    }

    spriteBatch.End();
    base.Draw(gameTime);
}
```

Again, step by step, here is what you do with this method:

1. Clean the old screen.

2. Draw the operations.

3. If you have more than one vertex, scroll the array of vertices, passing the coordinates of the current point and of the point immediately after as parameters to the drawLine method. (That's why you do this if you have more than one vertex.)

4. Show the results on video, thanks to the DrawString method, displaying the information that you have found for diagnostic purposes.

5. Close the batch data preparation and paint everything.

As you can see, we call a method named drawLine, the code for which is

```
void drawLine(Vector2 v1, Vector2 v2, Color color)
{
        float lenght = Vector2.Distance(v1, v2);
            spriteBatch.Draw(pointTexture,
                    new Rectangle((int)v1.X,
                    (int)v2.X, 1, 1), color);
}
```

The drawLine method does nothing more than create many small rectangles (1×1 pixels) at a position identified by the vectors that constitute your line.

Usage

From Visual Studio 2010, press Ctrl+F5 and wait for the application to be deployed and start on your device. Put the phone on your table. Begin to simulate an earthquake by hitting the table.

6-3. Indicating the User's Position on a Map

Problem

You want to create an application or game that gives information about where your user is located. (For a game, you could choose to let the user play in the city where she is located, against other players in the same region.)

Solution

To solve this problem, you'll use a control that uses Bing Maps tailored for Windows Phone. But much more important than how you will show data is how you will get them, which will be thanks to the GeoCoordinateWatcher class contained in the namespace System.Device.Location.

How It Works

The GeoCoordinateWatcher class provides location data based on coordinates of latitude and longitude. Like other sensors, the cycle is defined by the Start method (which enables you to access to the Position property and enable the PositionChanged event) and Stop (which prevents GeoCoordinateWatcher from providing events and data on the position).

The Code

As you can see in Figure 6-4, the constructor has an overload that enables you to specify the degree of accuracy that you want in determining the user's location (the property DesiredAccuracy is read-only). If you set the accuracy to High, you will have a more precise location of the user, but this requires more resources that will easily drain the battery. Therefore, use this setting only if needed, because you don't want to risk the user rejecting your application because it is too resource-intensive.

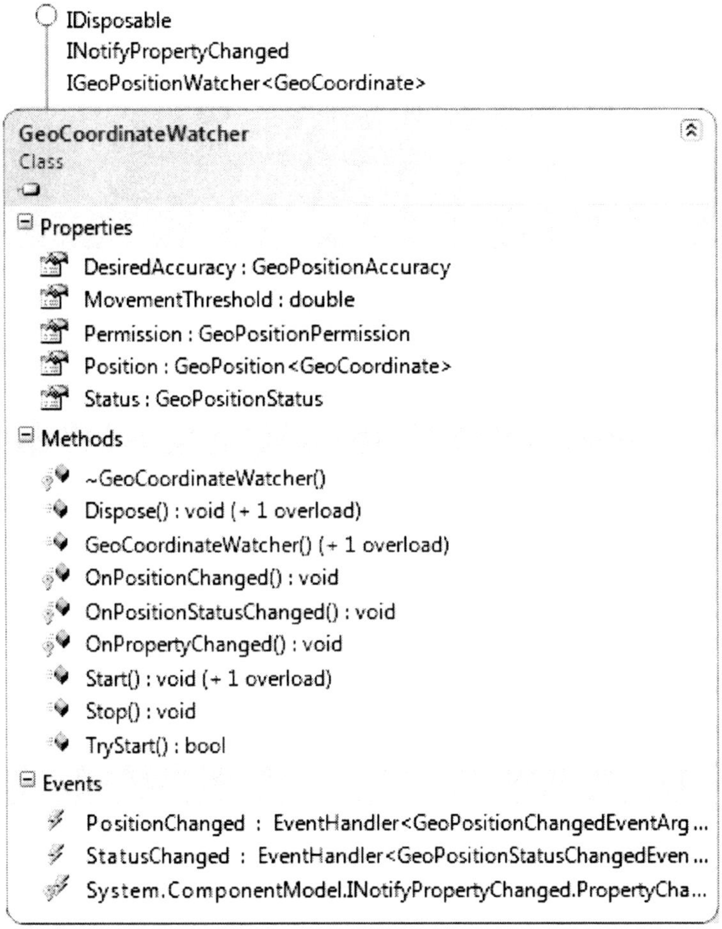

○ IDisposable
INotifyPropertyChanged
IGeoPositionWatcher<GeoCoordinate>

GeoCoordinateWatcher ⟨☆⟩
Class
⌐

⊟ **Properties**

⌦ DesiredAccuracy : GeoPositionAccuracy
⌦ MovementThreshold : double
⌦ Permission : GeoPositionPermission
⌦ Position : GeoPosition<GeoCoordinate>
⌦ Status : GeoPositionStatus

⊟ **Methods**

⚡ ~GeoCoordinateWatcher()
⚡ Dispose() : void (+ 1 overload)
⚡ GeoCoordinateWatcher() (+ 1 overload)
⚡ OnPositionChanged() : void
⚡ OnPositionStatusChanged() : void
⚡ OnPropertyChanged() : void
⚡ Start() : void (+ 1 overload)
⚡ Stop() : void
⚡ TryStart() : bool

⊟ **Events**

⚡ PositionChanged : EventHandler<GeoPositionChangedEventArg...
⚡ StatusChanged : EventHandler<GeoPositionStatusChangedEven...
⚡ System.ComponentModel.INotifyPropertyChanged.PropertyCha...

Figure 6-4. *Class diagram of GeoCoordinateWatcher*

There are two important events that you must take into consideration:

- PositionChanged

- StatusChanged

We start to see the private method that initializes the GeoCoordinateWatcher and subscribes the two events with our handlers:

```
private void InitWatcher()
{
  geoWatcher = new GeoCoordinateWatcher(GeoPositionAccuracy.High);
  geoWatcher.PositionChanged += new
      EventHandler<GeoPositionChangedEventArgs<GeoCoordinate>>(geoWatcher_PositionChanged);
```

```
geoWatcher.StatusChanged += new
    EventHandler<GeoPositionStatusChangedEventArgs>(geoWatcher_StatusChanged);
}
...
```

The respective handler is as follows:

```
...
void geoWatcher_StatusChanged(object sender, GeoPositionStatusChangedEventArgs e)
{
    //Handle here the change of status
}

void geoWatcher_PositionChanged(object sender, GeoPositionChangedEventArgs<GeoCoordinate> e)
{
    //Handle here the change of position
}
...
```

Let us explain the purpose of these event-handlers:

- geoWatcher_StatusChanged takes care of notifying that the status of GeoCoordinateWatcher has changed.

- geoWatcher_PositionChanged is the most important. The event handler is called when the PositionChanged event occurs, and communicates the new location via GeoCoordinate.

The GeoCoordinate class has several interesting fields that provide important information, as you can see in Figure 6-5. These include altitude, latitude, and longitude (for identifying the position) that will be set to NAN until the Watcher status will not become ready. Another interesting property is the speed, which would be useful if you wanted to create a navigation system.

All you need to do to resolve your problem quickly is to run this code:

```
...
void geoWatcher_PositionChanged(object sender, GeoPositionChangedEventArgs<GeoCoordinate> e)
{
    //BingMap is the Map control provided for the scope
    //14d is the level of zoom, this is good enough to have
    bingMap.SetView(e.Position.Location,14d);
}
```

It's really too simple, we know. Microsoft loves to allow developers to create applications as quickly as possible and has therefore integrated into its operating system some basic components to help developers focus on creating other aspects of their applications. Of course, we think it's important that you know that the use of Bing Maps implies that you are registered on Bing Maps service portal.

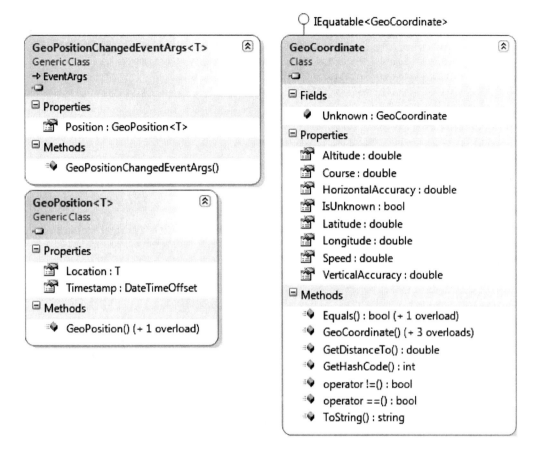

Figure 6-5. Classes used to handle GeoCoordinate

If you don't want to use Bing Maps to show the user's position on a map, you can use Microsoft Research Maps, available at `http://msrmaps.com/default.aspx`. In this chapter, you will not see how to interact with this service – look for that information in Chapter 9. Instead, your focus will be directed to the data, both at how to get it from Location Services and at how to use it to find the user's exact location.

After you add a reference to the service available from `http://msrmaps.com/TerraService2.asmx` (we will explain the configuration later), you can begin to look at the code.

The structure of the UI will look like this:

```
<Grid x:Name="LayoutRoot" Background="Transparent">
    <Grid.RowDefinitions>
        <RowDefinition Height="Auto"/>
        <RowDefinition Height="*"/>
    </Grid.RowDefinitions>

    <!--TitlePanel contains the name of the application and page title-->
```

```
        <StackPanel x:Name="TitlePanel" Grid.Row="0" Margin="12,17,0,28">
            <StackPanel Orientation="Horizontal">
                <TextBlock Text="Location Service"
                            Style="{StaticResource PhoneTextNormalStyle}"/>
                <TextBlock x:Name="LocationStatusTextBox" Text="..."
                            Style="{StaticResource PhoneTextNormalStyle}"/>
            </StackPanel>
        </StackPanel>

        <!--ContentPanel - place additional content here-->
        <Grid x:Name="ContentPanel" Grid.Row="1" >

        </Grid>
    </Grid>
```

There's something obviously strange in this interface at first glance. The Grid ContentPanel is empty, but only because inside the code you will create a kind of mosaic. In the code-behind, you will need a series of using statements:

```
...
using System.Device.Location;
using System.Windows.Media.Imaging;
using System.IO;
...
```

You will also need a private method that enables you to initialize the various services. In addition, you will need a proxy (and this will be the name of the object that we will use to interact with services, but we will not see the use of web services here) for TerraService and a GeoCoordinateWatcher:

```
TerraService proxy = null;
GeoCoordinateWatcher geoWatcher = null;

// Constructor
public MainPage()
{
  InitializeComponent();
  InizializeServices();
  Loaded += new RoutedEventHandler(MainPage_Loaded);
}

private void InizializeServices()
{
  proxy = new TerraService();
  geoWatcher = new GeoCoordinateWatcher();
}
```

In the event that fires when the page has finished loading, you will write the code to subscribe to events that are raised at the completion of an asynchronous request. This is because the service always works asynchronously, so you don't stop the UI too long while you wait for a response, and then your code will be notified that a request has been answered. This mode of operation is not new to anyone who has already worked with Silverlight on the Web side. Once again, this makes us appreciate how easy it is for developers to recycle their skills between technologies based on the .NET technologies stack.

```
void MainPage_Loaded(object sender, RoutedEventArgs e)
{
...
//Subscribe here webservice events
...
geoWatcher.PositionChanged += new
EventHandler<GeoPositionChangedEventArgs<GeoCoordinate>>(geoWatcher_PositionChanged);

geoWatcher.StatusChanged += new
EventHandler<GeoPositionStatusChangedEventArgs>(geoWatcher_StatusChanged);
//Start the geoWatcher
        geoWatcher.Start();
}
```

When the StatusChanged event of GeoCoordinateWatcher fires, you will change the text of the text box destined for this use, so you can have feedback onscreen that the location service is effectively launched and operational:

```
void geoWatcher_StatusChanged(object sender, GeoPositionStatusChangedEventArgs e)
{
this.LocationStatusTextBox.Text = e.Status.ToString();
}
```

The workflow of your application is as follows:

1. It will fire the event geoWatcher_PositionChanged and will make a request by calling the method GetAreaFromPt in the proxy.

2. Whether step 1 is successful or unsuccessful, the application will fire a proxy_GetAreaFromPtCompleted event.

3. In the case of a correct answer to step 2, this application will call the GetTile method of the proxy, with the consequent trigger of the event proxy _ GetTileCompleted.

Then we start from the first step, implementing geoWatcher_PositionChanged:

```
void geoWatcher_PositionChanged(object sender,
                            GeoPositionChangedEventArgs<GeoCoordinate> e)
{
        if (!e.Position.Location.IsUnknown)
        {
                proxy.GetAreaFromPt (
                    //the ActualPosition
                    new TerraService.LonLatPt()
                    {
```

```
                    Lat = e.Position.Location.Latitude,
                    Lon = e.Position.Location.Longitude
                },
                //the type of map
                1,
                //the scale of image received
                TerraService.Scale.Scale2km,
                (int)ContentPanel.ActualWidth,
                (int)ContentPanel.ActualHeight);
        }
}
```

This recipe showed you how the Location Service, which is based on a universal standard for localization, enables you to access without too much trouble information about the device's position in the world.

Usage

From Visual Studio 2010, press Ctrl+F5. Wait for the application to start on the phone and then wait to see whether the position is available. You can then look at that the position on the map and make changes relating your actual position.

6-4. Displaying Sunset and Sunrise

Problem

Your aim is to create an application that is able to tell the user what time the sun will rise and set today in his location.

Solution

There are several ways to find out the time of sunrise and sunset (for example, through web services, libraries, and complex calculations). This recipe shows how to access and use a certain property in order to explore the potential of Location Services. There are several ways to calculate the times from latitude and longitude values, and we will let you choose which best suits your needs.

How It Works

You will use information about the user's position, obtained from the device, to calculate the time of sunrise and sunset, simulating with a helper class the behavior of a service to calculate them.

The Code

To start writing code for this recipe we need two members field:

```
GeoCoordinateWatcher geo = new GeoCoordinateWatcher();
SuntimesHelper ssc = new SuntimesHelper();
```

SuntimesHelper is a class written by us, and its code is based on algorithms that are easily available on the Internet. This class exposes two methods, called GetSunRise and GetSunSet, as you can see in Figure 6-6.

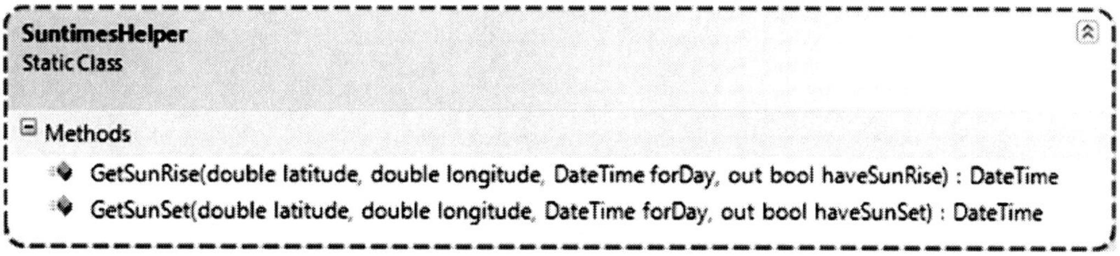

Figure 6-6. Class diagram of SuntimesHelper

```
void geo_PositionChanged(object sender, GeoPositionChangedEventArgs<GeoCoordinate> e)
{
            if (!e.Position.Location.IsUnknown)
            {
                bool isSunrise = false;
                bool isSunset = false;

                DateTime sunrise = SuntimesHelper.GetSunRise(e.Position.Location.Latitude,
e.Position.Location.Longitude, DateTime.Now, out isSunrise);
DateTime sunset = SuntimesHelper.GetSunSet(e.Position.Location.Latitude,
e.Position.Location.Longitude, DateTime.Now, out isSunset);
geo.Stop()
            }
}
```

It is important when working with the position to point out that the applications used for localizing consume battery power. Although we may sound repetitive, it is important to provide the best possible user interaction in our applications. Therefore, remember to stop the use of GeoCoordinateWatcher when you don't need it anymore.

Usage

From Visual Studio 2010, deploy the application to a physical device and watch it calculate sunrise and sunset from your position.

6-5. Indicating the User's Position via Coordinates

Problem

At application startup, you want to localize by position of the phone to see where in the world it is and what is the relative address.

Solution

The solution to this problem is very simple if you use classes available in Windows Phone. However, the official solution is unusable at this time, because `CivicAddressResolver` was scheduled to be included in Silverlight for Windows Phone, and using `CivicAddressResolver` you can disclose to obtain a `CivicAddress` by using the geo-coordinates. This method has not yet been implemented.

However, in this section, we will show you what to do, so when the method is implemented, you will be ready to integrate features that can use it. Meanwhile, we will show you an alternative implementation of this service.

How It Works

As in the previous recipe, retrieving the user's position on the map based on geo-coordinates will be simple. You will use certain classes in the namespace associated with the civic `System.Device.Location` to retrieve coordinates that we are providing.

The Code

As you can see in Figure 6-7, the `CivicAddressResolver` class implements the `ICivicAddressResolver` interface. Therefore, even if the service is not implemented yet, you might think to implement your own resolver, rather than wait for subsequent implementations, just as you will do shortly. But let's proceed step by step.

Figure 6-7. Class diagram for CivicAddressResolver *and its respective data class*

First, declare at the class level these two members:

```
GeoCoordinateWatcher geoWatcher = null;
ICivicAddressResolver civicResolver = null;
```

Next, create two private void methods dedicated to initialize the preceding members:

- InitWatcher()
- InitResolver()

The names we have chosen are self-explanatory, and tell you what they will do when implemented, as you can see here:

```
private void InitResolver()
{
  //for now we will use the default implementation
  civicResolver = new CivicAddressResolver();
  civicResolver.ResolveAddressCompleted += new
    EventHandler<ResolveAddressCompletedEventArgs>(civicResolver_ResolveAddressCompleted);
}

private void InitWatcher()
{
```

```
geoWatcher = new GeoCoordinateWatcher(GeoPositionAccuracy.High);
geoWatcher.PositionChanged += new
    EventHandler<GeoPositionChangedEventArgs<GeoCoordinate>>(geoWatcher_PositionChanged);
geoWatcher.StatusChanged += new
    EventHandler<GeoPositionStatusChangedEventArgs>(geoWatcher_StatusChanged);
        geoWatcher.Start();
}
```

The use of InitWatcher is clear, because you have seen it in previous recipes. InitResolver indicates that the class CivicAddressResolver will make a call to some external service, and will raise the OnResolveAddressCompleted event when it has finished finding the information you need.

```
void geoWatcher_PositionChanged(object sender,
                        GeoPositionChangedEventArgs<GeoCoordinate> e)
{
    var civic = civicResolver.ResolveAddress(e.Position.Location);
}


void civicResolver_ResolveAddressCompleted(object sender,
                            ResolveAddressCompletedEventArgs e)
{
    //do something with resolved address
    //here you can see the properties that you can access
    //e.Address.AddressLine1
    //e.Address.AddressLine2
    //e.Address.Building
    //e.Address.City
    //e.Address.CountryRegion
    //e.Address.FloorLevel
    //e.Address.PostalCode
    //e.Address.StateProvince
}
```

This is all you need to do to use CivicAddressResolver. It's simple to use this class, but is also useless because behind of this class there is no implementation. Therefore, we have given you a way to implement a service similar to what Microsoft has planned, only "homemade."

You will need to use a Bing Maps service from http://msdn.microsoft.com/en-us/library/cc966738.aspx and then add a service reference to the Geocode Service (if you don't know how to do that, see Chapter 9).

First, add a new class to your project and call it CustomCivicResolver:

```
public class CustomAddressResolver : ICivicAddressResolver
{
    public CivicAddress ResolveAddress(GeoCoordinate coordinate)
    {
        //…
    }
```

```
public void ResolveAddressAsync(GeoCoordinate coordinate)
{
    //…
}

public event EventHandler<ResolveAddressCompletedEventArgs> ResolveAddressCompleted;
{
    ...
}
```

You will implement only ResolveAddressAsync, simply because you are using Silverlight for Windows phone and are not interested in the synchronous pattern.

You declare at the global class level the proxy for the service:

```
GeocodeService.GeocodeServiceClient proxy = null;
```

And you must write the constructor of the class, where you will instantiate the proxy and subscribe to the event OnReverseGeocodeCompleted:

```
public CustomAddressResolver()
{
    proxy = new GeocodeService.GeocodeServiceClient("BasicHttpBinding_IGeocodeService");
    proxy.ReverseGeocodeCompleted += new
                    EventHandler<GeocodeService.ReverseGeocodeCompletedEventArgs>(
                                                proxy_ReverseGeocodeCompleted);
}
```

Then it's time to prepare your request to the service (and prepare your service to respond to the request that will come from the outside):

```
public void ResolveAddressAsync(GeoCoordinate coordinate)
{
    proxy.ReverseGeocodeAsync(
    new GeocodeService.ReverseGeocodeRequest()
      {
        Location = new Microsoft.Phone.Controls.Maps.Platform.Location()
        {
          Latitude = coordinate.Latitude,
          Longitude = coordinate.Longitude,
          Altitude = coordinate.Altitude
        },
        Credentials = new Microsoft.Phone.Controls.Maps.Credentials()
        {
          ApplicationId = "Put you app key here"
        });
}
```

The only row of this code that must be commented is the creation of a credential for the service. You must get an API key for your application from http://msdn.microsoft.com/en-us/library/ cc966738.aspx. Without this key, you will never have a response from the service. So remember to do this before you carry on.

```
void proxy_ReverseGeocodeCompleted(object sender,
                            GeocodeService.ReverseGeocodeCompletedEventArgs e)
{
  ResolveAddressCompleted(
    sender,
    new ResolveAddressCompletedEventArgs(
      new CivicAddress()
      {
        AddressLine1 = e.Result.Results[0].Address.AddressLine,
        AddressLine2 = e.Result.Results[0].Address.FormattedAddress,
        Building = "",
        City = e.Result.Results[0].Address.Locality,
        CountryRegion = e.Result.Results[0].Address.CountryRegion,
        FloorLevel = "0",
        PostalCode = e.Result.Results[0].Address.PostalCode,
        StateProvince = e.Result.Results[0].Address.PostalTown
      },
      e.Error,
      e.Cancelled,
      e.UserState));
}
```

When the ReverseGeocodeCompleted fires, you also fire the event ResolveAddressCompleted, which is a member of the ICivicAddressResolver interface, and which will be triggered by who uses this class.

As you can see, you can't add information in CivicAddress, such as Building and FloorLevel, but if you aren't writing an application to track the position of a courier, we think you can do well without this information (and it is still better than not having the ability to retrieve information).

Usage

From Visual Studio 2010, start the application. Wait for your position to become available and then look for retrieved addresses while you move around the globe. Remember, in order to use Position in your application, you must activate it in the settings or you will never have correct information to work from.

6-6. Using the Radio

Problem

You want to create a complete FMRadio application that is different from the standard radio included in the Windows Phone Music hub.

Solution

You must use the FMRadio class included in Windows Phone to access radio functionalities. In just a few steps, you can have a complete radio that you can tune into various stations.

How It Works

The Microsoft.Devices.Radio namespace contains the class FMRadio, which implements the singleton pattern. In this way, there is only one point of access to the radio API. To tune the radio, you must change the frequency property of FMRadio.Instance, and if you want to implement a seek functionality, you must check for Signal Strength, also known as a Received Signal Strength Indicator (RSSI).

The Code

Create a project for Windows Phone by using Visual Studio and call it Enhanced Radio. After the template is created, add a folder named Images to the solution. As you can imagine, in this folder you will add some pictures to create the user interface. In this case, you have the four pictures shown in Figure 6-8. After this preliminary operation, you will need to add a reference to the Windows Phone Toolkit assembly, to use the ToggleSwitch control.

Figure 6-8. *Our images*

At the top of your application, inside TitlePanel, you need two columns. In the first column will be a toggle button that starts and stops the radio (of course, if the radio is already started, the toggle must be selected). In the second column is a slider that represents the signal strength indicator.

To create this user interface, you will use the following XAML:

```
<Grid x:Name="TitlePanel" Grid.Row="0" Margin="12,17,0,28">
  <Grid.ColumnDefinitions>
    <ColumnDefinition Width="250" />
    <ColumnDefinition Width="*" />
  /Grid.ColumnDefinitions>
  <Slider Grid.Column="1" x:Name="SignalSlider" Foreground="{StaticResource
                                       PhoneAccentBrush}" Maximum="1" />

  <toolkit:ToggleSwitch x:Name="RadioSwitch" Header="Radio status"
                                       Margin="1,1,0,-1"/>
</Grid>
```

After creating the header, you will add a TextBlock to show the frequency and four buttons to add seek an single-step frequency change:

```
<StackPanel x:Name="ContentPanel" Grid.Row="1" Margin="12,0,12,0">
  <TextBlock Text="**.*" Style="{StaticResource FrequencyTextBlockStyle}"
                                       Name="FrequencyTextBlock" />
```

```
<StackPanel x:Name="ButtonsStackPanel" Orientation="Horizontal"
                            HorizontalAlignment="Center">
    <Button HorizontalAlignment="Right" Height="86" Width="106" Name="FastBackwardButton"
                                        Click="FastBackwardButton_Click">
        <Image Source="Images/FastBackward.png" />
    </Button>
    <Button HorizontalAlignment="Right" Height="86" Width="106" Name="BackwardButton"
                                        Click="BackwardButton_Click">
        <Image Source="Images/Backward.png" />
    </Button>
    <Button HorizontalAlignment="Right" Height="86" Width="106" Name="ForwardButton"
                                        Click="ForwardButton_Click">
        <Image Source="Images/Forward.png" />
    </Button>
    <Button HorizontalAlignment="Right" Height="86" Width="106" Name="FastForwardButton"
                                        Click="FastForwardButton_Click">
        <Image Source="Images/FastForward.png" />
    </Button>
  </StackPanel>
</StackPanel>
```

As you can see, you are creating image buttons by using the process you learned in Chapter 4. The only thing to explain in this XAML is the use of the style for the FrequencyTextBlock (another thing that you can see in Chapter 4). That is composed with the following XAML:

```
<Style x:Key="FrequencyTextBlockStyle" TargetType="TextBlock">
  <Setter Property="FontSize" Value="56"/>
  <Setter Property="FontFamily" Value="Meiryo UI"/>
  <Setter Property="VerticalAlignment" Value="Center"/>
  <Setter Property="HorizontalAlignment" Value="Center"/>
</Style>
```

Now, after you have created the interface, you can concentrate on the code-behind, the place where you interact with the FMRadio API.

First, declare at the class level six constants that will be the top limit and bottom limit of frequency ranges available in Europe, the United States, and Japan:

```
private const double minFrequencyEurope = 87.6;
private const double maxFrequencyEurope = 107.7;

private const double minFrequencyUnitedStates = 87.8;
private const double maxFrequencyUnitedStates = 108;

private const double minFrequencyJapan = 76;
private const double maxFrequencyJapan = 90;
```

After this, you need the instance of the radio:

```
FMRadio radio = FMRadio.Instance;
```

Because the radio could need up to three seconds to start, it is not convenient to launch it in the constructor. Other than that, we prefer to start the application as soon as possible, again to give control to the user.

```
public MainPage()
{
    InitializeComponent();
    this.Loaded += new RoutedEventHandler(MainPage_Loaded);
}
```

And inside the `MainPage_Loaded` event handler, you will start your application:

```
void MainPage_Loaded(object sender, RoutedEventArgs e)
{
    RadioSwitch.Checked += new
EventHandler<RoutedEventArgs>(RadioSwitch_CheckChanged);
    RadioSwitch.Unchecked += new
EventHandler<RoutedEventArgs>(RadioSwitch_CheckChanged);
}
```

At this point, you need something that will update the interface and at the same time check the current state of radio instance, and then declare at class level a `Timer` from `System.Threading` namespace to do an action at given time and you initialize `Timer` inside `Loaded` event handler:

```
private Timer signalCheckTimer;
...
signalCheckTimer = new Timer((o) =>
    {
        Deployment.Current.Dispatcher.BeginInvoke(() =>
        {
            this.SignalSlider.Value = radio.SignalStrength;
            this.FrequencyTextBlock.Text = radio.Frequency.ToString();
            this.RadioSwitch.IsChecked = radio.PowerMode == RadioPowerMode.On;
        });
    }, null, 100, 100);
```

Now that you have updated the interface, looking for any changes to the state of the radio, you can begin creating the event handler for the controls. The first is the `ToggleSwitch`, which when touched by the user, turns the radio on and off.

```
void RadioSwitch_CheckChanged(object sender, RoutedEventArgs e)
{
    try
    {
        bool powerCheck = RadioSwitch.IsChecked.HasValue
```

```
                     ? RadioSwitch.IsChecked.Value
                     : false;
             radio.PowerMode = powerCheck
                 ? RadioPowerMode.On
                 : RadioPowerMode.Off;
    }
    catch (RadioDisabledException ex)
    {
        ManageRadioDisabledException(ex);
    }
}
```

As you can see, you have introduced a method to manage what to do when the radio is not available. In this case, you show a message box. However, it is useful to do this, calling a method, because you will manage the exception that can come from all methods in only one point of your code.

Given that you can change the actual frequency of the radio in several places with different buttons, and that you have to verify the correctness of any modification, we prefer to use a method to do it from everywhere in your code. And this is called ManageFrequencyChange:

```
private void ManageFrequencyChange(double delta)
    {
        try
        {
            double frequency = radio.Frequency;
            do
            {
                frequency += delta;
                switch (radio.CurrentRegion)
                {
                    case RadioRegion.Europe:
                        if (frequency < minFrequencyEurope)
                            frequency = maxFrequencyEurope;
                        if (frequency > maxFrequencyEurope)
                            frequency = minFrequencyEurope;
                        break;
                    case RadioRegion.Japan:
                        if (frequency < minFrequencyJapan)
                            frequency = maxFrequencyJapan;
                        if (frequency > maxFrequencyJapan)
                            frequency = minFrequencyJapan;
                        break;
                    case RadioRegion.UnitedStates:
                        if (frequency < minFrequencyUnitedStates)
                            frequency = maxFrequencyUnitedStates;
                        if (frequency > maxFrequencyUnitedStates)
                            frequency = minFrequencyUnitedStates;

                        break;
                    default:
                      //Throw new ArgumentException();
                        break;
```

```
            }

        } while (!IsFrequencyCorrect(frequency));
        radio.Frequency = Math.Round(frequency, 1);

    }
```

As you can see here, you have introduced a new method, which checks whether a frequency is correct for the radio region available:

```
private bool IsFrequencyCorrect(double frequency)
    {
        string separator = CultureInfo.CurrentCulture.NumberFormat.NumberDecimalSeparator;
        bool isCorrect = false;
        string frequencyAsString = Math.Round(frequency, 1).ToString();
        switch (radio.CurrentRegion)
        {
            case RadioRegion.Europe:
             isCorrect = frequencyAsString.EndsWith(string.Format("{0}1", separator)) ||
             frequencyAsString.EndsWith(string.Format("{0}3", separator)) ||
             frequencyAsString.EndsWith(string.Format("{0}5", separator)) ||
             frequencyAsString.EndsWith(string.Format("{0}6", separator)) ||
             frequencyAsString.EndsWith(string.Format("{0}8", separator)) ||
             frequencyAsString.EndsWith(string.Format("{0}0", separator));
                break;
            case RadioRegion.Japan:
                //check here the correctness of frequency for this position
                break;
            case RadioRegion.UnitedStates:
                //check here the correctness of frequency for this position
                break;
            default:
                throw new ArgumentOutOfRangeException();
        }
        return isCorrect;
    }
```

The last thing to do at this point is to manage all the buttons' clicks, and look for a strong frequency:

```
private void ForwardButton_Click(object sender, RoutedEventArgs e)
    {
        ManageFrequencyChange(0.1);
    }

    private void BackwardButton_Click(object sender, RoutedEventArgs e)
    {
        ManageFrequencyChange(-0.1);
    }
```

```
        private void FastBackwardButton_Click(object sender, RoutedEventArgs e)
        {
            try
            {
                do
                {
                    ManageFrequencyChange(-0.1);
                } while (radio.SignalStrength * 100 < 65);
            }


            catch (RadioDisabledException ex)
            {
                ManageRadioDisabledException(ex);
            }
        }

        private void FastForwardButton_Click(object sender, RoutedEventArgs e)
        {
            try
            {
                do
                {
                    ManageFrequencyChange(0.1);
                } while (radio.SignalStrength * 100 < 65);
            }
            catch (RadioDisabledException ex)
            {
                ManageRadioDisabledException(ex);
            }
        }
```

The Seek functionality has now been implemented thanks to the do…while loop, which is stopped when the signal reaches at least 70 percent.

Usage

From Visual Studio, start the application by pressing F5. Start using the radio—changing the frequency, finding a strong signal, and then testing the signal strength as you move around.

6-7. Building an Augmented Reality Application

Problem

You want to create an application that provides augmented reality providing different information depending on the orientation of the phone.

Solution

You must use the PhotoCamera class to access real-time video and Motion API in order to access data about movements of the phone in a space, and then, depending on data provided by the Motion class, you will choose what function to start (e.g., if the user points the camera to the sky, you will retreive weather forecast information).

How It Works

As mentioned, Windows Phone supports a wide variety of sensors, which includes the gyroscope, accelerometer, and compass. But combining raw data that these sensors give to you could be difficult, because you must consider that accelerometer offers you more information than you may need. For example, it may be that you don't need the information on the force of gravity. For this reason you find in Motion API all you need to implement augmented reality without having to think about various mathematical calculations to extrapolate the data from the combination of sensors.

Not all devices support the Motion class, so when you use it you must check the property IsSupported (shown in Figure 6-9) in order to avoid InvalidOperationException if the sensor is not present on a device.

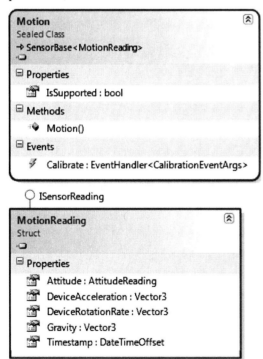

Figure 6-9. Motion class diagram

The Code

Your view will be really simple and will contain a rectangle filled by a VideoBrush and a textbox to show what operation you will do. The rectangle with the VideoBrush will have another rectangle as overlay, that will be filled depending on the forecast, enriching the reality with information that you will get via a service.

```xml
<phone:PhoneApplicationPage
    x:Class="AugmentedReality.MainPage"
    xmlns="http://schemas.microsoft.com/winfx/2006/xaml/presentation"
    xmlns:x="http://schemas.microsoft.com/winfx/2006/xaml"
    xmlns:phone="clr-namespace:Microsoft.Phone.Controls;assembly=Microsoft.Phone"
    xmlns:shell="clr-namespace:Microsoft.Phone.Shell;assembly=Microsoft.Phone"
    xmlns:d="http://schemas.microsoft.com/expression/blend/2008"
    xmlns:mc="http://schemas.openxmlformats.org/markup-compatibility/2006"
    mc:Ignorable="d" d:DesignWidth="728" d:DesignHeight="480"
    FontFamily="{StaticResource PhoneFontFamilyNormal}"
    FontSize="{StaticResource PhoneFontSizeNormal}"
    Foreground="{StaticResource PhoneForegroundBrush}"
    SupportedOrientations="Landscape" Orientation="Landscape"
    shell:SystemTray.IsVisible="False">

    <!--LayoutRoot is the root grid where all page content is placed-->
    <Grid x:Name="LayoutRoot" Background="Transparent">
        <Grid.RowDefinitions>
            <RowDefinition Height="*"/>
            <RowDefinition Height="50" />
        </Grid.RowDefinitions>
        <!--ContentPanel - place additional content here-->
        <Grid x:Name="ContentPanel" >
            <Grid.RowDefinitions>
                <RowDefinition />
                <RowDefinition />
            </Grid.RowDefinitions>
            <Canvas Width="640" Height="480">
                        <Rectangle Width="640" Height="480" Grid.RowSpan="2">
                    <Rectangle.Fill>
                    <VideoBrush x:Name="realityVideoBrush" />
                    </Rectangle.Fill>
                </Rectangle>
                        <Rectangle Canvas.ZIndex="100" Canvas.Left="0" Canvas.Top="50"
Width="640" Height="480" x:Name="WeatherRectangle" Grid.Row="0" Visibility="Collapsed" />
                </Canvas>

        </Grid>
        <TextBlock Name="InformationTextBlock" Grid.Row="1" />

    </Grid>

</phone:PhoneApplicationPage>
```

Now that we have a view, we must prepare all requirements to create a lot of good overlay animations in order to enrich the user experience, and then start creating a new folder in your project named Assets. Then create in this folder a dictionary named Style.xaml, and in this dictionary you will define resources like brushes to fill the overlay and show the forecast.

```xml
<ResourceDictionary x:Name="Styles"
        xmlns="http://schemas.microsoft.com/winfx/2006/xaml/presentation"
        xmlns:x="http://schemas.microsoft.com/winfx/2006/xaml">

  <ImageBrush x:Key="LightningBrush" ImageSource="../Images/Lightning.png" Stretch="Fill"/>
  <ImageBrush x:Key="SunBrush" ImageSource="../Images/Sun.png" Stretch="Fill"/>
  <LinearGradientBrush x:Key="FogBrush" EndPoint="0.5,1" StartPoint="0.5,0">
    <GradientStop Color="#55393939"/>
    <GradientStop Color="#55FFFFFF" Offset="1"/>
  </LinearGradientBrush>
</ResourceDictionary>
```

The first two brushes are ImageBrush, and then you must download images that you can apply as overlay of the reality on the device. You will find images in the project related to this recipe. For the fog, it's sufficient to have a LinearGradientBrush.

Now that you have the brushes, you can prepare storyboards to start when you want to apply effects to the view. In case of lightning, the storyboard will flash an image (with a transparent background) that simulates thunder; when the forecast is for sun, you will show a smiling sun across the sky, and when the fog comes a gray overlay will hide the camera. Then your storyboards will be similar to this:

```xml
        <phone:PhoneApplicationPage.Resources>
                <Storyboard x:Name="LightningStoryboard" RepeatBehavior="1x">
                        <DoubleAnimation Duration="0" To="174"
Storyboard.TargetProperty="(FrameworkElement.Height)" Storyboard.TargetName="WeatherRectangle"
d:IsOptimized="True"/>
                        <ObjectAnimationUsingKeyFrames
Storyboard.TargetProperty="(UIElement.Visibility)" Storyboard.TargetName="WeatherRectangle">
                                <DiscreteObjectKeyFrame KeyTime="0">
                                        <DiscreteObjectKeyFrame.Value>
                                                <Visibility>Visible</Visibility>
                                        </DiscreteObjectKeyFrame.Value>
                                </DiscreteObjectKeyFrame>
                                <DiscreteObjectKeyFrame KeyTime="0:0:0.1">
                                        <DiscreteObjectKeyFrame.Value>
                                                <Visibility>Collapsed</Visibility>
                                        </DiscreteObjectKeyFrame.Value>
                                </DiscreteObjectKeyFrame>
                                <DiscreteObjectKeyFrame KeyTime="0:0:0.2">
                                        <DiscreteObjectKeyFrame.Value>
                                                <Visibility>Visible</Visibility>
                                        </DiscreteObjectKeyFrame.Value>
                                </DiscreteObjectKeyFrame>
                                <DiscreteObjectKeyFrame KeyTime="0:0:0.4">
                                        <DiscreteObjectKeyFrame.Value>
                                                <Visibility>Collapsed</Visibility>
                                        </DiscreteObjectKeyFrame.Value>
```

```
                                        </DiscreteObjectKeyFrame>
                                        <DiscreteObjectKeyFrame KeyTime="0:0:0.5">
                                                <DiscreteObjectKeyFrame.Value>
                                                        <Visibility>Visible</Visibility>
                                                </DiscreteObjectKeyFrame.Value>
                                        </DiscreteObjectKeyFrame>
                                        <DiscreteObjectKeyFrame KeyTime="0:0:0.6">
                                                <DiscreteObjectKeyFrame.Value>
                                                        <Visibility>Collapsed</Visibility>
                                                </DiscreteObjectKeyFrame.Value>
                                        </DiscreteObjectKeyFrame>
                                        <DiscreteObjectKeyFrame KeyTime="0:0:0.8">
                                                <DiscreteObjectKeyFrame.Value>
                                                        <Visibility>Visible</Visibility>
                                                </DiscreteObjectKeyFrame.Value>
                                        </DiscreteObjectKeyFrame>
                                        <DiscreteObjectKeyFrame KeyTime="0:0:0.9">
                                                <DiscreteObjectKeyFrame.Value>
                                                        <Visibility>Collapsed</Visibility>
                                                </DiscreteObjectKeyFrame.Value>
                                        </DiscreteObjectKeyFrame>
                                        <DiscreteObjectKeyFrame KeyTime="0:0:1">
                                                <DiscreteObjectKeyFrame.Value>
                                                        <Visibility>Visible</Visibility>
                                                </DiscreteObjectKeyFrame.Value>
                                        </DiscreteObjectKeyFrame>
                                </ObjectAnimationUsingKeyFrames>
                                <DoubleAnimationUsingKeyFrames
Storyboard.TargetProperty="(FrameworkElement.Width)" Storyboard.TargetName="WeatherRectangle">
                                        <EasingDoubleKeyFrame KeyTime="0" Value="641"/>
                                        <EasingDoubleKeyFrame KeyTime="0:0:0.1" Value="640"/>
                                </DoubleAnimationUsingKeyFrames>
                                <DoubleAnimation Duration="0" To="0"
Storyboard.TargetProperty="(Canvas.Left)" Storyboard.TargetName="WeatherRectangle"
d:IsOptimized="True"/>
                        </Storyboard>
                        <Storyboard x:Name="SunStoryboard" RepeatBehavior="1x">
                                <DoubleAnimation Duration="0" To="100"
Storyboard.TargetProperty="(FrameworkElement.Height)" Storyboard.TargetName="WeatherRectangle"
d:IsOptimized="True"/>
                                <DoubleAnimation Duration="0" To="100"
Storyboard.TargetProperty="(FrameworkElement.Width)" Storyboard.TargetName="WeatherRectangle"
d:IsOptimized="True"/>
                                <ObjectAnimationUsingKeyFrames
Storyboard.TargetProperty="(UIElement.Visibility)" Storyboard.TargetName="WeatherRectangle">
                                        <DiscreteObjectKeyFrame KeyTime="0">
                                                <DiscreteObjectKeyFrame.Value>
                                                        <Visibility>Visible</Visibility>
                                                </DiscreteObjectKeyFrame.Value>
                                        </DiscreteObjectKeyFrame>
                                </ObjectAnimationUsingKeyFrames>
```

```xml
                            <DoubleAnimationUsingKeyFrames
Storyboard.TargetProperty="(Canvas.Left)" Storyboard.TargetName="WeatherRectangle">
                                <EasingDoubleKeyFrame KeyTime="0" Value="0">
                                    <EasingDoubleKeyFrame.EasingFunction>
                                        <CircleEase EasingMode="EaseOut"/>
                                    </EasingDoubleKeyFrame.EasingFunction>
                                </EasingDoubleKeyFrame>
                                <EasingDoubleKeyFrame KeyTime="0:0:1.5" Value="254">
                                    <EasingDoubleKeyFrame.EasingFunction>
                                        <QuinticEase EasingMode="EaseOut"/>
                                    </EasingDoubleKeyFrame.EasingFunction>
                                </EasingDoubleKeyFrame>
                                <EasingDoubleKeyFrame KeyTime="0:0:2.8" Value="536">
                                    <EasingDoubleKeyFrame.EasingFunction>
                                        <CircleEase EasingMode="EaseOut"/>
                                    </EasingDoubleKeyFrame.EasingFunction>
                                </EasingDoubleKeyFrame>
                            </DoubleAnimationUsingKeyFrames>
                            <DoubleAnimationUsingKeyFrames
Storyboard.TargetProperty="(Canvas.Top)" Storyboard.TargetName="WeatherRectangle">
                                <EasingDoubleKeyFrame KeyTime="0" Value="50">
                                    <EasingDoubleKeyFrame.EasingFunction>
                                        <CircleEase EasingMode="EaseOut"/>
                                    </EasingDoubleKeyFrame.EasingFunction>
                                </EasingDoubleKeyFrame>
                                <EasingDoubleKeyFrame KeyTime="0:0:1.5" Value="2">
                                    <EasingDoubleKeyFrame.EasingFunction>
                                        <QuinticEase EasingMode="EaseOut"/>
                                    </EasingDoubleKeyFrame.EasingFunction>
                                </EasingDoubleKeyFrame>
                                <EasingDoubleKeyFrame KeyTime="0:0:2.8" Value="52">
                                    <EasingDoubleKeyFrame.EasingFunction>
                                        <CircleEase EasingMode="EaseOut"/>
                                    </EasingDoubleKeyFrame.EasingFunction>
                                </EasingDoubleKeyFrame>
                            </DoubleAnimationUsingKeyFrames>
                    </Storyboard>
                    <Storyboard x:Name="FogStoryboard">
                            <DoubleAnimationUsingKeyFrames
Storyboard.TargetProperty="(Canvas.Top)" Storyboard.TargetName="WeatherRectangle">
                                <EasingDoubleKeyFrame KeyTime="0" Value="-600"/>
                                <EasingDoubleKeyFrame KeyTime="0:0:1" Value="0"/>
                            </DoubleAnimationUsingKeyFrames>
                            <DoubleAnimation Duration="0" To="0"
Storyboard.TargetProperty="(Canvas.Left)" Storyboard.TargetName="WeatherRectangle"
d:IsOptimized="True"/>
                            <ObjectAnimationUsingKeyFrames
Storyboard.TargetProperty="(UIElement.Visibility)" Storyboard.TargetName="WeatherRectangle">
                                <DiscreteObjectKeyFrame KeyTime="0">
                                    <DiscreteObjectKeyFrame.Value>
                                        <Visibility>Visible</Visibility>
                                    </DiscreteObjectKeyFrame.Value>
```

```
                        </DiscreteObjectKeyFrame>
                    </ObjectAnimationUsingKeyFrames>
                    <DoubleAnimation Duration="0" To="320"
Storyboard.TargetProperty="(FrameworkElement.Height)" Storyboard.TargetName="WeatherRectangle"
d:IsOptimized="True"/>
                    <DoubleAnimation Duration="0" To="640"
Storyboard.TargetProperty="(FrameworkElement.Width)" Storyboard.TargetName="WeatherRectangle"
d:IsOptimized="True"/>
                </Storyboard>
            </phone:PhoneApplicationPage.Resources>
```

Everything about the page is ready, so you can pass to the code behind, where you will use the Motion class to trap the user movements, a GeoCoordinateWatcher to retrieve the position of the user, a PhotoCamera in order to capture the reality to show to the user, and a lot of objects that will support you during the development.

```
        private Motion _motionHandler;
        private PhotoCamera _photoCamera;
        private GeoCoordinateWatcher _geoWatcher;
        private WeatherProxy _weatherProxy;
        private TimeSpan _minimumRequestTime;
        private DateTime _lastRequestTime;
        private Storyboard _executingStoryboard;
```

The first helps you to access the Motion API of Windows Phone. With PhotoCamera, you will access real-time use of the camera. You can see a class nowhere explained before; this class is WeatherProxy and simply acts as proxy between your client and a service that provides forecast information. WeatherProxy it's implemented in this way:

```
        public event GetWeatherCompletedEventHandler GetWeatherCompleted;

        public void GetWeatherAsync(GeoCoordinate coordinate)
        {
            weatherService.GetForecastCompleted += RetrieveCompleted;
            weatherService.GetForecastAsync(coordinate.Latitude, coordinate.Longitude);
        }

        private void RetriveCompleted(object sender, GetForecastCompletedEventArgs e)
    {
      if (GetWeatherCompleted != null)
        GetWeatherCompleted(this, new
GetWeatherCompletedEventArgs(DecodeWeatherStatus(e.Result)));
      }

        public delegate void GetWeatherCompletedEventHandler(object sender, GetWeatherComplete
dEventArgs e);

        public class GetWeatherCompletedEventArgs : System.ComponentModel.AsyncCompletedEventA
rgs
        {
            public GetWeatherCompletedEventArgs(Weather weather)
            {
```

```
            Weather = weather;
        }
        public Weather Weather { get; private set; }
    }
```

The GetWeatherCompletedEventArgs exposes a property of type Weather that is an enumeration (its values are Sun, Rain, Lightning, Clouds, Fog) that you use in the method DecodeWeatherStatus; the implementation of this method misses voluntary because it's the only part that depends on the forecast service that you choose to use.

Now that you have the necessary objects to implement augmented reality in OnNavigatedTo event handler, you will initialize _motionHandler and _photoCamera, then you will check if it's available on user device the support to Motion API, and so on the others objects.

```
protected override void OnNavigatedTo(System.Windows.Navigation.NavigationEventArgs e)
    {
        try
        {
            // Initialize the camera and set the video brush source.
            if (!Motion.IsSupported)
            {
                MessageBox.Show("the Motion API is not supported on this device.");
                return;
            }

            _photoCamera = new PhotoCamera();
            realityVideoBrush.SetSource(_photoCamera);

            _minimumRequestTime = TimeSpan.FromSeconds(8);

            _geoWatcher = new GeoCoordinateWatcher(GeoPositionAccuracy.High);
            _geoWatcher.Start();
            _weatherProxy = new WeatherProxy();
            _weatherProxy.GetWeatherCompleted += GetForecastCompleted;

            if (_motionHandler == null)
            {
                _motionHandler = new Motion
                                {
                                        TimeBetweenUpdates = TimeSpan.FromMilliseconds(20
)
                                };
                _motionHandler.CurrentValueChanged += MotionHandlerCurrentValueChanged;
            }

            // Try to start the Motion API.
            _motionHandler.Start();
        }
        catch (SensorFailedException)
        {
            MessageBox.Show("unable to start the Motion API.");
        }
        catch (Exception ex)
```

```
        {
            MessageBox.Show(ex.Message);
        }
    }
```

In this code you make a lot of initialization about "service" objects, then you check if Motion API are supported and you initialize the _motionHandler with a period of 20 milliseconds subscribing the CurrentValueChanged event.

```
void MotionHandlerCurrentValueChanged(object sender, SensorReadingEventArgs<MotionReading> e)
    {
        // This event arrives from a background thread. Use BeginInvoke
        // to call a method on the UI thread.

        Dispatcher.BeginInvoke(() =>
            {
                if (e.SensorReading.Gravity.Z > 0.6)
                {
                    if (DateTime.Now.Subtract(_lastRequestTime) > _minimumRequestTime)
                    {
                        _lastRequestTime = DateTime.Now;
                        GetForecast(_geoWatcher.Position);
                    }
                }
                else
                {
                    if (_executingStoryboard != null) _executingStoryboard.Stop();
                }
            });
    }
```

Because this event rises from a background thread, you must use BeginInvoke to do something on the UI thread.

When the user rotates the device to the sky, you check how long ago you made a request to retrieve a forecast, in order to not make too many requests, and then you store the time of the request, and you call a method GetForecast that uses the _weatherProxy object and its asynchronous method GetWeather.

```
    private void GetForecast(GeoPosition<GeoCoordinate> position)
    {
        InformationTextBlock.Text = "Looking for forecast...";
        _weatherProxy.GetWeatherAsync(position.Location);
    }


    private void GetForecastCompleted(object sender, WeatherProxy.GetWeatherCompletedEventArgs e)
    {
        Brush brush = null;
        switch (e.Weather)
        {
            case Weather.Sun:
```

```
                    brush = App.Current.Resources.MergedDictionaries.FirstOrDefault()["SunBru
sh"] as ImageBrush;
                    _executingStoryboard = SunStoryboard;
                    break;
                case Weather.Fog:
                    brush = App.Current.Resources.MergedDictionaries.FirstOrDefault()["FogBrus
h"] as LinearGradientBrush;
                    _executingStoryboard = FogStoryboard;
                    break;
                case Weather.Lightning:
                    brush = App.Current.Resources.MergedDictionaries.FirstOrDefault()["Lightn
ingBrush"] as ImageBrush;
                    _executingStoryboard = LightningStoryboard;
                    break;
                case Weather.Clouds:
                    break;
            }
            WeatherRectangle.Fill = brush;
            _executingStoryboard.Begin();
        }
```

After all that, don't forget to release the resources in this way:

```
        protected override void OnNavigatedFrom(System.Windows.Navigation.NavigationEventArgs
e)
        {
            if (_photoCamera != null) _photoCamera.Dispose();
            if (_geoWatcher != null) _geoWatcher.Stop();
        }
```

Usage

This recipe works only on a physical device, because an emulator doesn't support Motion API. In Visual Studio, select Windows Phone Device as target of delivery, then point the camera to the sky to retrieve forecast information. In this recipe we don't explain how the WeatherProxy class retrieves the information from the Web. There are a lot of services that enable you to do this, and you can choose your own. The application will give you an interaction as shown in Figure 6-10.

Figure 6-10. *The application while it works*

Media Management

In this chapter, you will find recipes dedicated to media management. Indeed, audio and video are two of the best resources provided by your phone, and as a developer, there are so many cool tricks and tips you should know in order to produce both ear-catching and eye-catching applications. The recipes in this chapter describe how to do the following:

- 7-1. Take a photo from your phone camera and upload it to the Flickr site

- 7-2. Capture and stream video using your phone camera and send images to Windows applications over the Internet

- 7-3. Pick a photo from your media library and upload it to the Flickr site

- 7-4. Use Picture Extensibility to integrate your application in the Windows Phone operating system

- 7-5. Use Windows Media Player to shuffle songs in your media library

- 7-6. Use a background audio agent to play music that is stored on SkyDrive

- 7-7. Use the microphone in the Funny Repeater application

- 7-8. Use the `MediaElement` control to play both music and video

- 7-9. Add integration with the Music-Videos hub

7-1. Taking a Photo from Your Phone Camera

Problem

You need to take a photo from your application without pressing the hardware Camera button provided by the phone.

Solution

You have to use the `CameraCaptureTask` chooser, which provides the `Show` method used to programmatically show the same camera application that is executed by the hardware Camera phone button.

How It Works

As you learned in Chapter 3, choosers are used to run external native Windows Phone applications or tasks. The main difference as compared to launchers is that choosers return data to your program. On the contrary, a chooser such as `CameraCaptureTask` opens the photo camera on the device and returns the photo taken from the camera to your application.

The `CameraCaptureTask` class provides the `Show` method, which is responsible for running the external application that enables you to take a picture from the camera and to set some options such as flash on/off, and zoom.

After the picture is taken, `CameraCaptureTask` raises the `Completed` event that your application can hook in order to have information on the photo. Indeed, the `PhotoResult` event argument provided by this event contains very important information about the photo such as the temporary path where it has been stored—the `OriginalFileName` property—and the stream containing the data of the phone—the `ChosenPhoto` property.

The Code

To demonstrate the use of the photo camera, we have created an application that enables us to take a picture and upload it to an account on the Flickr site. You have already seen part of this application in action in Chapter 3, Recipe 3-1, about animating a splash screen.

Open Visual Studio 2010 and load the `FlickrPhotoAlbum` application. In the `MainPage.xaml.cs` file, we defined a `CameraCaptureTask` object at the class level and we initialized it in the class constructor. The `Completed` event is managed by the `camera_Completed` event handler:

```
public partial class MainPage : PhoneApplicationPage
{
    CameraCaptureTask camera = null;
    Popup popup = null;

    // Constructor
    public MainPage()
    {
        InitializeComponent();

        camera = new CameraCaptureTask();
        camera.Completed += new EventHandler<PhotoResult>(camera_Completed);
```
. . .

The `camera_Completed` event handler contains the code that stores the image in a memory stream to be reused during the Flickr upload, and the code to show a preview by using the `Image` control defined in the `MainPage.xaml` file. Before performing any operation, the `TaskResult` property is checked to see whether the task has given a positive result returning OK. Next, the `ChosenPhoto` property containing the stream of picture data is copied to a byte array and, successively, to the memory stream. Finally, the `OriginalFileName` property is used by the `BitmapImage` class constructor to create a new image and set the `Image` control's `Source` property to it.

```
void camera_Completed(object sender, PhotoResult e)
{
    App app = Application.Current as App;

    if (e.TaskResult == TaskResult.OK)
    {
        byte[] data;
        using (var br = new BinaryReader(e.ChosenPhoto)) data =
                br.ReadBytes((int)e.ChosenPhoto.Length);
        app.settings.Image = new MemoryStream(data);

        BitmapImage bi = new BitmapImage(
                            new Uri(e.OriginalFileName));
        bi.CreateOptions = BitmapCreateOptions.DelayCreation;
        bi.SetSource(new MemoryStream(data));
        imgPhoto.Source = new WriteableBitmap(bi);
        btnUpload.IsEnabled = true;
    }
}
```

■ **Note** In the preceding code, you can see the `App` class having the `settings` property. This property points to an object from the `Settings` class that we added to contain useful information to be shared with all the pages within the application.

In the `MainPage.xaml.cs` code file, there is a button to take the photo that is enabled after you have successfully logged on to the Flickr site and given authorization to the phone application. In the `Click` event of this button, we call the `Show` method provided by the `CameraCaptureTask` class so that the Camera application is shown:

```
private void btnTakePicture_Click(object sender, RoutedEventArgs e)
{
    camera.Show();
}
```

That's all about camera usage from the code; let's focus our attention on Flickr functionalities. We have used the Flickr.NET library that you can download from the `http://flickrnet.codeplex.com` site. This library contains a lot of assemblies targeting almost all .NET systems, including Windows Phone 7.

To use this library in your code, you need to register your application on the Flickr site and receive an application API key and a security key. Then in your code you have to use both keys in the Flickr class's constructor, as shown in the following code.

> ■ **Note** Because API and security keys are private, you will not find ours in the code. You have to register your application on Flickr and use yours in the Flickr class's constructor.

```
public partial class App : Application
{
    /// <summary>
    /// Provides easy access to the root frame of the Phone Application.
    /// </summary>
    /// <returns>The root frame of the Phone Application.</returns>
    public PhoneApplicationFrame RootFrame { get; private set; }

    private FlickrNet.Flickr _flickr;
    public FlickrNet.Flickr FlickrService { get { return _flickr; } }
```

. . .

```
_flickr = new FlickrNet.Flickr("apiKey", "secureKey");
```

Because your application will be used by different users who want to upload photos on their accounts, the first thing you need to do in your code is to authenticate the user. This is accomplished adding a `WebBrowser` control to the `MainPage.xaml` page, to point to an URL calculated by the `AuthCalcUrl` method. This method accepts `Frob` as an input parameter; `Frob` is a sort of application identifier that we have to use in different API calls such as `AuthCalcUrl` ones. `Frob` is returned by a call to the `AuthGetFrobAsync` method. This is an async method that accepts a callback function as a parameter. We used a lambda expression in our code to create an inline callback function. Moreover, we used the `BeginInvoke` static method from the `Dispatcher` class so that the application is not stuck waiting for the Flickr API response and the user can continue to use it. The `r` parameter represents the result; we check whether there are errors by using the `HasError` property, and if there are no errors, we store the result in the `Frob` property from the `Settings` class. Finally, we call the `AuthCalcUrl` method to retrieve the calculated URL that we pass to the `Navigate` method provided by the `WebBrowser` control.

```
private void ConnectToFlickr()
{
    App a = Application.Current as App;

    Flickr flickr = a.FlickrService;

    flickr.AuthGetFrobAsync(r =>
    {
        Dispatcher.BeginInvoke(() =>
        {
            if (r.HasError)
            {
                MessageBox.Show(r.Error.Message);
            }
            else
```

```
            {
                a.settings.Frob = r.Result;
                string url = flickr.AuthCalcUrl(a.settings.Frob, AuthLevel.Write);
                Uri uri = new Uri(url);
                wbBrowser.Navigate(uri);
            }
        });
    });
}
```

The next step is retrieving the authentication token after the user is authenticated at the Flickr site. The AuthGetTokenAsync method accepts the Frob identifier and, like AuthGetFrobAsync, accepts a callback function that is called by this async method after the authorization process is finished. Even in this method we used a lambda expression as an inline callback function. If no errors occur, some buttons are enabled and the authorization token key is stored in the application settings.

```
private void btnAuthenticate_Click(object sender, RoutedEventArgs e)
{
    App app = Application.Current as App;

    app.FlickrService.AuthGetTokenAsync(app.settings.Frob, r =>
    {
        Dispatcher.BeginInvoke(() =>
        {
            if (r.HasError)
            {
                MessageBox.Show(r.Error.Message);
            }
            else
            {
                app.settings.Token = r.Result;
                btnTakePicture.IsEnabled = true;
                wbBrowser.Visibility = System.Windows.Visibility.Collapsed;
                imgPhoto.Visibility = System.Windows.Visibility.Visible;
            }
        });
    });
}
```

Finally, the photo uploading is accomplished by the UploadPictureAsync method. Among the many parameters it accepts, the ones worth noting are the first parameter (a Stream object containing the image data) and the third parameter (which is the name of the image that will be associated with the photo).

```
private void Button_Click(object sender, RoutedEventArgs e)
{

    if (txtName.Text == string.Empty)
```

```
    {
        MessageBox.Show("Please, specify the photo name");
        return;
    }

    App app = Application.Current as App;

    app.FlickrService.UploadPictureAsync(app.settings.Image,
                                txtName.Text,
                                txtName.Text,
                                txtDescription.Text,
                                txtTag.Text,
                                true,
                                true,
                                true,
                                ContentType.Photo,
                                SafetyLevel.None,
                                HiddenFromSearch.None, r =>
                                {
                                    Dispatcher.BeginInvoke(() =>
                                    {
                                        if (r.HasError)
                                        {
                                            MessageBox.Show("Ooops,
                                                error during upload...");
                                        }
                                        else
                                        {
                                            MessageBox.Show("Upload
                                                done successfully...");
                                        }
                                    });
                                });
}
```

Usage

With Visual Studio 2010 opened, set the target output to Windows Phone Emulator and press Ctrl+F5. The emulator starts, briefly showing the animated splash screen. Meanwhile, the application is requiring the Frob identifier and uses it to calculate the URL. When this process is accomplished, the main page is shown with the WebBrowser control filled with the Flickr page (see Figure 7-1).

Figure 7-1. *The* `FlickrPhotoAlbum` *application in action*

After inserting your Flickr credentials and accepting that the `FlickrPhotoAlbum` application can access your account, you can press the Authenticate button. If the process doesn't return errors, the Take A Picture button will be enabled. Press this button and you will see the emulator simulating the Windows Phone Camera application (see Figure 7-2). The emulator will show a moving square, simulating a moving target. By pressing the top-right icon, you can take a photo shot.

■ **Note** If you are using the Windows Phone device with Zune running and connected, you will not be able to accomplish this step, because Zune software locks the camera. You have to shut Zune down and use the WPConnect tool that you can find in the %Program Files%\Microsoft SDKs\Windows Phone\v7.1\Tools\WPConnect path.

Figure 7-2. The camera emulated by the Windows Phone Emulator

After taking the picture and accepting it, you can see that the Upload button is enabled. By pressing the Upload button, the Upload page is shown. Here you have to fill some text boxes with the picture's name, description, and tag (see Figure 7-3). Press the Upload button (maybe you can't see it because it is too small!) to start the upload process.

Figure 7-3. *The Upload page contains text boxes used to specify the photo's name, description, and tag.*

Depending on your Internet connection speed and its traffic, after a few seconds you will be informed by a dialog box that the upload has been accomplished (see Figure 7-4).

Figure 7-4. *The upload is done.*

7-2. Capturing Photo Camera Video Frames

Problem

You need to capture a video source from the phone photo camera and send the captured images to another application that will display them. Moreover, the captured images have to be sent to the destination application using the Internet and sockets. Since networking access and the photo-camera capturing process are battery-consuming, the application has to work only when the phone is connected to a power supply and using a WiFi connection.

Solution

You can use the `CaptureSource` class that provides the Start and Stop methods to start and to stop capturing from an audio and video source, respectively.

Also, the `CaptureSource` class provides the `CaptureImageAsync` method to capture an image from the photo camera with an asynchronous operation that is concluded when the `CaptureImageCompleted` event is raised. You can use a `DispatcherTimer` object to capture an image in a fixed period of time and send the image to a Windows application using network sockets.

The Windows Phone application can show the photo camera images on the main page using the `VideoBrush` brush associated with a rectangle.

Finally, you can use the `DeviceStatus` and `DeviceNetworkInformation` classes to retrieve phone-status information.

How It Works

In the previous recipe, you saw how to take a picture using the photo camera chooser. You can now also capture video using the photo camera.

The `CaptureSource` class is useful to capture video streaming from the phone video camera. The `Start` method is used to begin acquiring video frames that are captured by your application using the `CaptureImageAsync` method and the `CaptureImageCompleted` event. The `CaptureImageAsync` asynchronous method starts to capture the video image and raises the `CaptureImageCompleted` event when it ends to capture the video image. The `CaptureImageCompleted` event provides the captured video frame by the `Result` property of the `CaptureImageCompletedEventArgs` class.

■ **Note** You can also grab video stream with a `VideoSink` derived class that overrides the `OnSample` method. The `OnSample` method provides the raw bytes composing the captured image.

The `CaptureSource` class has the `VideoCaptureDevice` property that is initialized with default values when you create a new `CaptureSource` object. You can use the `VideoCaptureDevice` class to set video camera properties such as the image format, the capturing frame rate, and the capturing device (i.e. on phones providing more than one photo camera). Once you have created a `VideoCaptureDevice` object and set its properties, you can use the `VideoCaptureDevice` property provided by the `CaptureSource` class to use the customized video device.

■ **Note** You can retrieve the list of available audio and video sources querying the methods provided by the `CaptureDeviceConfiguration` class.

When the Windows Phone application is either deactivated or closed by the user, it is mandatory to release video camera source using the Stop method from the `CaptureSource` class, unregister the event handlers, and dispose all the objects.

Until now we focused attention on the classes used to capture the video stream and on the methods to store images in memory. Now we will look at how to use the `VideoBrush` class to show video from the photo camera on the Windows Phone page. The `VideoBrush` brush class works in the same way as other brush classes and can be used to paint the content of every control that has the Fill property (i.e. rectangles, textboxes, textblocks, etc.).

Creating a `VideoBrush` brush is easy; just create an object from the `VideoBrush` class and use its `SetSource` method. The `SetSource` method accepts a single parameter, the `CaptureSource` object.

The Windows Phone application can retrieve the phone status, querying the methods and properties provided by the `DeviceStatus` and `DeviceNetworkInformation` classes. The `DeviceStatus` class provides static properties to retrieve information on the device status. The main properties are `PowerSource`, which returns whether the phone is plugged to a power source or the phone is using the battery; and the `ApplicationCurrentMemoryUsage` and the `ApplicationMemoryUsageLimit` properties, which retrieve the amount of used memory and the memory usage limit for the application, respectively.

The `DeviceNetworkInformation` class provides static properties and methods to retrieve information on the network. Among the others, the main properties are `IsWiFiEnabled`, `IsNetworkAvailable`, and `IsCellularDataEnabled` properties, which return Boolean values indicating whether the WiFi is enabled on the phone, whether the phone is connected to the network, and whether the phone is set to use the network connection to retrieve data.

The final part of this huge recipe regards networking and in particular, sockets. You want the captured image to be sent over the Internet to a target (or client) application. The target application has to show the captured image using the `Image` control, updating the control content each time a new image arrives. So, theoretically, the Windows Phone application is the server application because it provides the service of sending images to a client application, which shows the images on its screen. Unfortunately, the Windows Phone SDK doesn't provide classes such as `TcpListener`, or methods such as `Bind` and `Listen`, from the `Socket` class to implement a TCP server application. The main reason is because the Windows Phone SDK is a Silverlight 4 porting and, usually, a Silverlight application is hosted in a web browser. A web browser application has a lot of constrains and one of them is that you can't open TCP ports and accept incoming connections.

By the way, this is a purely theoretical aspect because you can create the Windows Phone application as the client application that connects to the Windows server application and sends images without receiving any data from the server.

Since you are creating a Windows Phone application that shows and sends captured images, you have to use networking sockets in an asynchronous way in order to not lock the phone screen until the image is completely sent to the server. For this purpose you can use the `ConnectAsync` and `SendAsync` methods.

A connection between a TCP server and a client is based on the IP address and the port number. The `Socket` class has the `RemoteEndPoint` property useful to specify just the IP address and the port number using an object from the `DnsEndPoint` class. After either the connection or sending process is terminated, the Completed event is raised. You can attach an event handler to the `Completed` event so that you can send data to the server.

From the server side, you have to create an infinite loop waiting for an incoming client connection. Once the connection is established, the `BeginAccept` asynchronous method is used to accept the incoming connection. To begin reading data, you need to call the `BeginReceive` method. Every method is an asynchronous method because even the server application has to show images on the screen and cannot lock the user interface until a video frame is received.

Since the server application has to implement an infinite loop and the user interface has to be unlocked, you have to create a different Thread dedicated to listen for the incoming connection. Since the thread that manages the infinite loop is different from the thread that manages the user interface, you have to use the `Dispatcher` object and the `BeginInvoke` method to change user interface content from the looping thread.

The Code

To demonstrate this recipe, we have created a Windows Phone Silverlight application named `BabyMonitor`. We have also created a Windows Presentation Foundation application named `BabyMonitorViewer` to show images captured by the phone.

Let's start examining the Windows Phone application code. In the `MainPage.xaml` page, we have defined a Rectangle that fills the entire phone screen. The phone orientation is set to Landscape and the system tray is hidden to have only the camera images on the screen.

```
<phone:PhoneApplicationPage
. . .
    SupportedOrientations="Landscape" Orientation="LandscapeLeft"
    shell:SystemTray.IsVisible="False">

    <!--LayoutRoot is the root grid where all page content is placed-->
    <Canvas x:Name="LayoutRoot" Background="Transparent">
        <!--Camera viewfinder >-->
        <Rectangle
            x:Name="viewfinderRectangle"
            Width="640"
            Height="480"
            HorizontalAlignment="Left"
            Canvas.Left="80" />
    </Canvas>
</phone:PhoneApplicationPage>
```

In the `MainPage.xaml.cs` code, we added the `OnNavigatedTo` and `OnNavigatedFrom` methods useful to initialize and to dispose video capturing, respectively.

```
        protected override void OnNavigatedTo(NavigationEventArgs e)
        {
            base.OnNavigatedTo(e);

            InitializeVideoRecorder();

            captureSource.CaptureImageAsync();
        }

        protected override void OnNavigatedFrom(NavigationEventArgs e)
        {
            DisposeVideoRecorder();

            base.OnNavigatedFrom(e);
        }
```

In the `InitializeVideoRecorder` method we have created the `CaptureSource` object, set the event handlers and associate the captured source to the video brush so that the Rectangle in the main page is filled by captured images. Finally, we call the `Start` method to begin with the video source capturing.

```
public void InitializeVideoRecorder()
{
    if (captureSource == null)
    {
        captureSource = new CaptureSource();

        videoCaptureDevice =
            CaptureDeviceConfiguration.GetDefaultVideoCaptureDevice();


        captureSource.CaptureImageCompleted += new
                    EventHandler<CaptureImageCompletedEventArgs>
                    (captureSource_CaptureImageCompleted);

        captureSource.CaptureFailed += new
                    EventHandler<ExceptionRoutedEventArgs>
                    (OnCaptureFailed);

        if (videoCaptureDevice != null)
        {
            videoRecorderBrush = new VideoBrush();
            videoRecorderBrush.SetSource(captureSource);

            viewfinderRectangle.Fill = videoRecorderBrush;

            captureSource.Start();
        }
    }
}
```

In the `DisposeVideoRecorder` method, we stop the video capturing process, unregister the event handlers, and dispose the objects.

```
private void DisposeVideoRecorder()
{
    if (captureSource != null)
    {
        if (captureSource.VideoCaptureDevice != null
            && captureSource.State == CaptureState.Started)
        {
            captureSource.Stop();
        }
        captureSource.CaptureImageCompleted -=
                    captureSource_CaptureImageCompleted;
        captureSource.CaptureFailed -= OnCaptureFailed;

        captureSource = null;
        videoCaptureDevice = null;
        videoRecorderBrush = null;

        _timer.Stop();
    }
```

```
        }
```

The core of this code is in the **captureSource_CaptureImageCompleted** event handler where the **Result** property provided by the **CaptureImageCompletedEventArgs** parameter is used to retrieve the captured image. Before sending the image to the listening server, we have converted the image to the **Jpeg** format in order to reduce the image size in bytes. The **SaveJpeg** method provided by the **WriteableBitmap** class accomplishes the task very well, even asking for the quality of the resulting image. We set the quality parameter to 100 (the maximum value), but you can change this value to obtain the best compromise between quality image and size in bytes. Finally, the capturing and sending image process starts only when the phone is connected to a power source and the phone has the WiFi enabled and is connected to the Internet.

```
void captureSource_CaptureImageCompleted(object sender,
                               CaptureImageCompletedEventArgs e)
{
    // Avoiding to send data when the phone is not connected
    // to WiFi and power source
    if (DeviceNetworkInformation.IsWiFiEnabled &&
        DeviceNetworkInformation.IsCellularDataEnabled &&
        DeviceNetworkInformation.IsNetworkAvailable &&
        DeviceStatus.PowerSource == PowerSource.External)
    {
        // Convert WriteableImage to Jpeg
        WriteableBitmap wb = (WriteableBitmap)e.Result;
        using (MemoryStream ms = new MemoryStream())
        {
            wb.SaveJpeg(ms, wb.PixelWidth, wb.PixelHeight, 0, 100);

            // Send image to the client
            _client.SendData(ms);
        }
    }
}
```

The **CaptureImageCompleted** event is raised periodically by calling the **CaptureImageAsync** method with a timer. You can change the timer Interval property to increase the capturing time if you see the captured video animation is not smooth.

```
public MainPage()
{
...

    _timer = new DispatcherTimer();
    _timer.Interval = new TimeSpan(0, 0, 0, 0, 100);
    _timer.Tick += new EventHandler(_timer_Tick);

    _timer.Start();

...
}

void _timer_Tick(object sender, EventArgs e)
{
```

```
            if (captureSource.State == CaptureState.Started)
            {
                captureSource.CaptureImageAsync();
            }
        }
```

We have built the Client class and the SendData method to connect to the listening server and send data. In the SendData method, we built the Socket object, set its parameters to use the TCP protocol, and send the stream over the Internet. We created an object from the SocketAsyncEventArgs class that is passed as argument to the SocketEventArg_Completed event handler. In the SocketAsyncEventArgs object, we set the RemoteEndPoint property with the DnsEndPoint object pointing to the server address. Finally, the Socket object is passed to the SocketEventArg_Completed event handler using the UserToken property.

```
        public void SendData(MemoryStream data)
        {
            if (data == null)
            {
                throw new ArgumentNullException("data");
            }

            dataIn = data;

            SocketAsyncEventArgs socketEventArg = new SocketAsyncEventArgs();

            DnsEndPoint hostEntry = new DnsEndPoint(_serverName, _port);

            Socket sock = new Socket(AddressFamily.InterNetwork,
                                     SocketType.Stream,
                                     ProtocolType.Tcp);
            socketEventArg.Completed += new
                        EventHandler<SocketAsyncEventArgs>
                        (SocketEventArg_Completed);
            socketEventArg.RemoteEndPoint = hostEntry;

            socketEventArg.UserToken = sock;

            try
            {
                sock.ConnectAsync(socketEventArg);
            }
            catch (SocketException ex)
            {
                throw new SocketException((int)ex.ErrorCode);
            }
        }
```

In the SocketEventArg_Completed event handler, we simply check the LastOperation property to retrieve whether the event has been raised by a ConnectAsync method call or a SendAsync method call. In the former case, we call the ProcessConnect method and in the latter case we call the ProcessSend method.

```
        void SocketEventArg_Completed(object sender, SocketAsyncEventArgs e)
        {
```

```
        switch (e.LastOperation)
        {
            case SocketAsyncOperation.Connect:
                ProcessConnect(e);
                break;
            case SocketAsyncOperation.Send:
                ProcessSend(e);
                break;
        }
    }
```

In the `ProcessConnect` method, we have converted the `MemoryStream` object that stores the image into a byte array and used the `SetBuffer` method to store the byte array into the socket. Finally, after having retrieved the socket object previously stored in the `UserToken` property, we used the `SendAsync` method to send data to the server.

```
    private void ProcessConnect(SocketAsyncEventArgs e)
    {
        if (e.SocketError == SocketError.Success)
        {
            // Successfully connected to the server
            // Send data to the server
            byte[] buffer = dataIn.ToArray();
            e.SetBuffer(buffer, 0, buffer.Length);
            Socket sock = e.UserToken as Socket;
            sock.SendAsync(e);
        }
        else
        {
            clientDone.Set();
        }
    }
```

The `BabyMonitorViewer` application has been developed by using the Windows Presentation Foundation (WPF) framework. Building a Silverlight for Windows Phone application, as well as a pure Silverlight application, is very similar to build a WPF application, so you should not have problems understanding the code. By the way, you can learn more about WPF application development in *Pro WPF in C# 2010* (Apress, 2009) by Matthew MacDonald.

The `MainWindow.xaml` file contains the XAML code that builds the user interface. An `Image` control is added to the main page in order to display the incoming image. The Loaded and Closing events are used to start and to stop the TCP socket listener thread.

```
<Window x:Class="BabyMonitorViewer.MainWindow"
        xmlns="http://schemas.microsoft.com/winfx/2006/xaml/presentation"
        xmlns:x="http://schemas.microsoft.com/winfx/2006/xaml"
        Title="MainWindow" Height="480" Width="640" Loaded="Window_Loaded"
        Closing="Window_Closing">
    <Grid>
        <Image Width="640" Height="480" Stretch="Fill" Name="imgVideo" />
    </Grid>
</Window>
```

In the `Window_Loaded` event handler a new thread is created to run the TCP server listener code. This is necessary to prevent the user interface locking from the infinite loop contained in the `StartListening` method.

```
private void Window_Loaded(object sender, RoutedEventArgs e)
{
    tcpServer = new Thread(new ThreadStart(() =>
    {
        StartListening();
    }));

    tcpServer.Start();
}
```

The `StartListening` method defines an `IPEndPoint` object useful to specify IP address and IP port where the server is listening to incoming client connection. Then, a new `Socket` object is created and the `Bind` and `Listen` methods are used to bind the socket to the `IPEndPoint` object and to start listening for incoming client connection.

In the infinite loop, the code uses the `BeginAccept` asynchronous method to start accepting connection. The `AcceptCallback` method is called when a new client connection is established.

```
private string StartListening()
{
    IPEndPoint localEndPoint = new IPEndPoint(IPAddress.Any, 13001);

    Socket listener = new Socket(AddressFamily.InterNetwork,
        SocketType.Stream, ProtocolType.Tcp);

    try
    {
        listener.Bind(localEndPoint);
        listener.Listen(10);

        while (true)
        {
            allDone.Reset();

            listener.BeginAccept(
                new AsyncCallback(AcceptCallback),
                listener);

            allDone.WaitOne();
        }

    }
    catch (Exception e)
    {
        return e.Message;
    }
}
```

In the `AcceptCallback` method, we have used the `EndAccept` method to conclude the acceptance of the client connection. The `EndAccept` method returns the `Socket` object that owns the connection between server and client. We used this `Socket` object to begin receiving data from the client, calling the `BeginReceive` asynchronous method. The `BeginReceive` method accepts the buffer where storing incoming data and a callback method to call when the data reception is over. Finally, the `StateObject` is a private class that contains useful stuff to store incoming data. A `StateObject` object is passed through asynchronous method calling.

```
private void AcceptCallback(IAsyncResult ar)
{
    allDone.Set();

    Socket listener = (Socket)ar.AsyncState;
    Socket handler = listener.EndAccept(ar);

    StateObject state = new StateObject();
    state.workSocket = handler;
    handler.BeginReceive(state.buffer, 0, StateObject.BufferSize, 0,
        new AsyncCallback(ReadCallback), state);
}
```

Finally, the `ReadCallback` method is called by the `BeginReceive` method once the data are arrived. We used the `StateObject` object stored in the `AsyncState` property to retrieve the socket and call the `EndReceive` method. In this way we have obtained the number of read bytes that is necessary in the copying data process. The StateObject class has a `MemoryStream` object that is filled with incoming data using the Write method. We append the data stream into the memory stream until the end of file is reached. In the Jpeg format the end of file is defined by the pair `FFD9` hexadecimal values.

When the entire data stream has been stored in the memory stream, we create a `BitmapImage` object and assign it to the `Image` control so that the image will be displayed. The code that creates the image is contained in the `BeginInvoke` method provided by the `Dispatcher` class. This is necessary because the `ReadCallback` code is running in a different thread respective to the user interface thread. Thanks to the `Dispatcher` class, we can change the `Image` control content that belongs to the user interface thread from a different thread.

```
private void ReadCallback(IAsyncResult ar)
{
    StateObject state = (StateObject)ar.AsyncState;
    Socket handler = state.workSocket;

    int bytesRead = handler.EndReceive(ar);

    if (bytesRead > 0)
    {
        state.ms.Write(state.buffer, 0, bytesRead);

        if ((state.ms.ToArray()[state.ms.Length - 1] == 217) &&
            (state.ms.ToArray()[state.ms.Length - 2] == 255))
        {
            try
            {
                state.ms.Seek(0, SeekOrigin.Begin);

                Dispatcher.BeginInvoke(DispatcherPriority.Normal,
                (ThreadStart)delegate
```

```
        {
            BitmapImage bi = new BitmapImage();
            bi.BeginInit();
            bi.CacheOption = BitmapCacheOption.OnLoad;
            bi.StreamSource = state.ms;
            bi.EndInit();
            imgVideo.Source = new WriteableBitmap(bi);
        });
    }
    catch (Exception ex)
    {
        Dispatcher.BeginInvoke(DispatcherPriority.Normal,
        (ThreadStart)delegate
        {
            MessageBox.Show(ex.Message);
        });
    }
}
else
{
    handler.BeginReceive(state.buffer, 0,
            StateObject.BufferSize, 0,
            new AsyncCallback(ReadCallback), state);
}
    }
}
```

Usage

From the Solution Explorer window of Visual Studio 2010, select the BabyMonitorViewer project, right-click with the mouse, select Debug, and then the Start New Instance menu item. The server application will start, briefly showing a blank window. Now, from Visual Studio 2010 select Windows Phone Device as the output target and press Ctrl+F5. Remember to unlock the phone screen so that the application can be deployed to the phone correctly.

The BabyMonitor application will start showing images captured from the photo camera and you will see the same images in the Windows application, too (see Figure 7-5).

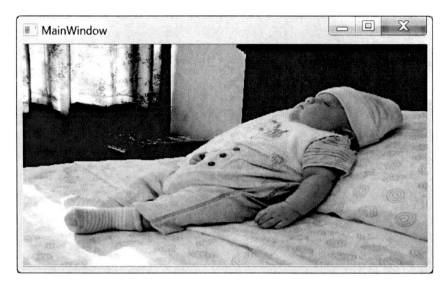

Figure 7-5. Watching Your Baby with BabyMonitor Window Phone Application

7-3. Picking a Photo from Your Media Library

Problem

You need to pick a photo from your media library and upload it to the Flickr site.

Solution

You have to use the PhotoChooserTask chooser.

How It Works

The PhotoChooserTask chooser class provides the Show method, which shows the picture library and lets you to pick a photo from it. When the photo has been chosen, the Completed event is raised. This event provides a PhotoResult object as a parameter; by using its properties, you can retrieve the stream data composing the photo by using the ChosenPhoto property, obtain the path and filename of the image by using the OriginalFileName property, and the get the result of the photo-picking operation by using the TaskResult property.

The Code

To demonstrate this recipe, we have enhanced the application written in Recipe 7-1, the `FlickrPhotoAlbum`. We added the Load button to the `MainPage`.xaml code, specifying that we want to manage its `Click` event.

```xml
<Grid x:Name="ContentPanel" Grid.Row="1" Margin="12,0,12,0">
    <Grid>
        <Grid.RowDefinitions>
            <RowDefinition Height="*" />
            <RowDefinition Height="Auto" />
            <RowDefinition Height="Auto" />
            <RowDefinition Height="Auto" />
            <RowDefinition Height="Auto" />
        </Grid.RowDefinitions>
        <phone:WebBrowser x:Name="wbBrowser" Grid.Row="0"
         Navigated="wbBrowser_Navigated"/>
        <Image x:Name="imgPhoto" Grid.Row="0" Stretch="UniformToFill"
         Visibility="Collapsed" />
        <Button x:Name="btnAuthenticate" Grid.Row="1" Content="Autenthicate"
         Click="btnAuthenticate_Click" IsEnabled="False" />
        <Button x:Name="btnTakePicture" Grid.Row="2" Content="Take a picture"
         Click="btnTakePicture_Click" IsEnabled="False" />
        <Button x:Name="btnLoad" Grid.Row="3" Content="Load" Click="btnLoad_Click"
         IsEnabled="False" />


        <Button x:Name="btnUpload" Grid.Row="4" Content="Upload"
         Click="btnUpload_Click" IsEnabled="False" />
    </Grid>
</Grid>
```

In the `MainPage.xaml.cs` code file, a `PhotoChooserTask` object is defined at the class level and created in the `MainPage` constructor. Finally, the `chooser_Completed` event handler is defined in order to respond to the `Completed` event.

```csharp
public partial class MainPage : PhoneApplicationPage
{
    CameraCaptureTask camera = null;
    Popup popup = null;
    PhotoChooserTask chooser = null;

    // Constructor
    public MainPage()
    {
        InitializeComponent();

        camera = new CameraCaptureTask();
        camera.Completed += new EventHandler<PhotoResult>(camera_Completed);
```

```
        popup = new Popup();
        popup.Child = new MySplashScreen();
        popup.IsOpen = true;

        chooser = new PhotoChooserTask();
        chooser.Completed += new EventHandler<PhotoResult>(chooser_Completed);
    }
. . .
```

In the `chooser_Completed` event handler, we call the private `DoCompletedTask` method. Because the code from Recipe 7-1 in the `camera_Completed` event handler is the same as that needed to load a photo from the media library, we have created `DoCompletedTask`, which accepts the `PhotoResult` argument, puts the image in a memory stream object, and shows a preview image.

```
        private void DoCompletedTask(PhotoResult e)
        {
            App app = Application.Current as App;

            if (e.TaskResult == TaskResult.OK)
            {
                byte[] data;
                using (var br = new BinaryReader(e.ChosenPhoto)) data =
                        br.ReadBytes((int)e.ChosenPhoto.Length);
                app.settings.Image = new MemoryStream(data);

                BitmapImage bi = new BitmapImage(
                                    new Uri(e.OriginalFileName));
                bi.CreateOptions = BitmapCreateOptions.DelayCreation;
                bi.SetSource(new MemoryStream(data));
                imgPhoto.Source = new WriteableBitmap(bi);
                btnUpload.IsEnabled = true;
            }           }
```

Finally, in the `btnLoad_Click` event handler, we call the `Show` method provided by the `PhotoChooserTask` class:

```
        private void btnLoad_Click(object sender, RoutedEventArgs e)
        {
            chooser.Show();
        }
```

Usage

The application usage is similar to Recipe 7-1. After having authenticated to the Flickr site and authorized our application to access the user's library, the Load button will be enabled.

Press the Load button, and the application will show the picture's library on your phone. In the emulator, you can access the library with some photos inside, as shown in Figure 7-6.

Figure 7-6. The picture library on the emulator

Now, select a picture of your choice, and you will see it in the FlickrPhotoAlbum application as a preview. The Upload button becomes enabled. Press the Upload button as you did in Recipe 7-1, and the picture loads into the Flickr site, as shown in Figure 7-7.

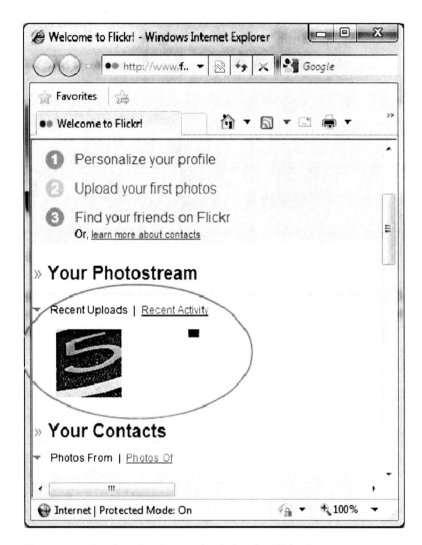

Figure 7-7. The photo has been uploaded to the Flickr site.

7-4. Add Integration Between Your Application and Windows Phone

Problem

You need to integrate your photo application inside the Picture Hub. In this way, when users select a photo, they can launch your application and see the selected photo inside your application.

Solution

You have to use the Picture Extensibility feature powered by the Windows Phone operating system.

How It Works

Your application can be integrated inside the Picture Hub in three different ways. The application can appear within the App page of the panorama control that is used by the Photo Hub application. The application can appear within the app menu that is shown after the user selects a photo. Or, the application can appear within the share menu that is shown after the user selects a photo.

In the first case, the App page of the Photo Hub application simply shows your application and the user can launch the application from there. This is the same as launching your application from the Start menu—but from the Picture Hub App page, the user knows that your application is dedicated to photo management.

In the second case, in the app menu that appears after having selected the photo, the user can execute your application and the URI of the selected photo is provided to the application using the query string.

The same for the third case, but the Photo Hub menu is called share.

You can add integration between your application and the Photo Hub application adding the Extension tag to the XML code in the WMAppManifest.xml file. You have to specify the Photos_Extra_Hub extension name when you want to show your image in the App page of the Photo Hub application. You have to specify the Photos_Extra_Viewer extension name when you want to show your image in the app menu. Finally, to show your application in the share menu, you have to use the Photos_Extra_Share extension name.

The Code

To demonstrate this recipe, we have enhanced the application written in Recipe 7-1, the FlickrPhotoAlbum.

In the WMAppManifest.xml file, we have added the Extensions section and specified two Extension elements. This will allow our application to be integrated with the App page and the app menu within the Photo Hub application.

```
    ...
    </Tokens>
    <Extensions>
      <Extension ExtensionName="Photos_Extra_Hub"
                 ConsumerID="{5B04B775-356B-4AA0-AAF8-6491FFEA5632}"
                 TaskID="_default" />
      <Extension ExtensionName="Photos_Extra_Viewer"
                 ConsumerID="{5B04B775-356B-4AA0-AAF8-6491FFEA5632}"
                 TaskID="_default" />
    </Extensions>
  </App>
</Deployment>
```

■ **Note** In the past, you had to create the `Extras.xml` and `E0F0E49A-3EB1-4970-B780-45DA41EC7C28.xml` file to obtain the integration between your application and the Photo Hub application. This is no longer necessary, so you can remove these files from your old project when you upgrade your application and use the new Picture Extensibilty feature.

When users select a photo from the Photo Hub application and they launch the `FlickrPhotoAlbum` application from the app menu, the local URI of the selected photo is provided to our application. We have added the `OnNavigatedTo` method to load and show the selected image in the `FlickrPhotoAlbum`. The photo will be shown after the user authenticates on the Flickr site.

By the way, the `OnNavigatedTo` method is called even when the user selects a photo from the `PhotoChooserTask` chooser. We used the `_doTask` Boolean flag to distinguish the calling between the Photo Hub and the chooser.

In the `OnNavigatedTo` method, we used the `ContainsKey` method to search for the token parameter inside the query string. Token is the name of the parameter provided by the Photo Hub application when the application is executed from the app menu.

■ **Note** The query string parameter name for the share menu is different from the app menu parameter name. It is called FileID.

If the application query string contains the token parameter, we use the `GetPictureFromToken` method provided by the `MediaLibrary` class. As you will learn from the next recipe, the `MediaLibrary` is contained in the XNA Framework. The Silverlight for Windows Phone application template doesn't include a reference to the XNA library, so we had to add a reference.

Finally, a `BitmapImage` object is created, set with Picture object data, and used to create the `WriteableBitmap` object that is associated to the `Image` control contained in the application page.

```
protected override void OnNavigatedTo(NavigationEventArgs e)
{
    if (this.NavigationContext.QueryString.ContainsKey("token")
        && !_doTask)
    {
        MediaLibrary library = new MediaLibrary();
        _token = this.NavigationContext.QueryString["token"];
        Picture picture = library.GetPictureFromToken(_token);

        BitmapImage bitmap = new BitmapImage();
        bitmap.CreateOptions = BitmapCreateOptions.DelayCreation;
        bitmap.SetSource(picture.GetImage());

        WriteableBitmap picLibraryImage = new
                        WriteableBitmap(bitmap);
        imgPhoto.Source = picLibraryImage;
    }
```

```
        }
```

Usage

From Visual Studio 2010, right-click the mouse on the `FlickrPhotoAlbum` solution name in the Solution Explorer window and select the Deploy menu item. Remember to connect the phone to the computer and to unlock the phone screen. Once the application has been deployed successfully, launch the Photo Hub from your phone and go through the panorama's pages until you find the App page. As you can see from Figure 7-8, the `FlickrPhotoAlbum` application appears within the App page and can be launched from there.

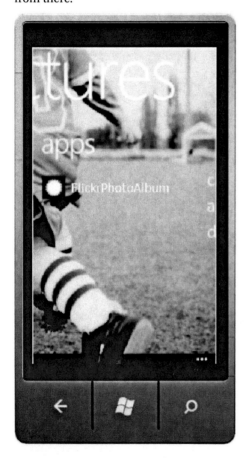

Figure 7-8. Our application is shown in the App page within the Picture Hub

Now come back to the main page, pick up a photo from your picture library, and expand the menu tapping on the ellipses button (see Figure 7-9).

Figure 7-9. *The ellipse button to show the picture menu*

Among the menu items is the app menu. Select the app menu and the App page will display and the FlickrPhotoAlbum item will appear inside the App page (see Figure 7-10).

Figure 7-10. *The App menu shows our application*

By tapping on the FlickrPhotoAlbum item, the application will launch; after you authenticate your account on Flickr, the selected photo will show in the FlickrPhotoAlbum application (see Figure 7-11).

Figure 7-11. The photo from PictureHub in the FlickrPhotoAlbum

7-5. Using Media Player to Shuffle Songs in Your Media Library

Problem

You need to retrieve songs from the media library of your Windows Phone device and play them in shuffle mode.

Solution

You have to use the `MediaLibrary` class provided by the XNA Framework and use its property collections such as `Songs` and `Albums`. Moreover, you can play a song by using the `Play` static method defined in the `MediaPlayer` class.

How It Works

The XNA Framework provides the `MediaLibrary` class, in the `Microsoft.XNA.Framework.dll` assembly, which enables us to retrieve information from the media library of your phone. The `MediaLibrary` class provides a lot of useful media collections such as Songs, Pictures, and Albums. After you have a `MediaLibrary` object instance, you automatically have those collections filled with related information.

In this recipe, you are going to reproduce a song, so you are interested to the Songs collection. By using the `Songs` property from the `MediaLibrary` class, you can obtain a `Song` object pointing to a specified collection index.

The `Song` class contains everything concerning a song in the media library. Indeed, you can find the `Album` property to retrieve information on the album containing the song. The `Artist` property retrieves information on the song's author. The `Duration` property indicates the song's duration. The `Genre` property contains information on the song genre. The `Name` property is the song name. The `TrackNumber` property represents the song number within the album. Finally, the `PlayCount` and `Rating` properties return the number of times the song has been played and the song's rating (if you have rated it), respectively. Figure 7-12 shows the pertinent class diagrams.

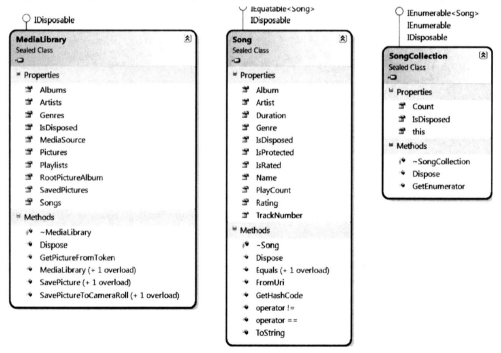

Figure 7-12. *The* `MediaLibrary`, `Song`, *and* `SongCollection` *class diagram*

The Code

To demonstrate this recipe, we have created the ShuffleMe application by using the Silverlight Windows Phone template from Visual Studio 2010.

Because the Silverlight application for Windows Phone doesn't have support for accessing the media library, the first thing we did was to reference the Microsoft.Xna.Framework.dll assembly. Indeed, the XNA Framework has everything necessary to query the media library for pictures and songs.

After shuffling the songs and retrieving a random one, you are going to play the selected song by using the Play method provided by the MediaPlayer class. But because we have a Silverlight application calling the Play method, you need to do an extra step: you need to call the Update static method from the FrameworkDispatcher class. This call should be done periodically, so the Microsoft official documentation suggests the creation of a class implementing the IApplicationService interface. This interface has two method definitions, to start and to stop the service. In the related methods, you are going to start and stop a DispatcherTimer timer object. This timer has an interval set to 30 times per second in which it raises the Tick event. By defining the Tick event handler, you can call the Update static method periodically.

```
public class XNADispatcherService : IApplicationService
{
    private DispatcherTimer frameworkDispatcherTimer;

    public void StartService(ApplicationServiceContext context)
    {
        this.frameworkDispatcherTimer.Start();
    }

    public void StopService()
    {
        this.frameworkDispatcherTimer.Stop();
    }

    public XNADispatcherService()
    {
        this.frameworkDispatcherTimer = new DispatcherTimer();
        this.frameworkDispatcherTimer.Interval = TimeSpan.FromTicks(333333);
        this.frameworkDispatcherTimer.Tick += frameworkDispatcherTimer_Tick;
        FrameworkDispatcher.Update();
    }

    void frameworkDispatcherTimer_Tick(object sender, EventArgs e) {
        FrameworkDispatcher.Update(); }
}
```

In the App.xaml file, you can add the namespace that contains the XnaDispatcherService class and include a tag so that the application itself will start and stop the timer, automatically:

```
<Application
    x:Class="ShuffleMe.App"
    xmlns="http://schemas.microsoft.com/winfx/2006/xaml/presentation"
```

```
    xmlns:x="http://schemas.microsoft.com/winfx/2006/xaml"
    xmlns:phone="clr-namespace:Microsoft.Phone.Controls;assembly=Microsoft.Phone"
    xmlns:shell="clr-namespace:Microsoft.Phone.Shell;assembly=Microsoft.Phone"
    xmlns:local="clr-namespace:ShuffleMe">

    <!--Application Resources-->
    <Application.Resources>
    </Application.Resources>
```

<Application.ApplicationLifetimeObjects>

```
        <!--Required object that handles lifetime events for the application-->
        <shell:PhoneApplicationService
            Launching="Application_Launching" Closing="Application_Closing"
            Activated="Application_Activated" Deactivated="Application_Deactivated"/>
        <local:XNADispatcherService />
    </Application.ApplicationLifetimeObjects>

</Application>
```

The `ShuffleMe` application has some requirements, which can be summarized as follows:

- It must continue to play and shuffle songs even when the screen is locked.

- When one song is over, a new one must be played, and it shouldn't be the same.

- When the application is tombstoned, it must save the song's properties such as its title and album cover.

- When the application is reactivated either from the dormant state or from a tombstone, it must not stop the current played song and must again display the song's properties.

- When the hardware Back button is pressed, the application must stop playing the song.

Let's examine the code and the solutions found to address those points.

As you saw in Chapter 2, you can set the `ApplicationIdleDetectionMode` property to `IdleDetectionMode.Disabled` so that your application doesn't stop working when the screen is locked:

```
// The shuffle routine has to work even when the screen is locked
PhoneApplicationService.Current.ApplicationIdleDetectionMode = IdleDetectionMode.Disabled;
```

Sadly, the `MediaLibrary` doesn't provide either a property or a method to retrieve when the song is over. Our solution has been to create a `DispatcherTimer` object set to 1 second more than the song duration. Indeed, when the song is over (plus 1 second), the timer raises the `Tick` event that is hooked by the related event handler, and the private `PlaySong` method is called:

```
public partial class MainPage : PhoneApplicationPage
{
. . .
```

```
        DispatcherTimer timer = null;

        // Constructor
        public MainPage()
        {
. . .
            timer = new DispatcherTimer();
            timer.Tick += new EventHandler(timer_Tick);


            // The shuffle routine has to work even when the screen is locked
            PhoneApplicationService.Current.ApplicationIdleDetectionMode =
                                                IdleDetectionMode.Disabled;
        }

        void timer_Tick(object sender, EventArgs e)
        {
            PlaySong();
        }
. . .
```

When the application is tombstoned—for example, after the application has been deactivated and put in dormant state the user launches other applications requiring phone memory—the application must store important data such the album cover and the song's author and title. Sadly, the Song class is not serializable, and the same is true for the BitmapImage class for the album cover. You need to create the AppSettings serializable class with specific information such as the Title property to store the application's title and the AlbumImage bytes array to store the image album. The latter is the way we found to serialize an image. Finally, in the SongNumber property, you store the song's number generated by the shuffle routine.

```
public class AppSettings
{
    public string Title { get; set; }
    public byte[] AlbumImage { get; set; }
    public int SongNumber { get; set; }
}
```

▨ **Note** You could store only the SongNumber value during the tombstoning and use it to retrieve the song when the application is reactivated from the tombstone. However, in this way you can learn different techniques to manage images' serialization.

An object from the AppSettings class is stored in the App application class, and you can retrieve it by using the related settings property:

```
public partial class App : Application
{
    /// <summary>
    /// Provides easy access to the root frame of the Phone Application.
    /// </summary>
    /// <returns>The root frame of the Phone Application.</returns>
    public PhoneApplicationFrame RootFrame { get; private set; }

    public AppSettings settings { get; set; }
```

. . .

Moreover, in the App class, you define the event handlers to manage the tombstoning. When the IsApplicationInstancePreserved Boolean value is equal to False the application has been resumed by a tombstone so we can retrieve the stored settings:

```
// Code to execute when the application is launching (e.g., from Start)
// This code will not execute when the application is reactivated
private void Application_Launching(object sender, LaunchingEventArgs e)
{
    settings = new AppSettings();
}

// Code to execute when the application is activated (brought to foreground)
// This code will not execute when the application is first launched
private void Application_Activated(object sender, ActivatedEventArgs e)
{
    if (e.IsApplicationInstancePreserved != true)
    {
        if (PhoneApplicationService.Current.State.ContainsKey("settings"))
        {
            settings =
              PhoneApplicationService.Current.State["settings"]
              as AppSettings;
        }
    }
}

// Code to execute when the application is deactivated (sent to background)
// This code will not execute when the application is closing
private void Application_Deactivated(object sender, DeactivatedEventArgs e)
{
    PhoneApplicationService.Current.State["settings"] = settings;
}
```

The other properties provided by the AppSettings class are set in the PlaySong method. The first operation in this method calls the DoShuffle method, which returns a Song object. This object is compared to a previous Song object stored as _lastSong variable. If the objects are equal, the PlaySong method is called again until a new Song object is retrieved. If the user has only one song in her library, the song is repeated each time until the application is closed.

■ **Note** You could use the SongNumber property to check whether the DoShuffle method picked the same song, but we used a Song object to demonstrate that this class supports object comparison.

The PlaySong method contains a couple of interesting code snippets. The HasArt property is checked to see whether the song has an associated album cover. If it does, the GetAlbumArt method is used to retrieve the stream data of the image. One way to use the Stream object with the Image control—and specifically its Source property—is to create a WriteableBitmap object with the static DecodeJpeg method from the PictureDecoder class defined in the Microsoft.Phone namespace. If the song does not have an associated album cover, a No Cover image is retrieved from the image folder within the ShuffleMe project.

The AlbumImage bytes array defined in the settings is filled with the GetAlbumArt data thanks to the BinaryReader class and its ReadBytes method.

Finally, the Duration property from the Song class is used to set the Interval property of the timer, and then the timer is started.

```
private void PlaySong()
{
    Song s = DoShuffle();
    if ((s != null && s != _lastSong)||(library.Songs.Count == 1))
    {
        App app = Application.Current as App;

        _lastSong = s;

        tbAuthor.Text = s.Artist.Name + ": " + s.Name;
        app.settings.Title = tbAuthor.Text;

        if (s.Album.HasArt)
        {
            WriteableBitmap wbimg =
                        PictureDecoder.DecodeJpeg(s.Album.GetAlbumArt());
            imgCover.Source = wbimg;
            using (var br = new BinaryReader(s.Album.GetAlbumArt()))
                    app.settings.AlbumImage =
                            br.ReadBytes((int)s.Album.GetAlbumArt().Length);
        }
        else
        {
            app.settings.AlbumImage = null;
            imgCover.Source = new BitmapImage(new Uri("/images/nocover.png",
                                            UriKind.Relative));
        }

        MediaPlayer.Play(s);
        timer.Interval = s.Duration + TimeSpan.FromSeconds(1);
        timer.Start();
    }
}
```

```
else
    PlaySong();
}
```

When the application either starts or is tombstoned, the `OnNavigatedTo` method for the `MainPage` page is called and the private `PlaySong` method is called. But before calling this method, you check whether the application has been launched for the first time. Only in this case do you call the `PlaySong` method, because you want to avoid having a new song played when the application is reactivated by either the dormant state or from the tombstoning. Indeed, when the application is reactivated, you simply rewrite the title and reset the album cover.

In the `OnNavigatedTo method code`, there is an interesting thing that is worth noting. After application reactivation occurs, the timer is not working anymore, and so you need to set its interval again. But this time you can't use the song duration because some time has passed. So the `PlayPosition` property from the `MediaPlayer` class is used to retrieve a `TimeSpan` object representing the song reproduction time. By subtracting this value from the song's duration, you obtain the new `Interval` value of the timer.

```
protected override void OnNavigatedTo(System.Windows.Navigation.NavigationEventArgs e)
{
    App app = Application.Current as App;

    if (e.NavigationMode == System.Windows.Navigation.NavigationMode.New)
        PlaySong();
    else
    {
        tbAuthor.Text = app.settings.Title;
        if (app.settings.AlbumImage != null)
        {
            MemoryStream ms = new MemoryStream(app.settings.AlbumImage);
            WriteableBitmap wbimg = PictureDecoder.DecodeJpeg(ms);
            imgCover.Source = wbimg;
        }
        else
            imgCover.Source = new BitmapImage(new Uri("/images/nocover.png",
UriKind.Relative));

        TimeSpan remainTime = library.Songs[app.settings.SongNumber].Duration -
MediaPlayer.PlayPosition;
        timer.Interval = remainTime + TimeSpan.FromSeconds(1);
        timer.Start();
    }

    base.OnNavigatedTo(e);
}
```

In the `DoShuffle` method code, you use the `Random` class to generate a number ranging from zero to the value of the `Count` property of the `Songs` collection, which returns the number of songs in the media library. Finally, this number is saved in the `SongNumber` property of the `settings` object, and the song at `songIndex` is returned from the `Songs` collection.

```
private Song DoShuffle()
{
    App app = Application.Current as App;

    int count = library.Songs.Count;

    Random rand = new Random();
    int songIndex = rand.Next(0, count);

    app.settings.SongNumber = songIndex;
    return library.Songs[songIndex];
}
```

The last requirement we have imposed on ourselves is that the application must end when the hardware Back button is pressed. In the PhoneApplicationPage class, you define the OnBackKeyPress method, which you can override so as to add your code before the back functionality is accomplished.

In this case, you stop the song that is playing and you stop the timer.

```
protected override void OnBackKeyPress(System.ComponentModel.CancelEventArgs e)
{
    MediaPlayer.Stop();
    timer.Stop();

    base.OnBackKeyPress(e);
}
```

Usage

From Visual Studio 2010, select the output target as Windows Phone Emulator and press Ctrl+F5. The emulator starts, briefly showing the application, as in Figure 7-13. The song you play could be different from the one shown in Figure 7-13, because of the shuffle mode. The emulator provides three songs with no covers, so if you want to see the application with album covers as well, you should run it on a physical device.

Figure 7-13. The ShuffleMe application running in the emulator

Press the hardware Back button to terminate the application and its song. Or press the hardware Start button and then the hardware Back button to reactivate the application from the dormant state. You should hear the song continuing playing without any interruption and see the title, as before the deactivation.

Now you can wait until the song ends in order to see that another (and different) song is played.

7-6. Playing Music Streamed from SkyDrive

Problem

You want to create an application that reproduces music stored on the SkyDrive. Your application does not locally copy remote files, but uses streaming music—allowing users to save storage space on the phone since the audio files are stored on the cloud.

Solution

You can use the `BackgroundAudioPlayer` agent that provides the `Instance` object useful to reproduce music in background. To connect your application to the SkyDrive on cloud hard disk you can use the `LiveConnectClient` class provided by the Live SDK.

How It Works

A background audio agent is a background process that reproduces media, such as a song, even when the phone screen is locked or the user launches other applications (this is true only if the launched application doesn't use media elements as well). A background audio agent is informed by Zune Media Queue—the phone native application that reproduces all the media—when a song is ready to be played, when the song is over, when the user wants to skip a song, and so on. You can create a class that derives from the `AudioPlayerAgent` class to manage all of these cases; for example, changing the song when the user taps the skip button from the Universal Volume Control (UVC). The UVC is a set of buttons within a panel that appears when the phone screen is locked and when the user presses the volume hardware buttons on the phone.

The `BackgroundAudioPlayer` class provides the `Instance` object that returns a reference to the active `BackgroundAudioPlayer` class instance. An application can have only one active `BackgroundAudioPlayer` class instance and you can use it to manage the music playback. The `BackgroundAudioPlayer` class provides the `Play`, `Stop`, `Pause`, `Rewind`, and `FastForward` methods. The `BackgroundAudioPlayer` class also has properties such as the `PlayerState` property, which is useful to retrieve the state of the player (Playing, Stopped, Paused, etc.); the `BufferingProgress` property, which retrieves the amount of buffered streaming; and the `Track` property, which is useful to get or to set the `AudioTrack` object that represents the audio track that you want to play.

The `AudioTrack` class contains all the necessary properties to set information on the audio you want to play. The most important property is the Source property, which is an `Uri` object pointing either to a local or remote file. In the former case, the file must be stored on the local isolated storage. In the latter case, the file can be stored on a remote web server. In both cases the file must have a supported media codec, such as MP3, MP4, WAV, WMA, etc. For the complete list of supported media codecs, go to `http://msdn.microsoft.com/en-us/library/ff462087(v=VS.92).aspx`.

Note If you want to create an application that reproduces media that is not supported by the provided codecs, you can use the background audio agent with `MediaStreamSource` class. You will be responsible to manage the raw data that will be sent by the background audio agent. You can learn how to implement `MediaStreamSource` from the official MSDN documentation at `http://go.microsoft.com/fwlink/?LinkID=226375`.

The Live SDK contains the necessary classes to connect your application to Microsoft Live services such as Hotmail, Windows Live ID, Messenger, and SkyDrive. The `LiveConnectClient` class contains the async methods useful to query information from the Microsoft Live service. More exactly, the `GetAsync` method allows developers to execute a REST command, which has results retrieved by the `GetCompleted` event.

The handler attached to the `GetCompleted` event provides an object from the `LiveOperationCompletedEventArgs` class. Among the others, the `LiveOperationCompletedEventArgs` class has the Result property that contains a `Dictionary<string, object>` object with the result of the REST command. For example, by executing the `me/skydrive/files?filter=folders,albums` command, you are querying all the folders within the SkyDrive cloud drive. The Result property will contain the dictionary filled with key/value pair items with information on folders. In particular, the `data` key contains a List<object> list that you can iterate by retrieving information on each folder. Once you have the folder object, you can retrieve some useful information, including folder id and folder name. In particular, you can use the folder id in conjunction with the `/files` command as a GetAsync method parameter to retrieve the list of all files of that folder.

The Live SDK provides the `SignInButton` control for Windows Phone. Placing the `SignInButton` control on the Windows Phone page, you can manage login and logout to Microsoft Live service without writing a line of code. The `SignInButton` control has some mandatory XAML attributes that you have to specify in the page. The `SessionChanged` attribute corresponds to the event handler that is called once the user completes the authentication process on Microsoft Live. The `Scopes` attribute represents the permission level of your application on the user files; for example, by setting the scope to `wl.skydrive` your application has read access to the user's documents and photos stored on SkyDrive.

Finally, the `ClientID` attribute must be set to the client identifier that is returned by the Live Connect App Management site once you register your application. You can reach the Live Connect App Management site going to `https://manage.dev.live.com/`.

■ **Note** At writing time, the Live SDK is a Developer preview; the final version expected a November 2011 release.

The Code

To demonstrate this recipe, we have realized the `BackgroundAudioSample` Windows Phone application. The Visual Studio 2010 solution is composed of two projects. The `BackgroundAudioSampleUI` project is a Silverlight for Windows Phone application used to show the user interface that plays music when the application is in the foreground. The other project is called `BackgroundAudioSample` and is created from the Windows Phone Audio Playback Agent template. This template creates a class derived by the `AudioPlayerAgent` class and is useful to play music when the application is running in background.

Let's start examining the application code. In the `MainPage.xaml` page, we added the `SignInButton` control to the main page together with a text block that shows the song title and author, and a couple of application bar buttons to play/pause and stop the media playback.

```
<phone:PhoneApplicationPage
```

```
    x:Class="BackgroundAudioSampleUI.MainPage"
. . .
xmlns:my="clr-namespace:Microsoft.Live.Controls;assembly=Microsoft.Live.Controls">

    <!--LayoutRoot is the root grid where all page content is placed-->
    <Grid x:Name="LayoutRoot" Background="Transparent">
        <Grid.RowDefinitions>
            <RowDefinition Height="Auto"/>
            <RowDefinition Height="*"/>
        </Grid.RowDefinitions>

        <!--TitlePanel contains the name of the application and page title-->
        <StackPanel x:Name="TitlePanel" Grid.Row="0" Margin="12,17,0,28">
            <TextBlock x:Name="ApplicationTitle"
                Text="BACKGROUND AUDIO PLAYER"
                Style="{StaticResource PhoneTextNormalStyle}"/>
            <TextBlock x:Name="PageTitle" Text="Player" Margin="9,-7,0,0"
                Style="{StaticResource PhoneTextTitle1Style}"/>
        </StackPanel>

        <!--ContentPanel - place additional content here-->
        <Grid x:Name="ContentPanel" Grid.Row="1" Margin="12,0,12,0">
            <TextBlock Height="77" HorizontalAlignment="Left"
                        Margin="-12,0,0,0" Name="txtPlaying"
                        VerticalAlignment="Top" Width="468"
                        Style="{StaticResource PhoneTextNormalStyle}"/>
            <my:SignInButton Name="btnSignin"
                ClientId="YOUR CLIENT ID HERE"
                Scopes="wl.skydrive"
                RedirectUri="https://oauth.live.com/desktop"
                Branding="Windows"
                TextType="SignIn"
                SessionChanged="btnSignin_SessionChanged"
                HorizontalAlignment="Left"
                VerticalAlignment="Top" Margin="150,429,0,0" />
        </Grid>
    </Grid>

    <phone:PhoneApplicationPage.ApplicationBar>
        <shell:ApplicationBar IsVisible="True" IsMenuEnabled="True">
            <shell:ApplicationBarIconButton
                IconUri="/Images/appbar.transport.play.rest.png"
                Text="Play" x:Name="btnPlay" Click="btnPlay_Click"/>
            <shell:ApplicationBarIconButton
                IconUri="/Images/appbar.stop.rest.png"
                Text="Stop" Click="btnStop_Click"/>
        </shell:ApplicationBar>
    </phone:PhoneApplicationPage.ApplicationBar>
</phone:PhoneApplicationPage>
```

When the user taps on the SignIn button, the main page shows the Windows Live ID authentication site. After the user inserts a username and password, and concludes the authentication process, the

SignIn button raises the SessionChanged event. The LiveConnectSessionChangedEventArgs parameter provided by the event handler contains the Session property, which must not be null, and the session Status has to be equal to the Connected value. Only in this case can the Session object be used with the LiveConnectClient constructor to create an object that manages the connection with the Microsoft Live service. After the LiveConnectClient object is created, the GetAsync method is called to retrieve information on the file that is stored on our SkyDrive account. Once the file information is retrieved, the GetCompleted event is raised and we have created the _client_GetMp3Url event handler to retrieve file information.

Note In the following code, we already know the file identifier for the song stored on SkyDrive. In a more complete application, you should show a user interface that lets users select the files they want to play.

```
private void btnSignin_SessionChanged(object sender,
                          LiveConnectSessionChangedEventArgs e)
{
    if (e.Session != null &&
        e.Session.Status == LiveConnectSessionStatus.Connected)
    {
      client = new LiveConnectClient(e.Session);

      client.GetAsync("file.9eca16521303e07a.9ECA16521303E07A!217");
      client.GetCompleted += new
    EventHandler<LiveOperationCompletedEventArgs>(_client_GetMp3Url);
    }
}
```

In the _client_GetMp3Url event handler, we check whether an error has occurred using the Error property. If the Error property is null (no errors are occurred), the Result property contains the file information. We are interested in the source dictionary item that contains the complete URL of the song file. We can use the song URL with the AudioTrack constructor to create an object that can be assigned to the Track property provided by the Instance object from the BackgroundAudioPlayer class. The track now is ready to be played.

```
void _client_GetMp3Url(object sender,
                    LiveOperationCompletedEventArgs e)
{
    if (e.Error == null)
    {
        Dictionary<string, object> file =
                          (Dictionary<string, object>)e.Result;
        string songURL = file["source"].ToString();
        Uri songUri = new Uri(songURL);
        AudioTrack at = new AudioTrack(songUri, "Title", "Artist",
                                      "Album", null);

        BackgroundAudioPlayer.Instance.Track = at;
    }
}
```

In the `MainPage` class constructor we have registered the `Instance_PlayStateChanged` event handler to catch the `PlayStateChanged` event that is raised when the media playback state changes. In the event handler code we called the `SetAppState` private method that manages the user interface displaying application bar buttons images and track information.

```
// Constructor
public MainPage()
{
    InitializeComponent();
    BackgroundAudioPlayer.Instance.PlayStateChanged += new
                        EventHandler(Instance_PlayStateChanged);
    btnPlay = ApplicationBar.Buttons[0] as ApplicationBarIconButton;
}

void Instance_PlayStateChanged(object sender, EventArgs e)
{
    SetAppState();
}

private void SetAppState()
{
    if (BackgroundAudioPlayer.Instance.PlayerState ==
        PlayState.Playing)
        btnPlay.IconUri = new
                Uri("/Images/appbar.transport.pause.rest.png",
                    UriKind.Relative);
    else
        btnPlay.IconUri = new
                Uri("/Images/appbar.transport.play.rest.png",
                    UriKind.Relative);

    if (BackgroundAudioPlayer.Instance.Track != null)
    {
        txtPlaying.Text = string.Format("Song: {0}\n\nAuthor: {1}",
                BackgroundAudioPlayer.Instance.Track.Title,
                BackgroundAudioPlayer.Instance.Track.Artist);
    }
}
```

Finally, in the Click event of the Play application bar button, we called the Play and Pause methods from the `Instance` object provided by the `BackgroudAudioPlayer` class.

```
private void btnPlay_Click(object sender, EventArgs e)
{
    if (BackgroundAudioPlayer.Instance.PlayerState ==
        PlayState.Playing)
    {
        BackgroundAudioPlayer.Instance.Pause();
    }
    else
    {
        BackgroundAudioPlayer.Instance.Play();
    }
```

```
}
```

The `AudioPlayer.cs` code file contains the `AudioPlayer` class derived from the `AudioPlayerAgent` class. This file is created by the Visual Studio template and contains the code to create the background audio agent. The code skeleton is ready to be modified and contains event handlers to catch events that occur; for example, when a media ends or when the user stops playing the media. The `OnPlayStateChanged` and `OnUserAction` events are raised by the Zune Media Queue native application when the media playing state is changed and when the user uses the UVC to change the media playback, respectively.

We haven't changed any code from the code skeleton generated by the template because it was not necessary. We have demonstrated how to play only one song stored on SkyDrive. But the code can be easily modified to create a playlist and respond to the `OnPlayStateChanged` event and check for the `TrackEnded` play state. When the track playing ends, you can pick up the next track from the playing list and set the Track property with the new track.

Usage

You can use this application both in the emulator and the physical device. Press Ctrl+F5 and wait for the application to be executed (see Figure 7-14).

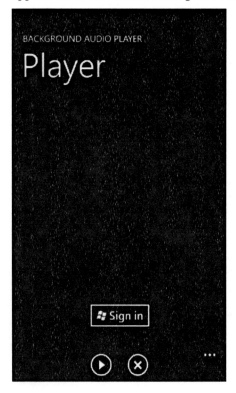

Figure 7-14. The BackgroundAudioSample application in action

Press the SignIn button and insert your SkyDrive user credentials (see Figure 7-15).

Figure 7-15. *The Windows Live user credentials page*

Once you have authorized your account, you have to allow access to the application to your SkyDrive cloud hard disk by tapping the Yes button (see Figure 7-16).

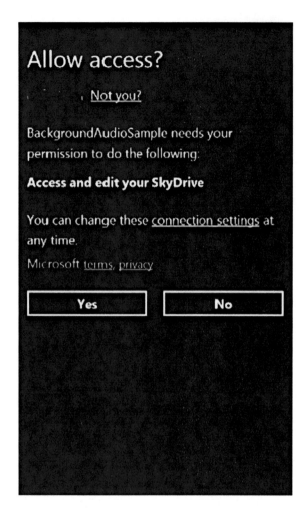

Figure 7-16. *Windows Live service asks to allow access*

Now you can press the Play application bar button and, hopefully, listen to the audio playing.

■ **Note** Remember you have to find the file identifier of your stored file (it is different than ours) and get your ClientID from the Live Connect App Management site at https://manage.dev.live.com/.

7-7. Using the Microphone in the Funny Repeater Application

Problem

You need to use the Windows Phone microphone to register your voice and reproduce it in a funny way.

Solution

You can use the `Microphone` class from the `Microsoft.Xna.Framework.dll` assembly and the `Play` method provided by the `SoundEffect` class.

How It Works

In the `Microsoft.Xna.Framework.Audio` namespace, the `Microphone` class is defined; this class provides access to the device's microphone. The `Microphone` class (see Figure 7-17 for the class diagram) has the `BufferReady` event that is raised at regular intervals depending on the `BufferDuration` setting. Within the `BufferReady` event handler, you can call the `GetData` method provided by the `Microphone` class in order to retrieve a portion of the registered audio buffer. This buffer has a fixed size that you can calculate by calling the `GetSampleSizeInBytes` method from the `Microphone` class.

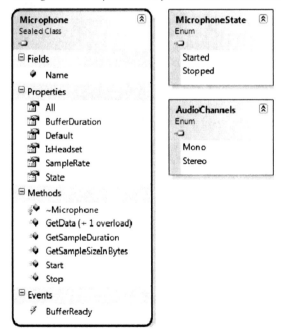

Figure 7-17. The `Microphone` class diagram

The microphone is started by using the `Start` method from the `Microphone` class and is stopped by the `Stop` method. The `Microphone` class is sealed, so you cannot create an instance from it; you have to call the static `Default` property from the `Microphone` class, which returns an instance of the `Microphone` object representing the default microphone.

To play the recorded audio, you have to use the `Play` method provided by the `SoundEffect` class. Before using this method, you need to create an object from the `SoundEffect` class by using one of the two provided constructors. The first constructor accepts the audio buffer as a bytes array, the audio sample rate, and the number of audio channels to use during the audio playing. The second constructor accepts—in addition to those three parameters— an offset value indicating from where the audio play has to start, the count representing the amount of data to play, and loops parameters to reproduce a looping sound.

The `SoundEffect` class provides a mix of static and instance methods. Among the static methods worth noting is the `FromStream` method, which retrieves a `SoundEffect` object from a stream. Among the instance methods worth noting is the `CreateInstance` method, which returns a `SoundEffectInstance` object. Before calling the `Play` method, you can use the `CreateInstance` method to return a `SoundEffectInstance` object and set its own 3D audio space parameters. Moreover, you can use the `SoundEffectInstance` object to set audio pitch, volume, and pan.

The Code

To demonstrate using the microphone and reproducing sound, we have created the `FunnyRepeater` Silverlight for Windows Phone application.

As you already learned in Recipe 7-5, the Silverlight application doesn't have support for audio recording, so you have to reference the `Microsoft.Xna.Framework.dll` assembly. Moreover, because the `Play` method needs repeated updates to the framework dispatcher, you add the `XnaDispatcherService`, which implements the `IApplicationService` interface (as seen in Recipe 7-5).

In the `MainPage.xaml` file, you add just a single button that starts and stops the audio recording from the microphone. You use the `PageTitle` TextBlock control to display the recording status.

```
<!--ContentPanel - place additional content here-->
<Grid x:Name="ContentPanel" Grid.Row="1" Margin="12,0,12,0">
    <Button x:Name="btnRecord" Click="btnRecord_Click" Content="Record" />
</Grid>
```

In the `MainPage.xaml.cs` code file, you start defining at the class level a `Microphone` object and some buffer data. In the `MainPage` constructor, you add the hook to the `BufferReady` event.

```
public partial class MainPage : PhoneApplicationPage
{
    Microphone mic = Microphone.Default;
    byte[] data = null;
    MemoryStream audio = null;

    // Constructor
    public MainPage()
    {
        InitializeComponent();
        mic.BufferReady += new EventHandler<EventArgs>(mic_BufferReady);
    }
```

When the `BufferReady` event is raised, you store the provided audio buffer into a `MemoryStream` object. This is necessary because this event is raised at regular intervals and provides slices of audio registration. Thanks to the `MemoryStream` object, you can store the entire audio recording.

```
void mic_BufferReady(object sender, EventArgs e)
{
    mic.GetData(data);
    audio.Write(data, 0, data.Length);
}
```

Behind the button click event handler stays the core of this application. First of all, to know when the button has either to start or to stop the audio recording, you check the `State` property provided by the `Microphone` class. When `State` is equal to the `MicrophoneState.Stopped` value, it means the microphone is not working and you can start it. When you want to start the audio recording, you set the `BufferDuration` property to 100 milliseconds—so that the `BufferReady` event is raised every 100 milliseconds. Then you prepare the bytes array buffer to receive audio data. This array will have a capacity equal to the value returned by the `GetSampleSizeInBytes` method provided by the `Microphone` class. The `GetSampleSizeInBytes` method accepts a `TimeSpan` object set equal to the `BufferDuration` property value. A fresh new `MemoryStream` object is created—so that each time a recording is started, you don't have the new recording appended to the old one—and the `Microphone` is started with the `Start` method. Finally, the `PageTitle` and the button's `Content` are set according to the new state.

If the button is used to stop the recording, you use the `Stop` method from the `Microphone` class to stop the microphone recording. Then the page title and button's content are set according to their new states, and the registration is played by calling the `PlayRecordedAudio` method. Finally, when the audio playing is over, `PageTitle` is set back to the original value.

```
private void btnRecord_Click(object sender, RoutedEventArgs e)
{
    if (mic.State == MicrophoneState.Stopped)
    {
        mic.BufferDuration = TimeSpan.FromMilliseconds(100);
        data = new byte[mic.GetSampleSizeInBytes(mic.BufferDuration)];
        audio = new MemoryStream();
        mic.Start();
        this.PageTitle.Text = "recording...";
        btnRecord.Content = "Stop";
    }
    else
    {
        mic.Stop();
        this.PageTitle.Text = "playing";
        btnRecord.Content = "Record";
        btnRecord.IsEnabled = false;
        PlayRecordedAudio();
        this.PageTitle.Text = "ready";
    }
}
```

In the private PlayRecordedAudio method, you create an object from the SoundEffect class providing the MemoryStream buffer. This buffer is converted to an array with the ToArray method. Finally, you provide the SampleRate microphone audio sample rate, and the mono audio channel. You play the recorded audio by using the Play method that accepts three parameters: the volume, the pitch, and the pan. All those parameters are float numbers but have different ranges. The volume parameter goes from 0.0 f (float) (no sounds) to 1.0 f (the volume is equal to the MasterVolume set in the phone). The pitch parameter is responsible for the funny effect. It reproduces the sound one octave higher than the original. The last parameter is the pan value, which represents the audio balancing heard from the left and right ears.

```
private void PlayRecordedAudio()
{
    SoundEffect se = new SoundEffect(audio.ToArray(), mic.SampleRate,
                                     AudioChannels.Mono);
    se.Play(1.0f, 1.0f, 0.0f);
    btnRecord.IsEnabled = true;
}
```

Usage

You can use this application both in the emulator and the physical device. If you choose the former, the PC's microphone will be used.

From Visual Studio 2010, press Ctrl+F5 so that the application is started. If you choose the emulator, the application will look like Figure 7-18.

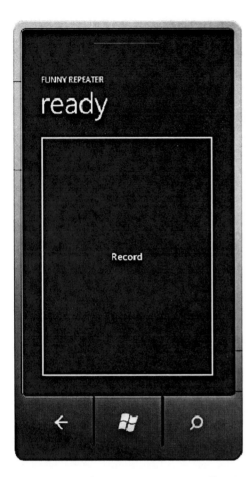

Figure 7-18. *The Funny Repeater application running in the emulator*

Now you can press the Record button and start to say what you would like to say. Press the Stop button, and hopefully you will hear your voice repeating your speech, but in a funny way.

7-8. Using the MediaElement Control to Play Both Music and Video

Problem

You need to play music, such as MP3 and WMA files, and videos by using the same Silverlight control.

Solution

You can use the MediaElement control within the System.Windows.Controls namespace.

How It Works

Within the Silverlight for Windows Phone controls library is the MediaElement control, which enables us to reproduce music and video available from remote sites and local resources. Obviously, in the latter case, the final distribution XAP package will be greater than the XAP package provided by the remote solution.

This path can be specified in the Source property that accepts the URI path of the file, or by using the SetSource method if the media file is stored locally in isolated storage.

■ **Note** In the following MSDN article, you can read about all media formats compatible with the MediaElement control: http://msdn.microsoft.com/en-us/library/ff462087(VS.92).aspx.

Other than the classic methods to start, stop, and pause the media playing, MediaElement provides some very interesting events. The CurrentStateChanged event is raised when the state of the media playing is changed. This event is used when you need to manage buttons to play, stop, and pause the media. For example, in this recipe, the event is used to change the Play icon of the ApplicationBarIcon to a Pause icon when the CurrentState property of MediaElement is equal to the MediaElementState.Playing value.

The BufferingProgressChanged event is raised during the buffering of the media file. Usually when the file is on a remote site, this event is used to inform the user that a buffering process is in progress. You can use the event to show the buffering percentage. The buffering progress can be retrieved from the BufferingProgress property, which returns a double value (from 0.0 to 1.0) that you can multiply by 100 to obtain the progress percentage.

The MediaOpened event is raised when the media is ready to be played (which means the header of the file has been read and the MediaElement properties are set). MediaEnded is raised when the media playing ends.

The AutoPlay property enables you to automatically start playing the media when its value is set to true. However, the Marketplace certification requirements (Section 6.5) indicate that you can't interrupt music that is already playing, so it is better to start with this value set to false and then check whether music is already playing on your device. This can be accomplished by calling the GameHasControl method provided by the MediaPlayer class.

The NaturalDuration, NaturalWidth, and NaturalHeight properties represent the media duration, width, and height (if the media is a video), respectively.

Finally, the Position property represents the media-playing position that you can read and set with a TimeSpan value. In this recipe, we used this property to update a Slider control position so to have visual feedback about the progression of the media playing.

The Code

To demonstrate the MediaElement usage, we have created a Silverlight for Windows Phone application that uses a MediaElement, a slider, to represent the progression of the media playing, and a TextBlock control to write the buffering percentage.

In the MainPage.xaml file, you add those three controls within the Content grid. Moreover, you define two ApplicationBarIconButton controls that enable us to play, pause, and stop the media playing (the Play button becomes the Pause button after being pressed).

```
<!--ContentPanel - place additional content here-->
<Grid x:Name="ContentPanel" Grid.Row="1" Margin="12,0,12,0">
    <Grid>
        <Grid.RowDefinitions>
            <RowDefinition Height="Auto" />
            <RowDefinition Height="*" />
            <RowDefinition Height="Auto" />
        </Grid.RowDefinitions>
        <TextBlock x:Name="tbBuffering" Grid.Row="0" />
        <MediaElement AutoPlay="False" x:Name="meVideo"
Source="http://mschannel9.vo.msecnd.net/o9/mix/09/wmv/key01.wmv" Grid.Row="1"/>
            <Slider x:Name="sPosition" Grid.Row="2"/>
    </Grid>
</Grid>

<phone:PhoneApplicationPage.ApplicationBar>
    <shell:ApplicationBar IsVisible="True" IsMenuEnabled="True">
        <shell:ApplicationBarIconButton IconUri="/Images/appbar.transport.play.rest.png"
        Text="Play" x:Name="btnPlay" Click="btnPlay_Click"/>
        <shell:ApplicationBarIconButton IconUri="/Images/appbar.stop.rest.png"
        Text="Stop" Click="btnStop_Click"/>
    </shell:ApplicationBar>
</phone:PhoneApplicationPage.ApplicationBar>
```

In the MainPage.xaml.cs code file, you start defining two class-level variables representing the media file duration and a DispatcherTimer timer to update the slider control position. In the MainPage constructor, you add event handlers and other initialization code. As you already learned in Recipe 3-2, even if you define a name for an application's icon button, you need to assign its own control's reference by picking the related index from the Buttons collection of the ApplicationBar class.

```
public partial class MainPage : PhoneApplicationPage
{
    private TimeSpan duration;
    private DispatcherTimer timer;

    // Constructor
    public MainPage()
    {
        InitializeComponent();
        meVideo.BufferingProgressChanged +=
                new RoutedEventHandler(meVideo_BufferingProgressChanged);
        meVideo.CurrentStateChanged +=
                new RoutedEventHandler(meVideo_CurrentStateChanged);
        meVideo.MediaOpened += new RoutedEventHandler(meVideo_MediaOpened);
        meVideo.MediaEnded += new RoutedEventHandler(meVideo_MediaEnded);
        btnPlay = ApplicationBar.Buttons[0] as ApplicationBarIconButton;
        timer = new DispatcherTimer();
        timer.Tick += new EventHandler(timer_Tick);
        timer.Interval = TimeSpan.FromMilliseconds(500);
        sPosition.Value = 0;
    }
. . .
```

The DispatcherTimer object is used to update the progress value of the slider control. Every half second, the Tick event is raised and the slider value property is set with the new Position value provided by the MediaElement class.

```
void timer_Tick(object sender, EventArgs e)
{
    if (meVideo.CurrentState == MediaElementState.Playing)
    {
        double currentPostition = meVideo.Position.TotalMilliseconds;
        double progressPosition = (currentPostition * 100) /
                                    duration.TotalMilliseconds;
        sPosition.Value = progressPosition;
    }
}
```

The duration variable is set in the MediaOpened event handler, where you are sure that the media header has been read and media properties are set.

```
void meVideo_MediaOpened(object sender, RoutedEventArgs e)
{
    duration = meVideo.NaturalDuration.TimeSpan;
}
```

In the `BufferingProgressChanged` event handler, you are going to update the text block `Text` property with the media buffering percentage that is retrieved by the `BufferingProgress` property of `MediaElement` and formatted with the `Format` method.

```
void meVideo_BufferingProgressChanged(object sender, RoutedEventArgs e)
{
    tbBuffering.Text = string.Format("Buffering...{0:P}",
                                        meVideo.BufferingProgress);
}
```

The `CurrentStateChanged` event is managed by the related event handler in order to change the Play icon button into the Pause icon button when `CurrentState` is equal to `Playing`.

```
void meVideo_CurrentStateChanged(object sender, RoutedEventArgs e)
{
    if (meVideo.CurrentState == MediaElementState.Playing)
        btnPlay.IconUri = new Uri("/Images/appbar.transport.pause.rest.png",
                                    UriKind.Relative);
    else
        btnPlay.IconUri = new Uri("/Images/appbar.transport.play.rest.png",
                                    UriKind.Relative);
}
```

In the `Play` and `Stop` event handlers, in response to the Play and Stop button clicks on the application bar, you call the `Play`, `Pause`, and `Stop` methods provided by the `MediaElement` class.

```
private void btnPlay_Click(object sender, EventArgs e)
{
    if (meVideo.CurrentState == MediaElementState.Playing)
    {
        meVideo.Pause();
        timer.Stop();
    }
    else
    {
        timer.Start();
        meVideo.Play();
    }
}

private void btnStop_Click(object sender, EventArgs e)
{
    meVideo.Stop();
}
```

Finally, you add some code to reset the media control when the media playing is over:

```
void meVideo_MediaEnded(object sender, RoutedEventArgs e)
```

321

```
    {
        meVideo.Position = TimeSpan.Zero;
        sPosition.Value = 0;
        btnPlay.IconUri = new Uri("/Images/appbar.transport.play.rest.png",
                                    UriKind.Relative);
    }
```

Usage

From Visual Studio 2010, select the Windows Phone Emulator as the target output and press Ctrl+F5 to start the application shown in Figure 7-19.

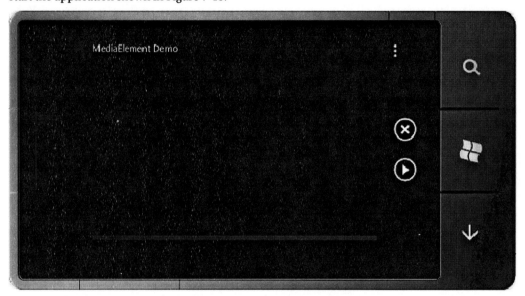

Figure 7-19. The `MediaElement` *demo application running in the emulator*

Now you can press the Play button on the application bar and see the buffering information on the screen. When the buffering is complete, the movie will start and the Play button will change into the Pause button.

7-9. Adding Integration with the Music-Videos Hub

Problem

You need to integrate your application with the Music-Videos hub in your Windows Phone device.

Solution

You have to use methods and properties provided by `MediaHistory` and `MediaHistoryItem` classes.

How It Works

The Music-Videos hub is an aggregator application available from the Windows Phone operating system. It groups all the applications installed on the phone that reproduce media files such as music and videos. The Music-Videos hub is composed of four sections:

> *Zune*: Contains links to music, video, podcasts, radio, and the Marketplace

> *History*: Contains recently played media and content from third-party providers

> *New*: Contains recent media either uploaded to the phone or downloaded from the Marketplace

> *App*: Contains the list of applications that manage media

So the last section is very interesting. How can your application be included in the App section of the Music-Videos hub? The MSDN official documentation says that the use of `MediaHistory` and `MediaHistoryItem` classes in your application will be detected during the certification process. If the application is accepted, the `WMAppManifest.xml` file is modified and the `HubType` attribute is added to the `App` tag. In this case, the application name will appear in the App section, and the user can execute it from there.

■ **Tip** You can manually add the `HubType="1"` attribute to the `App` tag in the `WMAppManifest.xml` file within your project in order to test the integration between your application and the Music-Videos hub.

The application must be developed to correctly respond to the Music-Videos hub interactions. These interactions can be summarized as follows:

- When a media file is played, it appears as Now Playing in the History section, next the Zune section. It appears as a 358×358 pixel image that you must provide in your solution. This image should represent your application, and you must provide a title for the media file being played.

- When another media file starts playing, the old one has to be inserted into the History section.

- When an item is picked from the History section, your application will be executed and a `QueryString` will be provided with the information you stored in the `PlayerContext` collection. Your application has to manage this query string information and play the related media.

- When your application is executed from the App section and a media file is already playing, the application has to continue playing that media.

Everything noted in the preceding list is available from the `MediaHistoryItem` and `MediaHistory` classes.

The `MediaHistory` class contains the `Instance` property, which returns the current instance of that class. Indeed, `MediaHistory` cannot be instantiated because it is a sealed class. After retrieving the instance of the `MediaHistory` class, you can use its methods to add items into the History section of the Music-Videos hub.

The `WriteRecentPlay` method writes a `MediaHistoryItem` item into the History section. The `WriteAcquiredItem` method writes the provided `MediaHistoryItem` into the New section.

Finally, the `NowPlaying` property is used to set the item that is presently playing in the Music-Videos hub. When the user selects the Now Playing icon in the hub, the application will be executed again (please note that we haven't said it is tombstoned). However, this time the `QueryString` collection property will contain the key/value pair you added via the `PlayerContext` property provided by the `MediaHistoryItem` class. You can retrieve its value in the `OnNavigatedTo` event handler so as to play the media again.

So you have encountered the first property from the `MediaHistoryItem` class. There are other very useful properties, such as `ImageStream` (which has to contain the image of 358×358 pixels, as stated in preceding bullet list).

■ **Caution** The image cannot be greater than 75 kilobytes. Otherwise, the following exception will occur: "System.ArgumentException: image stream size bigger than maximum allowed 76800."

The `Title` property enables you to set the string that will be displayed over the NowPlaying icon. Usually this will be set to the media name, such as a song's name. Even when you specify the item in the History and the New sections, you still have to set the `Title` property that will be displayed in the Now Playing section.

■ **Note** There is another property called `Source` that the official documentation defines as unsupported, but if you don't set this property to an empty string, you will not be able to add the item to the Music-Videos hub.

The Code

To demonstrate the Music-Videos hub integration, we have created the `MusicVideosHubIntegration` Silverlight for Windows Phone application. As you already learned in the previous recipes, you have to add the `Microsoft.Xna.Framework.dll` assembly and a class implementing the `IApplicationService` interface to periodically call the `Update` static method from the `FrameworkDispatcher` class.

The `MainPage.xaml` file contains just a label to show the author and song that is playing. The application bar provides buttons to play, pause, and stop the song.

In `MainPage.xaml.cs`, the core of the application code resides in the `OnNavigatedTo` method and in the Play button's `Click` event handler.

The `OnNavigatedTo` method is called when the application is either first launched or resumed from either the dormant state or a tombstone. The first operation to perform is to check whether the Media Player is already playing a song. If it is, the application must continue to play that song. The song can be retrieved via the `ActiveSong` property from the `MediaQueue` class. In turn, a `MediaQueue` object can be retrieved by the `Queue` property from the `MediaPlayer` class. Next, if the `QueryString` property contains the key you have previously stored, it means that the application has been executed from the hub. We previously stored the song index, so you can easily retrieve it by pointing to that index in the `Songs` collection. Finally, you update the text shown in the user interface and the related buttons' images. Please note that the `s` variable is a `Song` class-level field that is set through different classes' methods.

```
protected override void
        OnNavigatedTo(System.Windows.Navigation.NavigationEventArgs e)
{
    if (MediaPlayer.State == MediaState.Playing)
    {
        s = MediaPlayer.Queue.ActiveSong;
    }
    else if (NavigationContext.QueryString.ContainsKey(_key))
    {
        s = library.Songs[int.Parse(NavigationContext.QueryString[_key])];
        MediaPlayer.Play(s);
    }

    if (s != null)
    {
        tbSong.Text = "Now playing " + s.Artist + " " + s.Name;
        btnPlay.IconUri = new Uri("/Images/appbar.transport.pause.rest.png",
                                  UriKind.Relative);
    }

    base.OnNavigatedTo(e);
}
```

In the `btnPlay_Click` event handler, the main part of the code checks whether the `Song s` variable is null. If it is, either the song has not been provided by the hub or the user has stopped the song from playing. In either case, a shuffle is done to retrieve a song to be played.

The next operation is calling the `Play` method from the `MediaPlayer` class and calling the `UpdateNowPlaying` and `UpdateHistory` methods that accomplish the main Music-Videos hub integration job.

```
private void btnPlay_Click(object sender, EventArgs e)
{
    if (MediaPlayer.State == MediaState.Playing)
    {
        MediaPlayer.Pause();
    }
    else
    {
        MediaHistory history = MediaHistory.Instance;

        if (s == null)
```

```
        {
            s = DoShuffle();
            if (s == null)
            {
                MessageBox.Show("The media library doesn't contain songs");
                return;
            }
        }

        tbSong.Text = "Now playing " + s.Artist + " " + s.Name;
        MediaPlayer.Play(s);
        UpdateNowPlaying();
        UpdateHistory();
    }
}
```

These methods are pretty similar; you have to set mandatory properties of the `MediaHistoryItem` object and either call the `WriteRecentPlay` method or set the `NowPlaying` property from the `MediaHistory` class.

▓ **Note** You can't use the same `MediaHistoryItem` object, but you need to create more than one instance for each item you want to add in the hub's sections.

In the `UpdateNowPlaying` method, you use another way to retrieve the stream data composing the image: the `StreamResourceInfo` class. An object of this class is returned from the `GetResourceStream` static method provided by the `Application` class. The `GetResourceStream` static method accepts a URI object that specifies where to find the resource. The `StreamResourceInfo` class provides the `Stream` property containing the image's stream data that you can assign to the `ImageStream` property of the `MediaHistoryItem` class.

▓ **Note** We used a JPEG image so as to reduce the image definition and provide a compatible image size.

Finally, you set the `Source` and `Title` properties and you add the song index to the `PlayerContext` collection so that when the song is requested from the hub, your application can retrieve it from the query string. This new object is assigned to the `NowPlaying` property of the `MediaHistory` object that is retrieved with the `Instance` static property.

```
private void UpdateNowPlaying()
{
    MediaHistoryItem nowPlaying = new MediaHistoryItem();
    StreamResourceInfo sri = Application.GetResourceStream(
```

```
                              new Uri("NowPlayingIcon.jpg", UriKind.Relative));
        nowPlaying.ImageStream = sri.Stream;
        nowPlaying.Source = "";
        nowPlaying.Title = s.Name;
        nowPlaying.PlayerContext.Add(_key, songIndex.ToString());
        MediaHistory history = MediaHistory.Instance;
        history.NowPlaying = nowPlaying;
    }
```

The same code is used for the UpdateHistory method, except the final call is to the WriteRecentPlay method instead of the NowPlaying property setting.

```
    private void UpdateHistory()
    {
        MediaHistoryItem historyItem = new MediaHistoryItem();
        StreamResourceInfo sri = Application.GetResourceStream(
                              new Uri("NowPlayingIcon.jpg", UriKind.Relative));
        historyItem.ImageStream = sri.Stream;
        historyItem.Source = "";
        historyItem.Title = s.Name;
        historyItem.PlayerContext.Add(_key, songIndex.ToString());
        MediaHistory history = MediaHistory.Instance;
        history.WriteRecentPlay(historyItem);
    }
```

Usage

For this recipe, you need a physical device, because the emulator doesn't provide the Music-Videos hub. From Visual Studio 2010, select the Windows Phone Device target output and then press Ctrl+F5. The application deploys to the physical device and runs, as shown in Figure 7-20.

Figure 7-20. *The* `MusicVideosHubIntegration` *application running on the device*

You can press the Play button on the application bar so that a random song from your media library is picked and played. Now press the Start button and go to the Music-Videos hub, and you should see in the Now Playing section the application icon and the song title (see Figure 7-21).

Figure 7-21. *In the Music-Videos hub application, the History section shows the last played song.*

Press the Now Playing icon from the hub, and the application executes again playing the song. Now press the Stop button and then the Play button again so that another song is played. Stop that song and then press the hardware Start button. Go to the Music-Videos hub and see that the History section is populated with an item. Sadly, there is no title describing the item, but by clicking it, you can discover that our application is running and the first song is being played.

CHAPTER 8

Isolated Storage

The isolated storage in Silverlight for Windows Phone follows, in some ways, the architectural model used for the desktop version. The concept of this storage is to isolate the physical memory of one application from another. Isolated storage undoubtedly has its advantages: the application's data is available only to us, which means that no one else can compromise security by accessing it. Sure, you can also see disadvantages—our application will not be able to share data even partially with other apps, right? But to solve problems like this, you can just move the data to be shared "in the cloud." When the user chooses to download the latest version of your application, the update process will not modify your isolated storage or clean it.

The files that you choose to create and save in your application, as well as the settings of the application and the local database, are contained within isolated storage.

The recipes in this chapter describe how to do the following:

- 8-1. Save a file in isolated storage and load it

- 8-2. Save serialized data

- 8-3. Implement a local database

- 8-4. Modify the settings of your application

- 8-5. Save a photo in isolated storage

- 8-6. Use Isolated Storage Explorer

- 8-7. Implement a background file transfer

Note If your application is uninstalled, the relative isolated storage is completely removed. Therefore, if the application is installed once again, that installation occurs as if it were being done for the first time. Take care to notify the user of this issue and to save (with prior written permission of the user) the data that the user wants to keep on your server in the cloud.

8-1. Saving and Loading a File in Isolated Storage

Problem

You want to create a simple notepad so the user can store notes locally and easily retrieve them later.

Solution

You must use the `IsolatedStorageFile` class to access isolated storage.

How It Works

The class that provides the ability to access data in isolated storage is `IsolatedStorageFile`, contained in the namespace `System.IO.IsolatedStorage`, which in turn is contained inside the `mscorlib` assembly. As you can see from the class diagram shown in Figure 8-1, you are allowed a number of tasks, including creating directories. In this case, for example, you could ask the user whether to save data in a folder hierarchy.

Figure 8-1. *Isolated storage's class diagram*

The Code

You start from an interface that will be composed essentially of a main page and two buttons. In the main page, the user will insert the title of the note. In the application bar, you will have two buttons: one to save the note and another to display the page that contains the list of notes already written and saved in isolated storage. While on the list page, you will have only a list box in which every item will be a note that is already saved. When a note is selected from the list, it will be loaded on the main page.

```
...
<Grid x:Name="LayoutRoot" Background="Transparent">
      <Grid.RowDefinitions>
          <RowDefinition Height="Auto"/>
          <RowDefinition Height="*"/>
      </Grid.RowDefinitions>
      <StackPanel x:Name="TitlePanel" Grid.Row="0" Margin="12,17,0,28">
          <TextBlock x:Name="ApplicationTitle" Text="SIMPLE NOTE APPLICATION"
                             Style="{StaticResource PhoneTextNormalStyle}"/>
      </StackPanel>

      <Grid x:Name="ContentPanel" Grid.Row="1" Margin="12,0,12,0">
          <Grid.RowDefinitions>
              <RowDefinition Height="45" />
              <RowDefinition Height="*" />
          </Grid.RowDefinitions>
          <TextBox Grid.Row="0" Name="FilenameTextBox" Text="NoteName" />
          <TextBox Grid.Row="1" Name="NoteTextBox" Text="Write  your note here" />
      </Grid>
  </Grid>

<phone:PhoneApplicationPage.ApplicationBar>
      <shell:ApplicationBar IsVisible="True" IsMenuEnabled="True">
          <shell:ApplicationBarIconButton IconUri="/Images/save.png" Text="Save"
                  Click="SaveButton_Click" />
          <shell:ApplicationBarIconButton IconUri="/Images/notes.png" Text="Open"
                  Click="ListButton_Click" />

      </shell:ApplicationBar>
  </phone:PhoneApplicationPage.ApplicationBar>
...
```

In the SaveButton_Click handler you will use the IsolatedStorageFile and IsolatedStorageStream classes, which enables you to create a file in isolated storage and to write a text stream within it.

```
private void SaveButton_Click(object sender, EventArgs e)
{
  try
  {
    using (var store = IsolatedStorageFile.GetUserStoreForApplication())
    using (var stream = new IsolatedStorageFileStream(FilenameTextBox.Text,
                        FileMode.Create,
                        FileAccess.Write,
                        store))
    {
      StreamWriter writer = new StreamWriter(stream);
```

```
        writer.Write(NoteTextBox.Text);
        writer.Close();
      }
    }
    catch (Exception)
    {
      MessageBox.Show("Error saving the file");
    }
}
```

First you need the storage dedicated to your application, which will be automatically retrieved from the `GetUserStoreForApplication` method that is based on your application. Then you create a stream to a file that will store the content in your application. This filename is contained in the Text field of the control `FilenameTextBox`. At this point, you just have to write the stream you have available, with a `StreamWriter` (remember to close the stream after you are finished).

If errors occur in the preceding transactions, the application will show a message to the user indicating that there was a problem.

The other handler used to display the page with the list of notes already saved will not be anything other than a call to the `Navigate` method of the `NavigationService` class:

```
private void ListButton_Click(object sender, EventArgs e)
{
        NavigationService.Navigate(new Uri("/Notes.xaml", UriKind.Relative));
}
```

On the page where you will present the list, you will override the `OnNavigatedTo` event handler to load the list of all files created in your isolated storage:

```
protected override void OnNavigatedTo(System.Windows.Navigation.NavigationEventArgs e)
{
  using (var store =
        System.IO.IsolatedStorage.IsolatedStorageFile.GetUserStoreForApplication())
  {
    this.NotesListBox.ItemsSource = store.GetFileNames();
  }
}
```

Basically, you're passing as a source of list box items the list of filenames in your store that will be shown onscreen. (The list is created based on a data template that you will see in Chapter 10.)

Click an item within the list to pass it as parameter of the main page via the following code:

```
private void Notes_SelectionChanged(object sender, SelectionChangedEventArgs e)
{
  if (e.AddedItems.Count > 0)
    NavigationService.Navigate(new Uri(
                          string.Format("/MainPage.xaml?note={0}", e.AddedItems[0]),
                          UriKind.Relative));
     }
```

At this point, to complete the code of this application, you need to only override the OnNavigatedTo method in the main page. Then you manage the opening of the note by using the following code:

```
protected override void OnNavigatedTo(System.Windows.Navigation.NavigationEventArgs e)
{
  if (NavigationContext.QueryString.ContainsKey("note"))
  {
    string filename = this.NavigationContext.QueryString["note"];
    if (!string.IsNullOrEmpty(filename))
    {
      using (var store = System.IO.IsolatedStorage.IsolatedStorageFile
              .GetUserStoreForApplication())
      using (var stream = new IsolatedStorageFileStream(filename,
                          FileMode.Open,
                          FileAccess.ReadWrite,
                          store))
    {
      StreamReader reader = new StreamReader(stream);
      this.NoteTextBox.Text = reader.ReadToEnd();
      this.FilenameTextBox.Text = filename;
      reader.Close();
    }
   }
  }
}
```

There is not much difference between this code and the code used to save data, except that this time you first check whether a note to be opened has been passed. If it has, you aim to open it instead of creating a new note, as you did before when using a StreamReader to read and enter in the text box the body of the note that you read from the file.

Usage

From Visual Studio 2010, launch the application by pressing Ctrl+F5. The application displays, as shown in Figure 8-2. Write something and then click the button to save the note. Click to display the list of saved notes, as shown in Figure 8-3. (We had already saved some.) Click on another note that has been saved for loading and complete the cycle of the application, as shown in Figure 8-4.

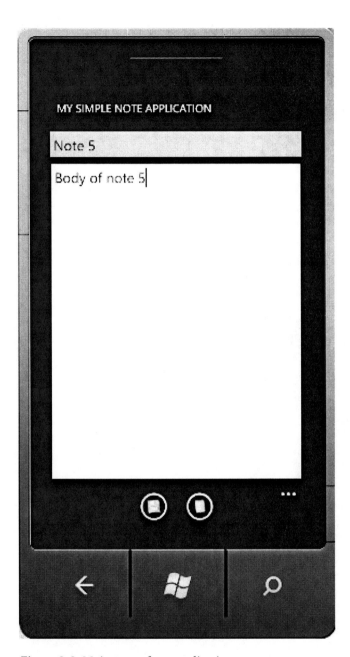

Figure 8-2. Main page of our application

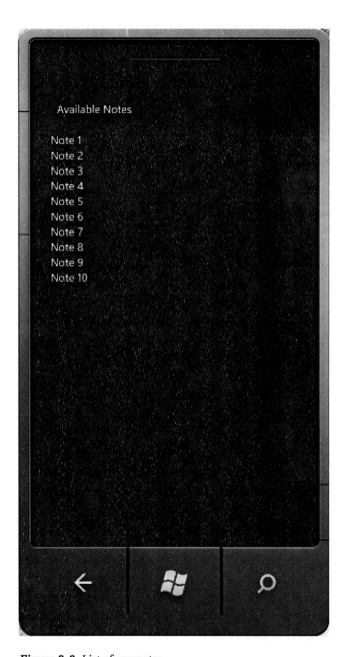

Figure 8-3. *List of our notes*

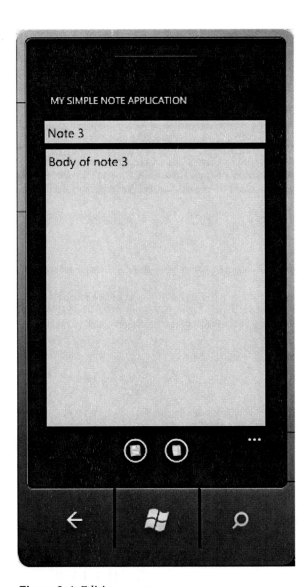

Figure 8-4. Editing a note

8-2. Saving Serialized Data

Problem

You want to serialize on disk the state of your objects, to load them later.

Solution

You must use XmlSerializer in combination with the IsolatedStorage classes to serialize the state of your objects in a file.

How It Works

The XmlSerializer class serializes (and deserializes) objects to and from XML documents. In serialization, we convert an object and its properties to a serial format (in this case, XML) that can be stored (in our case) or transported (in the case of services, for example). Deserialization is the process of re-creating the object from XML, by decorating the objects that correspond to XmlElement, and their properties that correspond to XmlAttribute.

The Code

For this recipe, we have chosen to complete the application logic of 7Drum by using the ExerciseManager class to save and load the exercises.

Just to refresh your memory, as you can see from the diagram in Figure 8-5, one of the entities involved in this recipe is ExerciseSettings, whose persistence logic (in this case, in the isolated storage) is handled by the ExerciseManager class, which deals simply with loading and saving a list of exercises.

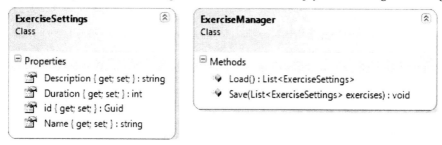

Figure 8-5. *Class Diagram of classes that works with exercise in 7Drum*

The first method that you want to consider is **Save**. The code is written as follows:

```
public static void Save(List<ExerciseSettings> exercises)
{
        using (var store = IsolatedStorageFile.GetUserStoreForApplication())
        using (var fileStream = store.CreateFile("exercises.xml"))
        using (var writer = new StreamWriter(fileStream))
```

```
        {
                XmlSerializer ser = new XmlSerializer(typeof(List<ExerciseSettings>));
                ser.Serialize(writer, exercises);
                writer.Close();
        }
}
```

This code, which makes extensive use of the construct using, behaves almost exactly the same way as the code of the previous recipe. In practice, you return the store associated with your application. Then in this store, you create the XML files for the exercises, you associate the StreamWriter to this fileStream, and finally, thanks to the XmlSerializer class, you write the XML serialization that results in the list of exercises. Closing the stream commits the changes, and the using statements coming at the end of the scope disposes the three variables: writer, fileStream, and store.

In this way, you just serialized into isolated storage a list of ExerciseSettings. It is obvious that if your application requires more than one entity domain, you will have no problem using this code. If you have any doubts, the only thing you need to revise is the use of the XmlSerializer class.

The other method to analyze now is the Load method, which will deserialize the data from the XML file in our class:

```
public static List<ExerciseSettings> Load()
{
  List<ExerciseSettings> exercises = new List<ExerciseSettings>();
  using (IsolatedStorageFile storage = IsolatedStorageFile.GetUserStoreForApplication())
  if (storage.FileExists("exercises.xml"))
  {
    using (IsolatedStorageFileStream stream = storage.OpenFile("exercises.xml",
                FileMode.Open))
    {
      XmlSerializer xml = new XmlSerializer(typeof(List<ExerciseSettings>));
      exercises = xml.Deserialize(stream) as List<ExerciseSettings>;
      stream.Close();
    }
  }
  return exercises;
}
```

This code is not so difficult to understand if you analyze it step by step:

1. Create a list of ExerciseSettings.

2. Return to our store (at this point, it's clear that if you want to access the isolated storage this is a necessary step).

3. If there is an XML file called exercises in the store, do the following:

   a. Open a stream pointing to the file.

   b. Create an XmlSerializer class to list the ExerciseSettings.

   c. Deserialize the stream in the list of ExerciseSettings.

> **d.** Close the stream.

At this point, our application `7Drum` is ready to save and upload lists of exercises, to keep them between sessions of our application.

Usage

After adding the implementation of the two methods of the class `ExerciseManager`, start the application from Visual Studio by pressing F5. To test if you have correctly written the code save a list of exercises and close `7Drum`. Then reopen and check that between sessions the whole list of exercises has been saved.

8-3. Implementing the Local Database

Problem

You want to create an application that manages and stores customer information in a database.

Solution

You must create the database in your isolated storage using the `DataContext` class and using LINQ to SQL to manage data.

How It Works

The local database for Windows Phone works on LINQ to SQL, which means that you can access relational data through an object-oriented approach, calling methods and accessing properties (the diagram in Figure 8-6 shows how it works). To access a database on Windows Phone you must extend `DataContext` (see Figure 8-7), implementing a class that works as a proxy between the application and the database and has many properties of type `Table<TSource>` for as many tables as you want in your database. Of course, you must remember that you can't access the database directly, and that your database will never be available if your application is not in foreground because the database is loaded with the application, and unloaded in the same way.

To connect to the database, you must provide to constructor of `DataContext` class a connection string that contains options to configure your database (even a password to protect it). First, you must define the `DataSource`, which could be one of the following:

- `isostore`: Your database file is located in isolated storage within your application. The format of this property is something like "`isostore:/Subdirectory/YourDbName.sdf`"

- `appdata`: The database is found in the installation folder of the application, as in "`Data Source = 'appdata:/YouDbName.sdf`"

You can also specify how the database will be opened, such as: `File Mode = <option>`, where `option` can assume the following values:

- *Read Write*: The default setting that allows you to access the database and modify its content

- *Read Only*: When using this setting, you can only read data from the database

- *Exclusive*: Other processes won't be allowed to access your database

- *Shared Read*: Allows other processes to access your database in read-only mode (remember that your database will be available only while you hold it open)

Another parameter that you can specify in your connection string is a password to encrypt your data, such as Password='YourPassword.' This way encrypts your entire database. This could be a good idea if you are writing an application that works on the user's reserved information to ask for a password and not sculpt it into the code.

You can also specify the `max buffer size` of your database that determines the amount of memory in kilobytes that your database uses before it flushes changes to disk; if you don't specify a value, the size will be the default value that is fixed to 384 KB, but if you specify a value, it can't be greater then 5,120 KB.

In the same way, you can specify a max database size that has a default value of 32 MB and a maximum value of 512 MB.

The last parameter that you can include in your connection string is the Culture Identifier, which formats language code, or the country/region code (for example, en-US). See `http://msdn.microsoft.com/en-us/library/hh202918(v=vs.92).aspx` for a complete list of supported languages and cultures.

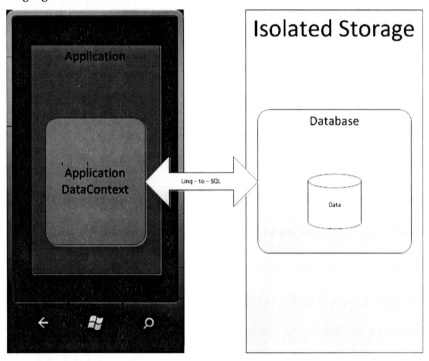

Figure 8-6. How the local database works on Windows Phone

The Code

First download the set of icons available at `http://metro.windowswiki.info/` in order to use these icons in your application; then start creating your project by adding the images add.png, delete.png, edit.png and save.png to a directory named `Images`.

After these preliminary steps have been completed, create a new folder named `Model`, where you will put all classes that will compose your application model. In this case you will add a class that represents your `Customer`.

```
using System;

namespace CustomersManager.Model
{
    public class Customer
    {
        public Guid Id { get; set; }

        public string Name { get; set; }

        public string TelephoneNumber { get; set; }

        public string Address { get; set; }
    }
}
```

We have not yet discussed how to create the database. It is really simpler than you might think. All you have to do is decorate classes that represent your model, as follows:

```
using System;
using System.ComponentModel;
using System.Data.Linq.Mapping;

namespace CustomersManager.Model
{
    [Table]
    public class Customer : INotifyPropertyChanged, INotifyPropertyChanging
    {
        [Column(IsPrimaryKey = true, IsDbGenerated = true, DbType = "GUID NOT NULL ",
CanBeNull = false, AutoSync = AutoSync.Always)]
        private Guid _id;

        public Guid Id
        {
            get { return _id; }
            set
            {
                NotifyPropertyChanging("Id");
                _id = value;
                NotifyPropertyChanged("Id");
            }
        }
```

```csharp
[Column]
private string _name;

public string Name
{
    get { return _name; }
    set
    {
        NotifyPropertyChanging("Name");
        _name = value;
        NotifyPropertyChanged("Name");
    }
}

[Column]
private string _telephoneNumber;

public string TelephoneNumber
{
    get { return _telephoneNumber; }
    set
    {
        NotifyPropertyChanging("TelephoneNumber");
        _telephoneNumber = value;
        NotifyPropertyChanged("TelephoneNumber");
    }
}

[Column]
private string _address;

public string Address
{
    get { return _address; }
    set
    {
        NotifyPropertyChanging("Address");
        _address = value;
        NotifyPropertyChanged("Address");
    }
}

#region Implementation of INotifyPropertyChanged

public event PropertyChangedEventHandler PropertyChanged;

private void NotifyPropertyChanged(string propertyName)
{
    if (PropertyChanged != null)
    {
        PropertyChanged(this, new PropertyChangedEventArgs(propertyName));
```

```
            }
        }
        #endregion

        #region Implementation of INotifyPropertyChanging

        public event PropertyChangingEventHandler PropertyChanging;

        private void NotifyPropertyChanging(string propertyName)
        {
            if (PropertyChanging != null)
            {
                PropertyChanging(this, new PropertyChangingEventArgs(propertyName));
            }
        }
        #endregion
    }
}
```

■ **Note** This way to work with database on Windows Phone will be more powerful used with MVVM pattern, where LINQ to SQL using POCO is your model.

As you can see, the decorations show that the Customer class represents a table in the database, and the properties are columns, where Id is the Primary Key. Once you have completed this first important step, you need to implement the data context of your application by extending the DataContext class (see Figure 8-7).

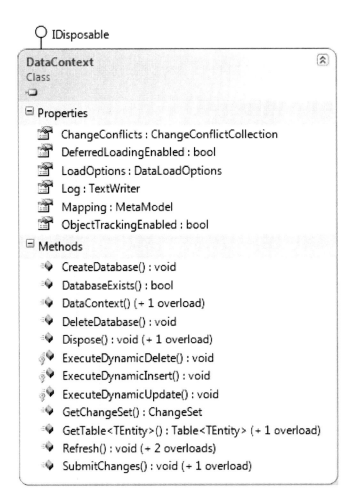

Figure 8-7. Class diagram of the DataContext class

Add another class to your application, naming it `CustomersManagerContext`, extending `DataContext`. The constructor of this class will call the one in the base class, passing it a connection string. Next, insert the instructions to create the database in the connection string, and then you will specify all the tables contained in your database.

```
public class CustomersManagerDataContext : DataContext
    {
        private const string DbConnectionString = "DataSource=isostore:/CustomerManager.sdf";

        public CustomersManagerDataContext()
            : this(DbConnectionString)
        {
        }
```

```
        public CustomersManagerDataContext(string connectionString)
            : base(connectionString)
        {
            if (!DatabaseExists())
                CreateDatabase();
        }

        public Table<Customer> Customers;
    }
```

As you can see, you can declare a private constant that is the default connection string used by your DataContext if you call the constructor without parameters. When you make a new instance of this class, the code inside the constructor controls whether the database exists and in this case starts creating the database, which will use all tables declared inside the class.

From here you are ready to start accessing the data inside your application, and then you must implement the rest of the application that interacts with the user. First, you must create a new page named Customers (as it appears in Figure 8-7) using the following xaml:

```
<Grid x:Name="LayoutRoot" Background="Transparent">
    <Grid.RowDefinitions>
        <RowDefinition Height="Auto"/>
        <RowDefinition Height="*"/>
    </Grid.RowDefinitions>

    <!--TitlePanel contains the name of the application and page title-->
    <StackPanel x:Name="TitlePanel" Grid.Row="0" Margin="12,17,0,28">
        <TextBlock x:Name="ApplicationTitle" Text="Customers Manager" Style="{StaticResour
ce PhoneTextNormalStyle}"/>
        <TextBlock x:Name="PageTitle" Text="Customers" Margin="9,-
7,0,0" Style="{StaticResource PhoneTextTitle1Style}"/>
    </StackPanel>

    <!--ContentPanel - place additional content here-->
    <StackPanel x:Name="ContentPanel" Grid.Row="1" Margin="12,0,12,0">
        <Grid>
            <Grid.ColumnDefinitions>
                <ColumnDefinition Width="*" />
                <ColumnDefinition Width="200" />
    <ColumnDefinition Width="50" />
            </Grid.ColumnDefinitions>
            <TextBlock Text="Name"/>
            <TextBlock Text="Telephone" Grid.Column="1" />
        </Grid>
        <ListBox x:Name="CustomersListBox">
            <ListBox.ItemTemplate>
                <DataTemplate>
                    <Grid>
                        <Grid.ColumnDefinitions>
                            <ColumnDefinition Width="*" />
                            <ColumnDefinition Width="250" />
                            <ColumnDefinition Width="50" />
                        </Grid.ColumnDefinitions>
```

```
                    <TextBlock Text="{Binding Name}"/>
                    <TextBlock Text="{Binding TelephoneNumber}" Grid.Column="1" TextAl
ignment="Right"/>

                    <Image Source="Images\edit.png" Grid.Column="2" Tap="Edit_Tap" />
                </Grid>
            </DataTemplate>
        </ListBox.ItemTemplate>
    </ListBox>
</StackPanel>
</Grid>

<phone:PhoneApplicationPage.ApplicationBar>
    <shell:ApplicationBar IsVisible="True" IsMenuEnabled="False">
        <shell:ApplicationBarIconButton x:Name="AddCustomerButton" IconUri="Images/add.png
" Text="Add " Click="AddCustomerButton_Click"/>
    </shell:ApplicationBar>
</phone:PhoneApplicationPage.ApplicationBar>
```

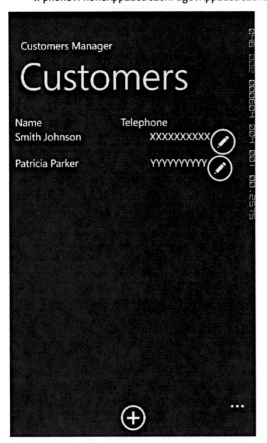

Figure 8-8. A screenshot of the Customers page

With this xaml, you will notice that you are using the binding of Silverlight (more information about binding in Chapter 10) to bind directly the content of textboxes to the columns of the table. The first step is to access the customer information into your database when this page is loaded, and then subscribe the Loaded event.

```
Loaded += Customers_Loaded;
```

And write the event handler as follows:

```
void Customers_Loaded(object sender, RoutedEventArgs e)
      {
          using (CustomersManagerDataContext dc = new CustomersManagerDataContext())
          {
              CustomersListBox.ItemsSource = from c in dc.Customers
                                             select c;

          }
      }
```

Again, you are using LINQ to access data inside your database, making it a simple query to enter customer information, and completing your first read operation on your database. If it's the first time that the application starts, nothing will be shown, so inserting is another basic step to implement. This is done in a page named CustomerDetails, which shows the customer information details. This page requires you to put in at least three textboxes for the user to input the information.

```
<Grid x:Name="LayoutRoot" Background="Transparent">
    <Grid.RowDefinitions>
        <RowDefinition Height="Auto"/>
        <RowDefinition Height="*"/>
    </Grid.RowDefinitions>

    <!--TitlePanel contains the name of the application and page title-->
    <StackPanel x:Name="TitlePanel" Grid.Row="0" Margin="12,17,0,28">
        <TextBlock x:Name="ApplicationTitle" Text="Customers Manager" Style="{StaticResour
ce PhoneTextNormalStyle}"/>
    </StackPanel>

    <!--ContentPanel - place additional content here-->
    <Grid x:Name="ContentPanel" Grid.Row="1" Margin="12,0,12,0">
      <Grid.ColumnDefinitions>
        <ColumnDefinition Width="140"/>
        <ColumnDefinition/>
      </Grid.ColumnDefinitions>
      <Grid.RowDefinitions>
        <RowDefinition Height="69"/>
<RowDefinition Height="69"/>
<RowDefinition Height="69"/>
<RowDefinition Height="69"/>
        <RowDefinition/>
      </Grid.RowDefinitions>
```

```
<TextBlock x:Name="NameTextBlock" Text="Name" VerticalAlignment="Center" HorizontalAlignment="
Right"/>

<TextBlock x:Name="AddressTextBlock" Text="Address" VerticalAlignment="Center" HorizontalAlign
ment="Right" Grid.Row="1"/>

<TextBlock x:Name="PhoneTextBlock" Text="Phone" VerticalAlignment="Center" HorizontalAlignment
="Right" Grid.Row="2"/>


<TextBox x:Name="NameTextBox" Text="{Binding Name, Mode=TwoWay}" VerticalAlignment="Center" Gr
id.Column="1"/>
            <TextBox x:Name="AddressTextBox" Text="{Binding Address, Mode=TwoWay}" VerticalAli
gnment="Center" Grid.Row="1" Grid.Column="1"/>
            <TextBox x:Name="PhoneTextBox" Text="{Binding TelephoneNumber, Mode=TwoWay}" Verti
calAlignment="Center" Grid.Row="2" Grid.Column="1"/>
        </Grid>
    </Grid>

  <phone:PhoneApplicationPage.ApplicationBar>
        <shell:ApplicationBar IsVisible="true" IsMenuEnabled="False">
            <shell:ApplicationBarIconButton x:Name="SaveButton" IconUri="Images/save.png" Text
="Save" Click="SaveButton_Click"/>

<shell:ApplicationBarIconButton x:Name="DeleteButton" IconUri="Images/delete.png" Text="Delete
" Click="DeleteButton_Click"/>
        </shell:ApplicationBar>
    </phone:PhoneApplicationPage.ApplicationBar>
```

Similar to the Customers page, you will bind a property of a customer object to the Grid's
DataContext, then every change made from user on the UI will reflect immediately on
CustomersManagerDataContext. Looking deeply inside this xaml, you can see that buttons in the
applicationBar subscribe two event handlers dedicated to save an object (insert or update) and delete it.

But before we look at the code to save and delete an item, check the QueryString to see if you have
invoked the page in insert or update mode, then subscribe the loaded event as before:

```
Loaded += CustomerDetailLoaded;
```

Declare at class level the following two members:

```
private Customer _customer;
private CustomersManagerDataContext dc = new CustomersManagerDataContext();
```

The Customer will represent the page's DataContext, while CustomersManagerDataContext as the
application data context.

Now implement the CustomerDetailLoaded event handler, looking for an Id key inside the
QueryString. If it is not present, create a brand-new Customer, else get it from the database, but in every
case, set it as a DataContext of the ContentPanel of the customer object, as follows:

```
private void CustomerDetailLoaded(object sender, RoutedEventArgs e)
{
```

```
        if (!NavigationContext.QueryString.ContainsKey("Id"))
        {
            _customer = new Customer();
        }
        else
        {
            Guid guid = Guid.Parse(NavigationContext.QueryString["Id"]);
            _customer = dc.Customers.FirstOrDefault(c => c == new Customer { Id = guid });
        }
        ContentPanel.DataContext = _customer;
    }
```

Now that you have a customer to work on, you can start implementing the SaveButton_Click and DeleteButton_Click event handlers, which will be based on two members that you must declare at class level, as follows:

```
    private void SaveButton_Click(object sender, EventArgs e)
    {
        if (!dc.Customers.Contains(_customer))
            dc.Customers.InsertOnSubmit(_customer);
        dc.SubmitChanges();
        NavigationService.Navigate(new Uri("/Customers.xaml", UriKind.Relative));
    }
```

In the first conditional statement, you control whether the customer is already inside the database to ensure if you are in the update or insert mode in case the customer doesn't exists. In this last case, you must call the method InsertOnSubmit that inserts an element into a table, changing from a detached state to attached, to make it persistent when the DataContext submits the changes. After the save operation, the user may need a delete operation, which can be implemented as follows:

```
private void DeleteButton_Click(object sender, EventArgs e)
{
  if (!dc.Customers.Contains(_customer))
    _customer = null;
  else
    if (MessageBox.Show("Are you sure?", "Confirm", MessageBoxButton.OKCancel) ==
MessageBoxResult.OK)
    {
      dc.Customers.DeleteOnSubmit(_customer);
      dc.SubmitChanges();
    }
    NavigationService.Navigate(new Uri("/Customers.xaml", UriKind.Relative));
}
```

Again, we look for the element inside the database; if it is not present you set to null the page's DataContext (that in this moment is the customer object) and you move to the Customers page, otherwise ask the user if they are sure they want to delete. If the customer is deleted from the database, submit the changes. You must take care of how this code works because you can simply call the method DeleteOnSubmit because the object _customer is already attached.

Now that your detail page is ready, all you need now is to implement the edit_tap EventHandler to pass the id of the element in QueryString, as follows:

```
        private void Edit_Tap(object sender, GestureEventArgs e)
        {
            NavigationService.Navigate(
                new Uri(string.Format("/CustomerDetail.xaml?Id={0}",
(CustomersListBox.SelectedItem as Customer).Id),UriKind.Relative));
        }
```

This is all you need to perform a Create, Read, Update and Delete (CRUD) operation.

Usage

Run the application from Visual Studio by pressing F5. The application can run on either the physical device or the emulator. From your `Customers` page, create a new `Customer`, save it, check that the customer appears on the list, then perform some of the basic operations, such as editing or deleting elements.

8-4. Modifying the Settings of Your Application

Problem

You want to locally save some settings about your application and then retrieve those settings later.

Solution

You must use the `IsolatedStorageSettings` class to access your application settings adding and deleting keys, like a `dictionary`.

How It Works

`IsolatedStorageSettings` enables you to easily and locally store user-specific data as key/value pairs in the object `IsolatedStorageFile`. You will see that the use of `IsolatedStorageSettings` is equal to the use of a dictionary `<TKey, TValue>`.

The Code

For this recipe, we want to show you how to complete another recipe that you can find in chapter 9 (in the cloud) by using push notification that will be displayed. A type of push notification is toast notification (more information in chapter 9). That requires that your application to be accepted and published on Marketplace must ask users whether they want to be notified with them. What better place for your application to store the user's choice than in the application settings?

To create this recipe, we have not focused on the application's user interface, but on the page of settings. Suppose that our application use notifications and sounds and we want to give to your user the possibility to disable or enable them

```
...
<phone:PhoneApplicationPage.ApplicationBar>
  <shell:ApplicationBar IsVisible="True" IsMenuEnabled="True">
    <shell:ApplicationBarIconButton x:Name="SaveSettingsButton"
      IconUri="/icons/appbar.save.rest.png"
      Text="Save" Click="SaveSettingsButton_Click" />
  </shell:ApplicationBar>
</phone:PhoneApplicationPage.ApplicationBar>


<Grid x:Name="LayoutRoot" Background="Transparent">
  <Grid.RowDefinitions>
    <RowDefinition Height="Auto"/>
    <RowDefinition Height="*"/>
  </Grid.RowDefinitions>

  <StackPanel x:Name="TitlePanel" Grid.Row="0" Margin="12,17,0,28">
    <TextBlock x:Name="PageTitle" Text="Settings" Style="{StaticResource
      PhoneTextNormalStyle}"/>
  </StackPanel>
  <ScrollViewer x:Name="ContentPanel" Margin="12,0,12,0" Grid.Row="1" >
    <StackPanel>
      <toolkit:ToggleSwitch Header="Toast Notification" x:Name="ToastSwitch"  />
      <toolkit:ToggleSwitch Header="Sounds" x:Name="SoundsSwitch" />
    </StackPanel>
  </ScrollViewer>
</Grid>
```

This xaml, inserted into the template of your page, will show an interface similar to that in Figure 8-9. We say *similar* because you might not be using the same icon or the same control to check the settings. For example, you could have chosen a check box or toggle button.

■ **Note** the control ToggleSwitch is contained in the Windows Phone controls toolkit, which is available on CodePlex.

Figure 8-9. *The Settings page*

In the code behind the page Settings, within the constructor you subscribe to the loaded event with Settings_Loaded event handler:

```
public Settings()
{
    InitializeComponent();
    this.Loaded += new RoutedEventHandler(Settings_Loaded);
}
```

And you define two class-level constant strings:

```
...
private const string _toastEnabledKey = "ToastEnabled";
private const string _soundsEnabledKey = "SoundsEnabled";
...
```

Why do you do this? Because basically, by accessing settings through a dictionary, you will have a number of key/value pairs that could potentially include everything.

The event handler Settings_Loaded will retrieve your settings and change the value of the switch with the following code:

```
void Settings_Loaded(object sender, RoutedEventArgs e)
{
  if (IsolatedStorageSettings.ApplicationSettings.Contains(_toastEnabledKey))
  {
    var toast = IsolatedStorageSettings.ApplicationSettings[_toastEnabledKey].ToString();
    this.ToastSwitch.IsChecked = bool.Parse(toast);
  }
  if (IsolatedStorageSettings.ApplicationSettings.Contains(_soundsEnabledkey))
  {
    var sounds = IsolatedStorageSettings.ApplicationSettings[_soundsEnabledkey].ToString();
    this.SoundsSwitch.IsChecked = bool.Parse(sounds);
  }
}
```

Line by line, what happens is as follows:

1. If the dictionary contains the key that you have associated with the settings for the toast notification,

    a. Recover the value from ApplicationSettings (as with a normal dictionary), getting it as a string (in fact, the type of value is an object).

    b. Assuming you have a Boolean value, you just do the Parse. If you can't be sure about what you will (God save you), you might opt for a tryparse. Finally, you associate the parsed value to the IsChecked property of the switch.

2. Repeat the preceding step for the key that relates the sounds.

In this way, you have loaded the settings related to your application, and so now you can see how to save them, with the handler SaveSettingsButton_Click:

```
private void SaveSettingsButton_Click(object sender, EventArgs e)
{
  IsolatedStorageSettings.ApplicationSettings[_toastEnabledKey] =
      this.ToastSwitch.IsChecked;
  IsolatedStorageSettings.ApplicationSettings[_soundsEnabledkey] =
      this.SoundsSwitch.IsChecked;
}
```

The only thing to do to save a setting of the dictionary is assign a key and a value, then thinks at all the class `IsolateStorageSetting`. In order to pursue this exercise further , consider at this point using the settings to save the BPM of the metronome of our application `7Drum`, for example.

Usage

Start the toast notification application by pressing F5 from Visual Studio. Open the Settings page. Change the settings and save them, thereby provoking the tombstoning of this application. Start the application again and open the Settings page to see that your settings have been saved.

8-5. Saving a Photo in Isolated Storage

Problem

You want to create a photo catalog application that captures from the camera device and saves locally, not in the media library.

Solution

You must work with the `PictureDecoder` class and store the data as an array of bytes, because an image is essentially a stream of bytes. Then you can use this array to write data inside an `IsolatedStorageFile` class.

How It Works

`PictureDecoder` is used to decode a JPEG file into a `WriteableBitmap` that provides a `BitmapSource` (constant set of pixels) that can be written.

The Code

In this recipe, you will play with some features of Windows Phone, combining them in an interesting application. At this point in the chapter, you know how isolated storage works and how you can add files to it and open them. Now you want to create an organized list of directories (1 directory : 1 album)

Our interface is composed of a home page, from which the user can start to take a photo, and the image gallery, where the user can navigate inside the storage structure.

`HomePage.xaml` contains this structure:

```
...
<Grid x:Name="LayoutRoot" Background="Transparent">
  <Grid.RowDefinitions>
    <RowDefinition Height="Auto"/>
    <RowDefinition Height="*"/>
  </Grid.RowDefinitions>
</Grid.RowDefinitions>
```

```
    <!--TitlePanel contains the name of the application and page title-->
    <StackPanel x:Name="TitlePanel" Grid.Row="0" Margin="12,17,0,28">
        <TextBlock x:Name="ApplicationTitle" Text="Photo App" Style="{StaticResource
            PhoneTextNormalStyle}"/>
    </StackPanel>

    <Grid x:Name="ContentPanel" Grid.Row="1" Margin="12,0,12,0">
        <Button Content="Capture a Photo" Height="72" Margin="47,6,76,0" Name="CameraButton"
            VerticalAlignment="Top" Click="CameraButton_Click" />
        <Image Height="337" HorizontalAlignment="Left" Margin="12,84,0,0" Name="image"
            Stretch="Fill" VerticalAlignment="Top" Width="438" />
        <TextBox Height="72" HorizontalAlignment="Left" Margin="-4,457,0,0"
            Name="FileNameTextBox" Text="TextBox" VerticalAlignment="Top" Width="460" />
        <TextBlock Height="30" HorizontalAlignment="Left" Margin="98,433,0,0"
            Name="textBlock1" Text="Choose a name and album" VerticalAlignment="Top" Width="242"
/>
        <ListBox Height="96" HorizontalAlignment="Left" Margin="6,522,0,0" Name="AlbumsListBox"
            VerticalAlignment="Top" Width="444" />
    </Grid>
</Grid>

<phone:PhoneApplicationPage.ApplicationBar>
    <shell:ApplicationBar IsVisible="True" IsMenuEnabled="True">
        <shell:ApplicationBarIconButton IconUri="/icons/appbar.save.rest.png" Text="Save"
            x:Name="SaveButton" Click="SaveButton_Click" />
        <shell:ApplicationBarIconButton IconUri="/icons/appbar.folder.rest.png" Text="Archive"
            x:Name="PhotosButton" Click="PhotosButton_Click" />

        <shell:ApplicationBar.MenuItems>
            <shell:ApplicationBarMenuItem Text="Create Album" x:Name="CreateAlbumButton"
                Click="CreateAlbumButton_Click" />
        </shell:ApplicationBar.MenuItems>
    </shell:ApplicationBar>

</phone:PhoneApplicationPage.ApplicationBar>
```

...

This xaml will be shown, as you can see in Figure 8-10. When the user clicks the CameraButton, you want to start CameraCaptureTask and show a preview. Then the user can choose an album and a filename.

Start analyzing the CreateAlbumButton_Click event handler, which shows a page where the user can create a new album:

```
...
private void CreateAlbumButton_Click(object sender, EventArgs e)
{
    NavigationService.Navigate(new Uri("/CreateAlbum.xaml", UriKind.Relative));
}
...
```

Figure 8-10. *A screenshot of the application's main page*

This code navigates to the `CreateAlbum.xaml` page, which is easy to understand because it's composed of only three elements: a text block, a text box, and a button.

```
<Grid x:Name="ContentPanel" Grid.Row="1" Margin="12,0,12,0">
  <TextBlock Height="30" HorizontalAlignment="Center" Text="Album Name"
    VerticalAlignment="Top" />
  <TextBox Height="72" HorizontalAlignment="Left" Margin="0,42,0,0"
    Name="AlbumNameTextbox" Text="Album" VerticalAlignment="Top" Width="460" />
  <Button Content="Create" Height="72" HorizontalAlignment="Left" Margin="12,120,0,0"
    Name="CreateAlbumButton" VerticalAlignment="Top" Width="438"
    Click="CreateAlbumButton_Click" />
</Grid>
```

The most important part of this code is the event handler associated with the click of CreateAlbumButton, because here you create the directory that will contain the new album:

```
private void CreateAlbumButton_Click(object sender, RoutedEventArgs e)
{
  using (var store = IsolatedStorageFile.GetUserStoreForApplication())
  {
    if (store.DirectoryExists(this.AlbumNameTextbox.Text))
      MessageBox.Show("Album already exists");
    else
    {
      store.CreateDirectory(AlbumNameTextbox.Text);
      NavigationService.Navigate(new Uri("/MainPage.xaml", UriKind.Relative));
    }
  }
}
```

Similarly, by creating a new file, the IsolatedStorageFile class allows us to access the functionality of the directories. So first you check whether an album with that name exists. If it does, you show a warning to the user. Otherwise, you create the album and move into the main window to enable the user to fill the new album.

At this point, it is time to show what happens in the main window when the user clicks CameraButton. But first there are some preliminary steps to be done, including editing the MainPage constructor in the usual way (in order to leave some actions not discriminatory for the operation of the application, when the page is loaded).

```
public MainPage()
{
  InitializeComponent();
  this.Loaded += new RoutedEventHandler(MainPage_Loaded);
}
```

And you declare at the class level the following member:

```
...
CameraCaptureTask cameraTask;
```

...

Now take a look at the implementation of the loaded event handler:

```
...
void MainPage_Loaded(object sender, RoutedEventArgs e)
    {
        cameraTask = new CameraCaptureTask();
        cameraTask.Completed += new EventHandler<PhotoResult>(cameraTask_Completed);
        AlbumsListBox.ItemsSource = IsolatedStorageFile.GetUserStoreForApplication()
                .GetDirectoryNames();
    if (AlbumsListBox.Items.Count > 0)
        AlbumsListBox.SelectedIndex = 0;
    }
...
```

You initialize cameraTask and associate it to the completed event on your event handler
cameraTask_Completed, but this hides the code that allows us to interact with the method
GetDirectoryNames, which retrieves the names of all directories in isolated storage. At this point, for the
first part of the interface, you complete the click handler for the CameraButton component:

```
private void CameraButton_Click(object sender, RoutedEventArgs e)
{
  cameraTask.Show();
}
```

That does nothing more than start the task to use the photo camera. Now assume that the user has
clicked a picture. You must provide a preview, because maybe you have implemented in your
application the capability to apply filters or other amazing features (we leave this to your imagination).
We'll show you the preview inside the image control with the code contained within the event
handler cameraTask_Completed, but before we do this, you must add another member at the class level:

```
...
byte[] _imageAsByte;
...
```

Then all you need to do with _imageAsByte is as follows:

```
void cameraTask_Completed(object sender, PhotoResult e)
{
    if (e.TaskResult == TaskResult.OK)
    {
        _imageAsByte = new byte[e.ChosenPhoto.Length];
        e.ChosenPhoto.Read(_imageAsByte, 0, _imageAsByte.Length);

        e.ChosenPhoto.Seek(0, SeekOrigin.Begin);
```

```
                    this.image.Source = PictureDecoder.DecodeJpeg(e.ChosenPhoto);
            }
        }
```

This code is responsible for checking that the user has actually accepted the photo from the interface. Then you create an array of bytes as large as the size of the photo taken, and you start reading the photo taken, instantiating the array, and filling it with the image. Finally, returned to the beginning of the image you convert it to JPEG, thanks to the support class `PictureDecoder` showing the image on the display.

The user is ready, in your case, to apply filters to the image or to edit it as desired (if you allowed that), and then to save it. In the application bar, you have a button that does just this—save the image in the library, according to the folder and filename chosen.

```
private void SaveButton_Click(object sender, EventArgs e)
{
  if (_imageAsByte == null)
  {
    MessageBox.Show("Nothing to Save");
    return;
  }

  using (var store = IsolatedStorageFile.GetUserStoreForApplication())
  {
    if (!store.FileExists(System.IO.Path.Combine(
                AlbumsListBox.SelectedItem as string,
                FileNameTextBox.Text)) ||
        store.FileExists(System.IO.Path.Combine(
                AlbumsListBox.SelectedItem as string,FileNameTextBox.Text))
          && MessageBox.Show("Overwrite the file?", "Question",
                        MessageBoxButton.OKCancel) == MessageBoxResult.OK)
    {
      using (var stream = store.CreateFile(System.IO.Path.Combine(
                AlbumsListBox.SelectedItem as string, FileNameTextBox.Text)))
      {
          stream.Write(_imageAsByte, 0, _imageAsByte.Length);
      }
    }
  }
}
```

First, by using this method, you ensure that it is legitimate for the user to save an image, because it is actually present. Then you access the isolated storage to ensure that in the selected directory (album), there isn't a file with that name. If there is, you ask the user to overwrite it. If one of these two conditions occurs, you create the file stream in the file contents in the directory specified and write the stream, by using the array of bytes that represents the image.

At this point, the photo has been saved and inserted in the gallery (your gallery and not the media library), and you just have to scroll down to discover the pictures you have saved. Then via the button click to `PhotosButton`, thanks to the usual `Navigation Service`, will lead you to that page Albums is the page used to show images

```
<Grid x:Name="ContentPanel" Grid.Row="1" Margin="12,0,12,0">
  <Grid.RowDefinitions>
    <RowDefinition Height="150" />
    <RowDefinition Height="*" />
  </Grid.RowDefinitions>
  <ListBox Height="150" HorizontalAlignment="Left" Name="AlbumsListBox"
          VerticalAlignment="Top" Width="460"
          SelectionChanged="AlbumsListBox_SelectionChanged" />
  <ListBox Grid.Row="1" Height="546" HorizontalAlignment="Left" Margin="-4,0,0,0"
          Name="PhotoListbox" VerticalAlignment="Top" Width="460" />
</Grid>
```

When a new album is selected, the directory changes to list the files in it. But first, you want to show all the directories in the same way in which you showed them on the main page:

```
void Albums_Loaded(object sender, RoutedEventArgs e)
{
  using (IsolatedStorageFile store =
            IsolatedStorageFile.GetUserStoreForApplication())
  {
    this.AlbumsListBox.ItemsSource = store.GetDirectoryNames();
  }
}
```

And when an element of the list AlbumsListBox is selected, you change the directory listing:

```
private void AlbumsListBox_SelectionChanged(object sender, SelectionChangedEventArgs e)
{
  using (IsolatedStorageFile store = IsolatedStorageFile.GetUserStoreForApplication())
  {
    this.PhotoListbox.ItemsSource = store.GetFileNames(string.Format("{0}\\*",
            this.AlbumsListBox.SelectedItem));
  }
}
```

As you can see, you've used a search function, which when used with a wildcard, could display all the files in a selected folder. However, you could apply a different pattern in other cases—for example, if the user wanted to do a search within the photos.

Usage

Run the application from Visual Studio by pressing F5. The application can run on either the physical device or the emulator. However, you will not be able to debug the application on the physical device if you are connected to Zune, because it stops the multimedia functionalities. To debug, use WPConnect. Start the application, create an album, take a picture with the camera, and save it in your album. Create another album and take another photo, and save that photo in the second album. Search through the albums in your application to verify the effective functioning of your gallery. The process is shown in

Figures 8-11 through 8-16 to give you an idea of how the application works. Notice that the pictures created and saved in this way will be not saved within the media library and Microsoft encourages to interact with Media hub, then consider a function that imports the image inside media library.

Figure 8-11. Creating an album   *Figure 8-12.* Selecting an album

Figure 8-13. Capturing the photo   *Figure 8-14. Creating another album*

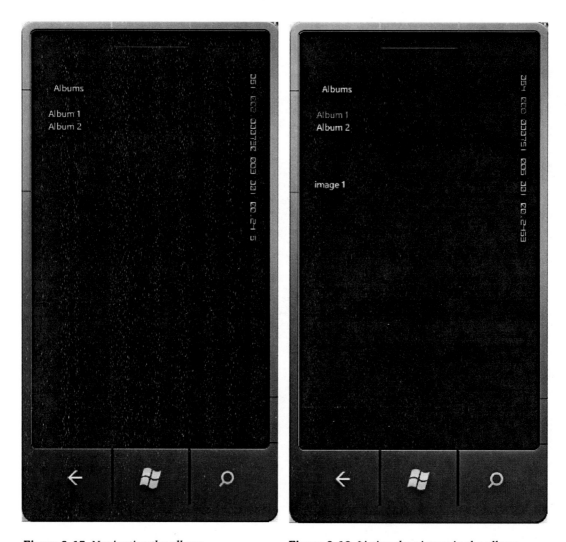

Figure 8-15. *Navigating the album*   **Figure 8-16.** *Listing the picture in the album*

8-6. Using Isolated Storage Explorer

Problem

You want to explore the isolated storage of your device, looking for files saved by your applications, and then download them onto your drive.

Solution

You must use Isolated Storage Explorer (`ISETool.exe`) to access data stored on your device; then you can edit information and upload the data to the isolated storage.

How It Works

`ISETools.exe` is a command line tool that enables you to access the isolated storage of your device. Of course, you can access the isolated storage of software that you have the unique identifier, and you can access both device and emulator.

By combining parameters, you can access all data (except databases and settings) on your device by using the following syntax:

```
ISETool.exe <ts|rs|dir[:device-folder]> <xd|de> <Product GUID> [<desktop-path>]
```

By choosing either `xd` (for emulator) and `de` (for physical device), you can specify the target of the operation on isolated storage, such as taking a snapshot of contents stored on the target using the `ts` parameter, or restoring a snapshot (replacing all files and directories) using the `rs`option, or simply listing the content of the isolated storage using the `dir`parameter. This parameter can be used to list files and folders in the root directory without specifying a folder or appending `:folder-name` to the list content of subdirectories. As part of targeting an isolated storage, you must specify the `GUID` of the application that you are pointing to. You can find the `GUID` of your application inside `WPAppManifest.xml` as a value of the attribute `ProductID`. The `desktop-path` parameter is mandatory if you take (or restore) a snapshot and specify the target (or the source) of files and directories.

The Code

Suppose that you want to access the isolated storage of the application created in Recipe 8-5. First identify the `ProductID`. Now open the command prompt (Windows key + R, then write `cmd`, and click OK), When you are ready, enter the directory that contains `ISETool.exe`. It could be `Program Files\Microsoft SDKs\Windows Phone\v7.1\Tools\IsolatedStorageExplorerTool` or `Program Files (x86)\Microsoft SDKs\Windows Phone\v7.1\Tools\IsolatedStorageExplorerTool`, depending on your operating system version. We will suppose that the `GUID` of your application is `{b6057858-0500-4af6-8316-377c232e7a25}`, and then remember to change this with the identifier of your application. To list files in a shared folder of your application, you will write something like the following:

```
>ISETool.exe dir:shared xd {b6057858-0500-4af6-8316-377c232e7a25}
```

▪ **Note** The command prompt must run with same privileges of the emulator if you want to access isolated storage inside it.

That will show you all files you have saved in this directory. Suppose that you want to save all files to path `C:\ISETools`. Then you must write the following:

```
>ISETool.exe ts xd {b6057858-0500-4af6-8316-377c232e7a25} c:\ISETools
```

That will produce a result as shown in Figure 8-17, which tells you whether the operation was done successfully or not.

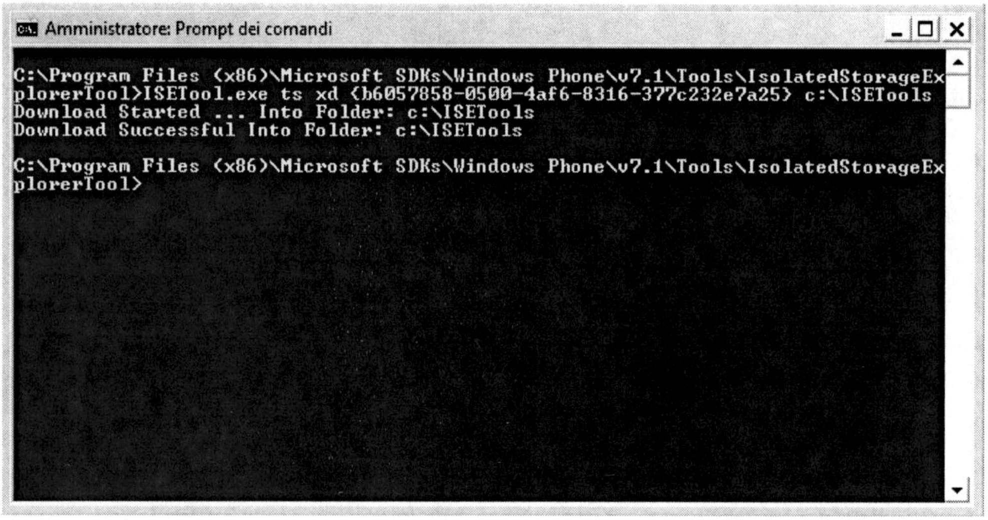

Figure 8-17. *Result of the first command*

Browsing to the C:\ISETool folder, you will find a folder named IsolatedStore, which contains the snapshot (remember that if you take another snapshot, all data will be overwritten). Now perform some operation on file (edit or rename, for example) then restore the snapshot as follows:

```
ISETool.exe rs xd {b6057858-0500-4af6-8316-377c232e7a25} c:\ISETools\IsolatedStore
```

All files inside the target isolated storage will be deleted and replaced with the content of the directory, even new data added.

Usage

Look for your application's identifier and start executing the steps described in the previous section; then download all files from isolated storage, modify them, and upload to the device.

8-7. Implementing Background File Transfer

Problem

You want to implement an application that downloads images from a server via a background transfer, but only when a WiFi connection is available.

Solution

You must create a page to show a list of files to download and a page to monitor uploads using the `BackgroundTransferService` class, which enables you to manage background transfer requests.

How It Works

Using the `BackgroundTransferService` class, you can manage a queue to download from or upload to a server. `BackgroundTransferService` exposes three important methods—**Add**, **Find**, and **Remove**—and a property named **Requests** (see Figure 8-18). The **Add** and **Remove** methods are self-explanatory, and the **Find** method simply looks for a request in the **Requests** collection of the `BackgroundTransferService` class. The reason to find a request is that you can have a maximum of five requests pending, and every request will not delete automatically when completed. It would be a good practice to delete an old request to make space for further requests.

For every operation that you want to start with `BackgroundTransferService`, you must use the class `BackgroundTransferRequest` (see Figure 8-18), which needs a URI to request when calling the constructor. Before you **Add** to the `BackgroundTransferService`, you can specify options like, `TransferPreferences` (see Figure 8-18), which helps you specify when the request can be processed. See `http://msdn.microsoft.com/en-us/library/microsoft.phone.backgroundtransfer.transferpreferences (v=VS.92).aspx` for a complete reference.

Note `BackgroundTransferRequest` supports both HTTP and HTTPS, but not FTP.

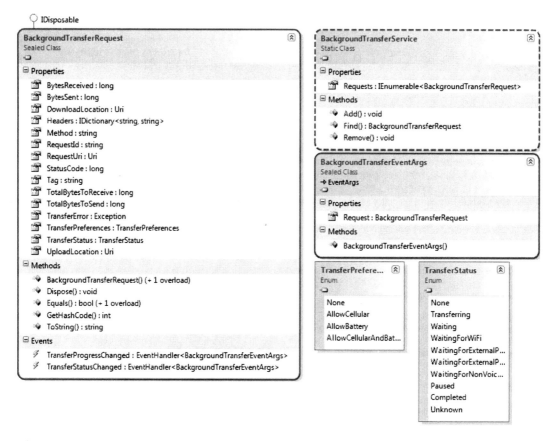

Figure 8-18. Microsoft.Phone.BackgroundTransfer namespace class diagram

As you can see in the class diagram shown in Figure 8-18, every request that you build in your application exposes the following two events:

- **TransferProgressChanged**: Fires every time one of the following properties changes its value

    - TotalBytesToReceive

    - BytesReceived

    - TotalBytesToSend

    - BytesSent

- **TransferStatusChanged**: This is raised when the **TransferStatus** property changes value with one of those exposed by **TransferStatus** enumeration

When you create a request, you can also set **TransferPreferences** that can be set with one of the values of the **TransferPrefences** enumeration, which has values that may be as follows:

- **AllowBattery**: Allows starting a request using a WiFi connection

- **AllowCellular**: Allows starting a request using a cellular or a WiFi connection only when the device is attached to external power

- **AllowCellularAndBattery**: Allows starting a request using a cellular or a WiFi connection whether or not the device is attached to external power

When you create a request, you must consider that the use of a cellular line discharges the battery, then you can choose to use the default behavior for your transfers (only with external power and connected to WiFi), and if you want to allow file download in every condition, consider asking the user what he or she prefers.

The Code

The application that you are going to create shows the user a list of image names of which he can choose what to download. Then, in another page, the user can see the state of the download and which images have already downloaded.

The first thing you need is a class that represents images that the user can download locally (treating it as the model of your application), then create a folder named Model, then add this folder in a new class called ImageResource, as follows:

```
public class ImageResource : INotifyPropertyChanged, INotifyPropertyChanging
{
    #region ImageUri
    private Uri _imageUri;

    public Uri ImageUri
    {
        get { return _imageUri; }
        set
        {
            RaisePropertyChanging("ImageUri");
            _imageUri = value;
            RaisePopertyChanged("ImageUri");
        }
    }
    #endregion

    #region Title
    private string _title;

    public string Title
    {
        get { return _title; }
        set
        {
            RaisePropertyChanging("Title");
            _title = value;
            RaisePopertyChanged("Title");
        }
    }
}
```

```
    #endregion

    #region Implementation of INotifyPropertyChanged

    public event PropertyChangedEventHandler PropertyChanged;

    public void RaisePopertyChanged(string propertyName)
    {
        if (PropertyChanged != null)
            PropertyChanged(this, new PropertyChangedEventArgs(propertyName));
    }

    #endregion

    #region Implementation of INotifyPropertyChanging

    public event PropertyChangingEventHandler PropertyChanging;

    public void RaisePropertyChanging(string propertyName)
    {
        if (PropertyChanging != null)
            PropertyChanging(this, new PropertyChangingEventArgs(propertyName));
    }
    #endregion
}
```

Now that you have a model, you need a repository to retrieve data from (it is not the purpose of this recipe to show you how to retrieve a list of images from the web), and to add a new static class to your project that will expose a collection of ImageResource (in your case you would contact a service that provides a list of available images, or parse a html page to find how many images are shown).

```
public static class ImagesRepository
    {
        private static ObservableCollection<ImageResource> _images;
        public static ObservableCollection<ImageResource> Images
        {
            get { return _images ?? InitImages(); }
        }

        private static ObservableCollection<ImageResource> InitImages()
        {
            _images = new ObservableCollection<ImageResource>
                        {
                            new ImageResource
                                {
                                    ImageUri = new Uri("http://www.plasmator.net/wallpaper/2
005-06-26.jpg",UriKind.Absolute),
                                    Title = "Fractal 1"
                                },
                            new ImageResource
                                {
```

```
                                          ImageUri = new Uri("http://t2.gstatic.com/images?q=tbn:A
Nd9GcRJC4aogaU6WhHqwp0_so0ia6IHiaG1EFLsxKQTk1H2c2TG6Ccp",UriKind.Absolute),
                                          Title = "Mango"
                                        },
                                        new ImageResource
                                        {
                                          ImageUri = new Uri("http://t0.gstatic.com/images?q=tbn:A
Nd9GcQrLsp_LHEHOeytMrBsa1_WLbwzF_XfWbNVjdwFljkv6_iOBy_rjw",UriKind.Absolute),
                                          Title = "Phone"
                                        },
                                        new ImageResource
                                        {
                                          ImageUri = new Uri("http://www.plasmator.net/wallpaper/s
tarBurst.jpg",UriKind.Absolute),
                                          Title = "Fractal 2"
                                        },
                                        new ImageResource
                                        {
                                          ImageUri = new Uri("http://s.camptocamp.org/uploads/imag
es/1265716960_373714172.jpg",UriKind.Absolute),
                                          Title = "Mountain 1"
                                        },
                                        new ImageResource
                                        {
                                          ImageUri = new Uri("http://s.camptocamp.org/uploads/imag
es/1290511517_554929250.jpg",UriKind.Absolute),
                                          Title = "Mountain 2"
                                        }
                                      };
                return _images;
            }
        }
```

Now that you have a source of data, you must show information to the user, then open the MainPage.xaml page, and modify it to contain a ListBox, as follows:

```xml
<phone:PhoneApplicationPage.Resources>
  <DataTemplate x:Key="ImagesItemTemplate">
    <Grid Height="50">
      <Grid.ColumnDefinitions>
        <ColumnDefinition Width="50"/>
  <ColumnDefinition Width="*"/>
      </Grid.ColumnDefinitions>
      <Image Tag="{Binding ImageUri}" x:Name="DownloadImage" Source="/08-
07BackgroundTransfer;component/Images/download.png" Stretch="Fill" Tap="DownloadImage_Tap" />
      <TextBlock Text="{Binding Title}" Grid.Column="1"  />
    </Grid>
  </DataTemplate>
</phone:PhoneApplicationPage.Resources>

<Grid x:Name="LayoutRoot" Background="Transparent">
  <Grid.RowDefinitions>
```

```xml
      <RowDefinition Height="Auto"/>
      <RowDefinition Height="*"/>
   </Grid.RowDefinitions>
   <StackPanel x:Name="TitlePanel" Grid.Row="0" Margin="12,17,0,28">
<TextBlock x:Name="ApplicationTitle" Text="MY BACKGROUND DOWNLOADER" Style="{StaticResource Ph
oneTextNormalStyle}"/>
   </StackPanel>

   <Grid x:Name="ContentPanel" Grid.Row="1" Margin="12,0,12,0">
      <ListBox x:Name="ImagesListBox" ItemTemplate="{StaticResource ImagesItemTemplate}" />
   </Grid>
</Grid>
```

This `xaml` shows a `ListBox` where every item appears with an image to tap to start the download, as well as the name of the image near it. You need to provide these items using the `ImagesRepository` class to set the `ItemsSource` property of the list box, and handle the tap event on `DownloadImage`.

```csharp
public partial class MainPage : PhoneApplicationPage
{
  // Constructor
  public MainPage()
  {
    InitializeComponent();
    Loaded += PageLoaded;
  }

  private void PageLoaded(object sender, RoutedEventArgs e)
  {
    ImagesListBox.ItemsSource = ImagesRepository.Images;
  }

private void DownloadImage_Tap(object sender, GestureEventArgs e)
      {
          if (ImagesListBox.SelectedItem is ImageResource)
          {
              var resource = (ImagesListBox.SelectedItem as ImageResource);
              var request = new BackgroundTransferRequest(resource.ImageUri)
              {
                  DownloadLocation = new Uri(string.Format("/shared/transfers/{0}.{1}", reso
urce.Title, resource.ImageUri.OriginalString.Substring(resource.ImageUri.OriginalString.Length
 - 3, 3)), UriKind.Relative),
                  TransferPreferences = TransferPreferences.AllowBattery,
              };
              NavigationService.Navigate(new Uri("/TransferStatus.xaml", UriKind.Relative));
              BackgroundTransferService.Add(request);
          }
      }
  }
```

In the `DownloadImage_Tap` you instantiate a `BackgroundTransferRequest` using a `RequestURI` (the URI associated with the selected `ImageResource`), then you set as `DownloadLocation` the isolated storage folder named `/shared/transfers`, because every download made using the `BackgroundTransferService` needs to use this folder as the root, and when it completes, you can move the file anywhere within your isolated storage.

Next, you navigate to another page that shows the status of transfers, giving the user the possibility to stop the operation in order to see the number of files that have already downloaded.

```xml
<phone:PhoneApplicationPage.Resources>
    <DataTemplate x:Key="ImageItemTemplate">
        <Grid Height="50">
            <Grid.ColumnDefinitions>
                <ColumnDefinition Width="50"/>
                <ColumnDefinition Width="*"/>
            </Grid.ColumnDefinitions>
            <TextBlock Text="{Binding Title}" Grid.Column="1"  />
        </Grid>
    </DataTemplate>

    <DataTemplate x:Key="DownloadingImageTemplate">
        <Grid Background="Transparent" Margin="0,0,0,30">
            <Grid.ColumnDefinitions>
                <ColumnDefinition Width="380"/>
                <ColumnDefinition Width="50"/>
            </Grid.ColumnDefinitions>
            <Grid Grid.Column="0">

                <StackPanel Orientation="Vertical">
                    <TextBlock Text="{Binding RequestID}"  Foreground="{StaticResource PhoneAccentBrush}" FontWeight="Bold"/>
                    <StackPanel Orientation="Horizontal">
                        <TextBlock Text="status: "/>
                        <TextBlock Text="{Binding TransferStatus}" HorizontalAlignment="Right"/>
                    </StackPanel>
                    <StackPanel Orientation="Horizontal">
                        <TextBlock Text="bytes received: "/>
                        <TextBlock Text="{Binding BytesReceived}" HorizontalAlignment="Right"/>
                    </StackPanel>
                    <StackPanel Orientation="Horizontal">
                        <TextBlock Text="total bytes: "/>
                        <TextBlock Text="{Binding TotalBytesToReceive}" HorizontalAlignment="Right"/>
                    </StackPanel>
                </StackPanel>

            </Grid>
            <Grid Grid.Column="1">
                <Button Tag="{Binding RequestId}" Click="CancelButton_Click" Content="X" VerticalAlignment="Top" BorderThickness="0" Width="50" Padding="0,0,0,0" />
            </Grid>
        </Grid>
    </DataTemplate>
</phone:PhoneApplicationPage.Resources>
```

```
<Grid x:Name="LayoutRoot" Background="Transparent">
    <Grid.RowDefinitions>
        <RowDefinition Height="Auto"/>
        <RowDefinition Height="*"/>
    </Grid.RowDefinitions>

    <!--TitlePanel contains the name of the application and page title-->
    <StackPanel x:Name="TitlePanel" Grid.Row="0" Margin="12,17,0,28">
        <TextBlock x:Name="ApplicationTitle" Text="My Background Downloader" Style="{Stati
cResource PhoneTextNormalStyle}"/>
    </StackPanel>

    <!--ContentPanel - place additional content here-->
    <Grid x:Name="ContentPanel" Grid.Row="1" Margin="12,0,12,0">
        <Grid.RowDefinitions>
            <RowDefinition />
            <RowDefinition />
        </Grid.RowDefinitions>
        <StackPanel>
            <TextBlock Text="Downloading Files"/>
            <ListBox Name="TransferListBox" ItemTemplate="{StaticResource DownloadingImage
Template}"/>

        </StackPanel>
        <StackPanel Grid.Row="1">
            <TextBlock Text="Downloaded Files"/>
            <ListBox x:Name="DowloadedFilesListBox" ItemTemplate="{StaticResource ImageIte
mTemplate}" >

            </ListBox>
        </StackPanel>
    </Grid>
</Grid>
```

This page is really simple; you have a root grid half-occupied by the list box of downloading items, and the other half occupied by the list box that shows the content of isolated storage. In the first data template, you bind textblocks to the properties of a transfer, such as:

- TransferStatus

- BytesReceived

- TotalBytesToReceive

■ **Note** TotalBytesToReceive will assume -1 as a value if the size of the file is unknown.

The part of the UI that shows information on the download needs to update the layout every time the progress changes. In the code behind it, you will subscribe to the TransferProgressChanged event and when a download ends, you want to move the file in the root folder of isolated storage; then you subscribe to the `TransferStatusChanged` event.

The other part of the UI shows the list of downloaded files refreshing the content of the list box every time a download finishes.

Note Remember that you must control the code of a request to see if it has successfully completed or not.

```
public partial class TransferStatus : PhoneApplicationPage
    {
        private ObservableCollection<ImageResource> _downloadedImages;

        public TransferStatus()
        {
            InitializeComponent();
            Loaded += TransferStatusLoaded;
        }

        private void TransferStatusLoaded(object sender, RoutedEventArgs e)
        {
            TransferListBox.ItemsSource = BackgroundTransferService.Requests;
            foreach (var request in BackgroundTransferService.Requests)
            {
                request.TransferProgressChanged += TransferProgressChanged;
                request.TransferStatusChanged += TransferStatusChanged;
            }
            GetDownloadedFiles();
        }

        private void TransferStatusChanged(object sender, BackgroundTransferEventArgs e)
        {
            switch (e.Request.TransferStatus)
            {
                case Microsoft.Phone.BackgroundTransfer.TransferStatus.None:
                    break;
                case Microsoft.Phone.BackgroundTransfer.TransferStatus.Transferring:
                    break;
                case Microsoft.Phone.BackgroundTransfer.TransferStatus.Waiting:
                    break;
                case Microsoft.Phone.BackgroundTransfer.TransferStatus.WaitingForWiFi:
                    break;
                case Microsoft.Phone.BackgroundTransfer.TransferStatus.WaitingForExternalPower
:
                    break;
                case Microsoft.Phone.BackgroundTransfer.TransferStatus.WaitingForExternalPower
DueToBatterySaverMode:
                    break;
```

```
                case Microsoft.Phone.BackgroundTransfer.TransferStatus.WaitingForNonVoiceBlock
ingNetwork:
                    break;
                case Microsoft.Phone.BackgroundTransfer.TransferStatus.Paused:
                    break;
                case Microsoft.Phone.BackgroundTransfer.TransferStatus.Completed:
                    if (e.Request.StatusCode == 200 || e.Request.StatusCode == 206)
                    {
                        BackgroundTransferService.Remove(e.Request);
                        using (IsolatedStorageFile isoStore = IsolatedStorageFile.GetUserStore
ForApplication())
                        {
                            string filename = e.Request.DownloadLocation.OriginalString.Split(
'\\').Last();
                            if (isoStore.FileExists(filename))
                            {
                                isoStore.DeleteFile(filename);
                            }
                            isoStore.MoveFile(e.Request.DownloadLocation.OriginalString, filen
ame);
                            GetDownloadedFiles();
                        }
                    }
                    break;
                case Microsoft.Phone.BackgroundTransfer.TransferStatus.Unknown:
                    break;
                default:
                    throw new ArgumentOutOfRangeException();
            }
            TransferListBox.ItemsSource = BackgroundTransferService.Requests;
        }

        private void TransferProgressChanged(object sender, BackgroundTransferEventArgs e)
        {
            TransferListBox.ItemsSource = BackgroundTransferService.Requests;
        }

        private void GetDownloadedFiles()
        {
            _downloadedImages = new ObservableCollection<ImageResource>();
            using (IsolatedStorageFile isoStore = IsolatedStorageFile.GetUserStoreForApplicati
on())
            {
                foreach (var fileName in isoStore.GetFileNames())
                    _downloadedImages.Add(new ImageResource { Title = fileName });
            }
            DowloadedFilesListBox.ItemsSource = _downloadedImages;
        }

        private void CancelButton_Click(object sender, RoutedEventArgs e)
        {
```

```
            var requestToCancel = BackgroundTransferService.Requests.FirstOrDefault(r => r.Req
uestId == (sender as Button).Tag.ToString());
            BackgroundTransferService.Remove(requestToCancel);
            TransferListBox.ItemsSource = BackgroundTransferService.Requests;
        }
    }
```

When a download finishes, you must check the `StatusCode` for a value of 200 or 206 that translates in `OK` status (depending on the configuration of your server); if this is the case, then every other value will be an error.

Usage

Run the application from Visual Studio by pressing F5. The application can run on either the physical device or the emulator. Then, start a download to see the advancing state in the next page, as shown in Figure 8-19.

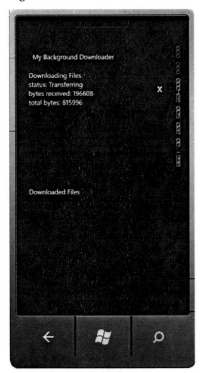

Figure 8-19. Application in execution

CHAPTER 9

In the Cloud

In recent years, the mobile device market has increased because modern phone devices encompass more than the simple necessity to make a call. This chapter covers interactions with services "in the cloud." You will see how Windows Phone is designed to enable users to always remain connected to the services they need.

The recipes in this chapter describe how to do the following:

- 9-1. Interact with WCF

- 9-2. Access OData Services

- 9-3. Create a feed reader

- 9-4. Create a Google API–based translator

- 9-5. Use push notification

9-1. Interacting with WCF

Problem

You want to build an application that interacts with a service by using Windows Communication Foundation (WCF).

Solution

You need to create your service (or get the address of the service that you want to query), and add a reference to that service so that you can query your methods and access the exposed `DataContract`.

How It Works

Windows Phone was created to use services, but you should always remember one thing when you work with it: service access is always asynchronous, because (as with the use of services in Silverlight for the Web) you must not freeze the user interface.

The implementation of Silverlight for Windows Phone provides a limited set of features to work on a network, as compared to its "big brother." Only Windows Communication Foundation, HttpWebRequest, and WebClient can be used with Silverlight for Windows Phone.

We will use web services, connecting your application to the Microsoft Research Maps service, which enables us to take pictures of the world (via satellite), based on GeoCoordinate.

The Code

Unfortunately, you cannot dynamically create a proxy to a service by using the ChannelFactory<TChannel> class, because it is not supported by this Windows Phone version. Therefore, to create a reference, you must use the command-line tool slsvcutil.exe to create a proxy for use at compile time.

Because creating a WCF service is not the goal of this book. In this section, you will complete Recipe 6-3 from Chapter 6 (which is about the use of the Microsoft Research Maps web service).

To complete the recipe, you need to see how to add a reference to the service (so that Visual Studio is running only the slsvcutil.exe utility to create a proxy), as in Figure 9-1.

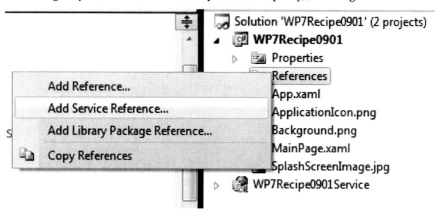

Figure 9-1. *Add a service reference*

As you learned in Recipe 6-3, to use Bing Maps, you must be registered as a Windows Phone developer. Therefore, you might prefer to use the map service offered by Microsoft Research.

Then you need to add a reference, calling it TerraService, to the service available at http://msrmaps.com/TerraService2.asmx, as shown in Figure 9-2. As you can see in the picture, there are many methods that you can call, but we are interested in GetAreaFromPt and GetTile.

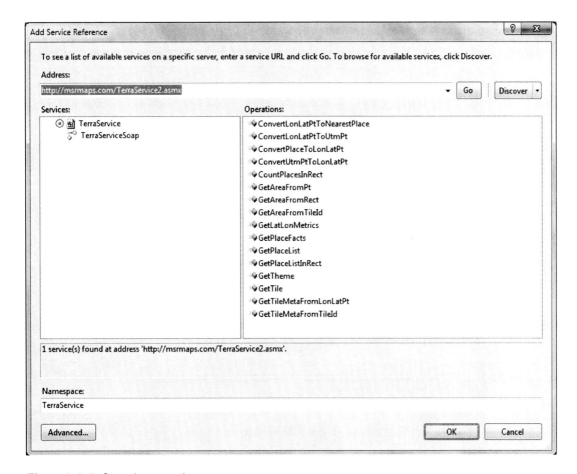

Figure 9-2. *Referencing a service*

At this point, you have a reference to your service and you can call the method that interests you. It's a best practice to instantiate the server proxy in the Loaded event handler, thereby ensuring that the application starts as soon as possible and that the user maintains control of the phone:

```
using Microsoft.Phone.Net.NetworkInformation;
...

  TerraService.TerraServiceSoapClient proxy = null;
  GeoCoordinateWatcher geoWatcher = null;

  // Constructor
  public MainPage()
  {
    InitializeComponent();
    InizializeServices();
```

```
        Loaded += new RoutedEventHandler(MainPage_Loaded);
    }

...

    private void InizializeServices()
    {
        proxy = new TerraService.TerraServiceSoapClient();
        geoWatcher = new GeoCoordinateWatcher();
    }

...

    void MainPage_Loaded(object sender, RoutedEventArgs e)
    {
        if (NetworkInterface.GetIsNetworkAvailable())
            MessageBox.Show("No Network available. The application will not work fine");

        proxy.GetAreaFromPtCompleted +=
            new EventHandler<TerraService.GetAreaFromPtCompletedEventArgs>(
                    proxy_GetAreaFromPtCompleted);
        proxy.GetTileCompleted +=
            new EventHandler<TerraService.GetTileCompletedEventArgs>(
                    proxy_GetTileCompleted);

        geoWatcher.PositionChanged +=
            new EventHandler<GeoPositionChangedEventArgs<GeoCoordinate>>(
                    geoWatcher_PositionChanged);

        geoWatcher.StatusChanged +=
            new EventHandler<GeoPositionStatusChangedEventArgs>(
                    geoWatcher_StatusChanged);

        geoWatcher.Start();
    }
```

As you can see in this code, you subscribe an event handler to two events (GetAreaFromPtCompleted and GetTileCompleted) because service calls are made asynchronously, because you are working with Silverlight (and this is the default way of working with Silverlight) and because it would make no sense to lock the phone interface for too long.

Then you look at the code to see whether a network connection is available. If you need access to a web service, it's a good idea to indicate that users will have access to a limited version of your software if they don't activate a network interface.

```
void geoWatcher_PositionChanged(object sender, GeoPositionChangedEventArgs<GeoCoordinate> e)
{
    if (!e.Position.Location.IsUnknown)
    {
        proxy.GetAreaFromPtAsync(
```

```
        //the ActualPosition
        new TerraService.LonLatPt()
          {
            Lat = e.Position.Location.Latitude,
            Lon = e.Position.Location.Longitude
          },
        1,
        TerraService.Scale.Scale2km,
        (int)ContentPanel.ActualWidth,
        (int)ContentPanel.ActualHeight);
    }
}
```

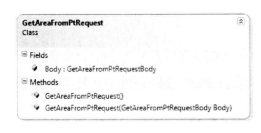

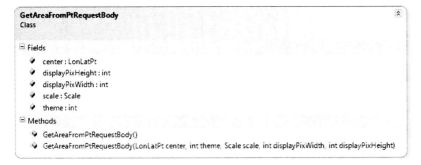

Figure 9-3. *Class diagram of classes used by GetAreaFromPt*

In Figure 9-3, you can see all the classes you need to prepare a `GetAreaFromPt` request, for whose response you must analyze the implementation of the event handler that handles the response.

```
void proxy_GetAreaFromPtCompleted(object sender,
                             TerraService.GetAreaFromPtCompletedEventArgs e)
{
  if (e.Error == null)
  {
```

```
            int startX = e.Result.NorthWest.TileMeta.Id.X;
            int endX = e.Result.NorthEast.TileMeta.Id.X;
            int startY = e.Result.NorthWest.TileMeta.Id.Y;
            int endY = e.Result.SouthWest.TileMeta.Id.Y;

            for (int x = startX; x < endX; x++)
              for (int y = startY; y >= endY; y--)
              {
                Image image = new Image();
                image.Stretch = Stretch.None;
                image.Margin = new Thickness(
                     (x - startX) * 200 - e.Result.NorthWest.Offset.XOffset,
                     (startY - y) * 200 - e.Result.NorthWest.Offset.YOffset,
                     0,
                     0);
                ContentPanel.Children.Insert(0, image);

                TileId tileId = e.Result.NorthWest.TileMeta.Id;
                tileId.X = x;
                tileId.Y = y;

                proxy.GetTileAsync(tileId, image);
              }
      }
    else
      MessageBox.Show(e.Error.Message);
  }
```

In this way, you will call the GetTile method as many times as needed to display each image according to the level of detail chosen. You will build a mosaic of images that are inserted as children of the container that you had prepared ad hoc in Recipe 6-3 in Chapter 6.

```
      void proxy_GetTileCompleted(object sender, TerraService.GetTileCompletedEventArgs e)
      {
          if (e.Error == null)
          {
              Image img = e.UserState as Image;
              BitmapImage bitmap = new BitmapImage();
              bitmap.SetSource(new MemoryStream(e.Result));
              img.Source = bitmap;
          }
      }
```

To further clarify, the use of this service presents some pros and cons:

Pros: The service allows you to retrieve maps for educational purposes without worrying about record in any place like happens when you use Bing Maps, but simply making requests. The service responses are rapid, and the service can be interrogated via different protocols.

Cons: The service provides no support for maps outside the United States.

Usage

Normally this application needs to run on a physical device, so change your output target to Windows Phone Device and start the application by pressing F5; then wait for your application to become available and look at the map charges.

9-2. Accessing OData Services

Problem

You want to access data exposed by an OData service—for example, a service exposed at Microsoft's MIX conference—and you want to show information about sessions in the main page of your application.

Solution

Unlike the first version of Windows Phone, you do not need to download any external tool; all you need to do is "use" (not directly) the two classes, `DataServiceContext` and `DataServiceCollection<T>`.

How It Works

First, we need to discuss OData, which is short for Open Data Protocol. The web site at `www.odata.org` describes it as an open protocol for sharing data. So, with OData you can access a set of data and make queries on it.

After you add a reference to the OData service, the proxy class generated will derive from the `DataServiceContext` class, which extends the behavior of this kind of service (that by its nature is stateless), but the class (which appears in Figure 9-4) tracks changes in order to manage entity updates. The `DeviceServiceContext` class exposes as many properties as an entity exposed by the service, and every property will be of the `DataServiceCollection<T>` type; for example `System.Data.Services.Client.DataServiceCollection<Speaker> Speakers`).

Figure 9-4. *OData service access classes*

The Code

Start creating a new project for Windows Phone, and just like in the first recipe, add a service reference using the address `http://live.visitmix.com/odata/`. The dialog will show you the entities exposed by the service, as in Figure 9-5. `eventsEntities` will be your `DataServiceContext` and `Files`, `Sessions`, `Speakers`, and `Tags` will be the collections exposed by the context in form of `DataServiceCollection<T>`.

Figure 9-5. *Entities exposed by the service*

⬚ **Note** This method of working expresses its full potential if used in combination with the implementation of the "Model-View-ViewModel" pattern (see Chapter 10), where the set of entities exposed by the service is your model.

Now you are ready to make a query against your model. First we're going to create the page that will host the list of sessions. In the `PhoneApplicationPage` declaration tag inside the `xaml`, we will subscribe to the `Loaded` event and interrogate the service.

```
<phone:PhoneApplicationPage
      x:Class="Accessing_OData_Services.MainPage"
      ...
      SupportedOrientations="PortraitOrLandscape" Orientation="Portrait"
      shell:SystemTray.IsVisible="True" Loaded="PhoneApplicationPage_Loaded">
```

Next, we'll create the rest of the application page, which will contain the list box, as follows:

```
<Grid x:Name="LayoutRoot" Background="Transparent">
  <Grid.RowDefinitions>
    <RowDefinition Height="Auto"/>
    <RowDefinition Height="*"/>
  </Grid.RowDefinitions>
  <StackPanel x:Name="TitlePanel" Grid.Row="0" Margin="12,17,0,28" >
    <TextBlock x:Name="ApplicationTitle" Text="List of Sessions" Style="{StaticResource
PhoneTextNormalStyle}"/>
  </StackPanel>

<Grid x:Name="ContentPanel" Grid.Row="1" Margin="12,0,12,0">
  <StackPanel>
    <Grid>
        <Grid.ColumnDefinitions>
          <ColumnDefinition Width="90" />
          <ColumnDefinition Width="50" />
          <ColumnDefinition Width="50"/>
          <ColumnDefinition Width="*"/>
        </Grid.ColumnDefinitions>
        <TextBlock Text="Code" />
        <TextBlock Text="Level" Grid.Column="1" />
        <TextBlock Text="Dur." Grid.Column="2" />
        <TextBlock Text="Title" Grid.Column="3" />
    </Grid>
    <ListBox Margin="0,25,0,-25" Name="SessionsListBox">
      <ListBox.ItemTemplate>
        <DataTemplate>
          <Grid>
            <Grid.ColumnDefinitions>
              <ColumnDefinition Width="90"/>
              <ColumnDefinition Width="50"/>
              <ColumnDefinition Width="50"/>
              <ColumnDefinition Width="*"/>
            </Grid.ColumnDefinitions>
          <TextBlock Text="{Binding SessionCode}" />
          <TextBlock Text="{Binding Level}" Grid.Column="1" />
          <TextBlock Text="{Binding Duration}" Grid.Column="2" />
          <TextBlock Text="{Binding Title}" Grid.Column="3" />
        </Grid>
      </DataTemplate>
    </ListBox.ItemTemplate>
  </ListBox>
</StackPanel>
</Grid>
```

```
</Grid>
```

Now you need to retrieve data from the service in the loaded event. The first step is to instantiate the data service contest class, as follows:

```
eventsEntities entities = new eventsEntities(new Uri("http://live.visitmix.com/odata"));
```

Because you want to show the list of sessions, you need to declare a collection of the type of sessions at class level, then in the code-behind, write as follows:

```
private DataServiceCollection<Session> sessions;
```

And in the loaded event handler, initialize it as follows:

```
sessions = new DataServiceCollection<Session>(entities);
```

You are ready to prepare a query against the model. To interact with OData, you need to use LINQ to prepare the request, and you will use the **Load** method of **DataServiceCollection** to materialize your query on the model. Your code will look like this:

```
var query = from s in entities.Sessions
            select s;
```

Now that the query is ready, you need to subscribe the **LoadCompleted** event to manage the **Async** call to the **Load** method.

```
// Register for the LoadCompleted event.
sessions.LoadCompleted += sessionsLoadCompleted;

// Load the customers feed by executing the LINQ query.
sessions.LoadAsync(query);
```

The **sessionsLoadCompleted** event handler is responsible to use the result from the service and checks if there are other elements to charge by accessing the **Continuation** property. If present, they will be loaded with the **LoadNextPartialSetAsync** method of **DataServiceCollection**.

```
 private void sessions_LoadCompleted(object sender, LoadCompletedEventArgs e)
{
  if (e.Error == null)
  {
    if (sessions.Continuation != null)
    {
      sessions.LoadNextPartialSetAsync();
    }
    else
    {
      this.SessionsListBox.ItemsSource = sessions;
    }
  }
  else
  {
```

```
        MessageBox.Show(string.Format("An error has occurred: {0}", e.Error.Message));
    }
}
```

Now we are ready to launch the application.

Usage

From Visual Studio 2010, press Ctrl +F5. The type of target is not important, as this recipe can work as well on the emulator as on the device. The application will start, briefly showing the splash screen and then the main page. After a few seconds (depending on your Internet connection), the list of sessions from the MIX 2011 conference will display, as shown in Figure 9-6.

Figure 9-6. The list of sessions

9-3. Creating a Feed Reader

Problem

You want to create a newsfeed reader that allows you to follow the links attached to every news story and view the articles within the browser.

Solution

You must use an object of the WebClient class and open the link using WebBrowserTask.

How It Works

For our application, we chose an Atom feed made available by the British Broadcasting Corporation (BBC), but it's clear that you can use all feeds in Atom format.

A feed is simply a document made available on the Web (we hope always at the same address) in an XML format that follows a specific syntax, described in this XSD:

```
<xs:schema xmlns:xs="http://www.w3.org/2001/XMLSchema" elementFormDefault="qualified"
                 xmlns:atom="www.atom.com">
  <xs:import namespace="www.atom.com" schemaLocation="atom.xsd"/>
  <xs:element name="rss">
    <xs:complexType>
      <xs:sequence>
        <xs:element ref="channel"/>
      </xs:sequence>
      <xs:attribute name="version" type="xs:string"/>
      <xs:attribute name="xmlns:atom" type="xs:string"/>
    </xs:complexType>
  </xs:element>
  <xs:element name="channel">
    <xs:complexType>
      <xs:sequence>
        <xs:element ref="link"/>
        <xs:element ref="title"/>
        <xs:element ref="link"/>
        <xs:element ref="description"/>
        <xs:element ref="language"/>
        <xs:element ref="copyright"/>
        <xs:element ref="item" maxOccurs="unbounded"/>
      </xs:sequence>
    </xs:complexType>
  </xs:element>
  <xs:element name="title" type="xs:string"/>
```

```
<xs:element name="link" type="xs:string"/>
<xs:element name="description" type="xs:string"/>
<xs:element name="language" type="xs:string"/>
<xs:element name="copyright" type="xs:string"/>
<xs:element name="item">
  <xs:complexType>
    <xs:sequence>
      <xs:element ref="title"/>
      <xs:element ref="description"/>
      <xs:element ref="link"/>
      <xs:element ref="pubDate"/>
      <xs:element ref="guid"/>
    </xs:sequence>
  </xs:complexType>
</xs:element>
<xs:element name="pubDate" type="xs:string"/>
<xs:element name="guid" type="xs:string"/>
</xs:schema>
```

The Code

You can start with the preceding XSD to generate classes that work to serialize/deserialize according to the structure defined by the schema. This is what you are going to do now. Create three classes in your project with the following names:

- Rss

- Channel

- Item

In Rss.cs, include the following code:

```
[XmlRoot(ElementName="rss",Namespace="")]
public class Rss
{
  private Channel _channel;

  private string _version;
  [XmlElement(ElementName="channel")]
  public Channel Channel
  {
    get
    {
      return this._channel;
    }
    set
    {
      this._channel = value;
    }
  }
}
```

```
  [XmlElement(ElementName = "version")]
  public string Version
  {
    get
    {
      return this._version;
    }
    set
    {
      this._version = value;
    }
  }
}
```

The attributes used on class and properties clearly say that you are going to use XmlSerializer to deserialize the response in your classes and then go up with Channel.cs.

```
[DataContract]
public class Channel
{
        private string _atomLink;
        private string _title;
        private string _link;
        private string _description;
        private string _language;
        private string _copyright;
        private Item[] _items;

        [XmlElement(ElementName = "atom:link")]
        public AtomLink AtomLink
        {
            get
            {
                return this._atomLink;
            }


            set
            {
                this._atomLink = value;
            }
        }

        [XmlElement(ElementName = "title")]
        public string Title
        {
            get
            {
                return this._title;
```

```csharp
        }
        set
        {
            this._title = value;
        }
    }

    [XmlElement(ElementName = "link")]
    public string Link
    {
        get
        {
            return this._link;
        }
        set
        {
            this._link = value;
        }
    }

    [XmlElement(ElementName = "description")]
    public string Description
    {
        get
        {
            return this._description;
        }
        set
        {
            this._description = value;
        }
    }

    [XmlElement(ElementName = "language")]
    public string Language
    {
        get
        {
            return this._language;
        }
        set
        {
            this._language = value;
        }
    }

    [XmlElement(ElementName = "copyright")]
    public string Copyright
    {
        get
        {
            return this._copyright;
```

```
        }
        set
        {
            this._copyright = value;
        }
    }

    [XmlElement(ElementName = "item")]
    public Item[] Items
    {
        get
        {
            return this._items;
        }
        set
        {
            this._items = value;
        }
    }
}
```

And last but not least, here is Item.cs (this is the most important class in our project as it will contain the news items in the feed):

```
public class Item
{
    private string _title;

    private string _description;

    private string _link;

    private string _pubDate;

    private string _guid;


    [XmlElement(ElementName = "title")]
    public string Title
    {
        get
        {
            return this._title;
        }
        set
        {
            this._title = value;
        }
    }
```

```csharp
        [XmlElement(ElementName = "description")]
        public string Description
        {
            get
            {
                return this._description;
            }
            set
            {
                this._description = value;
            }
        }

        [XmlElement(ElementName = "link")]
        public string Link
        {
            get
            {
                return this._link;
            }
            set
            {
                this._link = value;
            }
        }

        [XmlElement(ElementName = "pubDate")]
        public string PubDate
        {
            get
            {
                return this._pubDate;
            }
            set
            {
                this._pubDate = value;
            }
        }

        [XmlElement(ElementName = "guid")]
        public string Guid
        {
            get
            {
                return this._guid;
            }
            set
            {
                this._guid = value;
            }
        }
    }
e   }
```

Now that you have prepared the containers for your data, it's time to retrieve them from the cloud by using the `WebClient` class.

In your `MainPage.xaml`, you define a list box that will show all links to news and the titles:

```
<ListBox x:Name="NewsList">
  <ListBox.ItemTemplate>
    <DataTemplate>
      <StackPanel Margin="0,5,0,5">
        <TextBlock FontFamily="Tahoma" FontWeight="Bold" Text="{Binding Title}" />
        <HyperlinkButton Content="{Binding Link}"  Click="HyperlinkButton_Click"/>
      </StackPanel>
    </DataTemplate>
  </ListBox.ItemTemplate>
</ListBox>
```

The `Click` event of all `HyperlinkButton` controls created by the `ItemTemplate` will be handled by the `HyperlinkButton_Click` event handler, which will do the true work.

Then in the code-behind of your application, you will have the following:

```
...
WebBrowserTask webBrowserTask = null;
...
```

This declares at the class level your `WebBrowserTask` object, which will enable you to launch the web browser application.

As you can see in Figure 9-7 the two most important members of this class are the `Uri` property and the `Show` method. `Uri` represents the target address, while `Show` shows the browser. In Chapter 3 recipe 9, you can learn more about Launchers and Choosers in Windows Phone.

As with the other recipe, you do the work inside the `PageLoaded` event:

```
void MainPage_Loaded(object sender, RoutedEventArgs e)
    {
        WebClient wc = new WebClient();
        wc.OpenReadCompleted += new OpenReadCompletedEventHandler(wc_OpenReadCompleted);
        wc.OpenReadAsync(new Uri("http://feeds.bbci.co.uk/news/world/rss.xml"));
        webBrowserTask = new WebBrowserTask();
    }
```

Figure 9-7. *Class diagram for WebBrowserTask*

You instantiate a `WebClient` and then subscribe to the `OpenReadComplete` event, which fires after `OpenReadAsync` completely executes. `OpenReadComplete` only deserializes the result of the request in your object:

```
...
void wc_OpenReadCompleted(object sender, OpenReadCompletedEventArgs e)
{
  XmlSerializer xms = new XmlSerializer(typeof(Rss));
  Rss des = xms.Deserialize(e.Result) as Rss;
  NewsList.ItemsSource = des.Channel.Items;
}
...
```

At this point, all you have to do is to manage the click of the hyperlink button by the user opening the browser:

```
private void HyperlinkButton_Click(object sender, RoutedEventArgs e)
{
  HyperlinkButton hpb = sender as HyperlinkButton;
  webBrowserTask.URL = hpb.Content.ToString();
  webBrowserTask.Show();
}
```

Usage

From Visual Studio 2010, press Ctrl +F5. The type of target is not important, as this recipe can work as fine on the emulator as on the device. The application will start, briefly showing the splash screen and then the main page. After a few seconds (depending on your Internet connection), a list of news items will display. Click the hyperlink button to access the Browse function and open the link relative to the news.

9-4. Creating a Google API–based Translator

Problem

You want to create an application that interacts with a Representational State Transfer (RESTful) service that returns a response in JavaScript Object Notation (JSON) format.

Solution

You must use `WebClient` and `DataContractJsonSerializer`.

How It Works

`WebClient` provides common methods for sending and receiving data to and from a resource identified by a URI. In this case, the resource will give you a response in JSON format. Then you will use `DataContractJsonSerializer` to deserialize the response inside your object graph.

The Code

For the purposes of this exercise, you will use an API made available by Google for the translation of texts. (To use this API, you must have a key to access the service itself).

The application that you will create in terms of the UI is quite simple. It will have a text box for entering text to be translated, a button to start the interaction with the service, and a text block to show the result of your request (which in this case will be a translation from English to Italian).

Here is the XAML that composes our interface:

```
<Grid X:Name="ContentPanel" Grid.Row="1" Margin="12,0,12,0">
  <Grid.RowDefinitions>
    <RowDefinition Height="*" />
    <RowDefinition Height="Auto" />
    <RowDefinition Height="*" />
  </ Grid.RowDefinitions>
  <TextBox Name="TextToTranslateTextbox" Text="Translate Me" />
  <Button Name = "TranslateButton" Content = "Translate" Grid.Row = "1"
                  Click = "TranslateButton_Click" />
  <TextBlock Name="TranslatedTextblock" Grid.Row="2" />
</ Grid>
```

Then in the code-behind of your `PhoneApplicationPage`, add class-level member as follows:

```
WebClient proxy = null;
```

The `WebClient` class provides common methods for sending and receiving data from a resource identified by an URI, so it's perfect for our purpose:

```
private WebClient proxy = null;
```

And now in the constructor of your page you need to instantiate the proxy and prepare it to manage the response of an OpenRead request,

```
proxy = new WebClient ();
proxy.OpenReadCompleted + = new OpenReadCompletedEventHandler (proxy_OpenReadCompleted);
```

In the event handler, you will insert code to handle the response, but let's focus first on the request, which will be linked to the click of TranslateButton:

```
...
private void TranslateButton_Click (object sender, RoutedEventArgs e)
{
  try
  {
    if (String.IsNullOrEmpty (TextToTranslateTextbox.Text))
    {
      Uri request = buildGoogleTranslateRequest (TextToTranslateTextbox.Text);
      proxy.OpenReadAsync (request);
    }
  }
  catch (Exception ex)
  {
    // Do something with this exception
  }
}

...
```

And buildGoogleTranslateRequest(string) is our private method that creates the URI for your request:

```
private Uri buildGoogleTranslateRequest(string textToTranslate)
{
        return new Uri("https://www.googleapis.com/language/translate/v2?
                key=YOUR_API_KEY_HERE&
                q=" + textToTranslate + "
            &source=en
            &target=it
            &prettyprint=true");
}
```

As a result of this request, the application will give you an object serialized in JSON format—more precisely, the format is as follows:

```
{
```

```
    "Data": {
        "Translations": [
            {
                "TranslatedText": "Text"
            }
        ]
    }
}
```

That tells you that the root object of the object graph has an internal object of type `Date`, which in turn contains an array of objects of type `Translations`, which in turn contains a property of type `string` called `TranslatedText`. Figure 9-8 shows the class diagram.

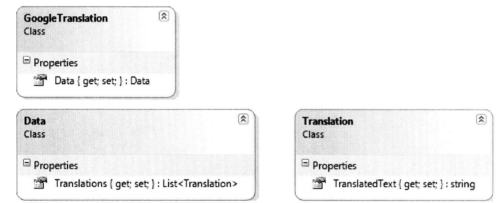

Figure 9-8. *Class diagram of classes used to deserialize the objects*

The implementation of `GoogleTranslation` is as follows:

GoogleTranslation.cs

```
[DataContract]
public class GoogleTranslation
{
    [DataMember (Name = "data")]
    public Data Data {get; set;}
}
```

Data.cs

```
[DataContract]
public class Data
{
    [DataMember (Name = "translations")]
    public List <Translation> Translations {get, set;}
}
```

Translation.cs

```
    [DataContract]
    public class Translation
    {
        [DataMember (Name = "translatedText")]
        public string TranslatedText {get, set;}
    }
...
```

The annotations on classes says you which type of serializer you will use —that is, `DataContractJsonSerializer`, which will be the focus of the implementation dell'eventHandler `proxy_OpenReadCompleted`. Il `DataContractJsonSerializer` `System.ServiceModel.Web` is contained in the assembly (so remember to add this reference to your project).

```
void proxy_OpenReadCompleted(object sender, OpenReadCompletedEventArgs e)
{
  var serializer = new DataContractJsonSerializer(typeof(GoogleTranslation));
  GoogleTranslation translation = serializer.ReadObject(e.Result) as GoogleTranslation;

  this.TranslatedTextblock.Text = translation.Data.Translations.FirstOrDefault() != null
  ? translation.Data.Translations.FirstOrDefault().TranslatedText
  : "error in translation";
}
```

As you can see, the interaction with a REST service is very simple, as is the use of JSON instead of XML. The only difficulty you may encounter is the interpretation of the object graph, to create a model for the deserialization of the response (or the serialization of a request).

Usage

Open Visual Studio and start deploying the application to the emulator. Write a sentence in the text box and look for the translation. Of course, you need to stay connected to the Internet to use this recipe.

9-5. Pushing Your Notification

Problem

You want to build an application that uses push notification to indicate to the user that something has changed in the cloud.

Solution

You must use the Push Notification Service to indicate the change that has happened.

How It Works

The Microsoft Push Notification Service in Windows Phone gives you the capability to send information and updates to an application from a web service. This new way of interacting with a service hides the lack of multitasking in Windows Phone 7. Push notification works as shown in Figure 9-9.

Another good reason to use push notification is the need to preserve battery power. If applications are continuously polling to check for new notifications, the device's battery will quickly run down.

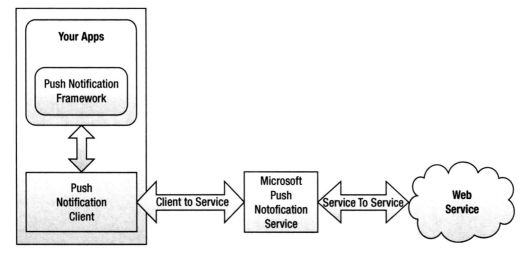

Figure 9-9. *Push notification architecture*

Your web service sends a notification to the Microsoft Push Notification Service , which routes the notification to the user's device interfacing with *push notification client* that notify to your application that something new is ready do know.

■ **Note** Your application will have only one channel available to establish a connection to the Push Notification Service. The user can activate a maximum of 30 applications that use push notification. If your application results in exceeding these quotas, an "InvalidOperationException (Channel quota exceeded)" error will be raised.

After your notification is delivered, the Push Notification Service sends a response to your service. But remember that you will not receive a confirmation that your notification was delivered.

There are three types of push notification that you can use—tile, toast, and raw—described as follows:

- *Tile notification*: Every application has a *tile.* A tile is a dynamic representation of the application that is displayed on the start screen if the user chooses this option. Figure 9-12 shows, inside the rectangle, the default settings that your application will use for tile notification. A tile is composed of the following six elements, which you can update:

- Count: An integer that can assume a value between 1 and 99 and that is displayed on the tile in a circle image (only if set or greater than 0).

- Title and BackTitle: A string set during development (see Figure 9-10).

- BackgroundImage and BackBackgroundImage: An image on the front or the rear of the tile that can be either a jpg or a png (see Figure 9-11). We recommend using local images in order to avoid an excessive use of the network, but nothing prevents you from using remote images (remember that the images must have a maximum size of 80 KB or will not be downloaded; and https connections are not supported).

- BackContent: A string less than 40 characters that appears in the body of the rear of a tile.

■ **Note** The title must fit on a single line of text. If you don't set this value, the pre-defined title will be displayed. Also, if no Count values are set, nothing will be shown. If you want to reset the count in the tile, you must use 0 (zero) as the value.

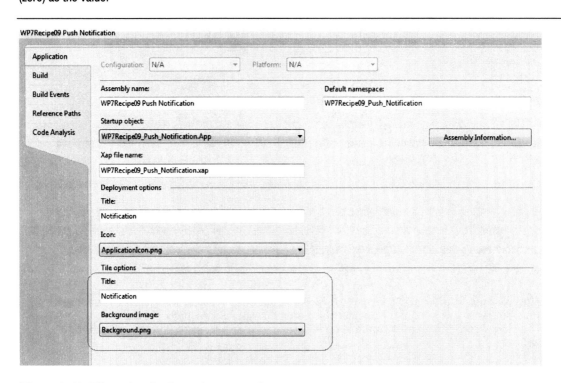

Figure 9-10. Tile options in the project properties

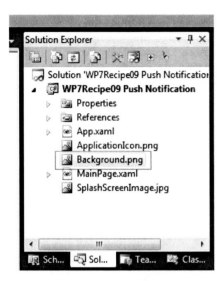

Figure 9-11. *The background image in Solution Explorer*

Figure 9-12. *The Background image pinned in the start page*

- *Toast notification*: This consists of a message shown in the top part of the screen and composed of a title and a subtitle. These two properties are simply strings, with the title having a bold weight and the subtitle appearing as normal text. You can see an example of toast notification when you receive a text message. The name of the person contacting is the title and the text is the subtitle.

- *Raw notification*: This notification is sent directly to your application and can be a maximum of 1 KB.

■ **Note** If you send a raw notification, and your app is not running, the Push Notification Service will discard your notification.

In this recipe, you will simulate a notification by sending a message to the Microsoft Push Notification Service via an application created by us. (This is only a simulation because it's not the purpose of this book to explain how to write a web service.)

The Code

Create a new solution, naming it **First Push Notification**. The first thing to do is define a constant as a string in the code, which identifies the channel that your application will use in the future. Add a new class to solution and call it `GlobalInformations`, declaring it as internal and static.

```
internal static class GlobalInformations
```

Inside this new class, add a constant that you will use to identify the `ChannelName`.

```
...
//Change this value with your channel name. You can prefer to use a GUID
private const string channelName = "NotificationTest";
...
```

Now you have the channel name, but you're missing `HttpNotificationChannel`, an object of the most important class. So you declare it, as follows:

```
...
private HttpNotificationChannel _notificationChannel;
...
```

`HttpNotificationChannel` is the class that supports (on the client side) the process of notification to the user, as you can see in Figure 9-13. This class puts at your disposal several methods, the first of which is `Find`. The `Find` method is used to check whether any notification channels with the name that you have set (`channelName`) already exists on the device, and if it exists, returns it. This method is very important for controlling the maximum number of channels that can be created on a device. You can also see in Figure 9-13 that `HttpNotificationChannel` doesn't have a parameterless constructor because you need to specify at least the channel name.

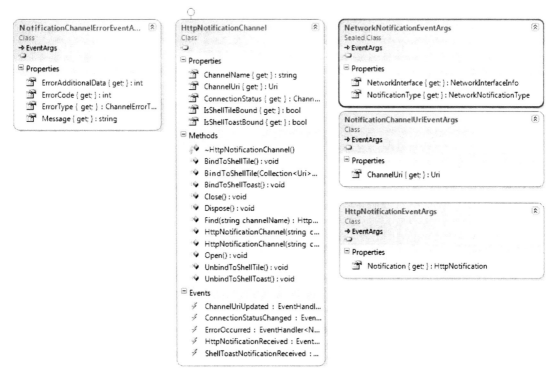

Figure 9-13. *Class diagram of HttpNotificationChannel and event args classes*

Now let's take a look at the method to call in the `Application_Launching` and `Application_Activated` event handlers to see the other important properties and events to subscribe to.

```
...
private void ActivateNotificationChannel()
{
  try
  {
    _notificationChannel =
HttpNotificationChannel.Find(GlobalInformations.NotificationChannelName);
    if (_notificationChannel == null)
    {
      _notificationChannel = new
HttpNotificationChannel(GlobalInformations.NotificationChannelName);
      _notificationChannel.ErrorOccurred += notificationChannel_ErrorOccurred;
      _notificationChannel.ChannelUriUpdated += notificationChannel_ChannelUriUpdated;
      _notificationChannel.Open();
    }

    if (!_notificationChannel.IsShellTileBound)
      _notificationChannel.BindToShellTile();
```

```
    if (!_notificationChannel.IsShellToastBound)
      _notificationChannel.BindToShellToast();

    _notificationChannel.HttpNotificationReceived +=
  notificationChannel_HttpNotificationReceived;
    _notificationChannel.ShellToastNotificationReceived +=
                    notificationChannel_ShellToastNotificationReceived;
  }
  catch (InvalidOperationException ex)
  {
    //notify the problem
    MessageBox.Show("If you want to use all functionality of this application, you must
  disable notification in others app, because you have too many channels opened");
    //disable Push Notification in your application
  }
}
```

As you can see, you call the `Find` method to determine whether a channel already exists—of course, because without a channel, nothing works.

If the channel is not present, you need to create one with the name that you decided to enter into the constant. (Keep in mind that it is not critical to insert the name of the channel in the constant, but it is a good way to avoid common errors.) `_notificationChannel` object initialization does not means that you opened it

Subscribe to events that might be raised during the opening of the first

- `ErrorOccurred` occurs whenever there is a problem in the use of class (and also later during the reception of notifications could be raised)

- `ChannelUriUpdated` will be raised after you receive the URI on Microsoft Push Notification Service of your channel that will allow you to send notifications directly on your device.

Next, open the channel. This may trigger the exception that we mentioned earlier, `InvalidOperationException`. This tells you that there are already too many applications that use push notification on the device. If you don't have permission to use notification in your app, you may want to notify the user (for example, with a message box) that having too many open channels on the device blocks the full use of your application (especially if your application is meant to make wide use of notifications).

In this example, you bind the channel directly to the notifications (tile and toast). However, remember that to use toast notification, you must allow the user to turn them off from the control panel of your application (see Chapter 10 for further explanation). After this, you subscribe to the two events, `HttpNotificationReceived` and `ShelToastNotificationReceived`.

The first will be raised when a raw notification is received. The second will be raised when the application receives a toast notification. (This event will occur only if the application is running in the foreground.)

Now take a look at the `ChannelUriUpdated` event handler. In this example, you write at the debug console the channel URI, but you have to add the logic to notify your web service of the address to which the push notification is sent.

```
...
void notificationChannel_ChannelUriUpdated(object sender, NotificationChannelUriEventArgs e)
```

```
{
        Debug.WriteLine(e.ChannelUri);
        //put here the code to notify your web service of the Uri of the channel
}
```

The channelUri object will be something like this:

```
http://db3.notify.live.net/throttledthirdparty/01.00/XXXXXXXXXXXXXXXXX...
```

You would replace all the Xs with the identification of your channel.

The concept is simple: you have received this channel, and now your service can send notifications. However, because it is not our aim to show you how to make a service, we will instead show you how to build a small test application to send notifications to the device.

Open Visual Studio. Create a desktop application and call it SendNotificationApplication. In the XAML of the main page, create the following structure:

```
<Window
        xmlns="http://schemas.microsoft.com/winfx/2006/xaml/presentation"
        xmlns:x="http://schemas.microsoft.com/winfx/2006/xaml"
        xmlns:d=http://schemas.microsoft.com/expression/blend/2008
        xmlns:mc=http://schemas.openxmlformats.org/markup-compatibility/2006
        mc:Ignorable="d"
        x:Class="SendNotificationApplication.MainWindow"
        Title="Main Window">
    <Grid>
        <Grid.ColumnDefinitions>
            <ColumnDefinition Width="100" />
            <ColumnDefinition Width="*" />
        </Grid.ColumnDefinitions>
        <Grid.RowDefinitions>
            <RowDefinition Height="25" />
            <RowDefinition Height="25" />
            <RowDefinition Height="25" />
            <RowDefinition Height="25" />
            <RowDefinition Height="25" />
            <RowDefinition Height="25" />
            <RowDefinition Height="25" />
            <RowDefinition Height="25" />
            <RowDefinition Height="25" />
            <RowDefinition Height="25" />
            <RowDefinition Height="25" />
            <RowDefinition Height="*" />
        </Grid.RowDefinitions>
        <TextBlock Text="Notification Uri" />
        <TextBox x:Name="NotificationUriTextBox" Grid.Column="1"/>
        <TextBlock Text="Text 1 " Grid.Row="1"  />
        <TextBox x:Name="FirstRowTextBox" Grid.Row="1" Grid.Column="1" />
        <TextBlock Text="Text 2 " Grid.Row="2" />
        <TextBox x:Name="SecondRowTextBox" Grid.Row="2" Grid.Column="1" />
```

```
        <TextBlock Text="Background" Grid.Row="4" />
        <TextBox x:Name="BackgroundTextBox" Grid.Row="4" Grid.Column="1" />

        <TextBlock Text="Count" Grid.Row="5" />
        <TextBox x:Name="CountTextBox" Grid.Row="5" Grid.Column="1" />

        <TextBlock Text="Title" Grid.Row="6" />
        <TextBox x:Name="TitleTextBox" Grid.Row="6" Grid.Column="1" />

        <TextBlock Text="(Back)Background" Grid.Row="7" />
        <TextBox x:Name="BackBackgroundTextBox" Grid.Row="7" Grid.Column="1" />

        <TextBlock Text="(Back)Contente" Grid.Row="8" />
        <TextBox x:Name="BackContentTextBox" Grid.Row="8" Grid.Column="1" />

        <TextBlock Text="(Back)Title" Grid.Row="9" />
        <TextBox x:Name="BackTitleTextBox" Grid.Row="9" Grid.Column="1" />
        <Button x:Name="SendTileNotificationButton" Grid.Row="10" Grid.ColumnSpan="2"
                Content="Send Tile Notification"
                Click="SendTileNotificationButton_Click" />
        <Button x:Name="SendToastNotificationButton" Grid.Row="3" Grid.ColumnSpan="2"
                Content="Send Toast Notification"
                Click="SendToastNotificationButton_Click" />
        <TextBlock x:Name="ResponseTextBox" Grid.Row="11" TextAlignment="Left"
                Grid.ColumnSpan="2" />
    </Grid></Window>
```

That will display something like Figure 9-14. Then you write the two event handlers for the two buttons. The first event handler is SendTileNotificationButton_Click, which takes the subscription URI from the text box and then creates the request. You must always remember that you can't send a notification via the GET method, but only with POST.

After this, the next step is to add headers to your request. Optionally, you can add an X-MessageID header that uniquely identifies your notification message, and will be returned in a response. Then, if something goes wrong with a message, you can associate the request with the response to know what's happened at a specific request. If a response doesn't satisfy your requirements, you can stop it from being sent to the user.

X-NotificationClass can assume three values: 1, 11, and 21. With 1 as the value, your notification will be sent immediately; with 11, you will have a delay of 450 seconds; and with 21, you will have a delay of 900 seconds.

```
private void SendTileNotificationButton_Click(object sender, RoutedEventArgs e)
        {
            string subscriptionUri = this.NotificationUriTextBox.Text;
            HttpWebRequest sendNotificationRequest =
(HttpWebRequest)WebRequest.Create(subscriptionUri);

            sendNotificationRequest.Method = "POST";

            sendNotificationRequest.Headers.Add("X-MessageID", Guid.NewGuid().ToString());
            sendNotificationRequest.ContentType = "text/xml";
```

```
            sendNotificationRequest.Headers.Add("X-WindowsPhone-Target", "token");
            sendNotificationRequest.Headers.Add("X-NotificationClass", "1");

            string tileTag = string.IsNullOrWhiteSpace(TileIdTextBox.Text)
                                ? "<wp:Tile>"
                                : "<wp:Tile Id=\""+ TileIdTextBox.Text +\">";

            string tileMessage = "<?xml version=\"1.0\" encoding=\"utf-8\"?>" +
                                    "<wp:Notification xmlns:wp=\"WPNotification\">" +
                                      tileTag +
                                        "<wp:BackgroundImage>{0}</wp:BackgroundImage>" +
                                        "<wp:Count>{1}</wp:Count>" +
                                        "<wp:Title>{2}</wp:Title>" +

"<wp:BackBackgroundImage>{3}</wp:BackBackgroundImage>" +
                                        "<wp:BackContent>{4}</wp:BackContent>" +
                                        "<wp:BackTitle>{5}</wp:BackTitle>" +
                                      "</wp:Tile> " +
                                    "</wp:Notification>";

            byte[] notificationMessage = new System.Text.UTF8Encoding().GetBytes(
                    string.Format(tileMessage,
                    BackgroundTextBox.Text,
                    CountTextBox.Text,
                    TitleTextBox.Text,
                    BackBackgroundTextBox.Text,
                    BackContentTextBox.Text,
                    BackTitleTextBox.Text));

            // Sets the web request content length.
            sendNotificationRequest.ContentLength = notificationMessage.Length;

            using (Stream requestStream = sendNotificationRequest.GetRequestStream())
            {
                requestStream.Write(notificationMessage, 0, notificationMessage.Length);
            }

            HttpWebResponse response = (HttpWebResponse)
                        sendNotificationRequest.GetResponse();

            StringBuilder sb = new StringBuilder();
            foreach (var item in response.Headers)
            {
                sb.AppendLine(string.Format("{0}-->{1}",
                        item.ToString(),
                        response.Headers[item.ToString()]));
            }

            ResponseTextBox.Text = sb.ToString();

        }
```

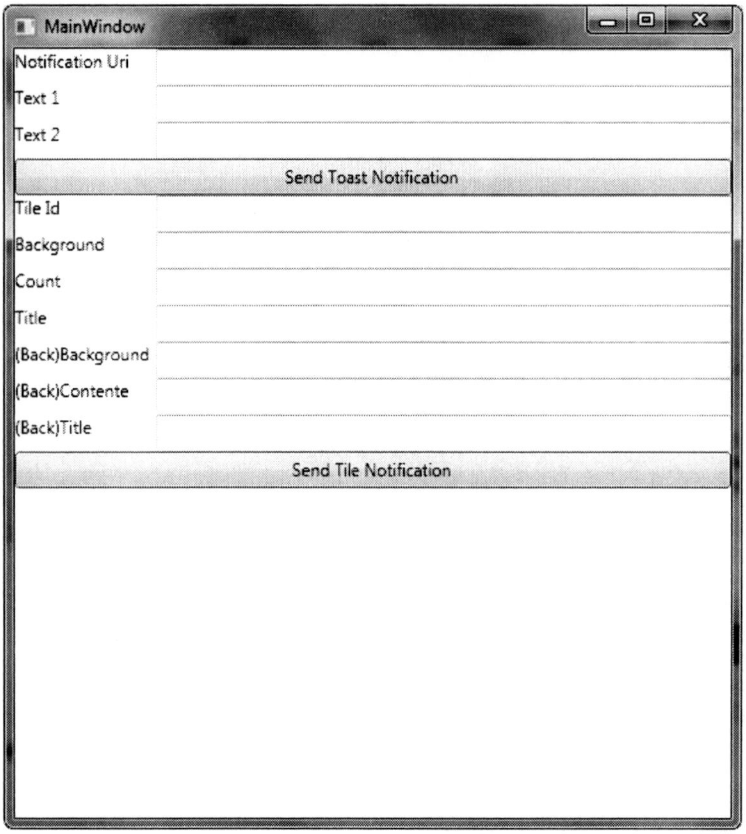

Figure 9-14. *The SendNotification application interface*

As you can see inside this interface you can specify a Tile Id that identifies a secondary tile, which is a tile created programmatically as result of user input.

On the other hand, inside the code behind you have the code to send a toast notification that appears largely similar to the code for the tile notification. The main difference is in the format of the XML that makes up the notification.

In this case, X-NotificationClass can take the value 2, 12, or22, reflecting a delay in sending the notification of 0, 450, and 900 seconds, respectively.

```
...
private void SendToastNotificationButton_Click(object sender, RoutedEventArgs e)
{
        string subscriptionUri = this.NotificationUriTextBox.Text;
        HttpWebRequest sendNotificationRequest = (HttpWebRequest)
                            WebRequest.Create(subscriptionUri);

        sendNotificationRequest.Method = "POST";
```

```
        sendNotificationRequest.Headers.Add("X-MessageID", Guid.NewGuid().ToString());
        sendNotificationRequest.ContentType = "text/xml";
        sendNotificationRequest.Headers.Add("X-WindowsPhone-Target", "toast");
        sendNotificationRequest.Headers.Add("X-NotificationClass", "2");
        string toastMessage = "<?xml version=\"1.0\" encoding=\"utf-8\"?>" +
                                "<wp:Notification xmlns:wp=\"WPNotification\">" +
                                    "<wp:Toast>" +
                                        "<wp:Text1>{0}</wp:Text1>" +
                                        "<wp:Text2>{1}</wp:Text2>" +
                                    "</wp:Toast>" +
                                "</wp:Notification>";

        byte[] notificationMessage = new System.Text.UTF8Encoding().GetBytes(
                    string.Format(toastMessage,
                                    FirstRowTextBox.Text,
                                    SecondRowTextBox.Text ));

        sendNotificationRequest.ContentLength = notificationMessage.Length;

        using (Stream requestStream = sendNotificationRequest.GetRequestStream())
        {
            requestStream.Write(notificationMessage, 0, notificationMessage.Length);
        }

        HttpWebResponse response = (HttpWebResponse)
                            sendNotificationRequest.GetResponse();

        StringBuilder sb = new StringBuilder();
        foreach (var item in response.Headers)
        {
            sb.AppendLine(string.Format("{0}-->{1}",
                            item.ToString(),
                            response.Headers[item.ToString()]));
        }

        ResponseTextBox.Text = sb.ToString();
    }
```

At this point you are ready to send notifications to your application. This version of Windows Phone introduces support of additional tiles created during an interaction with the user (you can create a tile only when the application is in foreground). Let's suppose that you want to create additional tiles to update. We start from the xaml of the Windows Phone application, which will appear as follows:

```
<Grid x:Name="ContentPanel" Grid.Row="1" Margin="12,0,12,0">
        <StackPanel>
                <TextBlock Text="Tile Id"/>
            <Button x:Name="CreateTileButton" Height="80" Content="Create tile" Click="Cre
ateTileButton_Click" />
                </StackPanel>
        </Grid>
```

The OnClick event of CreateTileButton will be handled from the CreateTileButton_Click method in the code-behind, which is responsible for creating the tile calling the static method **Create** exposed by the ShellTile class. This will create the tile, assigning it a Uri (that will identify the tile) and data relative to the tile.

```
private void CreateTileButton_Click(object sender, RoutedEventArgs e)
{
    ShellTile.Create(
        new Uri("/MainPage.xaml", UriKind.Relative),
        new StandardTileData
        {
            BackgroundImage = new Uri("\\ApplicationIcon.png", UriKind.Relative),
            Title = "New York"
        });
};
```

You're probably asking, "Why do I need a tile that will point to a single page?" The answer is really simple: because you can use the Uri to specify a query string, allowing you to pass a parameter to access, for example, the weather forecast for a particular zip code.

Usage

Open the two projects and start deploying the application to the Windows Phone Emulator. Get the notification URI from the debug console and then use it in SendNotificationApplication, which should work as shown in Figures 9-15 and 9-16. Remember that to see the toast notification, you must have your application running in the background.

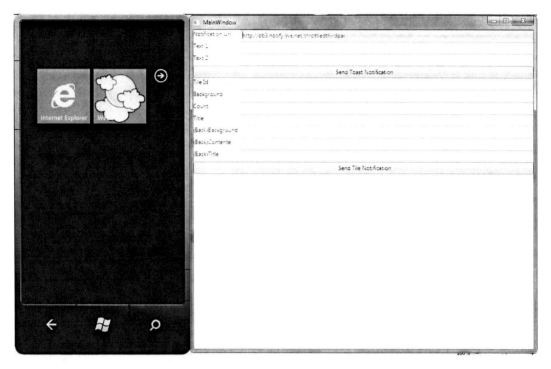

Figure 9-15. *The application before you send a notification*

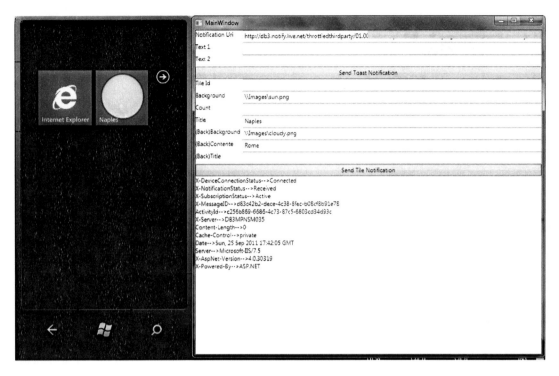

Figure 9-16. *The response from the push notification channel*

CHAPTER 10

Testing Windows Phone Applications

When your application is complete, you are ready to publish it (unless you have made it only as an exercise). Even if Microsoft were to raise the limit of free applications that you could publish to 100, none of those applications should be useless.

To be installed, your application must be signed by Microsoft with an Authenticode certificate. The best way to obtain an Authenticode certificate is to follow Microsoft's rules and understand the Application Certification Guidelines (which are available at `http://go.microsoft.com/?linkid=9730558`).

However, Microsoft's Authenticode certificate is only part of what is needed for a successful application. Say, for example, that Microsoft believes that your application complies with the rules of the marketplace, but for some "inexplicable" reason your application crashes while the user uses it. The user might not mind the first time, hoping that the crash was an extraordinary case. But if a crash occurs more often, the user will likely delete your application, and you will have wasted your time.

This chapter introduces you to concepts including Separation of Concerns and the Model-View-ViewModel pattern. These enable you not only to provide a separation of roles between your components, but also to make your application capable of undergoing unit testing. But first you must understand what is meant by SoC and unit testing.

Separation of Concerns (SoC) is one of the key principles of software engineering. To achieve software of a good quality—that is, software that has robustness, adaptability, maintainability, and re-usability—you must decouple the concern of one element from another. For example, it is the concern of the View to show information, and the way to do it, but ViewModel is responsible for retrieving information and preparing that information for View.

In *unit testing*, code is written to test a small piece of source code that represents a single functionality—or, to be more accurate, to test that functionality in a particular condition. Therefore, one method, or roughly a functionality, can have more than one unit test.

To underline the importance of unit testing, let's compare this approach with the debug approach. If you write a test and then change your code, you can run the test suite again to see whether something was broken by your modifications (this is known as regression testing). However, if you choose to always debug your application, you will not have the same result with the same velocity. Of course, you must perform integration testing and functional testing before you can say that your application was completely tested. Again, it's our opinion that the test must be written before you write the code, especially if the programmer who writes the code is the same person who will test the code.

In some recipes in this chapter, you will learn how to use Visual Studio tools to test your application in preparation for the marketplace and users. You will also learn how to avoid common errors that lead to the rejection of applications.

The recipes in this chapter describe how to do the following:

- 10-1. Implement MVVM on Windows Phone using MVVM Light
- 10-2. Implement MVVM on Windows Phone using Prism
- 10-3. Use MVVM and perform unit testing
- 10-4. Use application profiling
- 10-5. Follow certification test steps

10-1. Implementing MVVM on Windows Phone Using MVVM Light

Problem

You want your application implementation to have a consistent separation of concerns between modules. You want the view to have only the task of displaying information and to remove from the view everything that requires some logic or data access. You need to create a view with only a set of controls (such as `TextBlock`, `TextBox`, and `Button`) binding them with the `DataContext` (`ViewModel`) of the view. The view is not responsible for data-retrieving; this is a task reserved for the `ViewModel`, which will aggregate data if necessary, and put it in properties, bindable by the view.

Solution

You must implement the Model-View-ViewModel (MVVM) pattern, and because you don't want to reinvent the wheel, you'll also use the MVVM Light framework, which is available on the MVVM Light Toolkit CodePlex at `http://mvvmlight.codeplex.com`. MVVM Light provides some important classes and "gears" necessary to implement MVVM on Silverlight for Windows Phone, such as `EventToCommand` and `MessageBroker` (aka `Messenger`).

How It Works

MVVM (based on a specialization of Martin Fowler's Presentation Model) is a design pattern used to realize the separation of concerns. Elements of the MVVM pattern are as follows:

- *View* is responsible for showing information, as in other MV*x* patterns (where *x* could be C = controller, P = presenter, and so forth) to display controls (for example: buttons and text boxes).
- *ViewModel* is responsible for preparing data taken from the model for the visualization.
- *Model* represents the model of your application (that is, your data source).

In order to implement MVVM, you need to understand some basic concepts, such as commands and binding. Next, you'll learn about the basics of MVVM; and after that, we'll cover unit testing and its importance within your application lifecycle. Let's start with binding. A *binding* is simply an association between two properties of two different classes. You can bind the `Value` of a `Slider` with the `Text` property of a `TextBox`, or in the case of the MVVM implementation, you can bind the value of a property in our ViewModel with the property of a control on the view. Typically, you will use properties with the same or similar types. There are different options for binding:

- `Path`

- `Mode`

- `UpdateTrigger`

- `BindsDirectlyToSource`

- `Converter`

`Path` represents the path to the binding source property. For example, if your binding source is a product and you are binding `TextBox.Text` to show the category name, your path will be `Path=Category.Description`.

In Silverlight for Windows Phone, as in Silverlight for the Web, the `Mode` attribute can assume three values: `OneWay`, `OneTime`, and `TwoWay`. By default, the binding `Mode` is set to `OneWay`. This means that when you update the source of the binding, the target is updated. As you might guess from its name, `TwoWay` mode means that updating the target value will reflect on the source value, and vice versa. Finally, when you use `OneTime`, the target will be updated only the first time, when you create the binding.

`UpdateTrigger` in Silverlight for Windows Phone, as in its cousin for the Web, accepts only two values: `Default` and `Explicit`. With `Explicit`, you must indicate to the binding engine to update the source. `Default` mode updates the value when a lost focus (of the control) occurs. There is a way to use `UpdateOnPropertyChanged` as in WPF, by using Coding4Fun tools available on CodePlex (http://coding4fun.codeplex.com).

`BindsDirectlyToSource`, when set to `false`, causes `Path` to be evaluated relative to the data item; otherwise, `Path` is evaluated relative to the data source.

Last but not least is the concept of a *converter*. With a converter, you can bind properties of different types, defining the way in which the view must evaluate the value. For example, sometimes you will need to bind a Boolean property to the visibility of a control. As you know, visibility is an enumeration, so when you try to apply a Boolean, nothing happens. The solution? A converter! You will see this in the following "The Code" section.

Now you need to understand what a command is. The concept of a command comes from the command pattern, which allows you to isolate the part of code that executes an operation from the part that requests the execution. Inside the code of our ViewModel, a *command* is a class that implements the `ICommand` interface, which represents the contract to implement commanding. As you can see in the class diagram shown in Figure 10-1, `ICommand` exposes the methods `CanExecute` and `Execute`, and the event `CanExecuteChanged`. As you can imagine, `CanExecute` is the method that enables the control bound with the command to be enabled, and `Execute` is the method that describes what you want to do with that command. Unfortunately, in this version of Silverlight for Windows Phone, even if the `ICommand` interface is available, the command cannot be bound with controls without using `EventToCommand`, because the controls don't expose the `Command` property. However, we are confident that this capability will be introduced in future versions. It's important to remember that when you bind a command to a control through the `Command={Binding MyCommand}` syntax, where `MyCommand` is your command exposed by your ViewModel, this command refers to the default event of the control (for example, the `Click` event of a button).

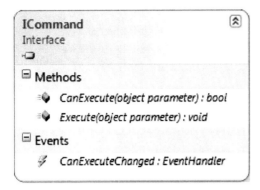

Figure 10-1. *Class diagram for ICommand*

The Code

Before you begin to create a new project, download the libraries indicated in the preceding "How it Works" section. Of course, if you want to get the most from MVVM Light, you should also install the templates for Visual Studio 2010 (Express or not, depending on your version) that the package contains.

To begin, create a new Windows Phone application, and add a reference to the MVVM Light DLLs and to the Coding4Fun libraries, as shown in Figure 10-2.

Figure 10-2. *Adding the MVVM Light and Coding4Fun DLLs to your project*

Your application is now ready for a quick implementation of the pattern, and to use a workaround notorious among people who work with Silverlight. This workaround helps you to update the source of the binding, every times a change occurs inside a textbox, then will be raised `PropertyChanged` event every time you write something in a text box, because as you know the default `UpdateSourceTrigger`, set the value of the source property only when the control has lost the focus.

To do this, you need to import the `Coding4Fun.Phone.Controls.Binding` namespace in the following way:

```
xmlns:local="clr-namespace:Coding4Fun.Phone.Controls.Binding;
            assembly=Coding4Fun.Phone.Controls"
```

Next, set `TextBoxBinding` .`UpdateSourceOnChange` to `True` as follows:

```
<TextBox Text="{Binding Text}"local:TextBoxBinding.UpdateSourceOnChange="True" />
```

Now we are ready to continue the implementation of the pattern. First, add the `ViewModelLocator` of MVVM Light to your application. Next, create the `ViewModels` folder and add a `ViewModelLocator` type, calling it `ViewModelsLocator`.

Immediately afterward, you must edit your `App.xaml` by adding the `ViewModelsLocator` namespace to it, creating a `ViewModelsLocator` type, as follows:

```
<Application
    x:Class="Wp7Recipe_10_2_MVVM.App"
    xmlns="http://schemas.microsoft.com/winfx/2006/xaml/presentation"
    xmlns:x="http://schemas.microsoft.com/winfx/2006/xaml"
    xmlns:phone="clr-namespace:Microsoft.Phone.Controls;assembly=Microsoft.Phone"
    xmlns:shell="clr-namespace:Microsoft.Phone.Shell;assembly=Microsoft.Phone"
    xmlns:vm="clr-namespace:Wp7Recipe_10_2_MVVM.ViewModels">

    <!--Application Resources-->
    <Application.Resources>
        <vm:ViewModelsLocator xmlns:vm="clr-namespace:Wp7Recipe_10_1_MVVM.ViewModels"
                              x:Key="Locator" />
    </Application.Resources>
    ...
</Application>
```

Now that you have a way of accessing your ViewModels, you can start creating them. You'll begin with the ViewModel for the main page.

■ **Tip** A naming convention for Views and ViewModels is important. If you have a view named `CategoriesView`, you could name the relative ViewModel `CategoriesViewModel`. Although you do not have to always have a 1:1 correspondence of Views and ViewModels, perhaps there is some case where you will have only one ViewModel for CRUD (Create, Read, Update, and Delete) operations for all your typological entities.

As before, add a new item, `MainPageViewModel`, to your `ViewModels`. As you can see in the constructor, this is a piece of code that has been commented out:

```
////if (IsInDesignMode)
```

```
////{
////     // Code runs in Blend --> create design time data.
////}
////else
////{
////     // Code runs "for real": Connect to service, etc...
////}
```

This is the first important feature to consider, because by using this code, you will have the ViewModel available at design time, and this is significant when you want to test your binding in DataTemplate. In addition, you must specify in ViewModelsLocator a MainPageViewModel property, and bind it as a DataContext of the view (MainPage, in this case).

```
#region MainPageViewModel
private static MainPageViewModel _mainPageViewModel;

  /// <summary>
  /// Gets the MainPageViewModel property.
  /// </summary>
  public static MainPageViewModel MainPageViewModelStatic
  {
    get
    {
      if (_mainPageViewModel == null)
      {
        CreateMainPageViewModel();
      }
      return _mainPageViewModel;
    }
  }

  /// <summary>
  /// Gets the MainPageViewModel property.
  /// </summary>
  [System.Diagnostics.CodeAnalysis.SuppressMessage("Microsoft.Performance",
  "CA1822:MarkMembersAsStatic",
  Justification = "This non-static member is needed for data binding purposes.")]
  public MainPageViewModel MainPageViewModel
  {
    get
    {
      return MainPageViewModelStatic;
    }
  }



  /// <summary>
  /// Provides a deterministic way to delete the MainPageViewModel property.
  /// </summary>
  public static void ClearMainPageViewModel()
```

```
{
  _mainPageViewModel.Cleanup();
  _mainPageViewModel = null;
}

/// <summary>
/// Provides a deterministic way to create the MainPageViewModel property.
/// </summary>
public static void CreateMainPageViewModel()
{
  if (_mainPageViewModel == null)
  {
    _mainPageViewModel = new MainPageViewModel();
  }
}

/// <summary>
/// Cleans up all the resources.
/// </summary>
public static void Cleanup()
{
  ClearMainPageViewModel();
}
#endregion
```

▪ **Tip** To quickly write these parts of the code, you must install snippets that are available inside the MVVM Light package that you download from CodePlex. The `mvvmlocatorproperty` snippet creates a property of ViewModel inside your `ViewModelLocator`. Another really helpful snippet is `mvvminpc`, which rapidly creates a bindable property in your ViewModel that raises `PropertyChangedEvent`.

Now you have the most important step to do: binding the data context of the view to your ViewModel. In this way, all properties exposed by the ViewModel will be available for binding controls inside the view. You do this with a simple binding, as you can see in the following code:

```xml
<phone:PhoneApplicationPage
    x:Class="Wp7Recipe_10_2_MVVM.MainPage"
    xmlns="http://schemas.microsoft.com/winfx/2006/xaml/presentation"
    xmlns:x="http://schemas.microsoft.com/winfx/2006/xaml"
    xmlns:phone="clr-namespace:Microsoft.Phone.Controls;assembly=Microsoft.Phone"
    xmlns:shell="clr-namespace:Microsoft.Phone.Shell;assembly=Microsoft.Phone"
    xmlns:d="http://schemas.microsoft.com/expression/blend/2008"
    xmlns:mc="http://schemas.openxmlformats.org/markup-compatibility/2006"
    mc:Ignorable="d" d:DesignWidth="480" d:DesignHeight="768"
    FontFamily="{StaticResource PhoneFontFamilyNormal}"
    FontSize="{StaticResource PhoneFontSizeNormal}"
    Foreground="{StaticResource PhoneForegroundBrush}"
```

```
            SupportedOrientations="Portrait" Orientation="Portrait"
            shell:SystemTray.IsVisible="True"
            DataContext="{Binding Source={StaticResource Locator}, Path=MainPageViewModel}">
...
```

In this way, you have the view (`MainPage`) data context bound to the property `MainPageViewModel` of the `Locator` resource that you have defined in `App.xaml`.

These are all the preliminary steps to start with MVVM, but it's clear that you must add properties at your ViewModel to bind them to the controls on the user interface, and you should start with simply the strings `ApplicationName` and `PageName`.

```
    ...
    /// <summary>
    /// The name of our application
    /// </summary>
    public string ApplicationName { get { return "Learning MVVM"; } }

    /// <summary>
    /// The name of the page
    /// </summary>
    public string PageName { get { return "Main Page"; } }
    ...
```

As you learned in the How It Works section, binding is an important in implementing MVVM; so bind the `ApplicationTitle` and `PageTitle` properties, as follows:

```
<StackPanel x:Name="TitlePanel" Grid.Row="0" Margin="12,17,0,28">
  <TextBlock x:Name="ApplicationTitle" Text="{Binding Path=ApplicationName}"
            Style="{StaticResource PhoneTextNormalStyle}"/>
  <TextBlock x:Name="PageTitle" Text="{Binding Path=PageName}" Margin="9,-7,0,0"
            Style="{StaticResource PhoneTextTitle1Style}"/>
</StackPanel>
```

At this point, if you use Microsoft Blend, you see MVVM Light supports "blendability," then you will see the `ApplicationTitle` `TextBlock` `Text` property valued with text of property `ApplicationName` of the ViewModel (Figure 10-3) and `PageTitle` set with `PageName`.

All of this introduces you to the concept of MVVM, but you want to use it in a real case—for example, with an application that helps the user to keep track of expenses. Then in `MainPage`, you would have a form for inserting data, with fields such as Date, Amount, and Motivation, and a button to bind to a command. Unfortunately, buttons in Windows Phone don't support "clean" commands (for example, `Command={Binding SaveCommand}`) in this release.

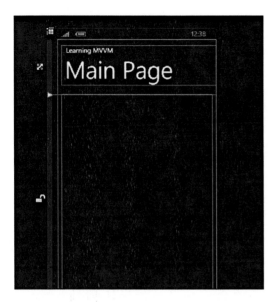

Figure 10-3. *MainPageViewModel supports blendability*

At this point, your view XAML will be something like this:

```
...
<Grid x:Name="ContentPanel" Grid.Row="1" Margin="12,0,12,0">
  <Grid.ColumnDefinitions>
    <ColumnDefinition Width="0.421*"/>
     <ColumnDefinition Width="0.579*"/>
  </Grid.ColumnDefinitions>
  <Grid.RowDefinitions>
    <RowDefinition Height="80"/>
    <RowDefinition Height="80"/>
    <RowDefinition Height="80"/>
    <RowDefinition Height="80"/>
    <RowDefinition/>
  </Grid.RowDefinitions>


  <TextBlock Margin="0" TextWrapping="Wrap" Text="Date" TextAlignment="Center"
          VerticalAlignment="Center"/>
  <TextBlock Margin="0" Grid.Row="1" TextWrapping="Wrap" Text="Amount"
          TextAlignment="Center" VerticalAlignment="Center"/>
  <TextBlock Margin="0" Grid.Row="2" TextWrapping="Wrap" Text="Motivation"
          TextAlignment="Center" VerticalAlignment="Center"/>
  <TextBox Margin="0" Grid.Column="1" Grid.Row="1" TextWrapping="Wrap"
          TextAlignment="Center" VerticalAlignment="Center"
          Text="{Binding Path=Amount, Mode=TwoWay}"
            local:TextBoxBinding.UpdateSourceOnChange="True" />
```

```
<TextBox Margin="0" Grid.Column="1" Grid.Row="2" TextWrapping="Wrap"
         TextAlignment="Center" VerticalAlignment="Center"
         Text="{Binding Path=Motivation, Mode=TwoWay}"
         local:TextBoxBinding.UpdateSourceOnChange="True"/>

<toolkit:DatePicker Grid.Column="1" VerticalAlignment="Bottom" Height="77"
                    HorizontalContentAlignment="Center"
                    Value="{Binding Path=Date, Mode=TwoWay}"
                    local:TextBoxBinding.UpdateSourceOnChange="True" />

<Button Content="Save It" Grid.Column="0" HorizontalAlignment="Center" Grid.Row="3"
        Width="152" Grid.ColumnSpan="2" >
  <i:Interaction.Triggers>
    <i:EventTrigger EventName="Click">
      <cmd:EventToCommand Command="{Binding SaveCommand}"/>
    </i:EventTrigger>
  </i:Interaction.Triggers>
</Button>
</Grid>
...
```

As you can see, you have two "new" namespaces, cmd and i, which come from the MVVM Light libraries. You have bound the Click event with a command (in ViewModel) named SaveCommand. When Button.Click raises, SaveCommand.Execute will be called. To use these namespaces, you must import them as follows:

```
...
xmlns:i="clr-namespace:System.Windows.Interactivity;assembly=System.Windows.Interactivity"
xmlns:cmd="clr-namespace:GalaSoft.MvvmLight.Command;assembly=GalaSoft.MvvmLight.Extras.WP7"
...
```

Your controls are bound to the ViewModel properties named Date, Amount, and Motivation. As before, you can use a snippet (mvvminpc) to create these properties in your ViewModel. The advantage of using this snippet is that you don't need to manually add any call to the RaisePropertyChanged method that raises the PropertyChanged event for subscribed handlers (in this case, by the binding engine).

■ **Note** The RaisePropertyChanged method call raises the PropertyChanged event in ViewModelBase (a class in the MVVM Light toolkit) that derives from the interface INotifyPropertyChanged. The binding engine will handle the event, looking for updated properties and informing the source of the binding that something has changed.

As you can imagine, the ViewModel has become a little longer because you have to bind more properties and a command:

...

```csharp
public class MainPageViewModel : ViewModelBase
{
    /// <summary>
    /// The name of our application
    /// </summary>
    public string ApplicationName { get { return "Learning MVVM"; } }

    /// <summary>
    /// The name of the page
    /// </summary>
    public string PageName { get { return "Main Page"; } }

    public GalaSoft.MvvmLight.Command.RelayCommand SaveCommand { get; set; }

    #region DateProperty

    /// <summary>
    /// The <see cref="Date" /> property's name.
    /// </summary>
    public const string DatePropertyName = "Date";

    private DateTime _date = DateTime.Now.AddDays(-4);

    public DateTime Date
    {
        get
        {
            return _date;
        }

        set
        {
            if (_date == value)
            {
                return;
            }


            var oldValue = _date;
            _date = value;

            // Update bindings, no broadcast
            RaisePropertyChanged(DatePropertyName);
        }
    }
    #endregion

    #region Amount Property
    /// <summary>
    /// The <see cref="Amount" /> property's name.
```

```csharp
        /// </summary>
        public const string AmountPropertyName = "Amount";

        private decimal _amount = 0;

        public decimal  Amount
        {
            get
            {
                return _amount;
            }

            set
            {
                if (_amount == value)
                {
                    return;
                }

                var oldValue = _amount;
                _amount = value;

                // Update bindings, no broadcast
                RaisePropertyChanged(AmountPropertyName);

            }
        }
        #endregion

        #region Motivation Property

        /// <summary>
        /// The <see cref="Motivation" /> property's name.
        /// </summary>
        public const string MotivationPropertyName = "Motivation";

        private string _motivation = string.Empty;

        public string Motivation
        {
            get
            {
                return _motivation;
            }

            set
            {
                if (_motivation == value)
                {
                    return;
                }
```

```
            var oldValue = _motivation;
            _motivation = value;

            // Update bindings, no broadcast
            RaisePropertyChanged(MotivationPropertyName);

        }
    }

    #endregion

    /// <summary>
    /// Initializes a new instance of the MainPageViewModel class.
    /// </summary>
    public MainPageViewModel()
    {
        SaveCommand = new GalaSoft.MvvmLight.Command.RelayCommand(SaveCommandExecute);
    }

    private void SaveCommandExecute()
    {
        //put your logic to save here
    }
    }
}
```

Usage

This application can run in the emulator or the physical device. This recipe is a good start point for a real financial tracking application; all you need to do is to add your preferred logic for saving data (look at Chapter 8 for inspiration) and start the application. Make sure that you have decoupled the view from the related ViewModel, so that the only interest of the view is to know how to show data (ViewModel is view-ignorant). In this way, if you change your logic for saving information, nothing must be done on your view. Furthermore, if you want to test your ViewModel, you can do it with unit tests without problems—as opposed to the events approach, that requires that an event be raised

10-2. Implementing MVVM on Windows Phone Using Prism

Problem

You want an application that implements the MVVM pattern using the Prism Library for Windows Phone.

Solution

You must download Prism from the CodePlex at `http://compositewpf.codeplex.com/` and reference its two projects, Microsoft.Patterns.Prism and Microsoft.Patterns.Prism.Interactivity, in order to create a concrete separation of concerns between Views and ViewModels.

How It Works

Prism is a class library that was born to resolve the problem of composite applications, where you have a shell application that hosts modules as part of a complete project. Prism helps you to write applications using a modular approach, rather than building monolithic applications. Separating your application into various modules helps you test a single aspect of your application without dependencies.

In the following list, you can find some of the core features provided by the library, which will help you implement MVVM pattern:

- `NotificationObject`: Acts as a base class to simply implement the `INotifyPropertyChanged` interface

- `CompositeCommand`: Acts as a commands grouping

- `DelegateCommand`: Acts like the `RelayCommand` of MVVM Light

- `DataTemplateSelector`: Allows you to select a `ContentTemplate` based on the content to display

The Code

Create a new project for Windows Phone. This application will show a list of news items and relative details so that `News` will be part of your domain. First, you must create the structure of folders inside the project, which includes the following:

- `Model`: Contains all classes that are part of your domain model

- `Repositories`: The location in your application from which you will retrieve data

- `ViewModels`: The folder where you will put all your `ViewModels`

- `Converters`: When you work with data binding, of course, you use a converter in your apps

Before you start creating your model, add a reference to `Microsoft.Practices.Prism` assembly, then add to the `Model` folder a class named `News.cs`, composed of four properties: `Id`, `Author`, `Title`, and `Body`, as follows:

```
using Microsoft.Practices.Prism.ViewModel;

public class News : NotificationObject
    {
        private int _id;

        public int Id
        {
```

```
            get { return _id; }
            set
            {
                _id = value;
                RaisePropertyChanged(() => Id);
            }
        }
    }


        private string _title;

        public string Title
        {
            get { return _title; }
            set
            {
                _title = value;
                RaisePropertyChanged(() => Title);
            }
        }

        private string _body;

        public string Body
        {
            get { return _body; }
            set
            {
                _body = value;
                RaisePropertyChanged(() => Body);
            }
        }

        private string _author;

        public string Author
        {
            get { return _author; }
            set
            {
                _author = value;
                RaisePropertyChanged(() => Author);
            }
        }
    }
}
```

Analyzing this code, you see that the News class extends the NotificationObject class shown in figure 10-4, which is part of the Prism Library. This class helps you to raise PropertyChanged.

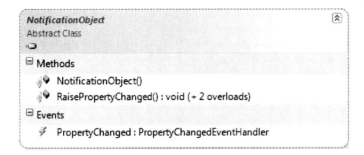

Figure 10-4. Class diagram for NotificationObject

The `RaisePropertyChanged` method has two overloads: one that accepts a string to specify a property name, and another that wants an `Expression` to work (it is our opinion that the use of the second overload results in fewer problems).

Now that you have a container for your data, you must provide content, which you will do by adding a repository to your application. Create a class named `NewsRepository`, making it static, as follows:

```
public static class NewsRepository
    {
        private static ObservableCollection<News> _news;
        public static ObservableCollection<News> GetNews()
        {
            return _news ?? (_news = new ObservableCollection<News>
                                {
                                    new News
                                    {
                                        Id = 1,
                                        Author = "Curabitur",
                                        Body = "Lorem ipsum dolor sit amet, conse
ctetur adipiscing elit. Fusce vulputate sollicitudin consectetur. Phasellus orci orci, pretium
 ut rutrum id, luctus ut mi. Morbi auctor nulla non dolor egestas rutrum dignissim nunc sceler
isque. Curabitur at nulla arcu, sit amet sollicitudin justo. Curabitur felis est, gravida eget
 faucibus sit amet, tempus tristique metus. Nam tincidunt lacus a velit mollis volutpat. Sed n
on mauris tempus magna ornare tincidunt. Suspendisse at lectus vel dolor vehicula laoreet.",
                                        Title = "Lorem ipsum dolor sit amet"
                                    },
                                    new News
                                    {
                                        Id = 2,
                                        Author = "Donec",
                                        Body = "Morbi consectetur blandit lorem.
Nulla facilisi. Praesent tristique accumsan velit, ac commodo justo malesuada non. Suspendisse
 scelerisque facilisis lacinia. Fusce luctus ipsum urna, sit amet commodo augue. Praesent at d
iam metus, non fermentum dui. Phasellus non nisl ante. Aliquam id magna purus. Aliquam aliquam
 varius diam a fermentum. Pellentesque sodales nunc ac turpis condimentum laoreet. Nunc augue
lacus, convallis commodo fermentum at, consectetur non eros. Nam in augue lectus, et hendrerit
 velit.",
                                        Title = "Morbi consectetur blandit lorem.
"
```

```
                                      },
                             new News
                             {
                                 Id = 3,
                                 Author = "Aenean",
                                 Body = "Aliquam rutrum, magna id vehicula
 varius, nisl augue convallis metus, ut dignissim massa nisl sit amet mi. Nam sit amet risus u
t ipsum sollicitudin cursus non vel lorem. Nullam hendrerit enim id sapien lobortis ultricies.
 Vivamus at odio in leo rhoncus tempus id vitae nisl. Etiam mattis porta nisi sed suscipit. Do
nec sed odio mi, eget dictum metus. Suspendisse tempor lacinia nisl quis cursus. Maecenas semp
er ipsum et nisl aliquet vulputate venenatis tortor eleifend. Etiam aliquam sem nec nulla temp
or lobortis.",
                                 Title = "Aliquam rutrum, magna id vehicul
a varius."
                             }
                     });
        }
    }
```

Now that you have a location to retrieve data from, you must prepare for viewing them. Right-click on the `ViewModels` folder and create a `ViewModel` by adding a class named `MainPageViewModel.cs`. This `ViewModel` will contain the following properties:

- `News`: An observable collection of news

- `SelectedNews`: The selected news in the list box

- `CloseDetailsCommand`: A `DelegateCommand` to close the detail grid

- `IsDetailsVisbile`: A Boolean that must be converted to a `Visibility` value

These properties translate in the following code:

```
public class MainPageViewModel : NotificationObject
    {
        public MainPageViewModel()
        {
            CloseNewsCommand = new DelegateCommand<News>(CloseNewsCommandExecute, CloseNewsCom
mandCanExecute);

        }

        #region Bindable Properties

        #region News
        private ObservableCollection<News> _news;

        public ObservableCollection<News> News
        {
            get { return _news ?? (_news = NewsRepository.GetNews()); }
        }
        #endregion

        #region IsDetailVisible
```

```
        private bool _isDetailVisible;

        public bool IsDetailVisibile
        {
            get { return _isDetailVisible; }
            set
            {
                _isDetailVisible = value;
                RaisePropertyChanged(() => IsDetailVisibile);
            }
        }

        #endregion

        #region SelectedNews
        private News _selectedNews;

        public News SelectedNews
        {
            get { return _selectedNews; }
            set
            {

                _selectedNews = value;
                RaisePropertyChanged(() => SelectedNews);
                IsDetailVisibile = true;
                CloseNewsCommand.RaiseCanExecuteChanged();
            }
        }

        #endregion

        #endregion

        #region Commands

        #region CloseNewsCommand
        public DelegateCommand<News> CloseNewsCommand { get; set; }

        private void CloseNewsCommandExecute(News news)
        {
            SelectedNews = null;
            IsDetailVisibile = false;
        }

        private bool CloseNewsCommandCanExecute(News news)
        {
            return IsDetailVisibile;
        }
        #endregion

        #endregion
```

```
                                     }
```

In this view, you certainly see that you need a converter to convert the value of the `IsDetailVisible` Boolean to a value of `Visibility` enumeration, before you pass to write the `View` (in a perfect world a designer works on the interface while you work on code, but this is the real world). The converter is really simple to write, and translates into one line of code:

```
                    return (bool) value ? Visibility.Visible : Visibility.Collapsed;
```

Now you have something to see, but you don't have a way to see it. For this recipe, you will create a `View` that contains a list box and an overlay composed by a grid to show the details of a news reader.

```xml
<phone:PhoneApplicationPage
    xmlns="http://schemas.microsoft.com/winfx/2006/xaml/presentation"
    xmlns:x="http://schemas.microsoft.com/winfx/2006/xaml"
    xmlns:phone="clr-namespace:Microsoft.Phone.Controls;assembly=Microsoft.Phone"
    xmlns:shell="clr-namespace:Microsoft.Phone.Shell;assembly=Microsoft.Phone"
    xmlns:d="http://schemas.microsoft.com/expression/blend/2008"
    xmlns:i="clr-namespace:System.Windows.Interactivity;assembly=System.Windows.Interactivity"
    xmlns:mc="http://schemas.openxmlformats.org/markup-compatibility/2006"
    xmlns:converters="clr-namespace:Wp7Recipe_10_2_MVVM.Converters"
    xmlns:toolkit="clr-
namespace:Microsoft.Phone.Controls;assembly=Microsoft.Phone.Controls.Toolkit"
    xmlns:vms="clr-namespace:Wp7Recipe_10_2_MVVM.ViewModels"
    x:Class="Wp7Recipe_10_2_MVVM.MainPage"
    mc:Ignorable="d" d:DesignWidth="480" d:DesignHeight="768"
    FontFamily="{StaticResource PhoneFontFamilyNormal}"
    FontSize="{StaticResource PhoneFontSizeNormal}"
    Foreground="{StaticResource PhoneForegroundBrush}"
    SupportedOrientations="Portrait" Orientation="Portrait"
    shell:SystemTray.IsVisible="True">
  <phone:PhoneApplicationPage.DataContext>
    <vms:MainPageViewModel  />
  </phone:PhoneApplicationPage.DataContext>
  <phone:PhoneApplicationPage.Resources>
    <converters:BooleanToVisibilityConverter x:Key="BooleanToVisibilityConverter"/>
    <Style x:Key="NewsItemContainer" TargetType="ListBoxItem">
      <Setter Property="Background" Value="Transparent"/>
      <Setter Property="BorderThickness" Value="0"/>
      <Setter Property="BorderBrush" Value="Transparent"/>
      <Setter Property="Padding" Value="0"/>
      <Setter Property="HorizontalContentAlignment" Value="Left"/>
      <Setter Property="VerticalContentAlignment" Value="Top"/>
      <Setter Property="Template">
        <Setter.Value>
          <ControlTemplate TargetType="ListBoxItem">
            <Border x:Name="LayoutRoot" BorderBrush="{TemplateBinding BorderBrush}"
BorderThickness="{TemplateBinding BorderThickness}" Background="{TemplateBinding Background}"
HorizontalAlignment="{TemplateBinding HorizontalAlignment}"
VerticalAlignment="{TemplateBinding VerticalAlignment}">
                <VisualStateManager.VisualStateGroups>
                  <VisualStateGroup x:Name="CommonStates">
```

```xml
                    <VisualState x:Name="Normal"/>
                    <VisualState x:Name="MouseOver"/>
                    <VisualState x:Name="Disabled">
                      <Storyboard>
                        <ObjectAnimationUsingKeyFrames Storyboard.TargetProperty="Background"
Storyboard.TargetName="LayoutRoot">
                          <DiscreteObjectKeyFrame KeyTime="0" Value="{StaticResource
TransparentBrush}"/>
                        </ObjectAnimationUsingKeyFrames>
                        <DoubleAnimation Duration="0" To=".5"
Storyboard.TargetProperty="Opacity" Storyboard.TargetName="ContentContainer"/>
                      </Storyboard>
                    </VisualState>
                  </VisualStateGroup>
                  <VisualStateGroup x:Name="SelectionStates">
                    <VisualState x:Name="Unselected"/>
                    <VisualState x:Name="Selected">
                      <Storyboard>
                        <ObjectAnimationUsingKeyFrames Storyboard.TargetProperty="Foreground"
Storyboard.TargetName="ContentContainer">
                          <DiscreteObjectKeyFrame KeyTime="0" Value="{StaticResource
PhoneAccentBrush}"/>
                        </ObjectAnimationUsingKeyFrames>
                        <ObjectAnimationUsingKeyFrames
Storyboard.TargetProperty="(UIElement.Visibility)" Storyboard.TargetName="rectangle">
                          <DiscreteObjectKeyFrame KeyTime="0">
                            <DiscreteObjectKeyFrame.Value>
                              <Visibility>Visible</Visibility>
                            </DiscreteObjectKeyFrame.Value>
                          </DiscreteObjectKeyFrame>
                        </ObjectAnimationUsingKeyFrames>
                        <ColorAnimationUsingKeyFrames
Storyboard.TargetProperty="(Shape.Fill).(SolidColorBrush.Color)"
Storyboard.TargetName="rectangle">
                          <EasingColorKeyFrame KeyTime="0" Value="Black"/>
                          <EasingColorKeyFrame KeyTime="0:0:0.2" Value="#FF2F2F2F"/>
                        </ColorAnimationUsingKeyFrames>
                        <ColorAnimationUsingKeyFrames
Storyboard.TargetProperty="(Control.Foreground).(SolidColorBrush.Color)"
Storyboard.TargetName="ContentContainer">
                          <EasingColorKeyFrame KeyTime="0" Value="#FF1BA1E2"/>
                          <EasingColorKeyFrame KeyTime="0:0:0.2" Value="White"/>
                        </ColorAnimationUsingKeyFrames>
                      </Storyboard>
                    </VisualState>
                    <VisualState x:Name="SelectedUnfocused"/>
                  </VisualStateGroup>
                  <VisualStateGroup x:Name="LayoutStates">
                    <VisualState x:Name="BeforeUnloaded"/>
                    <VisualState x:Name="BeforeLoaded"/>
                    <VisualState x:Name="AfterLoaded"/>
                  </VisualStateGroup>
```

```xml
                <VisualStateGroup x:Name="FocusStates">
                  <VisualState x:Name="Unfocused"/>
                  <VisualState x:Name="Focused">
                    <Storyboard>
                      <ColorAnimation Duration="0:0:0.3" To="Black"
Storyboard.TargetProperty="(Shape.Fill).(SolidColorBrush.Color)"
Storyboard.TargetName="rectangle" d:IsOptimized="True"/>
                      <ColorAnimation Duration="0:0:0.3" To="White"
Storyboard.TargetProperty="(Control.Foreground).(SolidColorBrush.Color)"
Storyboard.TargetName="ContentContainer" d:IsOptimized="True"/>
                    </Storyboard>
                  </VisualState>
                </VisualStateGroup>
              </VisualStateManager.VisualStateGroups>
              <Grid>
                <Rectangle x:Name="rectangle" Visibility="Visible" Fill="#FFB0FD46"
Stroke="Black"/>
                <ContentControl x:Name="ContentContainer" ContentTemplate="{TemplateBinding
ContentTemplate}"
                    Content="{TemplateBinding Content}"
                    Foreground="Black"
                    HorizontalContentAlignment="{TemplateBinding HorizontalContentAlignment}"
                    Margin="{TemplateBinding Padding}"
                    VerticalContentAlignment="{TemplateBinding VerticalContentAlignment}"/>
              </Grid>
            </Border>
          </ControlTemplate>
        </Setter.Value>
      </Setter>
    </Style>
    <ContentControl x:Key="content" Content="{Binding ''}"/>
    <ContentControl x:Key="content2" Content="{Binding ''}"/>
  </phone:PhoneApplicationPage.Resources>

    <!--LayoutRoot is the root grid where all page content is placed-->
    <Grid x:Name="LayoutRoot" Background="Transparent">
        <Grid.RowDefinitions>
            <RowDefinition Height="Auto"/>
            <RowDefinition Height="*"/>
        </Grid.RowDefinitions>

        <!--TitlePanel contains the name of the application and page title-->
        <StackPanel x:Name="TitlePanel" Grid.Row="0" Margin="12,17,0,28">
            <TextBlock x:Name="ApplicationTitle" Text="{Binding ApplicationName}"
Style="{StaticResource PhoneTextNormalStyle}"/>
            <TextBlock x:Name="PageTitle" Text="{Binding PageName}" Margin="9,-7,0,0"
Style="{StaticResource PhoneTextTitle1Style}"/>
        </StackPanel>

    <Grid x:Name="ContentPanel" Grid.Row="1" Margin="12,0,12,0">
```

```
            <ListBox ItemsSource="{Binding Path=News}" ItemContainerStyle="{StaticResource
NewsItemContainer}" SelectedItem="{Binding SelectedNews, Mode=TwoWay}">
                <ListBox.ItemTemplate>
                    <DataTemplate>
                      <StackPanel Orientation="Horizontal">
                    <!--<Button BorderThickness="0" Content=">>" Command="{Binding OpenNewsCommand,
Source={StaticResource MainPageViewModelDataSource}}" CommandParameter="{Binding}"
VerticalAlignment="Top" HorizontalAlignment="Right" />                                          --
>
                      <StackPanel>
                                    <StackPanel Orientation="Horizontal">
                                        <TextBlock Text="Title" />
                                        <TextBlock Text="{Binding Title}" />
                                    </StackPanel>
                                    <StackPanel Orientation="Horizontal">
                                        <TextBlock Text="Author" />
                                        <TextBlock Text="{Binding Author}" />
                                    </StackPanel>
                               </StackPanel>
                      </StackPanel>
                    </DataTemplate>
                </ListBox.ItemTemplate>
            </ListBox>
        </Grid>
        <Grid x:Name="DetailPanel" Grid.Row="1" Margin="12,0,12,0" Visibility="{Binding
IsDetailVisibile, Converter={StaticResource BooleanToVisibilityConverter}}" Background="Black"
>
            <StackPanel>
                <Button Command="{Binding CloseNewsCommand}"  Height="80" Content="Close"/>
                <TextBlock Text="{Binding SelectedNews.Body}" TextWrapping="Wrap" />
            </StackPanel>

        </Grid>
    </Grid>

</phone:PhoneApplicationPage>
```

Having written the view, you are ready to execute the application. Test to make sure that it all works fine.

Usage

This application can run in the emulator or the physical device. This recipe is a good start point for a real news reader, changing the repository with a service that gives you data, and using isolated storage to manage settings about source of data or caching data locally to your application. When the application runs, you will see the list of news items, as shown in Figure 10-5, and if you click on a news item, the detail panel will open, as shown in Figure 10-6.

Figure 10-5. List of news items

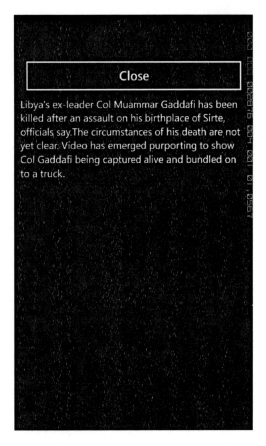

Figure 10-6. News details

10-3. Using MVVM and Performing Unit Testing

Problem

You want to write an application and test its logic by using a unit test, instead of using the F5 debug approach.

Solution

You must write your application using the MVVM pattern, and then you will be able to write a unit for each ViewModel. To test your ViewModels, you need to use the Silverlight Unit Test Framework.

How It Works

Unit tests are important for testing the singular functionality of your classes. In this recipe, you will build on Recipe 10-1 by creating logic for the `SaveCommandExecute` method. You will then create a test class with two test methods, one that always fails and another that always works. This way, you will learn how to run tests on your ViewModel and how to write them, with the scope of automatically test your business logic without any needs of interaction by you with the user interface (this is not completely exact, because Silverlight Unit Test Framework requires a couple of tap by you to run the Test).

The Code

Open the project created for Recipe 10-1. Add a reference to the two assemblies for unit testing contained in the package and mentioned in the Solution section of this recipe on Jeff Wilcox's (a senior software development lead on the Windows Phone team at Microsoft) site at `www.jeff.wilcox.name/2010/05/sl3-utf-bits/`. Now that you have these references, you need to add a little more logic to `MainPageViewModel` because without logic, you won't have anything to test.

Because the scope of this recipe is to show you how to unit test your Windows Phone applications, we added dummy logic to `ViewModel`, introducing the enumeration states:

```
public enum States : uint { Saved, Unsaved};
```

And a property in `MainPageViewModel` of the following type:

```
...
#region State Property

    /// <summary>
    /// The <see cref="State" /> property's name.
    /// </summary>
    public const string StatePropertyName = "State";


    private States _state = States.Unsaved;

    /// <summary>
    /// Gets the State property.
    /// </summary>
    public States State
    {
        get
        {
            return _state;
        }

        set
        {
            if (_state == value)
```

```
        {
            return;
        }

        var oldValue = _state;
        _state = value;

        // Update bindings, no broadcast
        RaisePropertyChanged(StatePropertyName);
    }
}

#endregion
```

...

As you can see, this property notifies the interface that a change has occurred, because when you save an object, it's good practice to let the user know what is being done.

Our last change to MainPageViewModel for this recipe is in SaveCommandExecute, which checks for the state of the ViewModel and sets the State property to "save" or "unsave" data.

```
private void SaveCommandExecute()
{
    State = (this.Amount == 0 || string.IsNullOrEmpty(Motivation))
        ? States.Unsaved : States.Saved;
}
```

Now that you have logic inside your ViewModel, you are ready to test it. Create a folder inside your project with the name UnitTests and add a class inside it named MainPageViewModelTest.

This class must be decorated with the TestClass attribute and needs to inherit from the SilverlightTest class contained in the namespace Microsoft.Silverlight.Testing, which is inside the assembly Microsoft.Silverlight.Testing.dll. We added three methods inside this class— TestSaveAlwaysFails, TestSaveOk, and TestSaveKo—decorating them with the TestMethod attribute. As you can guess from the names, the first test always fails, the second test results in a successful save, and the last results in an incorrect save

```
[TestClass]
public class MainPageViewModelTest : SilverlightTest
{
    [TestMethod]
    public void TestSaveAlwaysFails()
    {
            MainPageViewModel vm = new MainPageViewModel();
            vm.Motivation = string.Empty;
            vm.SaveCommand.Execute(null);
            Assert.IsTrue(vm.State == MainPageViewModel.States.Saved);
    }

    [TestMethod]
    public void TestSaveOk()
```

```
    {
        MainPageViewModel vm = new MainPageViewModel();
        vm.Motivation = "Shopping";
        vm.Amount = 200;
        vm.SaveCommand.Execute(null);
        Assert.IsTrue(vm.State == MainPageViewModel.States.Saved);
    }

    [TestMethod]
    public void TestSaveKo()
    {
        MainPageViewModel vm = new MainPageViewModel();
        vm.Motivation = string.Empty;
        vm.SaveCommand.Execute(null);
        Assert.IsFalse(vm.State == MainPageViewModel.States.Saved);
    }

}
```

The last thing you need to do is set the entry point for your suite of tests. Load the test execution page just after loading the main page of the application, as follows:

```
public MainPage()
{
    InitializeComponent();
    Loaded += new RoutedEventHandler(MainPage_Loaded);
}

void MainPage_Loaded(object sender, RoutedEventArgs e)
{
    SystemTray.IsVisible = false;
    var testExecutionPage = UnitTestSystem.CreateTestPage() as IMobileTestPage;
    BackKeyPress += (k, ek) => ek.Cancel = testExecutionPage.NavigateBack();
    (Application.Current.RootVisual as PhoneApplicationFrame).Content =
                                    testExecutionPage;
}
```

Now you are ready to test your application.

Usage

Run the project by using Visual Studio, targeting the emulator (if you run it on the device itself, some text blocks will be too small to read well, but we think that by the quantity of information shown inside the test page, there is nothing more to do). Wait a few seconds while the test page runs (see Figure 10-7). Then look for the result (see Figure 10-8). As planned, one test failed and the other two passed.

Figure 10-7. Starting the unit test

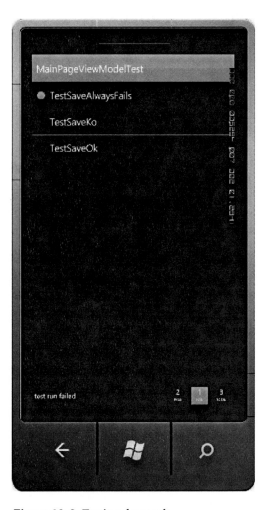

Figure 10-8. Testing the result

10-4. Using Application Profiling

Problem

You want to test your application performance in order to optimize your code, looking at CPU usage, memory, and the time spent to load images .

Solution

You must use your application's Windows Phone Performance Analysis testing performance tool to produce a report that will tell you how you need to change your code to make it more powerful and provide faster responses in interactions with users.

How It Works

Windows Phone Performance Analysis tool is part of the Windows Phone SDK. It helps you improve performance of your application. When you use the Windows Phone Performance Analysis tool, you can collect information about CPU usage in the form of a function call tree, grouped by modules, and much more.

The Code

In this recipe, we will profile the application written in Recipe 8-7 (background transfer), then open the project in Visual Studio.

Usage

From the Debug menu, select Start Windows Phone Performance Analysis (Alt+F1) as you can see in figure 10-9.

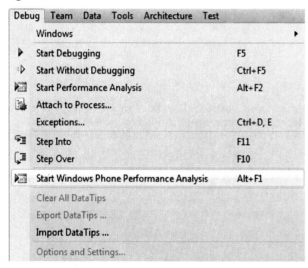

Figure 10-9. *Starting the profiling tool*

This will open the settings page, shown in figure 10-10, where you can specify if you want to collect information about execution or memory. This page will alert you that if you run test in the emulator, you will collect inaccurate information, so run the tests on your device (of course, this warning disappears if you select the physical device as the target of deployment).

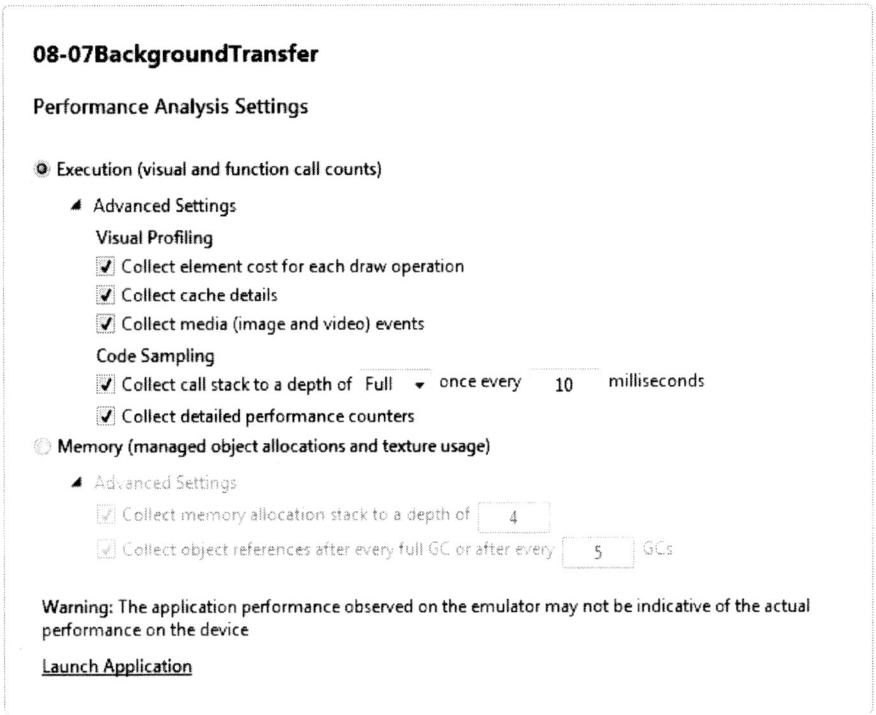

08-07BackgroundTransfer

Performance Analysis Settings

◉ Execution (visual and function call counts)
  ◢ Advanced Settings
    Visual Profiling
      ☑ Collect element cost for each draw operation
      ☑ Collect cache details
      ☑ Collect media (image and video) events
    Code Sampling
      ☑ Collect call stack to a depth of Full ▾ once every 10 milliseconds
      ☑ Collect detailed performance counters
◯ Memory (managed object allocations and texture usage)
  ◢ Advanced Settings
      ☑ Collect memory allocation stack to a depth of 4
      ☑ Collect object references after every full GC or after every 5 GCs

Warning: The application performance observed on the emulator may not be indicative of the actual performance on the device

Launch Application

Figure 10-10. Settings page

When you are ready, launch your application, and work with it by downloading an image (if you are profiling another application, interact concepts remain the same). Another page, shown in figure 10-11, will tell you that data collecting is in progress until you stop it or your applications become tombstoned.

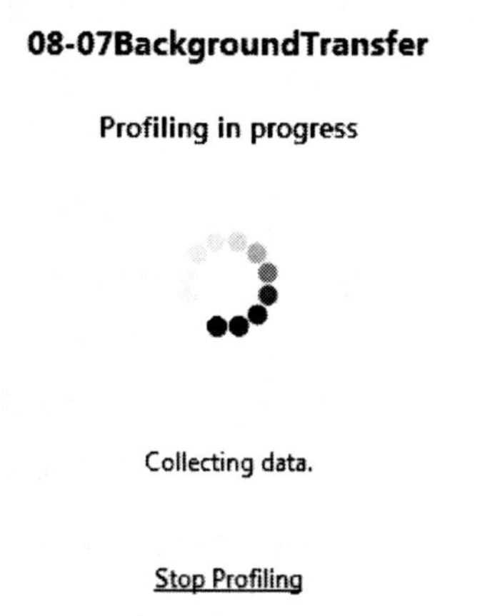

08-07BackgroundTransfer

Profiling in progress

08-07BackgroundTransfer

Analyzing the data

Collecting data.

Stop Profiling

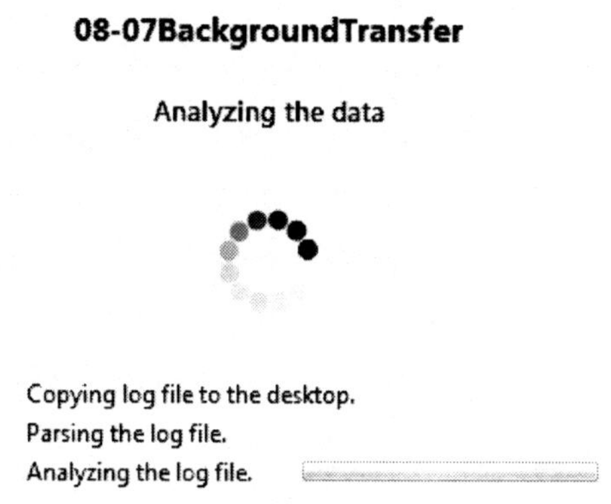

Copying log file to the desktop.
Parsing the log file.
Analyzing the log file.

Figure 10-11. Profiling in progress   *Figure 10-12.* Analyzing data

After the profile process has completed, a log file will be created (as in figure 10-12), and every time you launch the tool, this log file will be read from Visual Studio as a report that you can analyze, as shown in Figure 10-13.

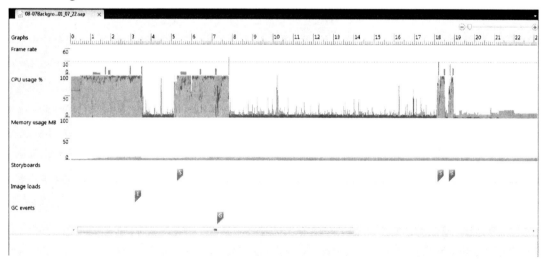

Figure 10-13. Profiling report

As you can see in Figure 10-13, a storyboard plays or garbage collector events happen. In the CPU usage row, you can see the CPU's usage percentage breakdown: the amount of time used by the UI thread is indicated in green; CPU usage by other threads, such as background worker or system threads are indicated in gray; the usage by threads not relative to the UI are indicated in purple; and idle CPU usage is indicated in white.

By selecting a range of time (at least 0.5 seconds), the tools help identify problems and suggests the best way to gain more information, as shown in Figure 10-14.

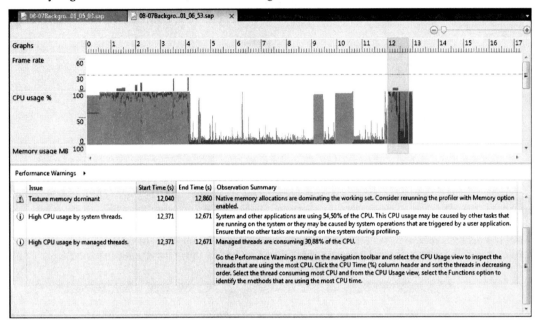

Figure 10-14. Profiling report with warnings details

Reading this report, you see three messages about the performance of software. The first is a warning that says the dominant set of data is memory allocation, suggesting you run the profiler using the Memory option. In Memory mode, you can perform the same operation, but in this case the report will be only relative to memory usage (see Figure 10-15).

By selecting a range of time, you can retrieve additional information; for example, you can see what module uses the most resources (as seen in Figure 10-16), and if this module is relative to your application, you must change something.

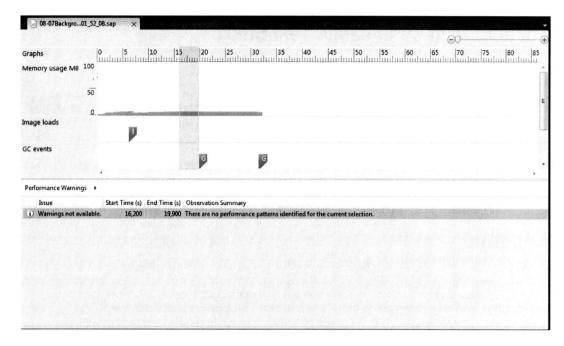

Figure 10-15. *Memory profile*

Method Name	Inclusive Samples	Exclusive Samples	Inclusive Samples %	Exclusive Samples %
▷ [Native Modules]	19	19	100,00 %	100,00 %
▷ System.Windows.dll	18	0	94,74 %	0,00 %
▷ mscorlib.dll	17	0	89,47 %	0,00 %
▲ 08-07BackgroundTransfer.dll	12	0	63,16 %	0,00 %
08_07BackgroundTransfer.App..ctor()	4	0	21,05 %	0,00 %
08_07BackgroundTransfer.App.InitializeComponent()	4	0	21,05 %	0,00 %
08_07BackgroundTransfer.MainPage..ctor()	8	0	42,11 %	0,00 %
08_07BackgroundTransfer.MainPage.InitializeComponent()	8	0	42,11 %	0,00 %
▷ System.dll	2	0	10,53 %	0,00 %
▷ System.Windows.RuntimeHost.dll	11	0	57,89 %	0,00 %
▷ Microsoft.Phone.dll	11	0	57,89 %	0,00 %
Microsoft.Phone.Interop.dll	1	0	5,26 %	0,00 %

Performance Warnings ▶   CPU Usage ▶   Modules ▶

Figure 10-16. *Resource using report*

10-5. Following Certification Test Steps

Problem

Before you submit your application, you want to test that you have considered all points that could make your application not in keeping with the rules of the marketplace.

Solution

You must use the Marketplace Test Kit in Visual Studio to run all automated tests that the validation team will perform on your application.

How It Works

There are a lot of rules to follow if you want your application published in the marketplace (for a complete list, see `http://msdn.microsoft.com/en-us/library/hh184843(v=VS.92).aspx`), but the greatest challenges to following these rules are testable before you submit your application. When self-testing your application, you can correct any problems that the Marketplace Test Kit will reveal.

Marketplace Test Kit is a tool that will guide you, step-by-step, in creating a good, presentable application.

The Code

Open the project relative to background transfers that was created in Recipe 8-7.

Usage

From the Project menu, select Open Marketplace Test Kit, which will open a view like that shown in Figure 10-17.

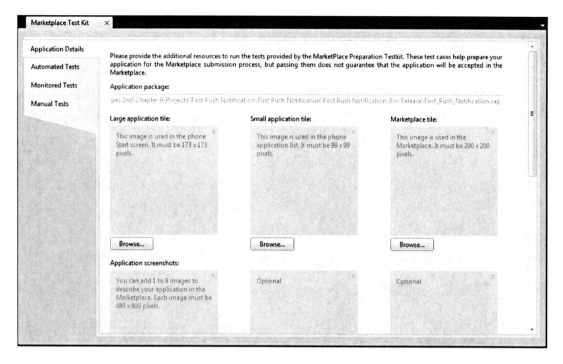

Figure 10-17. *The first page of the Marketplace Test Kit*

If at this time, your application doesn't have the necessary detail to be presentable to the marketplace, then select the images that will represent your project (in this case you will use images relative to a weather forecast or something that represents clouds or the sun). Next, open the second tab, Automated Test, click the button on top to run the test, wait a few seconds, and read the results. If your results appear like those in Figure 10-18, you can move on to Monitored Tests.

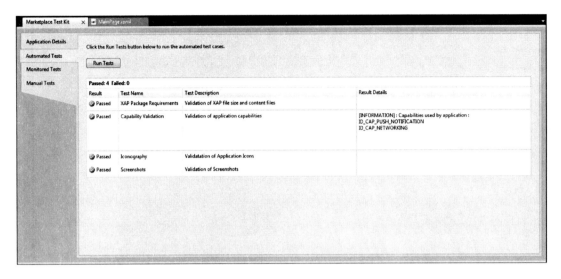

Figure 10-18. *Automated tests results*

In Monitored Tests (see Figure 10-19), you test your application's performance and correct exceptions. These tests help you avoid annoying problems that translate into an application uninstall by the user. To run this set of tests, you must connect your device, because application performances that run on an emulator are very different when they run on a physical device.

Start the application and simply use it. When you are done, close the application and navigate back in order to complete the final set of tests.

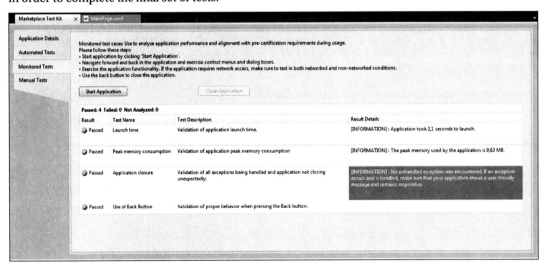

Figure 10-19. *Monitored tests results*

Finally, navigate to the Manual Tests tab. This tab contains a list of use cases, such as Multiple Devices Support, Phone Calls, Application Responsiveness, User-Initiated Background Transfers, and many others, any of which you must satisfy to be ready to successfully submit your application.

Index

M

V

W

CPSIA information can be obtained at www.ICGtesting.com
Printed in the USA
LVOW130243291211

261522LV00005B/17/P